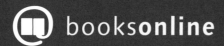 **books**online

Read this book online today:

With SAP PRESS BooksOnline we offer you online access to knowledge from the leading SAP experts. Whether you use it as a beneficial supplement or as an alternative to the printed book, with SAP PRESS BooksOnline you can:

- Access your book anywhere, at any time. All you need is an Internet connection.
- Perform full text searches on your book and on the entire SAP PRESS library.
- Build your own personalized SAP library.

The SAP PRESS customer advantage:

Register this book today at *www.sap-press.com* and obtain exclusive free trial access to its online version. If you like it (and we think you will), you can choose to purchase permanent, unrestricted access to the online edition at a very special price!

Here's how to get started:

1. Visit *www.sap-press.com*.
2. Click on the link for SAP PRESS BooksOnline and login (or create an account).
3. Enter your free trial license key, shown below in the corner of the page.
4. Try out your online book with full, unrestricted access for a limited time!

Your personal free trial **license key** for this online book is:

8rxp-wmfn-vgu2-kdqt

Efficient SAP NetWeaver® BW Implementation and Upgrade Guide

 PRESS

SAP PRESS is a joint initiative of SAP and Galileo Press. The know-how offered by SAP specialists combined with the expertise of the Galileo Press publishing house offers the reader expert books in the field. SAP PRESS features first-hand information and expert advice, and provides useful skills for professional decision-making.

SAP PRESS offers a variety of books on technical and business related topics for the SAP user. For further information, please visit our website: *www.sap-press.com*.

Mike Garrett
Using SAP Crystal Reports
2010, 500 pp.
978-1-59229-327-8

Jim Brogden, Heather Sinkwitz, Mac Holden
SAP BusinessObjects Web Intelligence
2010, 583 pp.
978-1-59229-322-3

Ingo Hilgefort
Reporting and Analytics with SAP BusinessObjects
2009, 655 pp.
978-1-59229-310-0

Larry Sackett
MDX Reporting and Analytics with SAP NetWeaver BW
2009, 380 pp.
978-1-59229-249-3

Gary Nolan and Debasish Khaitan

Efficient SAP NetWeaver® BW Implementation and Upgrade Guide

Galileo Press

Bonn • Boston

Galileo Press is named after the Italian physicist, mathematician and philosopher Galileo Galilei (1564–1642). He is known as one of the founders of modern science and an advocate of our contemporary, heliocentric worldview. His words *Eppur se muove* (And yet it moves) have become legendary. The Galileo Press logo depicts Jupiter orbited by the four Galilean moons, which were discovered by Galileo in 1610.

Editor Erik Herman
Copyeditor Lori Newhouse
Cover Design Jill Winitzer
Photo Credit iStockphoto.com/olm26250
Layout Design Vera Brauner
Production Editor Kelly O'Callaghan
Assistant Production Editor Graham Geary
Typesetting Publishers' Design and Production Services, Inc.
Printed and bound in Canada

ISBN 978-1-59229-336-0

© 2010 by Galileo Press Inc., Boston (MA)

1st Edition 2010

Library of Congress Cataloging-in-Publication Data
Nolan, Gary.
  Efficient SAP NetWeaver BW Implementation and Upgrade Guide / Gary Nolan, Debasish Khaitan. — 2nd ed.
     p. cm.
  Includes bibliographical references and index.
  ISBN-13: 978-1-59229-336-0 (alk. paper)
  ISBN-10: 1-59229-336-0 (alk. paper)
  1. SAP NetWeaver BW. 2. Data warehousing. 3. Business intelligence--Data processing. I. Khaitan, Debasish. II. Title.
  QA76.9.D37N65 2010
  005.74'5—dc22
                                                                                    2010012443

Contents at a Glance

Contents

3   Common SAP NetWeaver BW Implementation Mistakes   115

7   Preparing for Go-Live and the Go-Live Process 321

11   Epilogue 449

Acknowledgments

From Gary Nolan

The path to complete a book is a long and winding one. Many people have provided me invaluable help in completing this book. I would like to thank each of them for their help.

I offer thanks to my daughter Melanie who provided her dad with encouragement and support. May you always follow your dreams.

Thanks also go to my other daughter Vanessa, may your focus and drive lead you wherever you wish to go.

I also must thank my best friend and wife, Amy, for giving me the encouragement and the time to complete this book. Not only did she provide me the unending support needed to write, she also spent many hours giving editing suggestions to shape the presentation and content of this book. I thank her for her very valuable input. The end product reflects her dedication and I could not have completed it without her help.

Amy, I dedicate this book to you. I cannot thank you enough.

Other Thanks

I would also like to thank my extended family and friends for their various sacrifices to allow me time to complete this book.

Thanks to my colleagues and co-workers at my current and past projects for their feedback in helping make this book a reality. I wish to especially thank all the good folks at the Mercury Project for their constant support.

Special thanks to many of the staff members of Grom Associates, TekLink (TLI), and SAP America Inc. for providing me the information and support needed to complete this book.

From Debasish Khaitan

I am honored to have the opportunity to participate in the revised edition of this book. I would like to convey my sincere thanks to the editor of this book, Erik Herman, for giving me the opportunity and enormous support. I offer thanks to my parents for their support during the writing process. I thank all my colleagues who helped and reviewed the content of this book.

Last but not least, I must offer my thanks to my wife, Amrita, for her support while I was writing this book after my office hours.

Introduction

We are very happy to present the second edition of this book. This book has been revised from the earlier version, so it's up to date for the SAP NetWeaver® Business Warehouse (SAP NetWeaver BW) 7.0 component. In this edition, each chapter includes new information, including easy-to-remember process flows about SAP NetWeaver BW 7.0 implementation. We've also added a new chapter on SAP BusinessObjects and a new chapter about the Six Sigma methodology and processes. Using Six Sigma in your SAP NetWeaver BW support projects can reduce recurring technical and management issues.

The goal of this book is to help you understand and overcome the common SAP NetWeaver BW implementation issues and build an effective, adaptive, and responsive knowledge warehouse for your enterprise or your client.

How to Use This Book

Because successful, efficient implementations are of utmost priority to us, we wanted to write a book that provided valuable, timely advice. Therefore, the focus of this book is to give project advice to those who are implementing SAP NetWeaver BW, regardless of the release. We don't give specific advice on configuration, transformation, user-exits, etc, to keep the content of this book relevant to a wider audience and make the advice more universal.

In keeping the advice more project related, we emphasize that a well-planned project can quite easily attract the best and brightest developers and data architects. These individuals can provide the specific workarounds and configuration experience to help in the day-to-day issues that arise in any project. They should allow a project to overcome the software issues, and this book should help with process issues.

The advice in this book is useful to project management and project members on an SAP NetWeaver BW team, but it is also useful for those who are trying to understand the potential of an SAP NetWeaver BW project in their organizations.

Here is a quick overview of the contents of this book so you can determine how to read it and use the information contained in it.

Quick Overview

This book is divided into 10 chapters and 6 appendices. In this revised edition, we added two new chapters on Six Sigma and SAP BusinessObjects.

▶ **Chapter 1: The SAP NetWeaver BW Project Lifecycle**
This chapter gives you an overview of the SAP NetWeaver BW Project Lifecycle. You will get an understanding of the various complex challenges that are involved in such projects and will gain insight into the various steps that are involved in the implementation lifecycle. This chapter is the first step and establishes the contents of the rest of the book.

▶ **Chapter 2: Defining an Implementation Strategy**
This chapter helps you set your own implementation strategy. It helps you understand the importance of a sound strategy, while also taking you through the series of useful plans, steps, and actions needed to create a sound SAP NetWeaver BW implementation strategy.

▶ **Chapter 3: Common SAP NetWeaver BW Implementation Mistakes**
Few things are harder than having projects fail because of avoidable mistakes. This chapter takes you through commonly made SAP NetWeaver BW implementation mistakes, and how to avoid these common issues.

▶ **Chapter 4: Project Planning in SAP NetWeaver BW**
This chapter will help you understand and prepare for the various challenges that come up in SAP NetWeaver BW implementations. The steps of planning are outlined to help you in your own project planning endeavors.

▶ **Chapter 5: Gathering and Analyzing SAP NetWeaver BW Requirements**
For SAP NetWeaver BW projects to succeed, you need to know how to best gather and analyze requirements. In well-run SAP NetWeaver BW projects, people work together and use the information gathered to analyze and come up with the best methods and models needed.

▶ **Chapter 6: Sound SAP NetWeaver BW Development Strategies**
This chapter continues where Chapter 5 leaves off. It explains sound SAP NetWeaver BW development strategies. Some of the issues covered in this chapter include how to extract and load data, how to load data from non-SAP sources, how to extract data from SAP systems, and loading and transforming data into SAP NetWeaver BW.

▶ **Chapter 7: Preparing for Go-Live and the Go-Live Process**
You are now almost at the go-live stage and this chapter helps you see what's in store. It shows what needs to be done while preparing for go-live and how to

understand the go-live process. It covers topics such as documentation for SAP NetWeaver BW configuration, transport management, and testing.

▶ **Chapter 8: After SAP NetWeaver BW Go-Live**
Your work on an SAP NetWeaver BW implementation project is not complete after go-live. There is still important work to be done and this chapter shows you what and how to go about doing this. From setting up a Center of Excellence to transitioning from SAP NetWeaver BW development to production support and establishing a help desk, this chapter is packed with valuable information.

▶ **Chapter 9: Enhance Quality: The Six Sigma Way**
After SAP NetWeaver BW go-live, you may come across various support-related issues, some of which are repetitive in nature. In this chapter, we introduce a few of the Six Sigma tools that can help you better manage your SAP NetWeaver BW support project.

▶ **Chapter 10: Reporting and Analytics in a SAP NetWeaver BW Environment**
In this chapter, we focus on SAP BusinessObjects–related tools and their usage and best practices for using SAP BusinessObjects efficiently.

▶ **Chapter 11: Epilogue**
This summarizes the book and gives you important takeaways that you can use for your own SAP NetWeaver BW projects.

▶ **Appendix A: Sample Project Plan**
The sample project included in this appendix can be used as a template or a model for developing a plan for your own organization. The sections and subsections walk you through the SAP NetWeaver BW project plan, letting you know what needs to be done at each stage.

▶ **Appendix B: Important Checklists**
This appendix contains various important checklists that you can use to track the progress of your SAP NetWeaver BW project. These include: New BW System Validation Checklist, BW Query Development Checklist, BW Data Model Conceptual Review Checklist, BW Model Review Checklist, Cutover Plan Checklist, the BW Performance Checklist, ABAP performance checklist, and SAP BusinessObjects–related checklist.

▶ **Appendix C: Document Templates**
This appendix gives you detailed information about the various documents that need to be created for your SAP NetWeaver BW project, such as templates that you can use to create your own documents. They include: Functional Model template, DataStore template, InfoCube template, and the ETL template.

▸ **Appendix D: Common Issues When Upgrading from SAP NetWeaver BW Version 3.x to NW 2004s**
As the title of this appendix suggests, it lists commonly encountered issues during a typical upgrade from 3.x to NW 2004s. These include system-based issues, security-related issues, and portal-related issues.

▸ **Appendix E: Sample SAP NetWeaver BW Naming Standards Document**
Naming standards are important to maintain consistency in the approach to naming custom objects in SAP NetWeaver BW. This appendix lists some commonly used naming standards for your review and will act as a guide to create your own naming standards document.

▸ **Appendix F: SAP NetWeaver BW Integration Test Script**
This appendix gives you a document that can be used as an integration test script for the SAP NetWeaver BW data against the source data being loaded.

These chapters and appendices work together to give you a clear and practical understanding of how SAP NetWeaver BW projects work (and should work) and how to best implement SAP NetWeaver BW projects.

Conclusion

We hope you find great value in this book. It gives us pleasure to allow the information that has been kept in notebooks so long to be shared with people who can put it to good use. We welcome any questions or comments on the book and hope you enjoy reading it.

SAP NetWeaver BW can be a complex product. Its complexity lies in the many choices that are available when using it to provide business information. Understanding the product and its advantages and disadvantages is important for leading a project to success.

1 The SAP NetWeaver BW Project Lifecycle

The SAP Business Information Warehouse (BW) component has had many iterations and versions, but the core intention of the product and its designs have remained relatively unchanged since the first widely available version, 1.2B. The product now officially goes by the name SAP NetWeaver Business Warehouse (SAP NetWeaver BW).

Implementation of SAP NetWeaver BW has its challenges. There are many different sources of documentation to walk you through the functionality available in the product. Often, the most difficult task is not understanding the functionality of the SAP NetWeaver BW product, but rather applying that functionality to business situations and implementing the product to its fullest potential. Using the product is what allows you to provide the best advantages to your business for reporting and analysis.

There are many corporate uses for SAP NetWeaver BW; most involve gathering various data from different sources and analyzing this data in one place, SAP NetWeaver BW. Because SAP NetWeaver BW is fully configurable and quite flexible, the possibilities for reporting and analysis are virtually limitless. Among other things, companies use SAP NetWeaver BW to analyze sales to determine profitability, analyze headcounts, identify slow-moving materials, and track vendor performance.

The best way to start to look at SAP NetWeaver BW is to compare its related core transactional system, SAP R/3, the more recent version of that transactional system, SAP ERP Central Component (ECC). The SAP R/3 or SAP ECC systems provide optimal transaction processing in the organization while the SAP NetWeaver BW system provides optimal analysis of this transactional data. This data can source from the SAP ECC or SAP R/3 system or from other systems in the company's landscape. We refer to these sources of data by the SAP NetWeaver BW term, *DataSources*.

1.1 SAP ECC vs. SAP NetWeaver BW Implementations

A common analogy compares implementing SAP ECC or SAP R/3 vs. implementing SAP NetWeaverBW: Implementing SAP ECC is science, while implementing SAP NetWeaver BW is art. On the surface, this analogy sounds like a ploy to allow SAP NetWeaver BW project managers to make their projects sound more exciting (and perhaps gain more of the IT budget). However, as you examine the analogy, it does prove to be true in many SAP NetWeaver BW projects.

The art of implementing a SAP NetWeaver BW project lies in the extreme flexibility of the product and its diverse methods of delivering data. SAP NetWeaver BW was deliberately designed with this flexibility to allow maximum use. This flexibility of SAP NetWeaver BW allows many more choices in the implementation process than exist in a typical SAP ECC project. SAP NetWeaver BW can be implemented many different ways with few constraints on the sources or quality of data that is loaded. This allows a lot of creativity when solving business problems using SAP NetWeaver BW.

To compound the complexity, measures of success are less concrete with SAP NetWeaver BW projects. Most SAP ECC or SAP R/3 transactional systems have clear-cut requirements. For example, a common sales-system requirement might be to provide an order-to-cash process in support of business operations. The goal of an SAP NetWeaver BW implementation, to help people make decisions faster and better, is more subjective. This lends itself to a much more unstructured environment; thus, it is a more difficult project to implement and manage than those of a transactional system.

SAP NetWeaver BW lets an organization manage data from multiple sources to answer questions that previously may have been difficult or even deemed unanswerable. Thus, SAP NetWeaver BW, in many ways, should be considered a process, not a product. This complexity makes for a challenging implementation environment. To understand the environment, you must first understand the product, its strengths and weaknesses, and its overall development lifecycle.

1.2 Difference Between OLTP and OLAP Systems

SAP NetWeaver BW and SAP ECC systems are not the same from an architectural point of view or a processing point of view. The intensity of load and performance of the online transaction processing (OLTP) and online analytical processing

(OLAP) systems varies greatly. The processing in OLAP reaches its peak while data loads from the source system. The load in the OLTP system remains almost consistent because data loading does not happen in the OLTP system in a batch process; instead, data comes through executing different day-to-day enterprise operations. The main differences between OLTP and OLAP systems are shown in Table 1.1.

	OLTP	OLAP
Purpose	To carry out fundamental operations in a company	Helps to make strategic reporting and planning in a company
Source	Applications in the OLTP system	Data loaded from OLTP system directly in batch mode
History	OLTP systems contain very recent data.	OLAP systems contain present and historical data.
Data Type	Operational data	Summarized data
Database	Highly normalized and designed to write and update data in database	Highly de-normalized and designed to read data more efficiently from the database

Table 1.1 Difference Between OLTP and OLAP Systems

1.3   SAP NetWeaver BW from A to Z

Simply put, SAP NetWeaver BW is a data warehouse. A data warehouse is a logical collection of information gathered from many different operational databases to create business intelligence that supports business-analysis activities and decision-making tasks. Primarily, it is a record of an enterprise's past transactional and operational information, stored in a database designed for efficient data analysis and reporting.

SAP NetWeaver BW, as with other data warehouses, requires that data undergo specific steps: be gathered from the source system, put into a consistent state, stored, and presented to the end user for analysis. The main steps in the lifecycle of information in SAP NetWeaver BW are, in order in Figure 1.1:

1. Extraction

2. Staging and storage

3. Transformation and Harmonization

4. Presentation

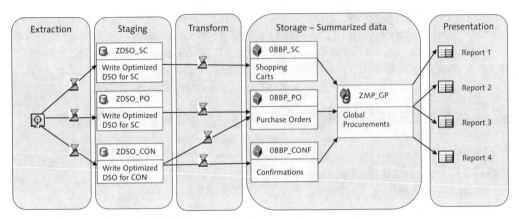

Figure 1.1 Sample SAP NetWeaver BW Data Journey Scenario

1.3.1 Extraction

Data can be extracted from source systems in a variety of ways. If the data required is in an SAP ECC source system, this data can be extracted via the *service applications and programming interface* (service API). In simple terms, the service API is the collection of pre-delivered extractors in SAP ECC. Almost all standard data in SAP ECC have delivered extractors called *DataSources*. These DataSources can load data into SAP NetWeaver BW. If SAP delivered data sources do not satisfy the requirement, you can create a custom datasource, named *Generic DataSources*. With these generic data sources, you can load data from different objects like transparent tables, database views, infosets, and function modules.

External systems do not have these DataSources, so this data must be extracted from these non-SAP systems in some other way. SAP NetWeaver BW has different types of adapters to load data to an external system (see Figure 1.2).

▶ **DB Connect**
This type of data source uses *Database Shared Library (DBSL)* to extract data. You can extract data from databases like IBM DB2, Oracle, and Informix using DB Connect.

▶ **UD Connect**
This type of data source uses a *Java database connectivity (JDBC)* engine to extract data. Because almost all existing databases have JDBC engines, SAP NetWeaver BW can extract data from any database with this adapter.

▶ **Web Services**
SAP NetWeaver BW can also load data in XML format directly from a website. Web Services also interact with XI systems.

▶ **File**

Typically, this is done via a custom extraction program on the external system that outputs files in a flat file format for loading into SAP NetWeaver BW. This extracted data can then be merged with other external data or SAP ECC data for reporting and analysis.

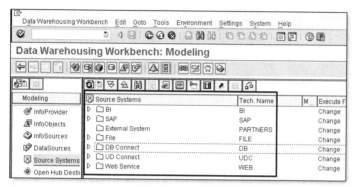

Figure 1.2 Different Types of SAP NetWeaver BW Source Systems

1.3.2 Staging and Storage

Staging and storage of data means that the data is kept in an environment that can handle large data sets and house them for further loading or for presentation to the end user. As you might expect, SAP NetWeaver BW implementations typically take up a lot of disk space.

A small SAP NetWeaver BW implementation can be as small as 50 to 75 gigabytes, while more complex environments can involve up to several terabytes of data. According to SAP, the average SAP NetWeaver BW implementation supports 200 users and is between 100 and 200 gigabytes in size.

A majority of this disk space is taken up with the Data Store Objects (DSO), formally known as an Operational Data Store (ODS), and the InfoCubes. Typically, the DSO is a repository for storing detailed, typically transactional data in the SAP NetWeaver BW system. The InfoCube typically contains aggregated summary information fed from either the DSO or other sources designed to present data in a clear and efficient manner.

> **Note**
>
> Data modeling decisions can severely affect the volume of data in SAP NetWeaver BW. This can have an adverse effect on performance. These data modeling decisions should always take into account the overall effect on data volume and system performance.

The DSO and InfoCubes set the foundation for data storage in SAP NetWeaver BW. Usually, the more voluminous the source, the more storage space is needed in SAP NetWeaver BW. However, this is not always the case. Decisions regarding redundancy of data and data granularity can either reduce or even exponentially increase the data volume in SAP NetWeaver BW.

Figure 1.1 shows data staging through the write optimized DSO; however, there is an option to stage the data in a Persistent Staging Area (PSA) layer also. If you want to use DSO as a staging layer, then you need to configure the deletion of PSA data often. Otherwise, too much disk space will be filled with redundant data.

1.3.3 Transformation and Harmonization

Data transformation is a large part of any SAP NetWeaver BW implementation. It is through data transformation that data from differing sources can be married to provide meaningful analysis. This transformation is necessary both for adding values that are not in the source data or altering values that may not be consistent with others. For example, users need to analyze data from both the legacy system orders and from SAP ECC system orders. These two data sets exist on separate systems. They both use completely different customer numbers, material numbers, etc. Users want to be able to see order history across the two systems. How can you provide this?

The only way to do this is to combine and harmonize the data together as if they all came from one system. This can be quite a difficult task. The customer numbers must be converted to a consistent number format from one source system. This must be done with all transactional fields until the data is stored in a consistent format.

This transformation is done in the SAP NetWeaver BW system using either update and transfer rules in SAP NetWeaver BW versions 3.0 to 3.5 or with the transformation area in the NW 2004s system. Data transformation can be time consuming and complicated, depending on the data that needs to be altered or appended.

Understanding and implementing harmonization of data requires a clear understanding of the sources of data. It involves combining the data in a logical format that can be re-used, often for other reporting purposes. You also need a clear understanding of all the data analysis needs of the organization. Fully understanding all of these areas can be quite challenging. Thus, transformation of data is a large task that often requires several iterations before the final version is complete (see Figure 1.3).

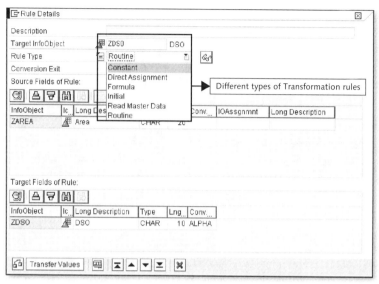

Figure 1.3 Different Types of Transformation Rules

The different types of Transformation Rules include:

▸ **Constant**
With this rule type, you can assign constant values. For each record, the assigned destination field will be populated with the constant value.

▸ **Direct Assignment**
The Direct Assignment rule type moves the source field to the destination field without any changes. This is basically one-to-one mapping between the source and the destination field.

▸ **Formula**
You can change the source field using this rule type. There are many standard formula exits in the formula editor. You also create your own formula using user exits.

▸ **Initial**
As name suggests, the destination fields will be populated with default values. For example, if the source field is of type character, then blanks will be moved in the destination field.

▸ **Read Master Data**
If the source field has a master data table and the destination field is required to be populated with an attribute of that master data, then you will use this type of transformation rule. For example, your destination field represents a cus-

tomer's address, and to populate this field, use the source customer field and apply the Read Master Data transformation rule type.

▶ **Routine**
Here, you will have full flexibility to write your own Advanced Business Application Programming (ABAP) transformation codes. If the above-mentioned rule type does not satisfy your requirement, then you have to use this transformation rule.

Rule types are executed for every record. However, you can also implement *Start Routines* and *End Routines.* These routines are executed for each data packet. The system executes the Start Routine before data packets pass through the transformation rule types. End Routine is executed after the transformation rules are executed.

> **Note**
>
> If you want to delete some records in the Data Packet before transformation, then you have to write that logic in Start Routine. Similarly, End Routines can delete the records based on the derived data in transformation. We also use End Routines for logging purposes.

1.3.4   Presentation

Presentation of data can come from a variety of different formats and methods (see Figure 1.4). Simply put, the presentation of data in SAP NetWeaver BW provides the data to the end user in a meaningful way. There are several different ways to present data in SAP NetWeaver BW, as seen in the following list:

▶ **BEx Reporting**
This is a tool to provide data analysis using Microsoft Excel as the basis for the delivery of the data.

▶ **Web Reporting**
This analysis uses reports with an HTML or Java frontend and is typically launched from a portal.

▶ **Third-Party Tools**
Various third-party tools provide information analysis in SAP NetWeaver BW.

▶ **SAP BusinessObjects**
This is a new addition to the business intelligence portfolio of SAP. Using this tool, you can report on the data from SAP NetWeaver BW as well as from external database systems.

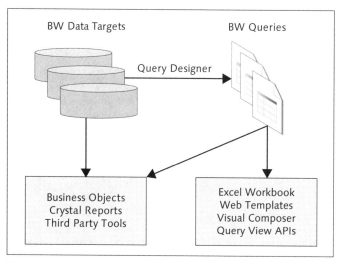

Figure 1.4 Presentation Layer

1.4   External Data: What is the Big Deal?

In most SAP NetWeaver BW projects, there are multiple sources of data. This data needs to be analyzed with various methods of discovery by a wide variety of users. To add to this complexity, most projects involve bringing the data from multiple sources and combining this data so it appears to come from one single source. This harmonization of data can require significant analysis as well as transformation of data to allow the analysis to take place.

Although some customers use SAP NetWeaver BW without any SAP data loaded into it, most SAP NetWeaver BW projects source a large majority of their data from the associated SAP transactional systems. This is because the transactional system of record for most projects involving SAP NetWeaver BW is usually SAP ECC or SAP R/3.

Most SAP NetWeaver BW implementations do not rely only on the SAP ECC system as their sole DataSource for SAP NetWeaver BWbecause of the best of breed and lifecycles of most IT organizations. Many IT organizations have multiple systems spanning many different processes and functions in their landscapes. Because these systems need to be analyzed together, SAP NetWeaver BW is often called on to provide this analysis.

Figure 1.5 shows the sources of data that can be accessed directly by SAP NetWeaver BW. There could be many other sources for which SAP NetWeaver BW does not have source systems, such as Mainframes. You can also extract data from there by writing legacy codes and extract them into a file and then load them in SAP NetWeaver BW.

> **Example**
>
> A large pharmaceutical company needs to analyze sales, shipments, and on-time delivery statistics. The SAP ECC system provides the sales and shipment data via the Sales and Distribution (SD) system. However, a legacy system provides the on-time delivery statistics. This on-time data must be loaded into SAP NetWeaver BW and married with the SAP ECC data so the analysis can span the entire data set. When users request this analysis, they should not need to know or care that the data came from a variety of systems. They simply expect a meaningful analysis of this data, regardless of its source.

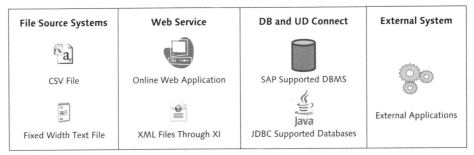

File Source Systems	Web Service	DB and UD Connect	External System
CSV File	Online Web Application	SAP Supported DBMS	External Applications
Fixed Width Text File	XML Files Through XI	JDBC Supported Databases	

Figure 1.5   Different Types of External Data Supported By SAP NetWeaver BW

1.5   Build for the Present, Keep an Eye on the Future

The SAP NetWeaver BW system must not only be designed with the current requirements in mind but must be flexible enough to allow for analysis of future data with requirements that may not even be known today. This is because the organization is constantly changing, and new ways of analyzing data emerge with the evolution of the users and the transactional source systems.

Implementation decisions that are made early in the SAP NetWeaver BW implementation cycle can provide significant challenges in the future. Much of the configuration in SAP NetWeaver BW is not easy to fix once data has been loaded. Data loaded into SAP NetWeaver BW InfoCubes or DSO structures can require significant effort to redesign.

Any significant changes usually require a purge or dump of the DSO or InfoCube in SAP NetWeaver BW, and a reload of this data. In many cases, a full reload of data in SAP NetWeaver BW requires the source system to be *quiet* during the reload. No users could perform transactions during this time.

As more and more organizations migrate toward a 24/7 uptime environment, it is much more difficult to schedule downtime on the transactional system. This type of disruption of business may not be possible in a dynamic environment or in one where the uptime of the system's transactional system is mission critical.

The challenge is to anticipate the core data that is needed for future requirements, and then build it into the data model to prevent a scheduled outage of the transactional systems and reload of the SAP NetWeaver BW system. This can present a burden on the SAP NetWeaver BW team to get it right the first time.

> **Example**
>
> The batch number, a field in the sales order, was not deemed appropriate for the sales-order reporting requirements, so the implementation team decided not to pull this field into SAP NetWeaver BW. It does not exist in the DSO order structures and therefore does not exist in the InfoCubes. Because it does not exist in the SAP NetWeaver BW environment, it cannot be used for reporting and analysis. The business users decide they now want to perform reporting in the batch number. How do you get the batch number into SAP NetWeaver BW?

Let's examine this example more thoroughly. If the data has not been mapped into SAP NetWeaver BW, and the batch number needs to be populated in all existing orders, including the history in SAP NetWeaver BW, you have some significant work to do. You must first purge the data in the SAP NetWeaver BW DSO and InfoCubes. You then need to add the field for the batch number to both the DSO and InfoCubes relevant for the reporting needs. Now, you have a place to store the batch number. You need to re-populate the InfoCubes and DSO to include the batch number.

To extract the data from SAP ECC, you must shut the users off from the SAP ECC system while you re-initialize the data and reload the data into SAP NetWeaver BW. This downtime on SAP ECC is required to make sure that the data is static in SAP ECC and the initial set-up of data is consistent and correct. There is no way to do this set-up while users are busy changing and adding sales orders. Depending on the volume of data in the SAP ECC transactional system, this downtime could be several hours or even days. This downtime is only required for the initial loading and setting up of the data; it is not required for each day's delta load into SAP NetWeaver BW.

This downtime can quickly become quite a burden on the transactional system, if a shutdown is required for each new data field that had not been mapped. Thus, the only way to prevent these outages is to anticipate the future needs of the analysis users and make sure that the fields that they might need are incorporated into the design.

The main storage of data in SAP NetWeaver BW is in the DSO structure. This DSO can contain a large volume of data and thus should be used to store the majority of the fields that are either specifically needed or may be needed into the future.

InfoCubes in SAP NetWeaver BW provide the main analysis structure for reporting in SAP NetWeaver BW. When the DSO data is loaded into the InfoCubes for eventual reporting, subsets of the DSO data are typically chosen based only on the current analysis requirements. This is useful, because the InfoCube can then contain only the data that is most pertinent for analysis. If the InfoCube is missing data needed for analysis, it can simply be reloaded from its source DSO in SAP NetWeaver BW. This does not require downtime on the transactional system. It simply requires some downtime of the SAP NetWeaver BW InfoCube. This is usually much less disruptive for the organization.

> **Note**
>
> The more complete the anticipation of future needs during the data-modelling process, the less impact new needs and changes will have on the transactional users and the more quickly and easily they can be implemented.

1.6 Dirty Data

Compounding the challenges facing a SAP NetWeaver BW project is that the source data has differing levels of quality. Delivering a SAP NetWeaver BW system with high-quality data is of utmost importance because once users determine that the data warehouse has data inaccuracies, it is difficult to win back the users' confidence.

The number one axiom for a SAP NetWeaver BW data warehouse must be: Get the data right, right from the beginning.

The Data Warehousing Institute estimates that data-quality problems cost U.S. businesses more than $600 billion a year. Yet, most executives are oblivious to the data-quality lacerations that are slowly bleeding their companies to death.

The challenge with data quality most often lies in the source of the data. This is best illustrated with the old (and often overused) analogy of garbage in/garbage out. Obviously, any data warehouse is a reflection of the quality of the source data that is loaded into it. However, because data in SAP NetWeaver BW is harmonized, the SAP NetWeaver BW user does not know or care where the source of data lies.

This presents an issue. If a user providing analysis in SAP NetWeaver BW *sees* incorrect or inconsistent data, he typically decides that SAP NetWeaver BW is wrong. Usually, this user does not understand or even care that the issues are often with *dirty* data at its source (Figure 1.6).

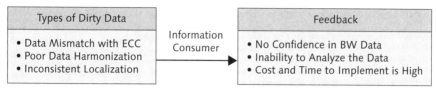

Figure 1.6 Consequences of Dirty Data

Data in a typical organization rolls downhill, and unfortunately SAP NetWeaver BW is at the bottom. Thus, any anomalies in the data that may not have surfaced in the transactional system now become part of SAP NetWeaver BW's territory.

Source system data issues provide a severe challenge to any project. Much time in a typical SAP NetWeaver BW project is spent analyzing data issues and meeting with the owners and representatives of the various source systems to get this data fixed. This significant part of the SAP NetWeaver BW implementation is difficult to quantify but must be budgeted as part of the SAP NetWeaver BW implementation lifecycle.

1.7   Can't SAP NetWeaver BW Just Clean the Data?

This question comes up frequently in a typical SAP NetWeaver BW implementation. The root of the question lies at the foundation of SAP NetWeaver BW. Is SAP NetWeaver BW simply a mirror of the sources of data in the various InfoCubes and DSOs? The answer to this question should be a resounding "Yes." This is because SAP NetWeaver BW is designed to house data from various source systems and presents this data the way the data is in those systems, right or wrong.

Because SAP NetWeaver BW does allow transformation of data, there are those who try to use SAP NetWeaver BW to *clean* data as it arrives in SAP NetWeaver BW. This is a mistake, because if the mission of a SAP NetWeaver BW project is to clean all data as it arrives in SAP NetWeaver BW, the project team will spend a great deal of time on this process. The best way to approach data is to expect that the data is clean at its source. This will allow the SAP NetWeaver BW team to concentrate on getting the data extracted and loaded into SAP NetWeaver BW, without worrying about keeping this source data consistent or correct.

> **Note**
>
> Any SAP NetWeaver BW implementation should stick to correcting the data at the source. Sometimes, fixing data in source systems is more costly than adding a validation check in SAP NetWeaver BW. But, using this kind of shortcut will result in inconsistencies in SAP NetWeaver BW and source systems. It may lead to disastrous circumstances. For example, if you correct the Organization Units hierarchy in user exit and do not correct those in HR source systems, this will create overall malfunctioning of the all workflows in HR applications.

1.8 Understanding SAP NetWeaver BW

It is difficult to talk about implementing software like SAP NetWeaver BW without clearly explaining what SAP NetWeaver BW does well and is designed to do, and to explain some things that SAP NetWeaver BW is clearly not designed to do. Simply put, SAP NetWeaver BW can provide aggregated reporting from one or many different DataSources. Typically, SAP NetWeaver BW is used for a more strategic view of data, while SAP ECC is designed for a more operational view of data. Although this is not mandatory, typically SAP NetWeaver BW fits better in an organization when it provides summary strategic data across the enterprise (Figure 1.7).

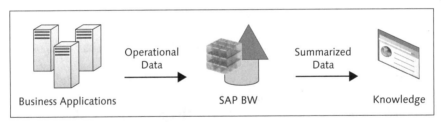

Figure 1.7 Understanding SAP NetWeaver BW

Recent releases of SAP BusinessObjects software also integrate the SAP NetWeaver BW system as well as other relational database systems. Using SAP BusinessObjects, you can report on any SAP NetWeaver BW queries and data providers. At the same time, reporting is also possible on SAP ECC operational data.

1.9 Reasons for Implementing SAP NetWeaver BW

Some popular questions often asked about SAP NetWeaver BW are: Why do I need SAP NetWeaver BW? Doesn't SAP ECC have reporting? Why do I need a separate system for reporting?

Understanding the strengths of the product and why most customers implement SAP NetWeaver BW allows you to gain a better understanding of its strengths. This allows you to make sure you implement in ways that optimize those strengths. The main reasons for implementing SAP NetWeaver BW are as follows:

▶ Concentrate the analytics of SAP NetWeaver BW rather than SAP ECC or SAP R/3

▶ Provide a single version of the truth

▶ Consolidate, harmonize, and centralize information

▶ Establish an enterprise data warehouse (EDW)

▶ Provide a competitive advantage

▶ Provide flexible analysis of information assets

▶ Make information available to more people in the organization.

To understand each of the above points, explore each reason for implementing SAP NetWeaver BW to reveal the motivation and how SAP NetWeaver BW provides the solution (see Figure 1.8).

Figure 1.8 Reasons to Implement SAP NetWeaver BW

1.9.1 Analytical System Access from the Transactional (SAP ECC) System

The reasons for implementing SAP NetWeaver BW vary, but the premise is the same. SAP ECC by its nature is an OLTP system. The system provides fast and efficient entering and retrieval of transactional data across the enterprise.

OLTP systems excel at transactional data processing and the timely delivery of data to support the transactional volume and users. Thus, most transactional systems use a relational database structure with multiple tables and fields, all connected by key fields and a complex number of join tables. This relational structure allows for fast transaction processing as the data is saved into the many tables in an OLTP system.

Figure 1.9 shows a common relational database view of the relationships among the tables in SAP R/3 or SAP ECC systems. The volume of tables and their relationships are quite complex.

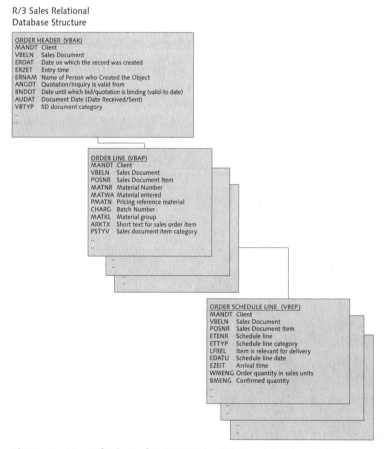

Figure 1.9 View of Subset of SAP ECC Sales Relational Database Tables

Often, after an organization has used the SAP ECC or SAP R/3 transactional systems for a while, it finds itself with a need to analyze the great volume of data that has accumulated. It is at this time that SAP NetWeaver BW is often considered as a solution to the need for analysis.

SAP NetWeaver BW is chosen because in any OLTP system, it is difficult to provide fast and efficient transaction processing while at the same time providing fast and efficient reporting. The two goals work against each other. Someone trying to enter transactions cannot afford to be slowed by a high-volume report analyzing data. However, the reports must be run. How can you make sure that you are able to analyze large volumes of data while also creating many diverse transactions in one system?

The answer is to remove the analytical data from the transactional environment and move it to a more suitable place to provide the analysis that is required by the users. Because there is no way to tune the transactional database optimally to serve both uses, it is vital that separation of the two systems provide both user groups what they were seeking. The separation allows each system to optimally provide their assigned tasks. The OLTP system (typically SAP ECC) continues to be designed to allow for fast transaction processing.

In contrast, SAP NetWeaver BW is considered an OLAP system. Data retrieval in a separate OLAP system can provide a quick and efficient analysis of data completely independent of the OLTP system.

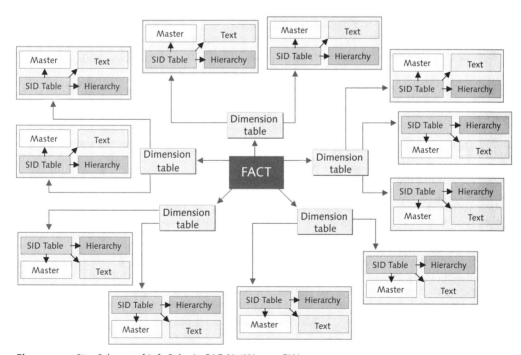

Figure 1.10 Star Schema of InfoCube in SAP NetWeaver BW

SAP NetWeaver BW's database structure is a star schema design (see Figure 1.10). The figure shows the main reporting structure in SAP NetWeaver BW. Rather than having hundreds of transactional data tables, SAP NetWeaver BW provides only a few. The main reporting structure in SAP NetWeaver BW, the InfoCube, is designed to allow the majority of data to sit in the central fact table. Dimension tables surround this fact table; the combination provides a key to the data and a link to the shared master data.

1.9.2 Transition to a Single Version of the Truth

Many organizations look to their data warehouses, in this case SAP NetWeaver BW, to provide a consistent view of the data in the organization. Because SAP NetWeaver BW can bring in data from multiple sources and harmonize this data, it can enforce one version of the data across the enterprise.

> **Example**
>
> There are many common statistics across an organization. To illustrate this, look at all the sales reports that report the key figure net sales. In an organization, many different reports often show net sales as a value on the report. However, net sales may be understood (or seemingly understood) in many different ways.

Some net sales values might include tax; others might exempt tax from the net sales value. Some may include returns values, while others may exclude these values. This situation can provide an unclear view of the organization. If many people are looking at one key value and defining it in different ways, this leads to incorrect assumptions and may, in turn, lead to invalid strategic decision making. How can you make sure that everyone in the organization who refers to a net sales value is always including the same values in his calculations?

This can be done by simply providing the data in SAP NetWeaver BW and mandating that the *net sales* value is always shown to have a consistent calculation to determine the results.

Thus, SAP NetWeaver BW does not necessarily provide a *single version of the truth*, but it does allow, through its implementation, an opportunity to enforce this thinking and keep the organization thinking of data in the same way. If everyone is running the same reports from the same systems, it is quite clear that their decision making would be the result of one set of agreed-on measures. The organization can then focus more on the decision-making process and not on the makeup of the statistical key values.

This consistency must be enforced from the beginning of an SAP NetWeaver BW project. It is difficult to retroactively make the SAP NetWeaver BW environment consistent after the implementation has become mature. In our example, gathering up all net sales key-figure values and determining what calculation is used to show these values and then fixing them is quite time consuming after implementation.

However, if these standards are determined and planned from the beginning, the data can be made consistent in the design. This allows for a firm data foundation for future analysis as more complex key performance indicators (KPIs) are developed.

1.9.3   Consolidation, Harmonization, and Centralization of Information

Consolidation, harmonization, and centralization of information simply refers to getting data from multiple places and merging that data cleanly so that it appears to have come from one source. Many companies meet information needs with small caches of data to support a number of small user groups. We usually refer to these small data stores as *data marts*.

Data marts may take the form of flat tables, spreadsheets, small data warehouses, Microsoft Access tables, etc. These provide raw analysis for the power users and even the end users. Depending on the environment, these data marts may exist all over the organization with many different sources and uses.

Figure 1.11 is based on a survey of 521 respondents conducted by Wayne Eckerson, Director of Research, TDWI. This figure shows that organizations have only consolidated about one-third of the analytic structures that exist in their organizations. The chart in Figure 1.11 gives an indication that organizations have many different data warehouses, independent data marts, data stores, and spreadsheets or spreadmarts. Many are in the process of consolidating and/or eliminating these data marts. This is especially true of the most common and most flexible spreadmarts.

The problem with having many different data marts is that the information in the data marts may not always follow a consistent format or standard. This becomes an even more complicated issue as people combine and aggregate data marts to make business decisions. Sometimes, the data that they are combining or aggregating is not consolidated properly, and thus business decisions are based on incorrect premises.

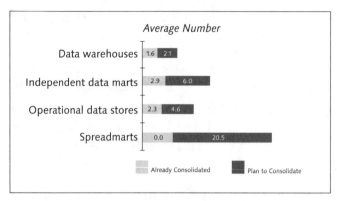

Figure 1.11 Completed vs. Planned Consolidation

Sometimes assumptions are made on the data as it is combined, and thus confusion results from these decisions. For example, if the user of the combined data mart data forgot to eliminate *intercompany sales*, this could skew the numbers improperly.

The only way to reduce this confusion in the organization is to centralize this data and establish some standards for extraction, loading, transformation, and presentation of the data. The next step is to eliminate the data mart completely.

There is an old legend about the pirate Blackbeard that says he would sometimes burn his own ship when engaging in combat with another ship. He did this, they say, so that his crew would have to fight harder to survive. Although you are not doing something as drastic as fighting another ship's sailors when implementing SAP NetWeaver BW, it does help to *burn the ships* in regard to data marts and reduce the number of places to go for information in the organization. You just have to make sure that those who relied on the ship that was burned can stay afloat elsewhere.

SAP NetWeaver BW allows for data standards to be created. These standards can help in the eventual reduction or elimination of these data marts from the organization. Thus, various users with differing goals for analysis can use one central tool for reporting.

That central tool, in this case SAP NetWeaver BW, then reduces the training needed for users to understand different tools for mining data from various data marts. It also makes sure that these users are all looking at the same data that has been consistently joined. This sets a firm foundation for information in the organization.

1.9.4 Establish an EDW

The next step in reducing the data marts is to have one, and only one, data warehouse in the organization for all reporting. This central or EDW is used not only for regional reporting but would also allow the data to be *rolled up* or aggregated for a global view of the data.

Many companies are facing more and more requests to view data at a global level. This presents a challenge in many organizations, especially those that do most of their data analysis locally rather than globally.

Many companies have data scattered across the organization or siloed in systems that do not allow for quick and easy roll-up to a global reporting instance. This often occurs because development of different systems took place at different times and with different objectives, without proper global governance and vision to assure that this data rolls up properly to a global EDW. Thus, data becomes difficult to analyze consistently and even more difficult to combine or harmonize.

This also happens when there are multiple SAP NetWeaver BW or multiple SAP ECC instances in the system landscape, because these systems often do not share common configuration or common master data.

Most companies, even without an EDW, are doing global reporting. However, this often involves a manual gathering of data from the various source systems and a manual synchronization of the data to a global view. This is typically resource and time intensive and lends itself to errors because it is not always performed consistently.

To standardize this practice, and to get more visibility of data across the organization, companies either consider or actually implement an EDW to perform global reporting. This EDW would gather data from differing source systems and provide reporting at both enterprise and operational levels.

Figure 1.12 shows an example of an EDW that combines data from multiple SAP ECC and legacy systems into three separate SAP NetWeaver BW systems and one legacy data warehouse. This data is consolidated into one EDW, and all reporting is then run from the EDW. This provides one version of the data and one place to go to gather data from the multiple sources.

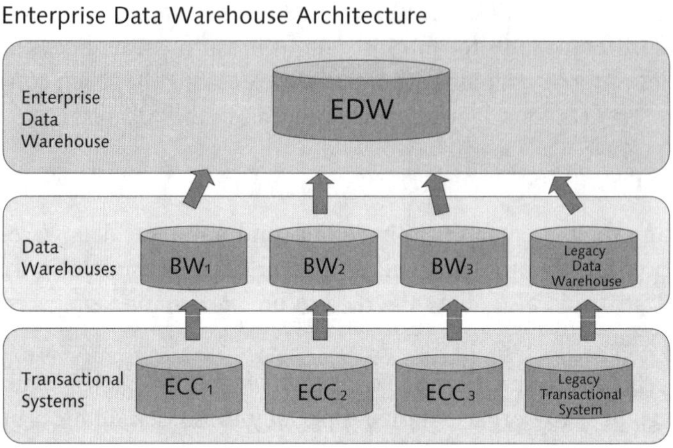

Enterprise Data Warehouse Architecture

Figure 1.12 Example of Enterprise Data Warehouse using SAP NetWeaver BW

Multiple SAP NetWeaver BW instances or legacy data warehouses do not have to be used to gather the data to consolidate. Many projects also provide one EDW that gathers data directly from the various source systems without an intermediate SAP NetWeaver BW system. The main goal is to consolidate data across the enterprise, and this can be implemented in many ways, as in Table 1.2.

Objective	Description
Single Point of Truth	All data mast pass through the EDW layer on its journey from source system to architected data mart layer. This will ensure the consistency and traceability of every master and transaction data.
Completeness	In EDW, layer data is not aggregated or overwritten with old data. Therefore, the EDW consists of the complete change history of a particular transaction.
Controlled Extraction	Data is extracted from source system only once. This ensures the least runtime load on OLTP systems.
Reusability and Flexibility	Because data is not manipulated in an EDW layer, it is projects and process area independent. If complete restructuring is required in a data mart, then all required data can be transferred from an EDW layer.
Integration	An EDW layer consists of all operational data of the organization without differentiating between process areas. Therefore, any integration of data from a different process area is possible through an EDW layer.

Table 1.2 Objectives of EDW Layer

1.9.5   Competitive Advantage

It has long been known that better information can mean a huge competitive advantage in business. There is no better example than Wal-Mart. Wal-Mart has one of the most sophisticated IT departments in the world. It not only gathers its own but also collaborates with customers and vendors to provide forecasting, planning, and logistical information.

Through Wal-Mart's constant focus on better information and better visibility in all phases of its supply chain, the company has forced many other organizations to also increase their information requirements. Remember: Better analysis means better decision making.

1.9.6   Provide Flexible Analysis of Information Assets

SAP ECC as a transactional system gets few fundamental criticisms. The system is extremely well engineered and flexible. The problems that organizations most frequently encounter with SAP ECC can be summed up in this quotation: "I know that the information that I need is somewhere in that huge system. I just can't seem to get it out."

SAP NetWeaver BW gathers up this transactional data in a more meaningful and summarized way than SAP ECC can provide. This gives the users the information that they need to analyze data. SAP NetWeaver BW is not designed to provide simple flat reports that might be long and cumbersome to read and distribute.

SAP NetWeaver BW presents the data in a drill-down format that allows users to take the data and slice and dice in the fashion that makes the most sense for their analytical needs. By pre-aggregating the data in a wide variety of ways, SAP NetWeaver BW lends itself to flexible analysis and thus to better visibility of the voluminous data in both the SAP ECC system and other legacy systems.

1.9.7   Business Information to More People in the Organization

Another advantage of SAP NetWeaver BW is that by providing one common tool and one common place to look for information, you can make the data in the organization available to more people. You may not want a large population of users getting access to the transactions to perform accounts receivable and ordering activities in your organization. However, if this data is extracted and stored in a meaningful format elsewhere, you may choose to allow the access of this data for strategic and even operational analysis.

Because the reporting in SAP NetWeaver BW can use one standard toolset, many users can be trained and have this functionality rolled out to them quickly. If the same users went to the transactional system reporting for this data, they would be forced to learn a variety of transaction codes to get the reports they desire. SAP NetWeaver BW allows these reports to be rolled out in a consistent format on an enterprise portal and even as Web reports.

Neither SAP ECC nor SAP R/3 excels at providing strategic analysis of transactional data. They cannot easily provide the organization with comparisons, trending, and graphing that is needed for strategic decision making. Without much customization, SAP ECC cannot provide the strategic data in a usable format that most companies need. It works well with the operational reports such as, "Give me all the deliveries that shipped yesterday." What it does not quickly and easily answer is, "What were my total sales for this product in the state of Pennsylvania last year vs. this year?"

SAP ECC keeps data at its most detailed form. In other words, virtually all data stored in SAP ECC is at the transactional level. Thus, to perform aggregated high-level reporting, the data must be aggregated by an SAP ECC report each time the report is run.

For example, in the report described above — "What were my total sales for this product in the state of Pennsylvania last year vs. this year?"— the system would have to go into the multiple sales tables, headers, detail, and other fields to gather up the various sales, filter out those for the state of Pennsylvania, and gather this data for two years.

Once the user finally gets back the totals that he requested, the next question that the user might ask is: "Now, let's see the same comparison for New Jersey." The system must then plough through the same volume of data to provide this analysis. Because each of these reports takes place on the transactional system, the transactional database server must be tuned to allow fast entry and saving of these transactions to provide the quickest turnaround of the system for the next transaction.

The gathering of the data in an aggregated format requires an on-the-fly joining of the data. In the case of analyzing the sales data in SAP ECC for the state of New Jersey, this can mean joining between 15 to 20 separate tables, gathering of data, sifting out the records that are irrelevant, and providing those sales for only New Jersey. This is a big load on the transactional system. Typically, this reporting would take place during the work day, at the same time the organization needs to process transactions. Thus, organizations limit the use of the transactional systems (typically SAP ECC) for large-volume data analysis.

Most large organizations do not have all their data in SAP ECC. Thus, only one small picture of the entire organization would be reported if all strategic analysis were done in SAP ECC. Because SAP NetWeaver BW allows for data to be brought in from many different DataSources, this provides a clearer and more complete picture of the enterprise. One of the most important features of SAP NetWeaver BW is that this data can be harmonized so that during reporting and analysis the user does not need to be aware, or even care, about the original source of the data.

1.9.8 The Report is Not the Only Output of SAP NetWeaver BW Implementations

The strongest feature of SAP NetWeaver BW is to present the corporate operational data in meaningful summarized information. However, there are more ways to explore the capability of SAP NetWeaver BW. Using *Open Hub*, SAP NetWeaver BW data can be transferred to other applications that do not have direct interface with the SAP platform. The most important area is Retail, where Open Hub is used for many important scenarios. SAP NetWeaver BW extracts the Retail sales data and stores them after performing complex transformations and harmonization. On the other hand, Retail Back Office systems will require SAP NetWeaver BW data to analyze sales on specific promotions, forecasting procurements, etc.

1.10   Why Not Another Data Warehouse?

There are several reasons why SAP customers choose SAP NetWeaver BW over other third-party data warehouse software. Let's examine these reasons in the subsections that follow.

1.10.1 Data Extraction From ECC is Much Easier with SAP NetWeaver BW

In each SAP ECC system, there is a package installed called a *plug-in*. Plug-ins can vary in their release levels and breadth of functionality, but each performs the same task. The plug-ins house the SAP NetWeaver BW DataSouces. A DataSource is a pre-delivered package on the SAP ECC system designed to extract data for loading into SAP NetWeaver BW. The advantages of these DataSources are vast. SAP has already provided an easy path to take data out of SAP ECC and into SAP NetWeaver BW. In the SAP ECC 6.0 version, the plug-in has been eliminated; the DataSources are incorporated as part of the releases of this version.

If the external data warehouse package cannot take advantage of the SAP NetWeaver BW DataSources, the effort becomes burdensome. In the absence of these Data-Sources, the data must be extracted manually out of the SAP ECC system. This is not an easy task in a relational database system. Often, complex function modules and ABAP programs are required to extract and gather the SAP ECC data in a meaningful way.

A great deal of knowledge is required to gather data from the various tables in SAP ECC and extract this data in a consistent form. The DataSources perform the task of gathering data for extraction. This significant task makes the implementation of SAP NetWeaver BW much easier than it would be for another data warehouse software package.

1.10.2 SAP NetWeaver BW Has Pre-configured Business Content Objects

With Business Contents, SAP provides pre-defined SAP NetWeaver BW object models to control and optimize the individual process areas both within as well as outside of the company (Figure 1.13).

Key Benefits of Business Contents:

▶ Ready-to-go reports, data models, extractors, transformations
▶ Significant cut down of implementation time and costs
▶ Rich set of standard key performance indicators
▶ Best practice models from over one thousand installations
▶ Easily extensible
▶ Covers a wide range of industry-specific and application-specific SAP NetWeaver BW objects.

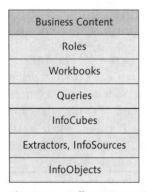

Figure 1.13 Different Types of SAP Delivered Business Content Objects

1.10.3   SAP NetWeaver BW is Already Part of the Landscape

In most cases, SAP NetWeaver BW is already owned (and paid for) as part of the licensing of the SAP ECC system. When an organization already owns the software, it makes little fiscal sense to purchase another data warehouse software package. Thus, many opt to use SAP NetWeaver BW for their data analysis and data warehousing needs.

Those who do not choose to use SAP NetWeaver BW sometimes take a hybrid approach to data warehousing in the organization. They may use the DataSources in SAP NetWeaver BW to gather data from SAP ECC and use functionality in SAP NetWeaver BW called the open hub or InfoSpoke to extract the data out of SAP NetWeaver BW and load this to another data-warehouse software package.

This technique is typically employed only by companies that already have a non–SAP NetWeaver BW data-warehouse package. Often, they need to provide some data from SAP ECC to an existing data warehouse but do not want to migrate to SAP NetWeaver BW. In these cases, the company might decide that the lengthy learning curve and implementation costs of transitioning completely to SAP NetWeaver BW from their legacy data warehouse make it too difficult. Otherwise, SAP NetWeaver BW is often used as the enterprise data warehouse.

1.10.4   SAP NetWeaver BW is the Foundation for Most SAP NetWeaver Products

SAP NetWeaver BW should be the cornerstone for many more products in the future. Some of the products that rely on SAP NetWeaver BW include but are not limited to: SAP Customer Relationship Management (SAP CRM), Advanced Planner and Optimizer (APO), SAP® Strategic Enterprise Management (SAP® SEM®), and SAP Supply Chain Management (SAP SCM). Simply put, many current and new products exist either in conjunction with or completely outside of the SAP ECC transactional environment. The reporting for these packages are usually best performed in the SAP NetWeaver BW environment rather than its source (see Figure 1.14).

Example

SAP APO creates plans for manufacturing or procuring products. This planning data is only useful if it is compared to actual data for analysis of the accuracy of the plan and for budgetary and manufacturing purposes. The actual data resides in SAP NetWeaver BW because this data is fed from the SAP ECC transactional system.

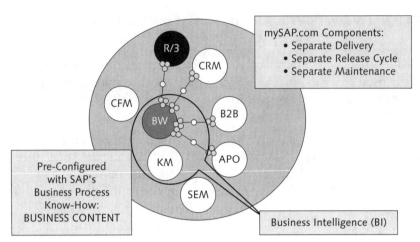

Figure 1.14 SAP NetWeaver BW as Integral Part of SAP NetWeaver Products

To compare the actual data to the plan data, the plan data is extracted from the SAP APO system and combined with the actual data extracted from the SAP ECC system and used for reporting. The end user does not need to be aware of the source of this data, because plan and actual data are presented together in SAP NetWeaver BW.

In the absence of SAP NetWeaver BW, the user would be forced to go to SAP APO for the planned data, then to the SAP ECC system to get the actual data, and then manually harmonize and compare this data. This would be quite labor intensive. It also forces SAP APO to do something that it was not intended to do. SAP APO is designed for planning. SAP NetWeaver BW is designed for reporting. By passing the data from SAP APO to SAP NetWeaver BW, we take advantage of the strengths of both products.

1.11   What SAP NetWeaver BW is Not Designed to Do

A complete understanding of SAP NetWeaver BW includes understanding what SAP NetWeaver BW is not designed to do, and the tasks that SAP NetWeaver BW does not excel. Read the following subsections to understand what SAP NetWeaver BW is not.

1.11.1   SAP NetWeaver BW is Not a Transactional System

Transactions should all be performed in the source systems and SAP NetWeaver BW will capture the transactional and associated master data values from these transactions. The best projects make it clear from the beginning that SAP NetWeaver BW is not the system of record for data. The system of record in the organization continues to live in the transactional systems that feed SAP NetWeaver BW. In most cases, this is SAP ECC, but it could be any other legacy system.

Projects fall into a trap when they try to use SAP NetWeaver BW to perform transactions. Sometimes, this comes in the terms of fixing missing data. For example, they may ask: "Can't we just load the data into a table in SAP NetWeaver BW, manually fix that table, and then load the data into an InfoCube in SAP NetWeaver BW?" The answer to this kind of request should *always* be "No." Alter the data in the source system in its original source transactions and the changed data can then flow into SAP NetWeaver BW. SAP NetWeaver BW is simply not designed as a transactional system for data.

Another common request is to provide transactions in SAP NetWeaver BW for entering data, or for tracking it against other data already in SAP NetWeaver BW. Because SAP NetWeaver BW is not designed to be a transactional system, these requests should be implemented in the transactional systems. Once these processes have been implemented in the transactional systems, SAP NetWeaver BW can extract and store this data and even provide some analysis of the data. The main goal is to keep SAP NetWeaver BW as an analytical system and not as a transactional system.

The more SAP NetWeaver BW's focus gets drawn away from its core value of storing, staging, and presenting data in an aggregated form, the more problems can arise with the project. To avoid these situations, it is important that everyone working on the project understands that SAP NetWeaver BW's role is to deliver information and that all transactions take place on the source system.

The only exception to this rule is planning. SAP NetWeaver BW does allow for planning transactions to take place directly in the SAP NetWeaver BW system. This allows the user to enter planning data. This planning data is saved directly into the SAP NetWeaver BW environment for analysis. Planning is usually done in a limited set of circumstances in SAP NetWeaver BW. This planning must be configured through either NW 2004s Integrated Planning module or Business Process and Simulation (BPS) functions in SAP NetWeaver BW.

For example, while analyzing the current year's actual sales values, it may be necessary to also plan next year's projected sales figures. This planning is performed by entering this planned data directly into the system. Although this is a transactional entry, it can and usually does occur in the SAP NetWeaver BW system itself.

1.11.2 SAP NetWeaver BW is Not the Only Reporting System

Although SAP NetWeaver BW does provide reporting, it should not be considered the only place to provide reporting in the organization. The source system's reporting is not automatically replaced by SAP NetWeaver BW. For example, a report such as *Credit Hold Orders* that shows all orders currently on credit hold is a report that would be better run in the SAP ECC system than SAP NetWeaver BW. SAP NetWeaver BW is typically updated in batch mode once a day. Information on which orders are on credit hold usually needs to be up to the minute. This report would not work well in SAP NetWeaver BW.

It is imperative that your organization understands that SAP NetWeaver BW does provide reporting, but there will always be some reporting requirements that should be met in the source transactional system. This situation will never go away. Not all reporting requirements are automatically SAP NetWeaver BW requirements.

1.11.3 SAP NetWeaver BW is Not Usually Updated in Real Time

SAP NetWeaver BW was designed as a batch system to gather data from source systems (Figure 1.15). In fact, if you were to survey all customers and their data in SAP NetWeaver BW, you would find that more than 99% of the data arrives in batches, not via real-time loading.

Recently introduced functionality has allowed SAP NetWeaver BW to get some data near real time. This should only be used in applications that absolutely require up-to-date, fresh reporting. Usually, this real-time reporting is better handled directly in the source system.

It is a significant challenge to verify the validity of real-time data, simply because the data is so dynamic. Users often have trouble performing analysis because the underlying data is changing even as the report is being run. A quick refresh of the data could yield completely new results. This can make for a difficult environment for decision making. For this and other reasons, many companies prefer an analysis method geared more toward a place in time than toward real time.

Extracting data in real time or close to real time can involve difficult configuration and decision making. To avoid confusion, it is usually recommended that teams with new projects not even talk about real-time reporting in SAP NetWeaver BW. They should convey that SAP NetWeaver BW does not do real-time reporting at all.

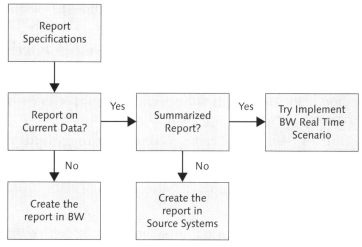

Figure 1.15 Decision Flow to Develop Reports in Source Systems

This avoids confusion and assumptions that people new to SAP NetWeaver BW sometimes make. If those gathering the business requirements assume that the data is updated in real time in SAP NetWeaver BW as a rule, their analysis requirements reflect this real-time requirement. If, on the other hand, everyone assumes that SAP NetWeaver BW is not real time but rather updated at most once a day, the SAP NetWeaver BW team can deal case by case with any circumstance where the data needs to be updated more frequently. In practice, this need turns out to be extremely rare.

1.11.4 BW is Not a Silver Bullet

Let's take a simple example to illustrate this premise.

> **Example**
>
> A large company wanted to use SAP NetWeaver BW to provide global reporting. The company had a complex environment with many different source systems. These source systems included multiple implementations of SAP ECC and several legacy systems. Therefore, the company wanted SAP NetWeaver BW to help provide some global reporting from these systems.

SAP NetWeaver BW is a perfect solution to provide the kind of reporting described in the example. However, this company thought that simply by implementing SAP NetWeaver BW it would automatically get global reporting. The company did not clearly understand that SAP NetWeaver BW can bring in data from many different sources, and this data can then exist together in one SAP NetWeaver BW system.

To have true global reporting, the data from the various sources must be harmonized into one common master data and transactional DataSource.

This can be quite a daunting task in some organizations. In this particular company, the different SAP ECC systems used different material codes for the same material. One SAP ECC system called a product A1, while a second SAP ECC system called the same product F1. Clearly, this data cannot be reported together as one unless there is some link between the two products.

This rule is also true for transactional data. There is no easy way to combine transactional data from many different systems with different configurations. Thus, a transformation process is required in SAP NetWeaver BW to create the harmonization, and in many cases, this can be quite tedious.

When this company realized the level of effort required in SAP NetWeaver BW, it was rather frustrated with what it perceived as a limitation of the SAP NetWeaver BW product. It was pointed out that there was no system that can automatically harmonize and combine data from multiple sources. Any data warehouse would require this work to bring this data together.

1.12   SAP BusinessObjects Capabilities

SAP BusinessObjects Information Management system is the new addition to the business intelligence portfolio.This tool can help you deliver integrated data from both SAP and non-SAP environments. SAP BusinessObjects solution is strongly tied up with SAP NetWeaver BW. Below is a list of important functionalities of SAP BusinessObjects Information Management system:

- ► **Data Integration**
  SAP BusinessObjects can access all types of structured and unstructured data from virtually any source, from databases to web forums. This tool delivers data in real time or in batches.

- ► **Data Quality Management**
  SAP BusinessObjects solution comes with numerous quality management tools to verify that your company's data is correct and consistent across your organization.

- ► **Metadata Management**
  SAP BusinessObjects Metadata Management software overcomes the difficulties of managing metadata from various source systems. This tool consolidates the metadata in relational repository.

1.13 Ingredients for a Successful SAP NetWeaver BW Project Manager

Now that you understand what the product is and what it does well, you can focus on how to implement SAP NetWeaver BW. The first step in any SAP NetWeaver BW project is to pick an SAP NetWeaver BW project manager. Nothing is more integral to the success or failure of a SAP NetWeaver BW project than the project manager. The project manager's many responsibilities are as follows:

▶ Gather requirements from business users

▶ Set priorities among business requirements

▶ Build a capable SAP NetWeaver BW team

▶ Oversee extraction data from various systems

▶ Implement SAP NetWeaver BW functionality to stage, store, and present information

▶ Communicate SAP NetWeaver BW scope and functionality to the organization

▶ Manage and organize transports between systems

▶ Manage testing and validation

▶ Track and resolve issues

▶ Coordinate go-lives

▶ Manage production support transition

▶ Filter, prioritize, and implement new requirements.

The tasks shown in this bulleted list are diverse. These tasks require a broad skill set. The remaining pages in this section discuss the most important qualities of a SAP NetWeaver BW project manager, to help you choose a project manager to manage your new project or upgrade (see Figure 1.16). These skill sets are identical for a new implementation and for an upgrade project. This is because upgrade projects and new implementations go through the same tasks shown above, just at different levels of detail and timing.

Communication skills are imperative when implementing any large-scale change in an organization. SAP NetWeaver BW is no exception. A major part of implementing or upgrading SAP NetWeaver BW is the selling of the system. It is up to the project manager to keep the steering committee, project sponsors, and business users in on the decision-making process of SAP NetWeaver BW. These people must understand what will be delivered with SAP NetWeaver BW and they must be involved, as much as possible, to give them some ownership of the system.

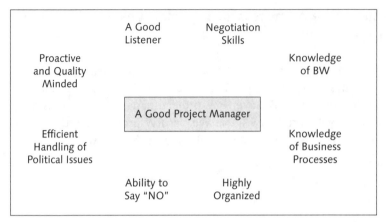

Figure 1.16 Qualities of a Successful SAP NetWeaver BW Manager

1.13.1 Good Communication Skills

The only way to foster ownership among others is to make sure that there is constant communication about the implementation. This communication can come from status reports, one-on-one meetings, and even prototype demos of the system. The project manager should do anything to make sure that the SAP NetWeaver BW project is not seen as an IT project run completely by the application's SAP NetWeaver BW team. The goal is for the business and project sponsors to become part of the process so that when inevitable issues arise, they are willing to work together toward a common solution, rather than waiting for the SAP NetWeaver BW implementation team to solve all the issues.

Continued and ongoing prototype demonstrations and design interviews help ensure that there are no surprises during the eventual handoff of the system to the business users. The more involved the business users and project sponsors are during the planning and development process, the more the SAP NetWeaver BW implementation will reflect their analysis needs.

It is not enough to simply foster the communication. The next step in the communication process is to have clear governance and documentation templates. These allow the SAP NetWeaver BW team to speak with one voice to the business and other units of the organization. This helps stop the scope assumptions and limits the scope creep that can cripple a project or cause project delays.

Once the documentation is complete, the best projects also require signoff on all major documents to make sure that the understanding of the business requirements are clear to all involved. This does not completely prevent the scope and design issues that arise. However, the signoff does help to mitigate and reduce the confusion.

Part of the communication process is the selling of the SAP NetWeaver BW project to the business. This involves generating excitement over the new features and functionality that may not currently be available in the reporting environment. After the initial implementation, the communication usually evolves into recruiting some *SAP NetWeaver BW champions* in the organization to help get the word out about SAP NetWeaver BW and create momentum in the organization. Simply put, the more users who rely on the tool and the more universal the acceptance of it, the more value in the implementation. This acceptance is only gained through awareness. The ultimate role of building this awareness falls on the SAP NetWeaver BW project manager.

1.13.2 Knowledge of SAP NetWeaver BW and Data Warehousing

There's no way to avoid the need to understand the SAP NetWeaver BW product and the various sources of data that are loaded into the system. Although this is not necessary right away, the quicker the project manager can become proficient with the SAP NetWeaver BW system and the various source systems that feed SAP NetWeaver BW, the more effective he will be.

This knowledge of the product helps when trying to quickly understand issues and their impact on the project. Suppose, for example, that a new requirement surfaces late in the development phase of the project. How quickly your project manager can determine the level of effort and impact of this change can help to determine if that requirement can be added to the scope of the project or delayed until a future phase of the project.

If the project manager has no SAP NetWeaver BW knowledge, this new requirement must be communicated to a product specialist, scoped, assessed, and then communicated back to the project manager for a decision. This can add significant time to the project.

Product knowledge is especially helpful because it provides another set of eyes on the issues. This can lead to quicker resolution of a problem and, if needed, a more appropriate escalation of an issue because of the understanding of its impact. If possible, it helps if the SAP NetWeaver BW project manager does some hands-on configuration of SAP NetWeaver BW. Depending on the scope and timeline, this is not always possible, but the more detailed the knowledge of the manager, the better the understanding of the issues faced.

A SAP NetWeaver BW project manager once bragged that he was going to complete an entire SAP NetWeaver BW implementation without logging into the system. He did all he could to stay away from the actual product. He saw his job as managing a SAP NetWeaver BW project. Despite constant prompting, he did not want to know the specifics of the product. Thus, when issues arose that escalated to SAP or the business management, it always slowed the process; we had to explain the issue, explain the impact, and the severity. We found ourselves keeping the project manager out of many of the issues because it simply took too much time to keep him up to speed. This made for an extremely ineffective manager, and as a result, the project moved slowly.

There are many sources that a product manager can go to for SAP NetWeaver BW knowledge. The best place to start is with the SAP education tasks. At minimum, the manager should attend SAP NetWeaver BW classes on the following:

- Data warehousing
- Data modeling
- Data extraction
- Presentation

This will provide a background of the product that should aid in the decision-making process. Make sure significant time is allocated for this training. With the current structure of the classes listed above, this involves more than 18 days of training. When you factor in travel and schedule time for these classes, you realize there is a large time allocation for SAP NetWeaver BW training. This illustrates the rather steep learning curve for the SAP NetWeaver BW product.

Make sure that the classes are representative of the release that will be used for development and go-live. There is little functionality difference between Versions 3.x and 3.5. Thus, those organizations that are planning an SAP NetWeaver BW release in Versions 3.0, 3.1, or 3.5 can attend the 3.x training. Any customer that plans to use the NW 2004s release of SAP NetWeaver BW should make sure that the class is specifically tailored to this release. There are rather significant changes between the 3.x releases and the NW 2004s release.

The next source of information on any project should come from the product and implementation know-how of the consultants on the project. As a consultant, the number one priority is knowledge transfer. This is an advantage in many ways for me. If a project manager and other employees are competent with the system, it makes issue resolution much easier and allows the client to take responsibility for issues and design concerns. It also means that the BW team can satisfactorily manage the system and deal with the inevitable issues that arise.

A good project manager ensures that there is time allocated throughout the implementation process to allow for this knowledge transfer.

When it is time for consultants to be moved off of the project, some project managers expect several months or even a few years' worth of knowledge transfer will take place in a few weeks. With a consultant who has one foot out the door, this will not happen. A roll-off knowledge transfer simply does not take place with the quality that would occur if the employees are part of the configuration from the beginning, have some ownership of the configuration, and stay involved in the process.

1.13.3 Knowledge of Business Processes and Analysis Goals

Knowing the business analysis goals can sometimes be a daunting task for a project manager. Often, even the organization does not completely understand its goals for data analysis. It is the job of the project manager to make sure that these goals are clearly defined and the implementation of the SAP NetWeaver BW system satisfies those goals. Thus, the more the project manager knows the business, the better he is able to be a voice for the business in the scoping and implementation of SAP NetWeaver BW.

There are many outstanding project managers who can quickly understand and evaluate the business user's requirements and help to explain them to the SAP NetWeaver BW team. You can usually know a project manager is especially effective if you hear him say things like: "The business users may say they want X, but I know what they really want is X+1 or even Y." This is not replacing the user's needs with something he does not want but more clearly understanding the goals of the business and helping them to get its needs communicated to the team.

It is this type of understanding of both the SAP NetWeaver BW tool and the business users' needs that help to make sure that the business is not only satisfied but also delighted with the implementation of the SAP NetWeaver BW product.

Knowledge of the organization is also helpful when there are leveraging opportunities. There are many circumstances where two groups in the organization are looking for the same type of information but with a slightly different view. SAP NetWeaver BW is outstanding at providing this kind of flexibility. Knowing the business helps to get several groups interested in the BW data. This not only expands the user base but also helps in funding the project across the organization.

1.13.4 The Need for Political Savvy

There is no way to avoid these inevitable political issues. SAP NetWeaver BW projects usually are quite political. This is because ownership of information in an organization makes one's position more powerful. SAP NetWeaver BW, if implemented properly, can be a powerful tool.

Setting the scope and priority of any project can cause political battles in many organizations. Many projects have been delayed because of simple decisions that could not be made due to an intensely political environment. Failure to properly escalate or champion issues through the political environment of any organization can cause significant delays that adversely affect a project. The project manager must be able to negotiate through these political hurdles.

> **Example**
>
> A client, in an early stage of an SAP NetWeaver BW implementation, spent several months deciding where their development and production servers should be physically located. This decision does not add any value to the implementation. However, in this organization, the location of the servers denoted the ownership of the box. This translated into resources for the technical and sustaining organizations. Each group was fighting for the servers to be located in their location to get some of the budget money.

The problem in the case described in this example was not as much the fight but the length of time that this delayed the project. The SAP NetWeaver BW project manager felt that this battle was too political and outside his domain. He decided that the best approach was to wait until the various technical groups determined the locations for the servers. This decision lasted a long time, and wasted a great deal of time. If the project manager had a clear path to the steering committee and/or project sponsors, he could have escalated this issue and forced a quicker decision, thus saving time and money.

The opposite is also true. Not including groups in discussions or not following the proper escalation channels can also land a project in a difficult situation. There have been many situations where potential allies in the implementation process were alienated early in the project because of a political squabble and thus did not give the project team the extra help that they could have used later.

The project manager also needs to be able to balance the team's strengths. For example, the best use of a SAP NetWeaver BW developer's time is as a tool to aid in the implementation of the SAP NetWeaver BW product. Typically, developers like to stay close to the product and work on the system because they do not like the day-to-day project management and the political struggles that come with a project. The better the project manager is able to keep these political issues from the developers and keep them focused on delivering and implementing the software, the more productive the team will be.

Often, you can spot a well-run project when developers find out about large political issues only after completion. The project manager was sheltering the developers from those battles and keeping the team focused on delivering the SAP NetWeaver BW system.

Keeping this delicate balance is a difficult and often overlooked talent that a SAP NetWeaver BW project manager must possess. However, the more politically in tune this manager is with his surroundings, the more efficient the entire implementation of SAP NetWeaver BW can become.

1.13.5 Highly Organized and Quality Minded

The multitude of issues, meetings, and requirements that are involved with a typical SAP NetWeaver BW project requires a detailed and organized and quality-minded individual. Developing a methodology to track requirements and issues is vital to a successful project.

1.13.6 Willing and Able to Develop and Enforce Standards

Any SAP NetWeaver BW project should be considered a foundation for the future. To ensure that this foundation is sound, governance must be established to make sure that the decisions of the past do not cause issues in the future. For instance, naming standards are important in SAP NetWeaver BW. The system allows for an extremely flexible naming of the InfoCubes and DSO structures.

It is up to the project manager to not only make sure that the naming standards are developed but also that these same standards are enforced in the SAP NetWeaver BW implementation.

As the number of InfoCubes and DSOs grow, the naming conventions become more important to track and understand the contents and purpose of the data in an InfoCube or DSO. The naming of the DSO and InfoCubes can also be used for security and authorizations. Thus, a well thought-out naming standards document and enforcement of the standards can make for easier authorizations.

Many projects wind up with a naming standards document that is not enforced. One example project had a naming standards document, yet most of the InfoProviders (InfoCubes and DSOs) did not follow the standards because there was no enforcement. Later the project team wanted to implement security based on their naming standards for each InfoProvider but, because of the lack of governance, it was much more difficult. These standards need to be built and enforced by the project manager.

1.13.7 Team Building

Building a good SAP NetWeaver BW team is a critical task for the project manager. Keeping a good mix between consultant resources and employee resources, and making sure these personalities work well together and fit into the overall corporate culture, is important. The project manager must be able to choose a productive team. This team consists of an SAP NetWeaver BW internal team and an external team. Let's discover what is involved in building these teams next.

Building an Internal Team

In a typical SAP NetWeaver BW project, there are two main groups helping on the implementation. These are considered *internal team* members, because they are performing the day-to-day implementation of the product.

These are usually called the applications and Basis teams. The applications team is focused on the day-to-day configuration of the SAP NetWeaver BW product. This includes the configuration, loading, and testing of the product. The Basis team handles the infrastructure of the implementation. This includes creating the environment, handling transports, patches, administering security, upgrades, etc.

The Basis and applications teams have a fundamental conflict in their goals. The Basis team is responsible for keeping the system at a stable, steady state, with maximum uptime. The applications team, when performing large data loads in SAP NetWeaver BW, can test the limits of the system environments in memory and disk space, thus placing a strain on the Basis goals of maximum uptime and steady state. This can cause conflict in some teams between the Basis and applications teams.

In a typical project, the Basis team and SAP NetWeaver BW application team must work together more closely than the SAP ECC teams and their Basis counterparts. This is because of the nature of the SAP NetWeaver BW product. It requires the Basis team to aid in connecting to the various source systems and handling file management, index creation, transport issues between systems, etc.

The project manager needs to bridge the gap between the Basis and applications team, and aid in the issue tracking and issue resolution between the two teams.

This will help make sure that the ownership of issues is clear and the constant communication keeps the priority issues on track for resolution.

Building an External Team

All projects have not only an SAP NetWeaver BW implementation team but also have various stakeholders who guide the requirements for the SAP NetWeaver BW project. Identifying and keeping these stakeholders part of the extended SAP NetWeaver BW team is important to make sure that stakeholders are satisfied with the implementation. These stakeholders might take the form of sponsors, users, managers, or other individuals or groups that have a stake in the success (or failure) of the SAP NetWeaver BW project.

The project manager must be able to understand the stakeholders' motivations and goals and make sure that the SAP NetWeaver BW project meets the various changing needs of these extended team members.

1.13.8   Budget Accountability

SAP NetWeaver BW, as with every project, has budget concerns. These include hardware, consulting, application, and production support. There are no available figures that detail the average total budget amounts for SAP NetWeaver BW projects. However, there are some surveys that give these figures for data warehouses in general. SAP NetWeaver BW projects are generally large, as compared to a typical data warehouse, because the volume of the source data is usually rather large.

The SAP NetWeaver BW budget, like the SAP ECC budget, is usually set at the beginning of the project before the scope is clearly established. As the scope gets more refined, the budget is typically not in line with the requirements. The SAP NetWeaver BW project manager is forced to re-allocate the resources based on the budget that has been allocated or seek to redefine the budget.

1.13.9   Willing to Say Both "Yes" and "No"

This is where the project manager needs to walk a fine line. If scope is set too rigidly and no changes are allowed, opportunities can be missed. For instance, a minor change in SAP NetWeaver BW could allow for a much more useful environment. Take the example of the InfoCube designed with no cost information included, because it was originally deemed out of scope. However, late in the implementation process, the cost values were requested by the project sponsor.

Adding the cost values to the InfoCubes would not have involved a large effort, but the scope was rigid, and the project manager declined the request. If the project manager had paused and assessed the workload of the new change, they could have included a much larger user base in SAP NetWeaver BW. In turn, SAP NetWeaver BW would have been more useful to the organization without a large budget impact. They were already planning a full regression test on the SAP NetWeaver BW data. This testing could easily have been adapted to include the costing figures and costing requirements.

There is another side to the same story. On one project, each small change that was requested was incorporated into the scope, even late in the build phase of the project. This caused many more hours of work as the new requirements were added and re-tested to fulfill the scope. For many of these requests, the project manager should have said "No" or should have taken time to reassess the scope as a whole rather than adding each request individually.

The only way to handle these requests is to have scope clearly documented. Thus, any new requirement can be clearly shown to be out of scope. All initial judgment should be withheld until a formal scope-management process can assess impact and benefit. Only through a formal process can a decision be made to include or exclude a request. The project manager is the one to head up the authorization of these requests.

1.14   Conclusion

In this chapter, we gave you a practical understanding of what is involved in a typical SAP NetWeaver BW project lifecycle. We hope that you can plan your own SAP NetWeaver BW implementation project with knowledge of the potential pitfalls. After reading this chapter, you should know what SAP NetWeaver BW can and cannot do and what your organization and project manager should be prepared for. In this chapter, we discussed the capabilities of SAP BusinessObjects software so that you will be able to choose an optimum business intelligence solution for your organization.

In Chapter 2, we will look at defining an implementation strategy.

Knowing the important questions to answer before starting any SAP NetWeaver BW project, will help ensure your project is planned, organized, and implemented as efficiently as possible.

2 Defining an Implementation Strategy

The first step in a project is to set the overall strategy. There are many factors that go into these decisions. Understanding the process and pitfalls in setting the strategy can make sure that a project has the best opportunity for success.

An SAP NetWeaver BW implementation strategy is a series of useful plans, steps, and actions to arrive at a clear and effective use of the SAP NetWeaver BW product. An implantation strategy of SAP NetWeaver BW can become quite complex. There are many factors involved in the decision making.

Common decisions that make up the implementation strategy involve scope, resources, technology, politics, culture, and change management. A sound implementation strategy should be able to answer the following questions in Table 2.1:

Areas of Involvement	Questions
Customer	► Who can leverage and get the most advantage from implementing SAP NetWeaver BW?
	► What kind of training is required for adapting the new technology?
	► What are the most significant barriers that end users need to overcome to get the full advantage of the change?
	► Is there sufficient commitment and involvement from the steering committee, project sponsors, and user community?
Business	► What are the business questions that SAP NetWeaver BW can answer? What are the assumptions?
	► What are the business and project risks?
	► How is the customer's business going to benefit with SAP NetWeaver BW implementation?

Table 2.1 Questions to be Answered Before Starting an SAP NetWeaver BW Project

Areas of Involvement	Questions
Data	▶ What is the scope of the data that will be in SAP NetWeaver BW?
	▶ What are the volume and sources of the data to be loaded into SAP NetWeaver BW?
	▶ How granular is the data to be in SAP NetWeaver BW, and what is the frequency of the update of data?
	▶ How many non-SAP source systems will be integrated with SAP NetWeaver BW?
	▶ How will the master data from various sources be integrated?
	▶ Do end users need real-time data? If yes, to what extent?
Presentation	▶ How will the current reporting environment be affected? Will it be retained, phased out, or replaced?
	▶ What type of presentation is expected for the end users?
Project	▶ What SAP ECC data is in scope? Is SAP NetWeaver BW being implemented at the same time as SAP ECC? Is SAP NetWeaver BW going live at the same time as SAP ECC? How will SAP NetWeaver BW interact with SAP ECC?
	▶ What is the technical landscape: hardware, software, network, etc.?
	▶ What testing and validation will be required?
	▶ What production support will be planned after go-live?
	▶ How is the scope to be documented and how will this be communicated to the business community?
	▶ If the project is implemented by an offshore team also, then what will be the ratio of work between onsite and offshore? And what will be the scope for these two teams?
Developer	▶ Who will be implementing SAP NetWeaver BW? How will these people become proficient with the product?
	▶ What are the experience levels of the SAP NetWeaver BW consultants?
	▶ In case of offshore teams, what will be the scope of the work?
Time	▶ What is the overall time line expected from SAP NetWeaver BW?

Table 2.1 Questions to be Answered Before Starting an SAP NetWeaver BW Project (Cont.)

Tip
Be particularly careful when talking about the reporting on real-time data with your customer. Never forget to implement scope change control to manage any further changes in scope.

2.1 Defining an Upgrade Strategy

A sound upgrade strategy should be able to answer the following questions in Table 2.2:

Areas of Involvement	Questions
SAP NetWeaver BW Version	▶ What version will be implemented? ▶ Why are we implementing the new version? ▶ What are the plug-in requirements in the SAP ECC system for this upgrade?
Time line	▶ What is the time line for the upgrade?
Landscape	▶ What is the technical landscape? Will the upgrade take place in a new development environment, or will the upgrade take place on the common development environment? ▶ How does this affect other components in the landscape? Will other components need to be upgraded, too?
Development	▶ What new functionality (if any) will be implemented immediately? ▶ What testing and validation are required? ▶ How does the upgrade affect other components of SAP NetWeaver BW? ▶ Is a conversion function needed to use new functionality in the release?

Table 2.2 Questions to be Answered Before an Upgrade Project

Tip

Don't upgrade your current implementation just because new versions of the software come up. There should be clear consensus within the organization for having an upgraded system. There could be multiple reasons to upgrade your system:

▶ The current system is not capable of handling the increased data load; the new version handles the data load better.

▶ There are many new features in the upgraded software that are critical for the current business scenario; the old version does not have those features.

SAP ECC systems are upgraded so it's also important to upgrade the SAP NetWeaver BW system. It is particularly important because most of the SAP NetWeaver BW projects use Business Content data sources to extract data from SAP ECC. So, using newer version of Business Content data sources with the old version of SAP NetWeaver BW will be a complicated development.

2.2   SAP NetWeaver BW Implementation Approach

Any SAP NetWeaver BW implementation approach can be distinguished in three types with respect to development of SAP R/3 system (Figure 2.1). Each of the approaches has its own pros and cons. Let's discuss each of the approaches.

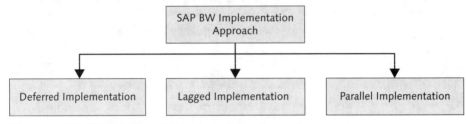

Figure 2.1   SAP SAP NetWeaver BW Implementation Approach

▶ **Parallel Implementation**
  In this type of approach, an SAP NetWeaver BW project and SAP R/3 projects are implemented in parallel. The main advantage of this type of approach is that customers can learn the SAP R/3 processes and SAP NetWeaver BW reports simultaneously. Thus, training cost is reduced significantly. Moreover, it is also easy to adapt to a new reporting environment when users are also learning to use the SAP R/3 system. However, this approach may face a considerable amount of difficulty in SAP NetWeaver BW objects modelling and testing because of the unavailability of the source system and test data.

▶ **Lagged Implementation**
  In this approach, SAP R/3 implementation and SAP NetWeaver BW implementation is scheduled in such a way that there is lag of phase in between two implementations. For example, after completing the blueprint phase of SAP R/3, the SAP NetWeaver BW blueprint phase starts. Most of the implementation projects are most suitable in this approach. With this approach, an SAP NetWeaver BW phase can start implementing while a phase of the corresponding SAP R/3 implantation is over. In this way, all SAP NetWeaver BW data flow scenarios can be modelled without waiting for SAP R/3 to be prepared. However, this approach requires much close coordination with both of the teams.

▶ **Deferred Implementation**
  Ideally, in this approach, SAP NetWeaver BW implementation starts after most of the implementation of the SAP R/3 systems. Many customers prefer this approach because of its simplicity and less coordination effort. SAP NetWeaver BW teams can implement the project almost independently. This approach also

ensures complete testing of each and every data flow scenario and transformation logics.

2.3 SAP NetWeaver BW Hardware Sizing

Sizing any SAP NetWeaver BW hardware requirement can be challenging and sometimes requires a lot of expertise and experience. This is an important strategy because SAP NetWeaver BW is considered corporate memory. Below are the different sizing methods that can be applied in your project:

▸ **Initial Calculation Method**
This is nothing but some educated guesses. Generally, an experienced SAP NetWeaver BW consultant who has several end-to-end SAP NetWeaver BW implementation experience takes this decision.

▸ **T-Shirt**
This sizing approach is based on algorithm and assumptions such as number of users, data loads, etc.

▸ **Formula**
With this approach, you create a formula to size the hardware. This is relatively transparent and closer to reality.

▸ **Quick Size**
This is a tool provided by SAP to its customers to estimate the hardware size. You can access this tool free of cost online in the SAP Service Marketplace. This is widely recognized and thoroughly updated by SAP.

Important Links on Web
SAP Developer Network: *www.sdn.sap.com* →Weblogs→Sizing
SAP Customer Services Network: *www.sap.com/services/*
SAP Sizing Tool: *http://service.sap.com/sizing*.

While working with the Quick Sizing tool in the SAP Service Marketplace, you will see that processor-related sizing is termed *SAPS*.

The *SAP Application Performance Standard (SAPS)* is a hardware-independent unit that describes the performance of a system configuration in the SAP environment. It is derived from the Sales and Distribution (SD) Benchmark where 100 SAPS = 2000 fully business processed order line items per hour.

Simplified estimates for an InfoCube:

```
Size in Bytes = {(n + 3)*10 Bytes + (m*17 Bytes)} * [Rows of Initial
Load + Rows of Periodic Load * Number of periods]
n = Number of Dimensions
m = Number of Key Figures
```

With the above result add following estimates:

```
+ 20% for PSA
+ 100% for Aggregates
+ 100% for Indexes
+ 10% for Master Data (Exception Retail, Utility etc)
+ Twice the memory space of the largest Fact table (at least 10 GB)
```

2.4   Landscape Strategy

The new system landscape strategy involves the following:

▶ The number of systems in the SAP NetWeaver BW landscape

▶ The purpose of each system

▶ Strategy for keeping the systems synchronized

▶ Strategy for development

▶ Strategy for production support.

The choice of the landscape for the SAP NetWeaver BW environment is one of the most important decisions made in an SAP NetWeaver BW implementation. In SAP NetWeaver BW, as with SAP ECC, systems are set up, each with their own purpose. The typical systems and their purposes in an SAP NetWeaver BW landscape strategy are as follows:

▶ **Development**
As the name implies, the development system is the SAP NetWeaver BW system where all new configuration and development is performed. Everything that will be eventually rolled out to the production user will begin here.

▶ **Testing and Quality Assurance (QA)**
Transports from the development environment typically land here first. All validation testing of the configuration takes place here before it is moved to production.

▶ **Production**
All live analysis will occur in the production instance.

▶ **Training**
This is an optional system that trains the end users.

▶ **Sandbox**
This is an optional system used for prototyping and playing.

▶ **Production Support**
This is an optional system used for testing production issues. This system is refreshed by copying the production system periodically.

There are several important elements that you can incorporate into your landscape strategy that will make a positive impact on your project. Recommendations for developing a landscape strategy are given in the following subsections.

2.4.1 Insist on a Sandbox System

When an SAP NetWeaver BW landscape is being determined, many feel that a sandbox is a luxury. They feel that having a three-tiered landscape environment (Development, QA, and Production) is enough to satisfy the needs of the development team.

The main advantage to the three-tiered landscape option shown in Figure 2.2 is in its simplicity. There are only three systems to install, maintain, back up, etc. This is the least expensive landscape option from a maintenance standpoint. It works fine if there is an extremely simple project with a tight timeline and a well-understood scope.

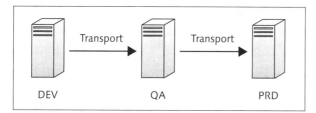

Figure 2.2 Typical Three-Tiered Landscape in SAP NetWeaver BW

However, this is rarely the case. Most configurations in SAP NetWeaver BW require some level of prototyping and building up of several scenarios to determine which is best. In the environment seen in Figure 2.2, there is no sandbox system for performing these prototypes. Because these are needed, the only place to do them is in the development system.

Quickly, the development system can become filled with many different prototypes and test objects, which pollute the environment with much unneeded configuration. The best way to prevent this is to have a sandbox system that allows configuration outside of the development environment.

Take the example of a client who had a Basis SAP NetWeaver BW sandbox but no development sandbox. In other words, they wanted a sandbox to be used to test support packages, upgrades, etc. only. This sandbox was not to be used for configuration testing. The Basis team could not be convinced that this added little value to the project.

They did not understand that any testing of support packages and upgrades needs to occur in conjunction with the development team and that having one sandbox for both teams would have made for a more useful prototyping environment for both the Basis and the development teams.

Figure 2.3 shows a landscape environment including a sandbox. In this environment, prototyping and testing can occur in the sandbox system outside of the development system and away from the final configuration.

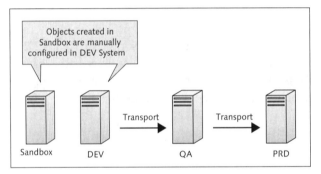

Figure 2.3 Typical SAP NetWeaver BW Environment Using a Sandbox

Unlike SAP ECC or SAP R/3, SAP NetWeaver BW does not support a multi-client system for doing testing. For example, in SAP ECC, it is possible to create another client on an existing development system that could be used for configuration and/or testing without impacting the development client. These clients allow for separate sets of master and transactional data on the SAP ECC system using the same set of configuration.

This is not possible in SAP NetWeaver BW. SAP NetWeaver BW allows only one client per SAP NetWeaver BW instance or system. This is an important distinction and one that somewhat limits the SAP NetWeaver BW system because multiple clients allow a lot more flexibility in the SAP ECC or SAP R/3 systems.

Because there is no way to have multiple clients, and because you need an area for prototyping, a completely stand-alone sandbox system should be created for the prototyping.

Of course, this sandbox can be refreshed as often as needed. This usually is accomplished via a client copy from either the development or the QA system. The assumption is that any configuration done in the sandbox will need to be manually replicated in the development instance.

The process of sending a configuration from one SAP NetWeaver BW system to another is called the *transport process*. This allows for the approved configuration to be moved from the development system to the QA system and then onto the production system. This is designed to make sure that only the functionality that was approved moves to the production and/or QA systems. The sandbox system is designed strictly for prototyping; therefore, transports should never be created from the sandbox system.

If the budget is the main factor not to have a sandbox system, you can use a sandbox system that is shared by other SAP NetWeaver BW projects, as in Figure 2.4. This can reduce the spending of having a dedicated sandbox system. However, take approval from your customer before using shared sandbox systems because of the security of data and configuration.

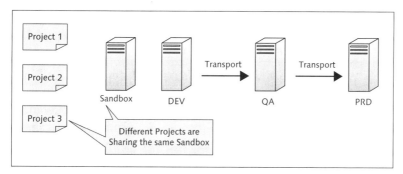

Figure 2.4 SAP NetWeaver BW Landscape where Sandbox is Shared with Many Projects

It must be clearly understood that any configuration done in the sandbox is fleeting and can be lost at any time to a system refresh. There have been many instances when team members did not know of an impending refresh and lost their work. As long as this is understood and the refresh schedule is clearly posted, this is typically not an issue.

Figure 2.5 shows a complete SAP NetWeaver BW environment including a sandbox. This is called a five-system landscape because the sandbox is not typically counted as part of the landscape. It is a stand-alone system that is not part of the transport path.

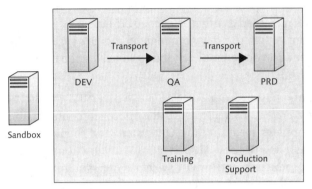

Figure 2.5 SAP NetWeaver BW Landscape with Sandbox, Production Support, and Training Systems

Objectives for Having a Sandbox
Prototyping and building up of several scenarios to determine which is best keeps development systems clean from unnecessary configurations designed for testing purpose.
Because SAP NetWeaver BW is not a multi-client system, it's hard to perform some R&D if you do not have sandbox systems.

2.4.2 Think About the Training Environment

Training in SAP NetWeaver BW is a task that is often not planned until well into the project lifecycle. This is a mistake. Because the configuration typically is not in production until cutover, training on new SAP NetWeaver BW functionality must occur outside of the production system. There are two popular strategies to provide SAP NetWeaver BW training:

► Use the Development or QA system for training
► Have a separate training system.

There are ramifications to both options. If you plan to provide the training on the development or QA system, conflicts inevitably occur. The queries, InfoCubes, DSO, and master data objects that are needed for training must be filled with valid data and kept fairly inactive during the training. This can be difficult for projects with tight schedules.

Constant changes make for a dynamic environment. To make matters worse, some of the configuration changes needed in SAP NetWeaver BW requires data to be dumped and reloaded. All of these factors mean that things are never at a steady state during the development and testing process.

To provide training, a steady state is needed. This causes conflict between the training group that is looking for a static environment to build test exercises, screen shots, etc., and the SAP NetWeaver BW development team that is trying to complete the SAP NetWeaver BW configuration. Essentially, this means that most development on these objects must stop during training.

The only way to alleviate this issue is with a separate, stand-alone training system. Figure 2.5 gave you a view of this landscape. Many companies opt for this landscape to have a static place for training. In my experience, this is usually the best option, but there are some drawbacks.

At some point, you must build the training system from the QA or development system based on the configuration at a certain point in time. Any changes after that time are not automatically reflected in the training system because that system must be at a steady state in which transports will not change the configuration.

Therefore, some of the issues that have been fixed in the development and QA systems are not included in training. These usually need to be manually fixed or worked around during training. The other most important factor is the time that it takes to build a separate training instance. Most projects underestimate the amount of time that it takes to get the training system ready.

The end users are getting their first view of SAP NetWeaver BW in this training environment, so it is very important to have this system perform as strongly as possible. This sometimes means creating manual flat file feeds to fill master data tables and InfoCubes/DSO in the training environment because the connected source systems do not yet have valid data.

Some level of performance tuning and testing should also occur on this training system. This is to ensure that the users have a positive view of the system during the training.

These efforts can be quite time-consuming. This significant time dedicated to training keeps the development team away from their development work and testing tasks, and thus can affect the schedule.

Tip

Significant time should be built into the project plan to build the training environment.

As long as the time can be dedicated to this environment, having a separate training system is the approach least disruptive to the project and the one that allows for more successful training of end users.

Objectives for Having a Training System
To give training to end users when new SAP NetWeaver BW system not rolled out in production.
A dedicated system for training ensures the stability of the SAP NetWeaver BW objects during training.
Sometimes, training can regenerate a production problem, which cannot be replicated in either development or a QA system.

2.4.3 Adding a Production Support System

Some companies also opt for another system in their environment called a *production support system*, as shown in Figure 2.5. This system is usually a complete copy of the production system that is refreshed periodically.

This stand-alone production support instance would allow for some limited prototyping and issue testing. For example, suppose a production support issue is reported in the sales InfoCube with return orders for a specific material type. There are few valid returns in the QA system, and none for that material type. You could attempt to create one in the SAP ECC QA system, but you might not be able to replicate it exactly.

Thus, in a scenario where there is little production data in a QA environment, it becomes difficult to test production support issues. This is because the data needed to replicate is simply not in the QA environment, and it can be cumbersome to create a specific scenario.

There is no better way of replicating the specific issue than with a copy of the production environment. The production support system serves as that copy. Typically, this system is open for configuration so scenarios can be tried to fix problems.

Tip
There should be no transports from the production support system. It is simply used as a system on which to test and re-test issues and prototypes with production data.

Periodic refreshes should occur to keep this system as close to production as possible. For a more complete environment, insist on a production support system in your SAP NetWeaver BW landscape. This system allows for quicker problem resolution and more complete prototyping of scenarios, and thus for a better overall environment for end users.

2.4.4 Keep Development, QA, Production Environments in Sync

One of the most important tasks in maintaining separate systems in a landscape is to keep them in sync. If these systems are not in sync, it is difficult to troubleshoot configuration, transports, and technical issues. If a function is working in development and QA, there is no reason that the same function should not work in production. If this is not the case, and the problem is not data related, the problem is usually that the systems are out of sync. This can happen for many reasons. For example, changes made to one environment may not have been performed in another. These changes can be manual changes or even transport changes.

> **Tip**
>
> Never, never, never let anyone pollute the environment by allowing configuration in a client other than the development client.

How can you keep these systems in sync to avoid wasting time chasing issues when something works in one environment and inexplicably does not work in another? The answer lies in having strict rules to make sure that all changes are performed in each system.

This recommendation sounds rather obvious. Anyone who has done any SAP ECC or SAP R/3 development knows that you would never perform any development in a client other than the development client. However, it's amazing that so many are willing to create exceptions to the rule.

Here is a typical scenario that causes someone to allow the landscape environment to be compromised, even if it unintentionally. An SAP NetWeaver BW developer is trying to build a rather complex InfoCube. He needs to perform significant transformation of data to arrive at a specified calculation and characteristic data in an InfoCube. This requires many iterations of testing to get the configuration correct.

The development system is linked to the development SAP ECC system; therefore, all the data that is fed to the development system comes from this system. The developer cannot test his work in development because the real data that he needs to verify the configuration is only found in the production SAP ECC system or QA system. Security and space requirements prevent the Basis team from connecting the production or QA SAP ECC system to the development SAP NetWeaver BW system, and so there is no way to test the new InfoCube transformation.

The developer could simply make a best attempt at the configuration, transport to QA or production, load the data there, and then—if results are incorrect—re-transport, etc. However, this adds a lot of time to the development process.

This is the point at which many project managers allow the development in the QA or productive environment. They ask for promises that any work that is done is then put into the development environment and transported again. They think that this will keep the systems in sync. They then ask the Basis system team to open up the QA or production system for configuration temporarily. Opening up the system is a simple process using Transactions SCC4 and SE06 that Basis performs to allow the manual configuration in these environments.

What inevitably happens is that as developers begin to get sloppy; they either forget or do not want to be bothered with making sure that all changes done go back to the development system. There is also the risk that they inadvertently change things in the QA or production system without really understanding the changes.

> **Note**
>
> Any time that you allow any manual configuration in any system other than the development system, you risk allowing the systems to get out of sync. Later, this can cause hours of work and troubleshooting issues.

There is one notable exception to this rule. Periodically, issues with transports necessitate allowing spot fixes in the QA or production environment. Read the section later in this chapter on transport strategies to understand more about this exception.

2.4.5   Assess New Phases of Development

New phases and releases of SAP NetWeaver BW cause the SAP NetWeaver BW landscape environment to become more complex. Issues and conflicts occur when you try to do new development in the production support landscape.

> **Example**
>
> You have a SAP NetWeaver BW landscape like the one depicted in Figure 2.6. You have gone live with the SAP NetWeaver BW system and everything is going well, users are active in our production environment, and the organization is happy. After the system stabilizes, they give you a list of things that they also want implemented into the SAP NetWeaver BW system. You decide to implement these changes and features and call it the resulting system SAP NetWeaver BW Release Two.

You can start doing the Release Two development directly into the SAP NetWeaver BW development system shown in Figure 2.6. However, some conflicts can occur with that strategy. If you've done some Release Two configuration changes to the productive sales InfoCube and later get a call from the users that there is a production problem with the very same InfoCube, you have an issue to resolve.

The changes that have already been done for the new development are not yet ready to go into production. However, you need to fix and transport the InfoCube to fix the production problem. How do you fix the production issue but still keep your newest configuration?

You must first back out any configuration changes to the InfoCube for Release Two, make the change needed for the production support issue, test, and transport the change up to production. You then have to reconfigure the Release Two configuration back into the InfoCube. This can get cumbersome if there are multiple production issues with that InfoCube.

You cannot simply avoid the issue by taking the InfoCube, DSO structure, and/or master data object and copy them to the newly named DSO, InfoCube, or master data objects. If you try to do this, you would have to implement a new InfoCube, DSO, and/or master data object each time you have any changes to these objects.

This is not practical. Changing an InfoCube technical name means switching the base cube name, which causes all InfoCube queries and favorites from the users to become invalid because they were built on the old technical InfoCube names. This would cause a disruption for the users because their favorites and bookmarks would no longer function and would have to be rebuilt.

The solution to this problem is to create a Release Two development and QA environment. This environment shown in Figure 2.6 and is used for new development. All configuration for Release Two occurs in the DEV2 system. All QA testing for Release Two occurs in the QA2 system.

This allows independent configuration of the system, while still allowing production support to take place. This is a popular landscape strategy where production support is outsourced to another group. The production support group *owns* the DEV1, DEV2, and the Production (PRD) systems, while the new development team *owns* the DEV2, and QA2 systems.

This landscape design raises an important question: How do changes made to the production support environment get into the new development environment? The answer is that any production support fixes or changes are manually added to the new development environment. This is because we cannot transport from one development to another development without a lot of analysis, and this can even be impossible if the two development releases are on different SAP NetWeaver BW versions.

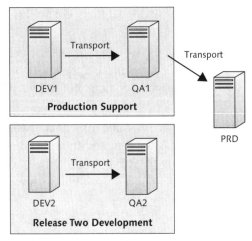

Figure 2.6 Release Two Development Environment Showing Dual Development and Dual QA

A process must be put in place to track the production support changes and make sure that these get into the new SAP NetWeaver BW development environment.

Once new development is complete, you are ready to cut over the new development landscape. For this, shut down production temporarily, transport the new development into the production system, and retire the DEV1 and QA1 systems. The DEV2 and QA2 systems now become the production support environment.

If a release three development is needed, make DEV1 and QA1 the new development landscape. During cutover, the DEV2 and QA2 are now retired and DEV1 and QA1 become the production support environment. Keep switching back and forth between the systems to allow development and production support to continue simultaneously.

The disadvantage to this approach is that there are more systems to maintain and support. However, this disadvantage is far outweighed by the flexibility of the landscape, if the new development is significant.

> **Note**
>
> If new development is minor, use the development system to perform changes, and manually back-out changes if needed for production support. If the release is significant, create a new development system as shown in Figure 2.6. Upgrades typically require a Release Two–type landscape strategy.

Figure 2.7 shows a Release Two landscape and cutover. This type of landscape is typically required during an upgrade. This is because you must upgrade the system, test the new release, and run regression tests on all parts of the system to make sure that the current configuration still works after the upgrade.

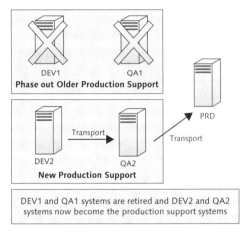

Figure 2.7   Release Two Cutover

Unless SAP NetWeaver BW can be shut down during the upgrade, there is really no clear way to provide an upgraded system and also perform testing. When the testing is complete, the production environment is shut down and upgraded. The DEV1 and QA1 systems on the old release are then retired after the production system has been upgraded. Some customers need to perform an upgrade to an existing environment. There are also several specific decisions that need to be made when determining the upgrade landscape.

Let's compare all the strategies in Table 2.3, so that you can take better decision for your landscape.

	Classic Three Tier	Landscape with Sandbox	Landscape with Training System	Landscape with Production Support System
Requirement	Mandatory	Optional	Optional	Good to have
Cost	Lowest	Low	High	Higher
Advantage	Mandatory	Highest	High	Higher
Effort to Implement	Least	Least	High	High

Table 2.3   Comparative Study on Different Landscape Strategy

2.5   Upgrade Landscape

An upgrade landscape refers to the series of systems that will be used to house the new development and production support when the system is being upgraded to a new SAP NetWeaver BW release. Because an existing environment is already in place, many decisions need to be made. A further challenge is that sending transports between systems of different releases is not a recommended practice.

The main focus of the upgrade effort should be on understanding how the upgrade can least affect the users who are using the system in production. Keeping this in mind, you need to make sure that the upgrade can be fully implemented and tested in a stand-alone environment, away from the end users. This allows for a full regression testing of the new release without affecting these users.

Typically, this is handled by a process known as *wave development*. This is a process in which two development environments are created and used simultaneously. One is used for production support. The other is used for new development tasks. The team moves from one to the other as new releases are planned. This allows the new upgraded environment to take place in one area and the existing production support to take place in a parallel but separate area.

During upgrades, organizations can opt to upgrade the existing development environment or opt for a new development environment. To upgrade the existing development environment, they must halt all production support fixes during the upgrade process. This is because SAP does not allow transports between different versions of the software.

If no freeze can take place in the production support environment for fixes, a new development environment like the one in Figure 2.6 is often implemented. Once new development is complete, as part of an upgrade or part of a new install, the configuration needs to be moved throughout the landscape. Having a clear and well-documented transport strategy is important to make sure that the systems stay in sync.

2.6   Transport Strategy

A transport is the method used to move configuration from one system to another in SAP systems. If all development is performed in the development system, the only way this configuration (InfoCubes, DSOs, etc.) is created in the QA and production environments is via the transport process.

A transport serves as a record in the system for what has been changed and when the change occurred. Each object that is activated in SAP NetWeaver BW has a development class. The development class is used by the system to track the status and type of development that has occurred. When a new object is created, the SAP NetWeaver BW system, by default, assigns the object a development package of $TMP.

This $TMP development-package indicator means that the development is currently deemed by the system as temporary. When the object is assigned to a transport via the transport system, the object can be assigned to a new development package. Once the object gets assigned a new non-$TMP development package and is attached to a transport, the object is locked for development. No other user may alter that object without being added to the transport that has been created.

Restricting the developers to save objects in $TMP is particularly important in SAP NetWeaver BW scenario because of dependency of several objects. For example, you have created a DSO that contains several newly created InfoObjects and by mistake one of the InfoObject is saved in $TMP. So, the transport request will contain all objects except InfoObject, which is saved under $TMP. If you don't check the request in the Transport Connection tool, then this request will fail in QA because of missing objects. This problem becomes worse in SAP NetWeaver BW queries where query elements are recorded by their GUID. You can restrict developers to save objects in $TMP with SE03 transaction or you can ask your Basis team to do the same (see Figure 2.8).

In most projects, there is a central group that actually sends the transports from one system to another. Typically, this group is part of the Basis or technical group. In most projects, the applications team is responsible for creating a transport, adding the necessary objects to the transport, testing, and then releasing the transport. The release part of the transport means that the objects are now ready to actually move, and the development lock on the objects is released.

Once the transport has been released, the applications team typically informs the Basis team to send the transport in a formal process or form. The Basis team then typically sends the transport and reports back if there are issues with the transport. The issues are handled by the applications team and/or the Basis team. A released transport is then imported into the desired destination system.

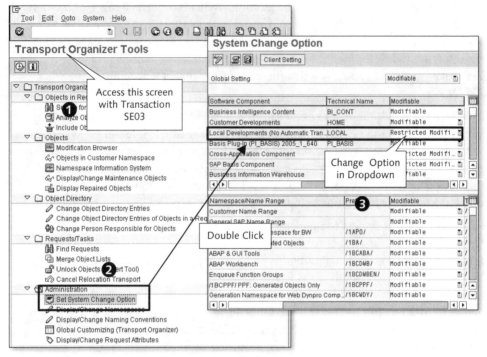

Figure 2.8 Restricting Development under $TMP

2.6.1 Develop and Communicate the Transport Path

The SAP NetWeaver BW transport path goes hand in hand with the SAP NetWeaver BW landscape, as shown in Figure 2.9. The transport path is the series of systems that are connected and the sequence in which these systems are involved in transporting configuration.

When developing a transport strategy, it is important to note the following:

▸ All SAP NetWeaver BW transports are sourced in the development system. Although this might sound like a simple statement, in designing landscapes, it often is forgotten that all transports are sourced from development. Because transports are sent to QA, and then sent to production, it is easy to assume that the transport moves from DEV to QA and then QA to production. This is not the case. The transport actually moves from development to QA and then from development to production.

To develop a sound transport strategy, you must develop a sound landscape strategy with each system's purpose clearly documented. Typically, the only systems that receive transports are the QA and PRD systems. Most other systems in an SAP NetWeaver BW landscape are developed and refreshed as copies from other systems.

▶ Transport process can be easier when sending transports to QA is delayed. Transport issues are minimized when there are fewer transports. There are fewer transports if the same InfoCube is not transported multiple times. This is not always possible, depending on the data. If, for example, you create an InfoCube in development, you unit-test the InfoCube and determine that the InfoCube passes the unit test. If you immediately send the InfoCube to QA for testing, any new requirements that are needed now must be transported.

There have been scenarios at organizations where they're transporting the same InfoCube 20 times at cutover. This happens because of the multiple issues discovered during testing and changing requirements from the business. The longer the InfoCube is kept in development, the more changes are included before transport to QA and the fewer transports are made. The fewer the transports, the less potential for issues.

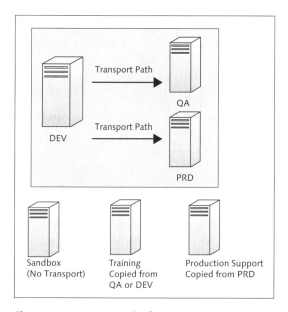

Figure 2.9 Transport Path of a Typical SAP NetWeaver BW Landscape

Sometimes, keeping the configuration in the development system as long as possible becomes difficult, or impossible. To fully complete the development, an integration test must be completed. If the only valid data for testing is in the QA system, the integration test cannot easily be performed. This means that transports are required earlier, and as a result, more transports are created and there is greater potential for issues.

So, if valid, system-ready data is available in the development system; some level of integration testing can be run in the development system. This allows many of the issues to be caught and fixed in the development system right away, rather than using the QA system for this work. If the QA system is used, any fixes need to be transported. This adds to the implementation time of the fix.

2.6.2 Implement Transport Approval Process from the Beginning

The approval process for transports is vital because, as many people start to work in an SAP NetWeaver BW environment, there will eventually be conflict in their development work. This is because SAP NetWeaver BW development usually involves sharing some objects and configuration as seen in the following typical scenario.

> **Scenario**
>
> Amy needs a new attribute to track the parent customer. She creates a new custom InfoObject ZPARENT and appends ZPARENT onto the common master data object of 0CUSTOMER. She is not ready to create a transport because she has not tested her configuration.
>
> Another developer, Greg, needs a new attribute ZGROUP on 0CUSTOMER, so he also appends his new InfoObject ZGROUP onto 0CUSTOMER. He tests and is ready to transport, before Amy is ready to send her transport. He adds his new InfoObject ZGROUP and 0CUSTOMER to a transport, releases it, and requests migration. When Greg's transport is sent, it fails because ZPARENT is appended to 0CUSTOMER but has not been transported.

This example illustrates a fairly simple scenario of conflict between developers. This can become more complex when you add DSO and InfoCube structures to the mix. As new fields are added, transformation is modified or configuration is changed in an SAP NetWeaver BW data model; it is easy for one developer to step on another's work. There really is no systematic way to prevent this from occurring, but we will now discuss some of the steps to minimize the problem.

2.6.3 Make Sure Each Developer Locks Objects

Locking means setting exclusivity on an object so no other developer may change it. This occurs automatically if an object has a development package assigned to it other than the default development package of $TMP. Once a user tries to change an object that has previously been locked or migrated, the system sees the development package and prompts the user with a transport request, forcing him to choose a transport number to assign the change.

Once assigned to that transport, the object is once again locked by that user for future change until the transport is deleted or released. Any new user who requires an additional change needs to either be added to the transport or have the original transport reassigned to that user.

This locking of objects helps to communicate and enforce all changes. For example, if you try to change an object that someone else is working with, you will get a prompt to join onto his transport. You should then find out why the other person is locking the object and the timing of the change. You can then decide if you want to join the other transport or wait until the transport is migrated and create another one for my change.

If an object has never been migrated, there is no locking. This is where developers can easily step on each other. The best way to avoid this is to set up a process that requires each developer to immediately add any new InfoCube, DSO, InfoObject, etc., to a transport immediately after it is created. This will force the developer to assign a development class and will minimize the conflicts of shared objects.

2.6.4 Transport Steward Process

Locking of the SAP NetWeaver BW objects is not the sole strategy for resolving development conflicts. The most efficient SAP NetWeaver BW development groups establish an individual or a group as the transport steward. This person keeps track of the transport and helps to determine potential conflict in development before it occurs. This requires organization and an understanding of the entire SAP NetWeaver BW development group and its work. The steward process can help in seeing problems and setting the priority of transports. In the previous examples, the steward would recommend that one of the conflicted parties wait on his configuration until the first group is complete.

> **Example**
>
> A project had such a complex environment that developers could not create their own transports. Every time new development was to occur, the transport steward had to get a new transport. Only he could create new transports. They then attached the new object to the transport and locked the object during development. This process made sure that the transport steward could track the transports and new development by all the developers in the group.

This is a rather extreme example of managing change; your situation might not be this complex. Your level of transport and change management depends completely on the complexity of your environment, the size of the team, and the amount of shared development that is occurring.

In smaller SAP NetWeaver BW projects, this is simply handled by word of mouth or informal emails. The important thing is to be aware of others when doing shared development and to understand that if heavy shared development is expected, a process should be developed.

2.6.5 Keep a Thorough Log of Transports

Transports in SAP NetWeaver BW are much more complex than in SAP R/3 or SAP ECC environments. This is because SAP NetWeaver BW transports typically generate multiple objects on the destination system. SAP R/3 or SAP ECC transports usually involve adding one entry to this table and replicating that entry in the same table in the destination system.

Because SAP NetWeaver BW transports are performing so many tasks behind the scenes, there is a much greater possibility for transport failure. It is important to keep good notes of each transport that has been created, released, and migrated.

Any special instructions or notes on the transports should be clearly documented. These notes will be used as the notes for the cutover process. To cutover to production, these instructions must be followed exactly.

This means that if a transport has been sent to the QA system and it failed because of missing objects, and a new transport was migrated following that transport, both transports need to be sent to production. The first transport should be sent; it should be expected to fail, and then the next transport should be sent again.

The failed transport is sent because even though the transport failed overall, there may have been objects that were transported successfully. If you ignore the transport and only send the second transport, you risk some objects being missing in the destination system. By sending all transports to production in the exact order they were sent to the QA system, you keep the two systems in sync. When tracking the transports, the following must be recorded:

- Transport number
- Requestor
- Creation date
- Transport date and time (to track order of transports)
- Comments on transport, failure, etc.

2.6.6 Develop a Process for Troubleshooting Failed Transports

There are many reasons a transport can fail, some of which are described here:

- **Objects Missing from Transport**
  If you try to migrate an InfoCube without first migrating all InfoObjects in the

InfoCube, the transport will fail. This is the most common reason for SAP NetWeaver BW transport failure.

▸ **Replication of DataSources Did Not Occur**
If there are dependent objects in the SAP R/3 or SAP ECC systems, a replication may be required before the transport can succeed.

▸ **No Logical Reason**
There are times that transports fail without any clear explanation or logical reason.

A clear process should be developed to troubleshoot transports with clear roles and responsibilities. This can be a time-consuming job involving both the Basis and development teams. Troubleshooting transports is a technical and specialized job. In most projects, you centralize this job with one or two experienced consultants.

There have been projects that have assumed that the Basis group would do most of the troubleshooting of transports. This is typically not the case. Instead, the Basis group informs the applications group of a failed transport. The applications group researchs the reason for the problem and suggests a solution. Quickly diagnosing and fixing failed transports is an important, but not easily acquired, skill.

Troubleshooting transports is a project task that an experienced hands-on consultant can fix in a few minutes what may take an inexperienced consultant several days to correct, see the example in Figure 2.10.

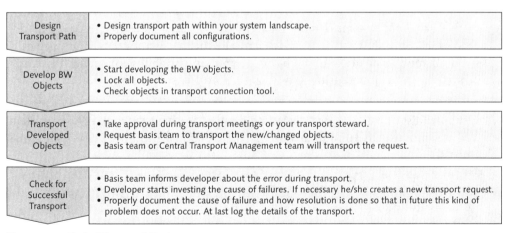

Figure 2.10 Typical Transport Strategy

Because SAP NetWeaver BW transports are much more complex than that of SAP R/3, never release any transport from development before checking it in a Transport Connection tool. Most of the problem happens in SAP NetWeaver BW query elements. Query elements are saved as their internally generated IDs, which are not easy to track. The Transport Connection tool can be accessed from RSA1 Transaction "Transport Connection" tab.

2.6.7   Some Objects will be Changeable

To develop a sound transport strategy, it is important to understand and determine those objects that will not be transported at all. These objects are bypassed in the transport process.

Example

InfoPackages are used to kick off loading in SAP NetWeaver BW. The InfoPackage contains information such as the file name and location, selection criteria, destination information, job name, etc. The InfoPackage settings can change each time the data load is run. Most projects require the flexibility to change the InfoPackage in production.

As a result, most projects do not transport InfoPackages. They set these objects to changeable in the production system. This allows the InfoPackages to be created and changed in the production system without the necessity of a transport.

The Object Changeability button on the Transport Connection screen, seen in Figure 2.11, allows for objects to be edited in a closed system. A closed system refers to those systems that do not allow configuration, like the QA or Production systems. This allows a subset of objects to be changed without transport. Typically, this involves a small group of objects that require the ability for change in a closed system. This is found using RSA1 Transaction Transport Connection.

Table 2.4 shows all objects that can be set as changeable. In most cases, there is a limited list of those objects that should be set to changeable in a closed system. Thus, in most QA and Production systems, a limited list of these options should be set.

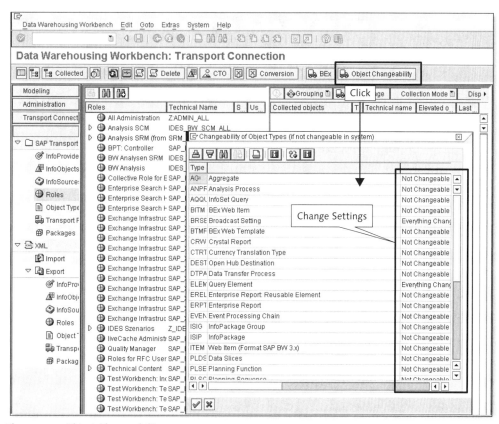

Figure 2.11 Object Changeability

Object	Description
AGGR	Aggregate
ANMO	Mining model
ANPR	Analysis process
ANSO	Model source
AQQU	Infoset query
BRSE	Broadcast setting
CRWB	Crystal report
CTRT	Currency translation type
DEST	Open hub destination

Table 2.4 Changeable Options in a Closed System

Object	Description
DMMO	Data-mining model
ELEM	Query element
EVEN	Event processing chain
ISIG	InfoPackage group
ISIP	InfoPackage
ITEM	Web item
QVIW	Query view
RAPA	Reporting agent scheduling package
RASE	Reporting agent setting
RRCA	RRI InfoCube receiver
RRQA	RRI query receiver
RSPC	Process chain
RSPT	Process chain starter
RSPV	Process variants
SPOK	InfoSpoke
TMPL	Web template name
XLWB	Workbook

Table 2.4 Changeable Options in a Closed System (Cont.)

2.6.8   Transport Organizer Tool

In connection with transport strategy, let's discuss the transport management tool. During the entire project lifecycle, these tools will be useful to manage SAP NetWeaver BW transports (see Figure 2.12). The Transport Organizer tool can be accessed through the SE03 Transaction.

▶ **Search for Objects in Requests/Tasks**
This tool is useful when you need to find out the request number that locked a particular object.

▶ **Include Objects in a Transport Request**
This tool can add an object in a transport request. This is particularly useful when dependent objects are not changed but need to be transported.

▶ **Object Directory Tools**
These tools are useful to change the package of a developed object. You can also change responsible persons for a changed object.

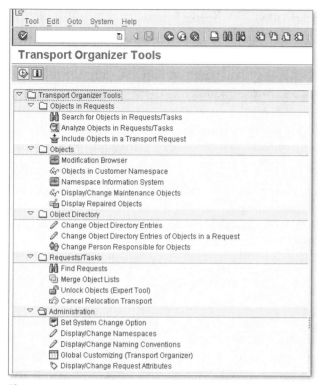

Figure 2.12 Transport Organizer Tools

▶ **Merge Object Lists**
Using these tools, you can merge several transport requests into one transport request.

▶ **Unlock Objects**
An object locked by a transport request can be unlocked by this tool. But, be careful while using this tool because unlocking objects means you are compromising with consistency in SAP NetWeaver BW objects.

▶ **Set System Change Options**
You can set the changeability of SAP NetWeaver BW objects using this tool.

2.7   New Release Rollout Strategy Challenges

There are various challenges for rolling out SAP NetWeaver BW, and the SAP NetWeaver BW rollout strategy should clearly navigate these challenges. Let's examine these in the following subsections.

2.7.1 Timing of SAP NetWeaver BW Rollout

A significant challenge exists when SAP NetWeaver BW is being configured at the same time as the transactional system, such as SAP R/3 or SAP ECC. This is because decisions made in the transactional system configuration have a rather profound effect on the SAP NetWeaver BW configuration.

SAP NetWeaver BW must have a steady transactional system to determine mapping and analysis needs. If these keep changing, this places an extreme burden on the SAP NetWeaver BW team to constantly adjust SAP NetWeaver BW to match this changing environment.

It is also difficult to get the project teams to provide valid master and transactional data because they are constantly changing the configuration. When they finally have valid test data, it may be well after the SAP NetWeaver BW team needs to have its data model completed.

Compounding the issue is that the transactional project teams typically do not want to devote a lot of time for reporting when they are trying to configure the process.

Most projects find that this burden is significant enough to delay the SAP NetWeaver BW go-live by several months after the SAP R/3 or SAP ECC go-live. This gives the SAP NetWeaver BW team an opportunity to configure SAP NetWeaver BW based on final SAP R/3 or SAP ECC configuration, which allows for a more sound SAP NetWeaver BW system.

2.7.2 Rollout Scope

The scope of SAP NetWeaver BW and the timing of this rollout is an important decision that is largely based on the analysis needs and availability of source data for extraction. A comprehensive rollout strategy should be developed, and this should be coordinated with each of the teams.

The process teams need to make sure that they can deliver the transactional data in a valid form to support the rollout data. The technical and Basis teams must make sure that the infrastructure and systems can support the rollouts both from sizing and system-build perspectives.

If possible, this strategy should be developed for as far into the future as possible. The most recent rollouts should have a more detailed plan. In the distant future, a multi-generational plan can be developed.

Rolling out a new system inevitably involves the rollout of an upgrade. In order to provide these upgrades to the end users, an upgrade rollout strategy must be developed. This strategy is used to plan and determine how the end users will acquire the new upgraded system and how their jobs will be directly affected. These all become part of the upgrade rollout strategy.

2.8   Upgrade Rollout Strategy

There are several key decisions defining the upgrade strategy (see Figure 2.13) that are discussed in the following subsections.

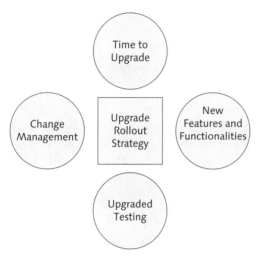

Figure 2.13   Key Decisions for Upgrade Rollout Strategy

2.8.1   Timing

The most common reason for upgrading in SAP R/3 or SAP NetWeaver BW is: "SAP made me." This is because there is always pain and cost in the upgrade process. Timing of the upgrade should reflect significant time to do a full regression test, and some contingency plan should be created for issues and rework that result from the upgrade. Typically, during the upgrade process, no new development can occur. This restriction needs to be built into the development schedule and time line.

2.8.2   Features and Functionality

Most successful upgrade projects do not use new functionality right away. The goal is simply to get the system upgraded to the new release and regression tested. New features and functionality can be rolled out later. Trying to implement new functionality while performing an upgrade can cause the complexity of the upgrade to be increased significantly, and thus, stretch the time line.

2.8.3 Upgrade Testing Strategy

A regression testing strategy makes sure that the existing functions and processes continue to function without issues following the upgrade. This should include plans for creating test scripts, executing tests, reporting issues, and issue resolution. The testing strategy should include volume and stress testing to ensure that adding a large amount of data or many users to the system will not cause new issues.

2.8.4 Upgrade Change Management Strategy

There are many new features in the new release of SAP NetWeaver BW. The look and feel of the system differs, so a sound change-management strategy to communicate the changes and differences is important to a successful upgrade. Another important area to understand in SAP NetWeaver BW is the strategy for the database. There are many parts to the database strategy. Let's learn more about the database strategy now.

2.9 Database Strategy

SAP NetWeaver BW is database independent. This allows for decision-making flexibility with respect to the underlying database system in the technical environment. Typically, the type of database used for SAP NetWeaver BW does not matter. Database design comes into play only for various features, such as MOLAP aggregates, that are only available in specific database systems.

SAP as a company will always state that it will not influence a customer's database decision and will try not to steer a customer toward or away from any database system or company. This allows SAP to remain neutral in the database-selection process of a company.

Typically, the database system of SAP NetWeaver BW mirrors that of the SAP R/3 or SAP ECC systems in the landscape. Rarely is SAP NetWeaver BW of a different database system than that used in the rest of the landscape, simply because of the burden that this would place on the database administration and Basis teams to maintain different database systems.

There are many organizations with many different database systems, but experience tells us that the organizations that have had the fewest database issues and most stable SAP NetWeaver BW environments own Oracle databases.

This is because Oracle is a popular option for database designs in SAP NetWeaver BW, and thus is tested by many users on a daily basis. It's also been found that the overall design of the Oracle database seems to fit well with SAP NetWeaver BW's design and you are likely to experience fewer performance and database specific issues when using Oracle than with any other database system.

The issues that are common with other database platforms and not as common with Oracle involve the many dynamic joins that SAP NetWeaver BW data uses when running a query. It has been observed that Oracle has a better data-access process than other database systems. This makes for better query performance and better load performance.

Some database platforms, especially DB2, perform poorly if the database statistics are not pristine. Without warning, a load that took several minutes each day suddenly takes several hours to complete. To prevent these issues, you may have to spend much of your batch-loading time in the evening running statistics to make sure that the loading windows were not affected by outdated statistics.

> **Note**
>
> Oracle is better at handling outdated database statistics, and a more stable environment occurs as a result. Even with new releases of other databases, Oracle continues to be ahead of the curve in this area.

In whatever database system you are using, seek out the other customers who are also using your database and keep in communication. One idea is to have customers participate in periodic conference calls to go over specific issues and their resolution. It's likely that many of the issues brought up could be incorporated into patches and future design. Once the database strategy is complete, there are other decisions that have a global reach on the SAP NetWeaver BW system. One of these involves an EDW strategy.

2.10   EDW and Global Rollup Strategies

An SAP NetWeaver BW EDW is a system that gathers data from multiple sources and serves as a global reporting system. This can be quite complex, depending on how regionalized a company's culture and development functions are. This strategy takes into account any global data needs and regional aggregations and transformation of data into a global view. A global EDW project dramatically benefits the following departments of a company:

▶ **Marketing**
An EDW brings visibility to sales and marketing program effectiveness and product line profitability across the entire organization.

▶ **Pricing and Contracts**
These departments can better understand pricing and usage to optimize negotiation.

▶ **Forecasting**
An EDW provides timely visibility of global demand.

▶ **Sales**
The sales department can better determine sales profitability and productivity for all territories and regions. It can use results by geography, product, sales group, or individuals across the enterprise.

▶ **Financial**
This department receives daily, weekly, or monthly results quickly, enhancing financial management throughout the organization.

▶ **Supply Chain**
An EDW enables faster, thorough analysis of purchase quantities and prices.

▶ **Inventory Management**
This department gains a holistic view, which helps identify ways to manage inventory more effectively.

▶ **Customer Service**
Service staff can deliver consistent customer service metrics for all facilities.

▶ **Information Technology**
This team can reduce its manual consolidation workload by providing each user with fast and easy access to regularly used queries, reports, or analyses.

An EDW project can be a difficult and sometimes painful process in many organizations because it combines many diverse groups. An EDW strategy should meet the following goals:

▶ Assessing of data from multiple source systems

▶ Extraction of data from these systems

▶ Aligning and cleansing the data as necessary

▶ Loading this data into a new EDW environment so data appears to come from a single source.

The source systems may be multiple SAP ECC systems, SAP NetWeaver BW systems, other legacy systems, or a combination of these. Many different groups may own the transactional or master data, which increases the complexity. The overall challenges of an SAP NetWeaver BW EDW surface in the following categories of Figure 2.14:

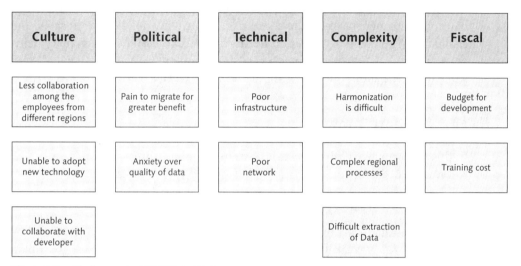

Figure 2.14 Challenges to EDW Global Rollup

▶ **Cultural**
The culture of the organization may not be ready for an EDW. Although management may feel that an EDW will bring great benefits, the organization may not agree and/or follow the EDW standards.

▶ **Political**
Many organizations do not want to give up their local reporting flexibility to enter into global standards. The EDW might also reduce the number of reporting systems in an organization. The prospect of retiring formerly essential systems may cause anxiety among users.

▶ **Technical**
Sometimes, the technical infrastructure that supports an EDW is not robust enough to handle the data volume. An EDW may require a network upgrade or enhanced hardware to support global reporting. Technical problems may arise when trying to consolidate the disparate systems.

▶ **Complexity**
Some global organizations have such a complex environment that it's virtually impossible or difficult to harmonize data in a single system.

> **Fiscal**
> An EDW effort can cost a great deal of money because of the significant challenges with data integration, consolidation, and cleansing. This process is most successful if funded as its own project.

The global EDW strategy is important to determine from the beginning of the project because it dictates how data should be rolled into a global data view and affects harmonization of data across the enterprise. This can involve significant scope and challenges. The entire organization needs to have a clear and concise query delivery strategy to allow consistent access of data. In the next section, we will discuss some decisions about query development in SAP NetWeaver BW.

2.11   Report Strategy

In this section, we will discuss various strategies on the presentation layer of SAP NetWeaver BW. This includes Query strategy and Web Template strategy.

2.11.1   Query Strategy

There has been an ongoing debate in SAP NetWeaver BW that started from the earliest SAP NetWeaver BW systems ever implemented. The issue: Where should queries be developed? There are two options:

> Create and develop queries in the development system, and require transport of all queries to the production environment.
> Create queries directly in production.

Experience tells us that customer preference is split evenly between the two options. However, the option to develop queries in development and transporting is slightly more popular.

So, what is the right answer for this question? As with most decisions in SAP NetWeaver BW (and SAP overall), the answer is: "It depends." We will provide the advantages and disadvantages of each approach to help your decision-making process.

Pros and Cons of Developing Queries Directly in Production

There are several pros discussed below:

> **Increased Speed and Flexibility**
> This allows new queries and changes to be rolled out quickly. No waiting for a transport to be created, approved, and migrated. Query development is not owned by the IT department.

- ▶ **Easier Development**
  All data needed for testing is available in the production environment. There-fore, the tasks of creating a query and testing the formula, filters, etc., are much easier than in a development environment with limited data.
- ▶ **Reduced Transport Activity**
  Transports for queries would not be required if these are developed directly in production.

Now, let's take a look at the cons:

- ▶ **Auditing Effort**
  It's difficult to audit reports to make sure that they conform to standards.
- ▶ **Data Quality Issues**
  Quality and consistency issues can arise. For example, a user creates a query with a key figure called net sales, and they forget to filter out the intercompany sales. This skews the net sales number.
- ▶ **Performance Issues**
  Performance problems can arise because power users are not always aware of the data and its volume. They can create queries that allow unfiltered access and thus create performance concerns.
- ▶ **Data Redundancy**
  Duplication of data is inevitable. After many years of using SAP NetWeaver BW, this can become a rather significant burden.

How Do I Allow Development of Queries in Production?

Here, you set the object changeability using the functionality as previously described in Figure 2.6. To allow the development of queries in production, you must set the changeability flag of the following options in the production system. This will allow the changeability of these objects. See Table 2.5 for a look at some of these options.

Object	Description
AQQU	InfoSet query
ELEM	Query element
QVIW	Query view
XLWB	Workbook

Table 2.5 Object Changeability Options for Query Processing

Create Central Key Figure Matrix

The most successful projects have central documents that detail all key figures or KPIs in the organization. This key figure matrix gives the name of the key figure value and the calculation used throughout the organization to arrive at the value. This makes sure that each time someone sees a particular name, such as days of supply, everyone understands how this is calculated.

The key figure matrix can either be published on the portal or a link can be established for each query, workbook, or Web report. If this key figure matrix is properly maintained and adhered to, there is no confusion with different people or groups calculating data differently.

If a situation arises where the finance group calculates the same key figure differently than the sales group, simply make a new name for one of the key figures. This keeps the consistency of the environment and makes it easier for users to understand the data that they are viewing in a query.

Develop a Validation Process

To keep a clean and consistent production environment, the queries that are developed directly in production should be validated. This process starts with thorough training of the power users in the data and standards for development.

Once queries are created, these queries also go through a validation process either with the SAP NetWeaver BW team or peer evaluation before they are rolled out to the end user community. This ensures that the query has been reviewed for standards, key figure consistency, and quality.

Developing Queries in Production vs. Development

There have been projects that have been successful using both approaches. The projects that perform all development of queries in the development system and transport all queries are able to keep strict control on the number of queries and are able to verify and test all queries for data quality and consistency before they are transported to production. This reduces the redundancy and makes the environment much stronger because the queries have been validated.

However, these projects sacrifice the flexibility and speed that development in production allows. This can become a serious concern when a vice president calls the SAP NetWeaver BW department and says: "I need analysis on the following values, and I need this quickly." The team is forced develop, test, create the transport, transport approval, migration, etc. This can be rather frustrating for the vice president who is waiting for his data (and quite stressful for the SAP NetWeaver BW development team, too!).

Those customer environments that have allowed production to be opened up for development can quickly spin out of control as the number of queries explodes and the support of so many queries becomes crippling.

Those customers that are the most successful either do not develop queries in the production system or they allow only limited development of queries in production. They limit the creation of queries in production to a certain naming convention and to a very, very small group of well-trained power users.

This allows them to quickly know the difference between those queries that are developed in production and those that have been migrated. The development and production support teams offer only limited support for those queries that are developed directly in production.

This approach reduces the redundancy because the small team can create a process to determine if a query has already been developed. This approach allows the flexible development of queries while also allowing the discipline needed for a consistent, high-quality, and efficient environment.

2.11.2 Visual Composer

Beginning in SAP NetWeaver BW Version 3.5, SAP delivered the Visual Composer software. This was enhanced significantly for SAP NetWeaver BW version 2004s. This enhancement changes the options significantly when reporting and querying data in SAP NetWeaver BW.

Visual Composer is a Web-based solution that allows the linking of objects by dragging and dropping the objects and establishing links between them. Visual Composer generates code to establish the link and passing of data between applications. It is independent of any platform, technology, or language.

This greatly improves the analysis in SAP NetWeaver BW because through Visual Composer you can link third-party or legacy systems views to SAP NetWeaver BW queries. The goal of the tool is to reduce the effort involved in bringing this data into SAP NetWeaver BW directly, harmonizing it, and presenting it. This allows the data to be visually reported and even some interaction of the data through the Drag & Drop functionality.

This can be a good addition to the SAP NetWeaver BW reporting strategy because it allows for a flexible view of data in outside systems together with data in SAP NetWeaver BW. The user does not have to even be aware of the source of this data.

2.11.3 Web Template Strategy

Web Application Designer (WAD) is the robust tool to create Web templates for SAP NetWeaver BW queries. In this section, we will discuss the strategy for Web templates so that information consumers can see the report uniformly and with all possible features of navigations.

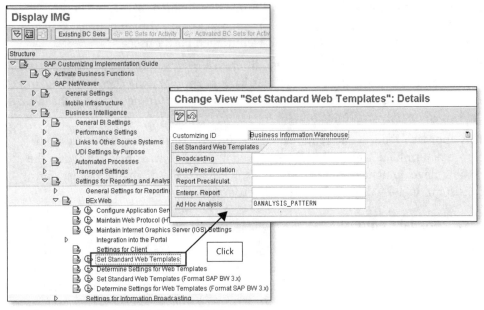

Figure 2.15 Standard Web Template Settings

Create Master Web Template

There are many projects that create as many different Web templates as the queries created. The logic behind this approach is to display each query differently as their content. So, if there are 50 queries and corresponding 50 Web templates, it becomes difficult to maintain each of the Web templates. Additionally, this approach incurs extra effort for development, maintenance, and training. Trainings to end users could be a biggest overhead for developers because end users will require document or training for each of the report. To alleviate this problem, we can set a standard Web template that can be used to display each SAP NetWeaver BW queries (see Figure 2.15). By default, SAP uses 0ADHOC Web template as standard. You can use this template to create your own organization specific Web template. Below are the steps to create a standard Web template:

- Open the Web application designer tool. Save 0ADHOC as another name.
- Change the your saved template according to the requirement of your organization.
- Change the technical name of the master template in SPRO.

In your standard Web template, you can add few of the most important features:

- Ability to export data in Microsoft Excel, CSV, Adobe
- Access to the query documentation
- Access to views created on the query
- Ability to create, activate, and deactivate exceptions and conditions.

2.11.4 SAP BusinessObjects Strategy

Although SAP BusinessObjects is the latest addition to SAP's SAP NetWeaver BW portfolio, the SAP BusinessObjects tools have had a prominent existence before acquisition by SAP. Below are a few points that can be considered driving factors to adopt the SAP BusinessObjects tools as your primary reporting strategy:

- Customer was using SAP BusinessObjects and Crystal Reports even before implementation of SAP NetWeaver BW. This will cut down significant cost in training moreover; end users will be happy seeing the same reporting interface.
- Using SAP BusinessObjects tools that you can present SAP NetWeaver BW reports with intuitive look and feel.
- End users need to look at data from a non-SAP system and from SAP NetWeaver BW within the same reporting interface.

Part of any sound reporting strategy is to make sure that the data being accessed is done in the most efficient way. One way to make sure this occurs is by keeping the system up-to-date with support packages. These support packages allow for periodic fixes of software issues. Understanding and keeping a clear support-package strategy is important to keeping the system healthy.

In the next section, we will discuss this strategy.

2.12 Support Package Strategy

All SAP NetWeaver BW teams must have a documented support-package strategy to document the process and timing of support package applications. SAP releases SAP NetWeaver BW support packages periodically, and these need to be applied to fix various issues in SAP NetWeaver BW.

The SAP NetWeaver BW support team prefers to release fixes only as part of a support package, not as an individual SAP Note fix. This ensures that they can test the quality of the fix with other fixes, and they aren't often forced into a situation where one notes fixes one thing but breaks several others. A team is then required to put in more notes to fix the old note.

You might run into an issue in SAP NetWeaver BW where the support group refuses to provide fixes in SAP Notes at all and directs you to the newest support package to fix the issue. This can be quite difficult because applying an SAP Note requires a full regression test of the SAP NetWeaver BW environment.

Most organizations are not able to do a full regression test often. Thus, we often find ourselves working around issues until we can apply support packages. There are several different kinds of support packages in SAP NetWeaver BW, which are discussed here.

▶ **SAP NetWeaver BW Application Support Package**
These are support packages released periodically by SAP to fix various issues in the SAP NetWeaver BW system.

▶ **SAP NetWeaver BW Front-End Support Package**
These are support packages designed to fix issues in the query processing tool in SAP NetWeaver BW. They are installed as a separate component, so the support packages are administered separately. The SAP NetWeaver BW front-end support packages are backward compatible with previous releases of SAP NetWeaver BW. They are loaded on each individual PC that runs SAP NetWeaver BW.

▶ **Plug-in Release**
The plug-in release is not really a support package but rather the release of the DataSources (extractors) on the SAP ECC system. Prior to SAP ECC Version 6.0, the plug-in release was independent of the release or SAP ECC support packages. It is now included as part of the SAP ECC release and will automatically have the latest plug-in.

To see the most recent support package and plug-in compatibility go to: *http://service.sap.com/bi*.

2.12.1 Recommendation

The most successful companies using SAP NetWeaver BW stay as up-to-date as possible on the support packages. These support packages differ in their quality and the number of issues they fix (and new issues they cause). However, to keep a system performing at its best, keeping current on support packages is vital.

The best way to roll out new support packages is with a new release of SAP NetWeaver BW. Piggyback all SAP NetWeaver BW support packages with each new release of functionality.

Thus, when you plan a new phase of development for your system, the first thing that you should do is to move the development environment to the newest support package and keep all development and testing on that support package. This allows for the support package to be regression tested fully, as part of a project release strategy. Migrating to the support package can occur with minimal disruption to the business.

This strategy typically forces the SAP NetWeaver BW system to lag several support packages behind. By the time an SAP NetWeaver BW functionality release gets to production in a project, SAP has released at least one new support package. Thus, we usually accept that we cannot use the newest support package at all times in production; we just stay as close as possible with minimal disruption.

A process should be developed for any support package that is needed to fix a critical issue.

Sometimes, there are critical issues that are only fixed in support packages. SAP, on occasion, cannot provide these fixes as part of an SAP Support fix. Thus, an emergency support package upgrade is necessary. As part of the support-package strategy document, a strategy for this should be clearly defined.

2.12.2 Front-End Support Packages

The SAP NetWeaver BW front-end support packages are the most difficult and cumbersome support packages to deploy. This is because, unlike the SAP NetWeaver BW application packages, these are not deployed in one place. They must be deployed to each PC that is accessing SAP NetWeaver BW. Rolling this patch out to the individual users can become quite a task.

Prior to the NW 2004s release of SAP NetWeaver BW, the front-end patches were developed separately from the application support packages and thus were released independently. In the NW 2004s version, the front-end patches are in sync with the application-support package. Starting with NW 2004s, the front-end patches are renamed to *BW Front-End Add-On Support Packages*.

Any fix in between support packages will be released as a Hotfix. The Hotfixes that are released in between regularly scheduled support packages are now named *BW Front-End Add-On Patches*.

Most customers use a centralized software package to push the front-end patches to each user. They do this periodically to keep all users on the latest front-end patch.

2.13 Authorization Strategy

An authorization strategy involves making decisions about the SAP NetWeaver BW environment and determining what parts, if any, need to be secured. This helps to keep sensitive data away from unauthorized parties, while still allowing analysis by those who need the data.

Developing an authorization strategy for SAP NetWeaver BW is important to consider from the earliest stages of a project because many of the decisions regarding the implementation of SAP NetWeaver BW can be guided based on these requirements. An authorization strategy in SAP NetWeaver BW takes into account the security of the following areas:

- Functional security within the SAP NetWeaver BW tool
- Data security
- Presentation security
- Profile and role strategy.

To define an authorization strategy, you must first look at the scope of data that will be loaded into SAP NetWeaver BW. You need to know if there is data that will be loaded that will be sensitive and should not be viewed by some of the users of SAP NetWeaver BW.

2.13.1 SAP NetWeaver BW Security

SAP NetWeaver BW security is based on a roles and authorization concept. Users are assigned to one or many roles. These roles contain authorizations. Authorization objects are assigned to the objects in SAP NetWeaver BW. The system checks the authorization objects against the authorizations for the user.

This concept differs from SAP ECC or SAP R/3 because these systems are transaction based. The transaction-based systems secure values based on transactions or specific field values to determine what tasks a user can perform.

SAP NetWeaver BW is based on analysis-based security. This is driven by InfoProviders, queries, and data. Basically, this means that you look at the analysis methods and determine which analysis is sensitive. You secure the sensitive data by user role.

To establish an authorization strategy, you do not need to know exactly how security is to be configured; you simply need to know what data needs to be secured and by whom. If this has been determined early in the project cycle, these needs can be incorporated into the data model design.

You should create an authorizations strategy document and revisit this document each time you roll out functionality in SAP NetWeaver BW. This document should clearly state what data is to be secured and the roles that should be included and excluded from the data.

The document should also detail the authorization strategy within the SAP NetWeaver BW tool. This would show what SAP NetWeaver BW developers and production support users are allowed to do, and not allowed to do.

The strategy document also should reference what security is required on the raw data loaded into SAP NetWeaver BW such as flat files and direct connection to legacy databases, XML, XI, etc. This needs to be a living document, because as new data and users come onto the system, new security needs evolve.

2.13.2 Authorizations for Upgrade to NW 2004s

There has been a significant redesign of the authorization concept in the NW 2004s release. SAP has converted from reporting authorizations to an analysis authorizations concept for SAP NetWeaver BW data security. This redesign of authorizations allows for much more flexible data-security functionality.

No new development will be done to the BW 3.x authorization functionality in SAP NetWeaver BW. SAP strongly encourages customers to move to the new security design. There are tools to migrate the security in the Version 3.5 reporting authorizations to the NW 2004S analysis authorization.

If you are using the 3.x security (any SAP NetWeaver BW data security at all), you should plan to upgrade to the new security concept. However, the 3.x security will continue to function in the NW 2004s environment. Because no new development will be performed on this security method and it is somewhat limited in its flexibility, the new analysis method of authorizations is preferred.

Time should be allocated in the upgrade process to migrate the security to the new analysis authorization. The redesign only affects the data security in SAP NetWeaver BW. There is still a transactional-based security to provide security for the SAP NetWeaver BW administrator and developer activities within the SAP NetWeaver BW system. For example, SAP still provides the ability to secure transactions in SAP NetWeaver BW, such as RSA1 and SPRO. This is covered by the standard security and will remain unchanged in SAP NetWeaver BW.

> **Note**
>
> Execute report RSEC_MIGRATION for migration assistance. Using this tool, you can migrate about 80% of the authorization objects for rest of the authorization you may need to migrate manually. It is highly recommended to conduct intense testing before the migrated settings go-live.

2.14   Conclusion

If the different strategies mentioned are planned, organized, and implemented, it allows for a much smoother project overall. Because many if not all of the areas will come up in any SAP NetWeaver BW project, getting in front of the demand and planning for the decisions in each of the areas allows for a more-efficient SAP NetWeaver BW planning process, and thus a smoother implementation.

In this chapter, we discussed what are important questions need to be answered first before starting any SAP NetWeaver BW projects.

You learned various ways to design your SAP NetWeaver BW landscape based on your requirements. Additionally, you also learned how to adopt a clear strategy for transports, support packages, and reporting tools.

Now, let's proceed to Chapter 3, where we'll review the most common mistakes made when implementing SAP NetWeaver BW.

By understanding the key challenges associated with an SAP NetWeaver BW project; you can often avoid many of the most common mistakes.

3 Common SAP NetWeaver BW Implementation Mistakes

This chapter details common mistakes that are often made on SAP NetWeaver BW project implementations. Throughout this chapter, we will detail some of the most important ones and provide insight to how to address, or better yet, avoid them.

3.1 Unclear Definition of Goals and Scope

Implementing SAP NetWeaver BW, as with any project, you must start with clear goals and a clearly defined and documented scope. While it seems that any project manager would admit this is the most important task in SAP NetWeaver BW project management, its absence is the most common reason that projects miss their scheduled go-live date or are cancelled altogether. How can you make sure that the goals of SAP NetWeaver BW are clearly defined and communicated?

3.1.1 Develop Clear Project Scope Documentation

SAP NetWeaver BW scope definition needs to be agreed to and signed off on by all parties before any development can begin. The more detailed the scope documentation, the better the understanding of the requirements, timing, and implementation of SAP NetWeaver BW, and thus the more likelihood for success.

The scope document should be considered the most important document in the SAP NetWeaver BW project. The SAP NetWeaver BW scope should be first established as part of an initial scoping exercise, then refined through an interview process, and finally be subject to a scope document signoff (see Figure 3.1). This scoping exercise is part of the earliest phase of the project, the project-preparation phase.

Figure 3.1 SAP NetWeaver BW Scope Development Process

There are multiple subsequent documents that will establish the scope in even greater detail. However, these documents will come in the analysis phase of the project, not in project preparation. The critical components of the scope document include:

▶ Information that will be included in SAP NetWeaver BW
▶ Subject areas, with their priority status
▶ Scope of each subject area
▶ Summary of transformation needed
▶ Summary of the level of aggregation and summarization of data
▶ Description of the presentation tools.

The initial scoping document should provide information on the following critical areas in the scope process in Table 3.1.

Business Areas	Description
Business Requirements	Business reasons for the project and business questions answered by the implementation
Stakeholders	Roles and responsibilities of those in the implementation process
Critical Success Factors	Determinants and measures for a successful project
Source Systems	The source systems that are involved in the project and the sources of data in these systems
Data Access	The intended audience of the SAP NetWeaver BW project and their use of the information
Transformation	Any transformation that is needed to provide the data in its desired format

Table 3.1 Critical Areas in Scope Process

Business Areas	Description
Security	The data-access security requirements to prevent unauthorized use of the information
Batch Window	The frequency of load and approximate timing of loads
Archiving/History	How much historical data is needed, and how long will this information be kept in SAP NetWeaver BW?
Testing Procedures	The basic process for testing and some testing and validation parameters
Master Data Requirements	The master data tables and information that are needed to support the reporting in SAP NetWeaver BW
Change Management	Strategy for rolling out the process changes to the organization
Timing	Project schedule and time line
Transition to Production Support	Some information on the go-live process and transition from development to production support

Table 3.1 Critical Areas in Scope Process (Cont.)

3.1.2 Establish Milestones

Establishing milestones and measuring these milestones is one of the most important measures of a project's chances for success. Setting these milestones allows the SAP NetWeaver BW team to understand and work to these goals. This process is called *setting micro goals*. The micro goal is a small, attainable goal that can track a project week to week. Examples are setting up connectivity with a source system, doing a test pull of data, and transformation of data in one area.

If you measure the micro goals, you can make sure that the project is on track. You can then quickly add resources to those areas where the micro goals are not being met. Often, project teams find themselves simply measuring against a macro goal, such as completing the analysis phase. Often, projects that focus too highly on larger goals do not know that they are behind schedule until it is too late to act.

How you will be setting the milestones is completely dependent on the nature of the SAP NetWeaver BW project. However, any SAP NetWeaver BW project can be divided in smaller parts based on the following criteria.

▶ **Business Area**

If you are implementing SAP NetWeaver BW on various business areas like MM, SD, FI, don't implement them at once. Instead, implement those business areas one-by-one.

▶ **Source Systems**

If your SAP NetWeaver BW implementation involves many source systems, then dividing your milestones based on source systems will be a helpful approach.

Figure 3.2 shows that by breaking up the SAP NetWeaver BW project into smaller, more digestible chunks, it is much easier to see the whole picture, understand dependencies on other groups, and make sure that the SAP NetWeaver BW project will make its scheduled go-live date.

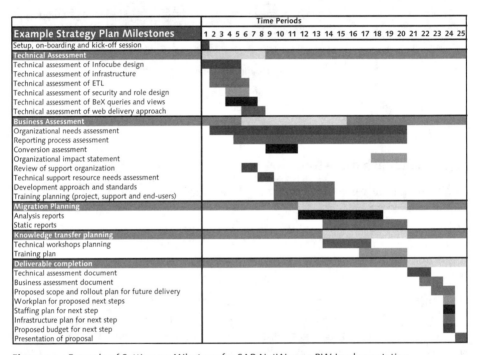

Figure 3.2 Example of Setting up Milestone for SAP NetWeaver BW Implementation

3.1.3 Avoid Scope Creep

Scope creep can occur in an SAP NetWeaver BW project just as easily as an SAP R/3 or SAP ECC project. The best way to prevent the scope creep in SAP NetWeaver BW is to have a firmly established scope right from the beginning and require signoffs on the scope document. Adding more detailed governance, such as the functional model process, further establishes the intended scope.

Keeping to and tracking against the scope is one of the more difficult challenges facing a SAP NetWeaver BW project, and there are no easy solutions to scope creep other than to clearly document all requirements.

A functional model is a document that clearly states the scope and delivery of the data in an SAP NetWeaver BW functional area. Chapter 5 walks through the functional model process in detail. This process helps to establish the SAP NetWeaver BW requirements, business questions, and needs. The functional model serves as the most important scope-management document, and a signed-off functional model can help avert scope creep and keep the project on track.

> **Note**
>
> The best way to avoid scope creep is to allow end users to participate in the design phase and incorporate their suggestions.

3.1.4   Establish a Scope Change Control Process

As tightly as any SAP NetWeaver BW project team would like to control scope, changes inevitably occur. These could be the result of missed scope areas, new opportunity, changing business environment, or newly discovered challenges. Thus, scope cannot be assumed to be unchanging. A scope review and management process to allow for changes is vital to communicating and accepting these changes. This should involve review, communication, and escalation.

3.1.5   Take Advantage of Existing Legacy Systems

Many SAP NetWeaver BW projects are mainly upgrades from existing legacy reporting systems. This happens when a customer upgrades its legacy transactional systems with SAP R/3 or SAP ECC systems. To create a robust scope document, you can refer to the existing reports that the customer was using before migration. For example, a customer was using Mainframe for materials management when they migrated to the SAP R/3 MM module. They also adopted SAP NetWeaver BW as their reporting environment. The initial scope document was developed quickly based on the older system. When the customer saw the scope, they quickly agreed on that scope and subsequent SAP NetWeaver BW–related features were implemented in the next release.

You should always be aware of certain pitfalls of using legacy systems as a template for your SAP NetWeaver BW project, including:

▶ Extensive industry and SAP R/3 knowledge is required to map with SAP and legacy fields.

▶ Do not use fields from a legacy system. In your scope document, you should always define SAP-related fields.

▶ The customer is upgrading the system because they need new features, so don't always stick to older systems.

Controlling the scope helps to avoid another common issue, an over-ambitious scope. This can often be the result of simply trying to do too much, too fast. Let's find out more about over-ambitious scope now.

3.2   Over-Ambitious Scope

As with many SAP R/3 or SAP ECC projects, the failures that occur in SAP NetWeaver BW projects are often the result of attempting to implement too much at one time. SAP NetWeaver BW has the power to pull significant amounts of data from multiple source systems both in the SAP landscape and outside of this landscape. This freedom to bring almost any data into SAP NetWeaver BW tempts many organizations to become overly ambitious.

There are several things that need to be learned and accounted for in any SAP NetWeaver BW implementation. A developer must understand the information requirements, the data, and the presentation and loading needs, and must reconcile all these needs with the SAP NetWeaver BW tool. Thus, any overly ambitious scope forces the team to take shortcuts on the analysis and understanding of the data and information needs and thus can cause the SAP NetWeaver BW project to stall.

3.2.1   Start Small

How can an overly ambitious scope be avoided? The only answer is to start the SAP NetWeaver BW implementation plan with a small go-live scope and build from a small but well-designed base. This allows the process of implementing SAP NetWeaver BW to be firmly established. The lessons-learned from the first implementation can be used to make each subsequent implementation that much stronger.

A good example of a small project is one that limits the data to one source system, typically and most often the SAP R/3 or SAP ECC transactional system. Within that transactional system, the scope should also be reduced to one subject area, such as sales tracking or SAP General Ledger postings.

The smaller the scope, the more focused the team can be on understanding the requirements and delivering these as a quality deliverable on time. As previously stated, once the user loses confidence in the SAP NetWeaver BW solution and the information provided from SAP NetWeaver BW, it is extremely difficult to win the user back.

Thus, a small scope allows a robust user signoff and testing process. This makes sure that any data anomalies that occur on the source systems are fixed in that source system and that SAP NetWeaver BW is aggregating and reporting the data in the most effective manner.

Many organizations will opt to start with some small financial or sales reporting. They set up the extraction process to bring this data into SAP NetWeaver BW and present it with a limited number of queries. The users can then look at these queries and formulate the requirements for the next phases of rollout.

Because SAP NetWeaver BW is independent of the SAP R/3 or SAP ECC source system, in some cases new SAP NetWeaver BW functionality can be created and rolled out to the end users without coordination or synchronization with the SAP R/3 or SAP ECC rollout schedules. In other words, if the source data is available, SAP NetWeaver BW can allow the reporting on this data to go live without tying it to an overall project phase go-live involving the SAP ECC or SAP R/3 teams.

SAP NetWeaver BW can have many mini–project go-lives to stagger delivery of functionality, thereby preventing a big bang overly complex scope from crippling the SAP NetWeaver BW team. Often, a small go-live provides the momentum (and funding) needed for subsequent go-lives.

Advantages with Small Go-Lives
Team members can concentrate on business logic effectively.
Rigorous testing can be performed.
Quality delivery is assured.
Small go-lives allow robust user signoff.

3.2.2 Be Wary of Implementing SAP NetWeaver BW at the Same Time as SAP ECC or SAP R/3

Projects that attempt to implement SAP NetWeaver BW at the same time as the source SAP ECC or SAP R/3 system face especially big challenges. This can be compared to trying to climb a mountain whose summit is constantly moving. No sooner do you get a foothold and start to climb then the goal changes.

Having a constant and steady source system when implementing SAP NetWeaver BW helps ensure consistent rules for the data. When the SAP ECC or SAP R/3 system is evolving at the same time as the SAP NetWeaver BW system, this causes severe frustration and delays in the SAP NetWeaver BW project.

Take the example of a large company that was implementing the Materials Management (MM) module of SAP R/3 to enter and track its purchases. They set their transactional configuration and pricing for the purchase orders, and the data was first extracted into SAP NetWeaver BW. The purchasing data was configured into a sound data model.

As more data was extracted, the purchase order price fields became inconsistent. The net price was in one key figure value; later, this same key figure value included the freight charges. It took a lot of testing to determine that the issue was a result of a last-minute pricing configuration change on the SAP R/3 transactional system. A small decision in the source system can have huge ramifications for the SAP NetWeaver BW system.

The problem is that few of the people configuring pricing were aware of the impact of their decisions. Waiting until after their configuration was complete would have mapped the freight and net sales consistently and saved a great deal of time.

Many projects look to SAP NetWeaver BW to become the place for reporting of data for an SAP ECC or SAP R/3 implementation. However, when developing SAP NetWeaver BW at the same time as the source area in SAP ECC or SAP R/3, challenges are inevitable.

There are advantages to developing both systems at the same time. By developing both systems together, it is possible to have a clear integrated test process in conjunction with the SAP R/3 or SAP ECC systems.

Implementing SAP NetWeaver BW with SAP R/3 or SAP ECC also eliminates some of what would be throwaway work on the transactional systems. This is because the reporting functionality is often needed on the source system. If SAP NetWeaver BW is not there to provide this reporting, there must be some other system to provide this reporting.

In some cases, custom ABAP reports are created for temporary use on the transactional systems. Some, if not all, of these could be eliminated if the SAP NetWeaver BW system were there from the beginning to provide this type of reporting.

The biggest challenge is to try to implement SAP NetWeaver BW on a changing source system platform. Good communication and change management are needed to coordinate the transactional team and the SAP NetWeaver BW team.

In most SAP NetWeaver BW implementations, the SAP NetWeaver BW team usually lags the transactional team by four to six weeks (see Figure 3.3). This allows the transactional team to be more firmly established and create some sample configuration and data to configure, load, and test the SAP NetWeaver BW system.

> **Note**
>
> To assure that the SAP NetWeaver BW project budget does not get exhausted waiting for SAP R/3 or SAP ECC configuration to finish, the SAP NetWeaver BW project should not kick off until four to six weeks after the associated SAP R/3 or SAP ECC project.

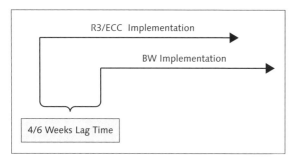

Figure 3.3 SAP NetWeaver BW Implementation Lagging Time with Respect to SAP R/3 or SAP ECC Implementation.

Setting the time line for an SAP NetWeaver BW project in coordination with the SAP ECC or SAP R/3 teams often means adjusting the SAP NetWeaver BW time line if the transactional time line shifts. It also means setting a realistic time line that can be achieved. Issues often occur when projects have an unrealistic time line.

3.3 Unrealistic Time Line

Some projects start with a time line that is either unintentionally or intentionally unrealistic. Project teams have been known to provide what they knew was an unrealistic time line simply to get management's buy-in. This gets management on board, but then slowly the dates are moved into a more realistic time line.

Naturally, we don't suggest this for long-term project management. Let's look at another example. A project manager intentionally sets unrealistic time lines to motivate the team to act. The project managers felt that if they didn't put a *stake in the ground,* the team would never move forward. This strategy backfired because most of the team members knew that the time table would never be met and therefore ignored the fact that their deliverables would be late.

A clear realistic time line is the most honest way to ensure longer-term success and keep the team motivated toward the goal of a successful go-live, within budget and on time.

Once a clear timeline is established, it needs to be clearly communicated to the team. This communication and other project-related standards become part of the project governance. This governance helps ensure that there are common standards for the project.

3.3.1 Don't Forget the Time for Documentation and Training

There are some projects that calculate the time line based on development and testing of the system. Project managers simply don't give much importance on documentation or training material for end users. This kind of approach should not be adopted at all. The success of any SAP NetWeaver BW implementation lies on usability of reports. If users are not properly trained, they will be able to run the reports and overall objective of having SAP NetWeaver BW fails.

There are several ways to manage SAP NetWeaver BW documents and display them to end users whenever they need. One option is to leverage the Document Management tool in RSA1 (see Figure 3.4). Here, you can create tutorials/user guides for several objects of SAP NetWeaver BW. These documents then can be accessed from reporting environment on demand.

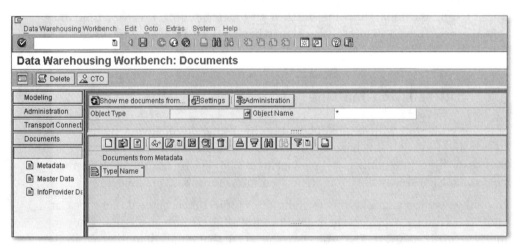

Figure 3.4 Document Management Tool in SAP NetWeaver BW

You can create document for the SAP NetWeaver BW object types in Table 3.2.

Object Type	Description
CTRT	Currency Translation Type
UOMT	Quantity Conversion Type
IOBJ	InfoObject
IOBC	InfoObject Catalog
ODSO	DataStore Object
CUBE	InfoCube
AGGR	Aggregate
ISET	InfoSet
MPRO	MultiProvider
ALVL	Aggregation Level
ISTD	3.x InfoSource
TRCS	InfoSource
UPDR	Update rules
ISFS	3.x DataSource
RSDS	DataSource
ISMP	Transfer Rules
TRFN	Transformation
ISIP	InfoPackage
ELEM	Query Element
RASE	Reporting Agent Setting
RAPA	Reporting Agent Scheduling Package
XLWB	Workbook
DDAS	Data Access Service
QVIW	Query View
EREL	Enterprise Report: Reusable Element
ERPT	Enterprise Report
ITEM	Web Item (Format SAP BW 3.x)
BITM	BEx Web Item
TMPL	Web Template (Format SAP BW 3.x)
BTMP	BEx Web Template

Table 3.2 Object Types for SAP NetWeaver BW Documentation

Object Type	Description
ACGR	Role
CRWB	Crystal Report
DMOD	Data model
DTPA	Data Transfer Process
PLST	Planning Function Type
THJT	Key Date of Type Derivation
RSPV	Process Variants
RSPC	Process Chain
RRUL	Remodeling Rule

Table 3.2 Object Types for SAP NetWeaver BW Documentation (Cont.)

3.4 Governance

Governance in any project covers the various templates, tools, documents, and standards that keep the consistency and communication of the project sound. You can compare the governance of a project to the laws in society. Governance helps to make sure that there is a certain standard and uniform way of doing things to help everyone configure and communicate effectively.

In many ways, the governance of a project defines the culture of the project (see Figure 3.5). Take the example of a project with extremely lax standards, with many of the SAP NetWeaver BW developers doing their own thing and configuring SAP NetWeaver BW in many different styles. Other projects have governance so strict that making any changes requires approval from many layers of management.

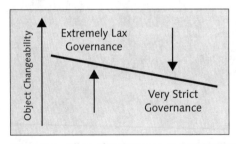

Figure 3.5 Effect of Governance on SAP NetWeaver BW Object Changeability

Striking a good balance between a clear and consistent governance document and stiflingly rigid standards allow the project to keep standards while also allowing for rapid change.

A clear set of governance standards are necessary to achieve project success. This governance is achieved through processes and clear documentation. There are several important documents that must exist in any SAP NetWeaver BW implementation. These are discussed in Table 3.3.

Project Charter	The project charter states the reason for the project, main deliverables, sponsors, success measures, etc.
Stakeholder Document	This document lists all stakeholders and the roles that the stakeholders have in the success of the project.
Project Plan	Two types of project plans are typically used in an SAP NetWeaver BW implantation. There is the SAP NetWeaver BW project plan and the overall project plan. Typically, the SAP NetWeaver BW project plan is managed locally and has detailed tasks, timelines, etc. The overall project plan integrates the SAP NetWeaver BW plan with the Basis, transactional, and other system projects to ensure that the SAP NetWeaver BW project goals and milestones can be met.
BW Organization Chart	This document shows the SAP NetWeaver BW team and their roles.
BW Development Standards Document	This document spells out the methodology and strategy for the SAP NetWeaver BW implementation. The development standards document states the master data and transactional data strategy and the different SAP NetWeaver BW rules and conventions that are followed. These include, for example, how the Persistent Staging Area (PSA) is typically used, how transformation is performed, whether function modules are used to house Advanced Business Application Programming (ABAP) code, or whether multi-level data store object (DSO) structures are used to store data.
Naming Standards Document	The naming standards document is used to define the convention used to name custom objects in the SAP NetWeaver BW system. This document is important to ensure some consistency in the design. This spells out how the naming will be used for InfoProviders, InfoObjects, Queries, etc.
Landscape Document	The landscape document details the different systems in the landscape and the transport path of those systems. For example, the landscape document shows the sandbox, development, QA, production, training, and production support systems in the BW landscape.

Table 3.3 Important SAP NetWeaver BW Project Governance Documents

Transport strategy Document	This document shows the strategy and timing for transports and the documentation and procedure for transport approval.
Architecture Document	This document shows the different InfoProviders and the flow of data through the system. This document shows all source systems and all Infoproviders and the flow of data from the source systems to the InfoProviders and to the presentation of data.
Disaster Recovery Document	This document details the disaster recovery standards, restore plan, etc. This document is used by the project to plan to deal with issues that occur. For the Basis organization, this involves backup and recovery. For the SAP NetWeaver BW applications team, this often means preparing to dump and reload data from the source, if needed.
System Copy—Refresh Document	The copy/refresh document shows the schedule and strategy for refreshing and copying systems from one system to another. For example, it shows when the sandbox system will be refreshed, and how often.
Review Checklist	This document is used as a checklist to review the design of a process in SAP NetWeaver BW before transport occurs. This document shows all things that should be checked, implemented, and documented prior to transport.
Functional Model Document	The functional model document shows the requirements and scope of a subject area.
Functional/Technical Specifications	These documents define and detail the design of SAP NetWeaver BW and the specific details of the implementation.
Security Standards Document	This document details the security standards and methodology.
Change Management Strategy Document	This document gives the strategy, roles, and templates for change management in the organization.
Glossary	A document with commonly used SAP NetWeaver BW terminology, defined for both the project team and the business.
Cutover Plan	This documentation is a list of all things needed before go-live can occur.
Communications Documents	These are for various communications, such as status reports, issues lists, etc.

Table 3.3 Important SAP NetWeaver BW Project Governance Documents (Cont.)

Having the documents is important, but even more important is making sure that these are living documents. It should be assumed that these documents will be modified and changed based on the needs of the project and the issues that arise.

This flexibility allows for the documents to be used to familiarize new developers and also to communicate to the business the different processes and methodologies of the project.

Big Mistakes Related to SAP NetWeaver BW Project Governance

▶ Naming standards do not exist. If they exist, they are followed partially or not followed at all.

▶ No clear transport strategy adopted.

▶ Developers can change Quality or Production systems without transport. This means DEV, QA, and PROD are not in sync.

▶ Security-related strategy is not implemented.

These can prevent the most common communication issues that occur in a project. We will now explore some of these communication issues.

3.5 Communication Issues

Many SAP NetWeaver BW projects face challenges in communication. These communication issues occur within the SAP NetWeaver BW team and between the SAP NetWeaver BW team and the various other transaction process teams in the project.

Communication issues may not occur just due to lack of management efforts. There are several challenges on effective communication and these barriers need to be overcome, as in Figure 3.6. The most important of them are language and cultural.

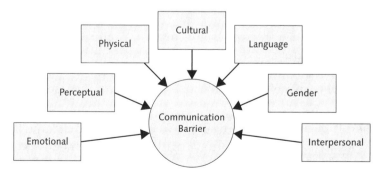

Figure 3.6 Barriers to Effective Communication

The best way to minimize these issues is to have checkpoints throughout the project. These serve as milestones and also allow for people inside and outside of the project to understand the progress and status.

3.5.1 Insist on Weekly Status Reports

Weekly status reports help the groups communicate what has been done. This practice allows the team to report on their statuses and also allows the organization to see what each other have been working on.

3.5.2 Encourage Informal Discussion

Sometimes, after-hours or lunchroom discussions lead to the most innovative ideas for issue resolution. These should be encouraged whenever possible. Some of the strongest teams are able to solve issues when they are physically apart from the situation. This experience results in bonding that develops trust and helps build a stronger team.

3.5.3 Locate Centrally

It's not uncommon that you'll be able to resolve many issues by simply overhearing someone speaking about something they were encountering. Locating a team close to one another allows this to happen and keeps communication more free and open, and thus allows for faster resolution of issues.

3.5.4 Centralize Issues List and Use It

The issues list should be considered a place where project challenges can be communicated and brought to the attention of all parties. Communicating the issues through weekly or even daily issue meetings allows the SAP NetWeaver BW issues to be understood.

In the past, many consultants have found themselves working on projects where the issues list either was not reviewed often enough by the project teams, or where individuals were unable or unwilling to add their issues to the central list, instead listing and managing their issues locally. This was the result of a culture where issues were seen as a weakness and process teams avoided making issues visible. Thus, many of the issues lingered on local lists for a long time awaiting resolution before they were centrally reported.

Many of these issues, if reported quickly, would have been resolved quickly. It is important that issues are managed centrally and tracked centrally. The project-management organization should encourage issues to be reported on the list and schedule meetings to resolve and escalate issues as necessary.

An important part of issue tracking is to clearly assign ownership of the issues to ensure that issues are addressed and escalated, if needed. The more clear the ownership of the issues, the better the action plan. Establishing clear ownership across the project also allows for a better action plan in the implementation. However, a lack of ownership can be one of the more common mistakes.

3.6   Ownership Issues

One of the quickest ways to keep a project successful is to spread the ownership of the project across the enterprise (see Figure 3.7). The more involved the business users are in the project, the more the project reflects their needs. Some of the least cost-effective and most tedious projects are staffed mainly with IT resources and have almost no user involvement.

In projects like this, with the same basic flawed methodology, the SAP NetWeaver BW team would briefly meet with user representatives. These teams would present their requirements, and then the SAP NetWeaver BW team would independently interpret those requirements and translate them into an SAP NetWeaver BW data model. They would then deliver a prototype, and finally present it to the users. The users would look at the prototype, redesign it, and suggest many changes. The process would begin again.

In some cases, this iterative design works because the users are simply presenting their small changes to the model. However, in many cases, because there was little interaction between the SAP NetWeaver BW team and the user representatives, the prototype was far from what the users actually wanted. A lot of reworking of the prototype was needed to meet the requirements.

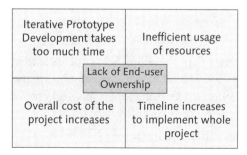

Figure 3.7 Problems Raised due to Lack of End-User Ownership

This extremely inefficient methodology was repeated again and again at different phases of the project. Rather than insisting that the development of the solution include active involvement of the users, the SAP NetWeaver BW team simply involved them only at the beginning and the end.

Most of the time, the project managers agreed that this was an inefficient use of resources. However, they found that getting the users' time to work with them on the design was not possible. This was mainly due to the perceptions of the user representatives. These individuals felt that minimal time was required from them to deliver the model. Once this perception was established, it was difficult to change.

The problem was in not getting the users to agree and sign off on a level of involvement from the beginning. Rather than allow this iterative development, the SAP NetWeaver BW project manager must insist on time from the user community, and get this commitment before any scoping begins.

> **Tip**
>
> The more ownership the business has in the SAP NetWeaver BW solution, the more support they give when issues occur (and they will).

3.6.1 Insist on Signoff of Documents

To keep the involvement of the users and give them some stake in the project, a simple signoff process on all requirement documents helps greatly to keep the scope and development clear to all parties involved. Typically, once stakeholders are forced to sign off on a document, their involvement increases.

3.6.2 Have the Power Users Develop the SAP NetWeaver BW Queries

Another great way to keep the users responsible for business processes involved in the development process is to have them develop all queries. This gives them an understanding of the reporting tool, its advantages, and limitations and helps them to understand the data, filtering, etc.

There is nobody who knows the queries better than these business process teams. The best way to start involving them is to identify those business users who are the most adept at understanding the requirements and learning new tools and groom them as the power users. The power user has three main roles:

► Develop, test, and roll out queries to the end user community
► Aid in training the other users
► Act as the first level of support for issues.

Below are the most important benefits of involving power users in the development process:

▶ **Ability to Understand Business Language**
The business user community often responds well when trained by someone who understands his business and can speak to its requirements. These power users can help to answer some of the business questions that inevitably come up during the training process. They also reduce the load on the help desk after go-live because he can often assist his peers with issues.

▶ **Acting as First Level of Support**
Many end-user queries can be answered by power users and they can act as first level support.

▶ **Part of the Implementation Team**
More important, this work helps to make sure that they are part of the process and own some of the development, as well as the issues when they occur.

It is important to make sure that power users are acknowledged by management for their roles in the project throughout the process. There have been many projects that simply would not have been successful without the extremely good power users testing and helping deal with issues. This is a very difficult role, so the proper recognition from management is imperative.

These power users help to address and solve some of the biggest issues on the project. Often, these issues are the result of problems with data quality. Understanding the issues that can occur as a result of data quality concerns cannot be overstated, because these often represent some of the biggest challenges in any SAP NetWeaver BW project.

3.7   Data Quality Issues

Data quality refers to the fitness of the data for use by the end user. Data quality is a subjective measure, so it is not always easy to quantify. However, poor data quality is the quickest way of losing user confidence in SAP NetWeaver BW. Many SAP NetWeaver BW issues after go-live occur because of bad master data.

For example, a user runs a query to see the total sales by division. In this case, the user is running the report based on the division found as an attribute on the material master. To run the report, the system does not show the division from the transactional data; instead, it looks to the master data attributes of the material reported. A small percentage of the master data division values are mistakenly left blank on the material master data. These values would not appear on the report by division; thus, to the user, the data in SAP NetWeaver BW is incorrect. This user starts to lose faith in the SAP NetWeaver BW system because the data is wrong.

Let's take another example. When a new material master record is created in SAP NetWeaver BW, the configuration team has the option to set select fields as mandatory. However, there are no rules checking the validity of the fields, just that the values are filled.

There is also very little checking on the SAP ECC or SAP R/3 system for conflicting or illogical values. This would occur on fields that relate to one another, such as making sure that any material master that is priced by weight has a net and gross weight populated in the material master. Rules to check for validity of various master data fields are often missed or not implemented in the SAP ECC or SAP R/3 system.

Because it is not easy to verify the master data and its validity, in most organizations, there are huge mistakes and missing data in master data. This becomes a problem for SAP NetWeaver BW because queries in BW are often based on this master data. Those queries that are not based on the master data are often referencing the transactional data that was filled from the master data in the transactional system.

This user starts to lose faith in the SAP NetWeaver BW system because the data is wrong. The user is correct that the data in SAP NetWeaver BW is indeed wrong. However, it is consistent with the values in the SAP ECC or SAP R/3 systems. If this master data is wrong, then SAP NetWeaver BW will be wrong, too.

Many of the SAP NetWeaver BW issues are the result of this kind of error. In many projects, much of the time is spent screen-dumping the incorrect data values in the SAP R/3 or SAP ECC system to prove that SAP NetWeaver BW matches the SAP R/3 or SAP ECC data. In many cases, it is this source data that is incorrect. This issue is then passed on to those teams to correct.

Data quality is a big topic; it helps to break the topic up into the following types of issues:

▶ **Data Integrity**
   Data must be of the proper level of granularity and must be extracted, transformed, and harmonized correctly with other data.

▶ **Data Completeness**
   Data must be extracted at the right frequency at the right time for data availability with the proper level of history for analysis.

▶ **Data Timeliness**

Data extraction must include timely, fresh data with a response time that is acceptable to the user for analysis.

A good master data strategy takes into account all the possible errors and develops means to keep this data consistent.

3.7.1 Don't Completely Rely on the Source Systems to Ensure Data Quality

The goal of configuring the various transactional systems is to make sure that a transaction can be entered completely, correctly, and quickly. Keeping the master data consistent is part of this job. However, even the best-configured systems end up with some bad master data.

Users do not always follow the rules and guidelines when entering master data or they inadvertently place incorrect values into the master data. To ensure that the SAP NetWeaver BW system has the best data possible, it is often necessary to build some testing and checking tools in SAP NetWeaver BW.

Create Transformation Rules to Check Master Data During Load

When data is loaded, it may be necessary to use rules to verify and check the data during the data loading process. The system provides many places to put transformation rules to determine the validity of the data. These allow for simple or complex checks of this data against established rules or against the data's source.

This is not always easy to do. However, if there are specific fields or rules that need to be applied to the master data, the master data can be checked during data loading for consistency. There are several different means and functions in SAP NetWeaver BW to check this master data and determine its validity.

Create Reports to Manually Check Master Data and Spot Anomalies

All master-data InfoObjects can be turned on for reporting. This allows SAP NetWeaver BW queries to be run against the master data. The queries allow checking of the master data for incorrect or inconsistent values. Although this governance is quite tedious, it does allow a more proactive checking of the master data in SAP NetWeaver BW and a way to avoid some future issues with incorrect or incomplete master data.

3.7.2 Establish Active Governance of Data

Active governance refers to an active process to keep master data as accurate and complete as possible. Unfortunately, the SAP R/3 and SAP ECC systems have few tools to ensure that the master data is kept consistent. There are some tools to make sure that mandatory master data values are filled, but it is difficult to configure rules in SAP R/3 or SAP ECC to make sure that the various fields in master data are consistent with each other.

For instance, when a new material master record is created in SAP NetWeaver BW, the configuration team has the option to set select fields as mandatory. However, there are no rules checking the validity of the fields, just that the values are filled.

There is also little checking on the SAP ECC or SAP R/3 system for conflicting or illogical values. These would occur on fields that relate to each other. These include making sure that any material master priced by weight has a net and gross weight populated in the material master. Rules to check for the validity of various master data fields are often missed or not implemented in the SAP ECC or SAP R/3 system.

Because it is not easy to verify the master data and its validity in most organizations, there are often mistakes and missing data in master data. This becomes a problem for SAP NetWeaver BW because queries in SAP NetWeaver BW are often based on this master data. Those queries not based on the master data often reference the transactional data that was filled from the master data in the transactional system.

This puts the SAP NetWeaver BW team at an extreme disadvantage. The master data is an integral part of the success of SAP NetWeaver BW, yet the master data rules and data are filled on the SAP R/3 or SAP ECC systems. The SAP NetWeaver BW team has very little say on the configuration of that data. Thus, in most SAP NetWeaver BW projects, much time is spent chasing missing or incorrect master data.

One way to do this is to work with the SAP ECC or SAP R/3 teams to develop active governance on their master data. This consists of running audit reports periodically on the master data to ensure its correctness.

3.7.3 Don't Keep Data Mismatch Issues Open for Long Time

When a user finds any mismatched data between SAP NetWeaver BW reports and source systems, try to fix these problems with the highest priority. Lingering issues of this nature can lower user confidence and it's difficult to regain lost user confidence.

3.7.4 Leverage the SAP BusinessObjects Data Services Tool

The SAP BusinessObjects Data Services tool provides a broad set of tools for ETL and Data Quality (see Figure 3.8). Especially for Data Quality, Data Services goes way beyond the capabilities available in SAP NetWeaver BW. Hence, using it in conjunction with SAP NetWeaver BW does leverage the quality of the data in the enterprise enormously.

Figure 3.8 Dataflow Through Business Objects Data Services

Using this tool, you can perform various data quality–related activities, which may be difficult to implement in SAP NetWeaver BW.

▶ **Data Profiling**
The Profiling feature in Data Services allows for detecting patterns in the data at hand, which columns contain potentially invalid values, and how often certain values occur in particular columns. Profiling can be executed on single or multiple objects.

▶ **Data Cleansing**
You can use Data Cleanse to assign gender codes and prenames, split records with dual names into individual records, create personalized greetings, and generate standards used in the match process. Data Cleanse can also parse and manipulate various forms of international data, as well as operational and product data.

▶ **Enhancement**
Completes records with directory information by appending name, address, phone number, or email address. It also provides geo-coding capabilities for geographic and demographic marketing initiatives.

▶ **Matching and Consolidation**
The Matching and Consolidation component of Data Services solution matches and consolidates data elements based on user-defined business rules. Duplicate records can be identified and eliminated.

▶ **Continuous Monitoring**
This feature allows monitoring and measuring the activities within Data Services at any time. It can be customized for periodic assessment. Thresholds can be set, and notification can be sent on exceeding the defined thresholds. There are also various reports available to analyze and track the Data Quality process.

If your master data quality requirements are not met with the existing SAP tools, you can also turn to various third-party vendors.

3.7.5 Turn to a Third-Party to Help with Validation

Let's look at the example of a third-party vendor that helped a project with active governance on its ECC system. Basically, its software sat on top of the SAP ECC or SAP R/3 system. Master data was entered into the BackOffice system, checked for rules, completeness, etc., and then BackOffice saved the master data into the SAP ECC or SAP R/3 system.

If data is incorrect or missing, the system does not allow the data to be entered. It also has a component to make sure that if there are several roles involved in establishing the master data, each user can perform his own role and notify the next role group. Thus, if a new product requires information from purchasing, finance, and the warehouse groups, each one can enter its part, and the data can be verified and passed on to the next group.

This process, whether handled manually using workflow in SAP ECC or SAP R/3 or handled via a third-party vendor, can safeguard the integrity of the master data and thus help the overall quality of the reporting solution that is built with this master data at its core.

If a third party system cannot be implemented, a significant effort should be planned before each new SAP NetWeaver BW implementation to check and fix the master data to make sure that SAP NetWeaver BW has the most complete and consistent master data for reporting.

Processes should also be put in place to ensure that data is checked periodically for completeness and consistency.

Validata from Validata LLC is another third-party vendor that provides a good tool to validate data from the SAP source systems and the SAP NetWeaver BW system. See the section in this chapter on third-party tools for more information on this product, or visit their website at *www.validatabw.com*.

Once data has been validated and found to clearly match its source, the next step is to assimilate this data together into a clear and consistent SAP NetWeaver BW data model. This process is often called *harmonization of data* or *data alignment*. The process of aligning data can be quite challenging, and is a frequent source of challenges.

3.8   Data Alignment Issues

Data alignment involves taking data from various source systems and harmonizing that data so that it is consistent and appears to have come from one source. It is common to overlook the complexity of aligning data from different systems and performing the transformation to keep this data consistent.

3.8.1   Master Data Alignment

There are several strategies for combining master data in SAP NetWeaver BW. You need to combine master data when there is more than one source system providing master data values for SAP NetWeaver BW. For instance, a company may have two different purchasing systems: one for external orders and another for internal orders. The transactional data from each of the systems will be loaded into SAP NetWeaver BW, so the associated master data also needs to be loaded into SAP NetWeaver BW.

These two systems are independent of each other and the master data values are not in sync between the two systems. How can you make sure that the master data is loaded but also make sure that there are no collisions between the streams of data? A collision occurs when each system has the same master data key. If this occurs, the values would overwrite and cause inconsistent values in the master data.

Master data alignment refers to the process of removing duplicates and bringing data together with a common key. For example, to perform global reporting on Wal-Mart, a common Wal-Mart customer number needs to be determined, and all Wal-Mart locations must then reference that number. This is not always easy because of the many ways that each of the local systems has stored customer data.

Often, these differing systems do not use a common master data key. However, for a global SAP NetWeaver BW project to be successful, the master data must use a common key. This would guarantee that reporting across the enterprise can occur with a common material number, customer number, etc. This effort requires taking existing master data, removing the duplicates, determining commonality, and centralizing this data into one structure. This effort is often a difficult task.

Typically, most data alignment efforts must take place outside the SAP NetWeaver BW system. This is because it is difficult for SAP NetWeaver BW to provide active governance and perform merging and matching of master data objects when these are loaded into SAP NetWeaver BW from several source systems.

This alignment is vital to ensuring that data from different source systems do not overwrite each other. For example, without master data alignment, one SAP R/3 system can have customer 1234 identified as Wal-Mart and another SAP R/3 system could have customer 1234 as Target. If both SAP R/3 systems load customer data into SAP NetWeaver BW, these customer numbers need to be handled to ensure that there is no overwriting of master data in the EDW.

Master Data Maintenance (MDM)

The most popular tool for master data alignment in SAP is master data maintenance (MDM). Although this tool is not related to SAP NetWeaver BW, the results of common master data governance with common master data keys provide a great opportunity to allow for global reporting and global alignment of data. The MDM tool allows for this central monitoring and governance of master data. The goals of MDM are shown in Figure 3.9.

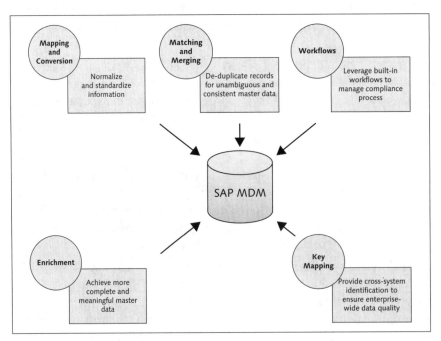

Figure 3.9 MDM Capabilities and Goals

These goals fit in well with the reporting goals of SAP NetWeaver BW.

> **Tip**
>
> The more effort spent keeping master data aligned, correct, and less redundant, the better the resulting reporting is in SAP NetWeaver BW.

Concatenated Keys or Compound Keys?

If data cannot be easily harmonized, many SAP NetWeaver BW projects look for a way to make the data unique, even if it is not unique at its source. Because the data cannot be loaded verbatim without facing collisions of data with the same keys, a new approach is needed.

The most common approach to making the data unique is to use either a compound or concatenated key (see Figure 3.10). Both of these processes change the key structure of the data to make each loaded value unique from its source. This allows data from two different sources that otherwise would collide to be harmonized into one master data table.

The compound master data key approach appends a key onto the master data values with a designator for the source system. The concatenated approach increases the size of the master data key and prefixes the value with a source-system identifier. Both approaches ensure that no data is duplicated when data is loaded into SAP NetWeaver BW.

The differences in the two approaches center on establishing the data integrity and keeping the two sets of data separate. When using a compound master data key, the system is added to the master data key to make a new compound key. For example, material A1 can be the same in two source systems. Thus, if the key is not just material number A1, but material A1 and a source-system designator, the two values remain unique.

Concatenating the data would simply change the existing key value by giving the value a prefix with the source system. In this case, material A1 would be SYS01_A1 and SYS02_A1. These ensure that the two values also remain unique.

The concatenation approach is much less invasive and allows more flexibility with the data model than the compounding approach, so in general terms it makes sense to favor the concatenation approach. A compound key is much more difficult to remove. The compound key value must always be shown in queries. Without it, a user can make an incorrect assumption because—without the source system being shown—the system can and will aggregate values based on the customer number. This can be a problem if the values are not consistent. This problem does not occur with the concatenation approach.

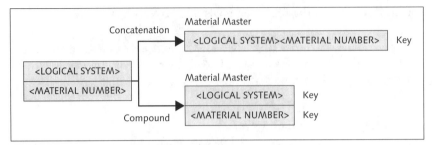

Figure 3.10 Concatenation and Compound Harmonization Approach

However, both approaches affect how the data is stored in SAP NetWeaver BW. In many cases, the user is not presented with the compound values or concatenated values in their queries. Another field is added as an attribute of the master data and shows the value to the user independent of the concatenation. The filters in the query make sure the same material does not appear twice.

A better and more long-term approach is to harmonize these values into one material code. This requires work to analyze the data, decide on a common value, and provide the change management to move to this common value. This can be difficult and time consuming.

3.8.2 Transactional Data Alignment

Transactional data alignment can also prove to be a difficult effort. For example, suppose a company has orders coming in from two different systems: one SAP ECC and the other a legacy system. The company wants to be able to report these ordered together. This causes significant challenges.

The two systems may have radically different ways of treating and saving transactional data. They may also have different values for master data elements such as the customer or the material. Therefore, the effort to bring the data into SAP NetWeaver BW involves creating complex transformation logic to bring the data into a common format. This often involves a series of cross-reference tables that must be read to convert this data.

The level of effort for this process can be easily overlooked. There is no easy way to perform the data harmonization other than to clearly understand both sources of data and map together the fields one by one. This is a tedious and lengthy process.

To make the process easier, we recommend that the original sources of data be first loaded unchanged into their own DSO structures. Thus, there are two DSO structures: one with the legacy data and one with the SAP ECC data. This data can then be combined into a second level or subsequent DSO. The transformation rules are used to transform data into the second-level DSO.

This allows for a much easier reconciliation and reload of data because each source exists unchanged from the source in its own SAP NetWeaver BW DSO. If there is an issue with the harmonization of the data, the second-level DSO can be purged and reloaded from the two sources of data once the transformation rule or cross-reference table is adjusted to fix the error.

Even the best efforts to align data can lead to incorrect results. When the data in SAP NetWeaver BW is incorrect, it is usually not easy to fix. Most often, this means dumping out the data and reloading from the source. For obvious reasons, this needs to be avoided as much as possible in any SAP NetWeaver BW project. Anticipating the realignment needs and avoiding realignment as much as possible helps to make the project more successful. In the next section, we will describe some common issues with realignment and show how these can be avoided.

> **Note**
>
> Transactional Data alignment is tightly dependent on how master data is harmonized. If you are using concatenation method of master data harmonization, then you have to follow the same logic for characteristics while loading transactional data.

3.9   Data Realignment

Realignment is a nasty word in an SAP NetWeaver BW project. Realignment refers to the process of taking data that has already been loaded into SAP NetWeaver BW and changing some of the attributes of the data so that it can be presented differently to the end user. The problem with data realignments in SAP NetWeaver BW is that many of these realignments require a full dump and reload of SAP NetWeaver BW data. This can cause a severe interruption of the data warehouse.

In a typical realignment scenario, the InfoProviders need to be purged of all data, the rules for aligning data need to be adjusted, and the data needs to be reloaded. Often, this means a shutdown of the transactional system while the data is reloaded. Downtime of the SAP R/3 or SAP ECC systems can be substantial, depending on the volume of data that needs to be reloaded.

The complexity and pressure of shutting out the users from the transactional system and effort to test and validate the data in SAP NetWeaver BW make for an extremely difficult realignment process.

3.9.1 Realignment Without Reload—Is It Possible?

Many organizations handle realignments often without ever reloading master data. This is done by preparing the SAP NetWeaver BW data model for the realignment in the design phase of the project. If an SAP NetWeaver BW project team can find out where and on which fields the realignments typically take place, they can often make sure that the fields needed for realignment are part of the master data objects, thus making it possible to realign without performing a dump and reload of the transactional data values. Let's look at two possible realignment scenarios.

Scenario 1
Sales order data is loaded into SAP NetWeaver BW by sales division, and the sales division is loaded into the transactional data from the master data. This data is stored directly into the InfoCube and used for reporting by the users.

The sales department now gets a new vice president and he decides to change the sales division rollups for reporting. In Scenario 1, to realign the data, the transactional data must be purged and reloaded. This is because the values are loaded into the transaction data values with an *as-posted view*. This as-posted view hard-codes the value of the sales division into the transactional data of the InfoCube at the time it is saved. Thus, to change these values, the data must be reloaded.

In Scenario 2, a dump and reload of data is not required. In fact, during realignment in the second scenario, there is nothing that needs to be done. The realignment occurs naturally because as the divisions change in the master data in the SAP ECC or SAP R/3 systems, the master data in SAP NetWeaver BW would automatically change.

When this data changes, the resulting queries would then show the new values rather than the as-posted values in the transactional data. The two sample scenarios show that realignments in SAP NetWeaver BW can be avoided if:

▶ You anticipate the fields that will be needed for realignment.

▶ The users accept the restated field in their queries.

The second bullet point can be a complex and heated debate among users. The design of SAP NetWeaver BW and the shared master data allow for both an as-posted view of data and a restated view of data. As the two scenarios show, the as-posted view hard-codes values into the InfoProvider, because the values existed at the time of the transaction. The restated view represents the values from the master data, as it currently exists.

It is important to make sure that users understand that they have this option when viewing data in SAP NetWeaver BW. When a query is created, both options are possible. You can use a display attribute to show a value, or the same value might also appear in the transactional data.

Using the display attribute from master data always ensures that the user is seeing the most current view of the data and will automatically realign the data via the normal master data changes. When an SAP ECC or SAP R/3 user changes the division, the new division will automatically appear in the associated SAP NetWeaver BW reports.

There is a performance concern with the restated view. This view is typically much slower than the corresponding query on the transactional data because the system must access the master data table to provide the data. This can be offset by adding database indices or SAP NetWeaver BW aggregates, if needed.

Any SAP NetWeaver BW system with significant data loaded has the potential for performance issues. Understanding and avoiding these as much as possible can circumvent many common SAP NetWeaver BW issues. In the next section, we'll discuss some of the common performance issues and their impact on SAP NetWeaver BW.

3.9.2 Remodeling Toolbox

The Remodeling Toolbox is delivered with NW 2004s. When you can't avert adding a new characteristics or key figure in an InfoCube, you can use this tool (see Table 3.4). Using this tool, you don't have to empty the InfoCubes and re-design; rather, new InfoObjects, Key Figures, can be added or deleted when the InfoCubes have data (see Figure 3.11). However, it is recommended to make a backup of the existing data in another InfoCube. The Remodeling Toolbox can be used with the following scenarios:

▶ A new Key Figure must be added to a particular InfoCube with initialized values.

▶ A new characteristic should be added or replaced with an existing one. Data can be filled with old characteristics, other InfoObject values, attribute of an InfoObject, constant, or customer exit.

Conversion	Rule
Key Figure	▶ Add any Key Figure initially filled with constant or customer exit. ▶ Replace Key Figure, filled with customer exit. ▶ Delete Key Figure.

Characteristics	▶ Add/Replace Characteristics
	    – with Constant or Customer Exist
	    – with Attribute of an InfoObject of same dimension
	    – with same value of another InfoObject of same dimension
	▶ Delete Characteristics.

Table 3.4 Conversion Rules in Remodeling Toolbox

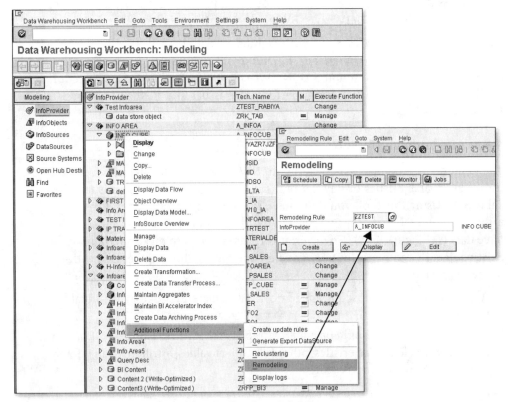

Figure 3.11 Accessing Remodeling Toolbox from InfoCube

> **Note**
>
> With the current version of SAP NetWeaver BW implementation, the Remodeling Toolbox can be applied for InfoCubes only. However, DSO and InfoObject remodeling will be possible in future SAP NetWeaver BW releases.

3.10 Performance Issues

Outside of data quality, performance is the most important concern in SAP NetWeaver BW. What makes performance tuning in SAP NetWeaver BW so challenging is that many of the decisions made early in the project affect the performance significantly.

> **Note**
>
> Unlike the SAP R/3 or SAP ECC systems, the majority of the performance problems in SAP NetWeaver BW are not the result of the database or Basis system setup. They occur because of the data modeling decisions made by the applications team.

In this respect, SAP NetWeaver BW is unlike almost all other SAP modules. Usually there are few decisions that the applications team can do to affect the performance of a module in SAP R/3 or SAP ECC. When performance is slow, it is due to a network, database, or Basis issue. In SAP NetWeaver BW, the performance tuning must be built into the application during the configuration.

Unfortunately, this is not always done, or done well. One project manager once described performance planning and data modeling in SAP NetWeaver BW as a young man getting a tattoo: "Sometimes a decision that you make when you are young and new to the world is one that you may regret later, and they aren't always easy to change."

> **Tip**
>
> Data modeling is an area where good advice can make a data model performance optimal not only for the current needs but also for future growth. Invest in a good data architect for your SAP NetWeaver BW project and hold on to that resource.

3.10.1 Establish Clear Goals for Performance

Performance is a nebulous topic. One user could perceive a performance issue where another does not. The only way to understand and prioritize performance issues is to develop a method for tracking and measuring performance and, most important, goals for performance in the organization.

These goals should be established for both query-presentation and loading performance. This best statement of goals comes in the form of a service level agreement (SLA) with the end users. The SLA should state the average goal for query performance and uptime of SAP NetWeaver BW. This sets the goal for measurement and tracking of the SAP NetWeaver BW system.

An SLA at one organization sets the overall query performance to stay under 30 seconds, on average. Because the implementation had large volumes of data, it was a challenge to maintain aggregates and queries so that they would bring back smaller amounts of data to the users to keep the overall performance of the system within the goal. The SLA in an organization depends on many factors; however, after the system has been stable for a few weeks, it is usually a good time to assess goals and reset the SLA, if needed.

Data Load Performance Goals

In most SAP NetWeaver BW projects, the majority of data loading occurs each evening. The loads are usually designed to be complete by the next morning so the users can query the data. If the data loading performance is sub-standard, or runs late, the InfoCubes and DSO structures aren't loaded in time for the users to perform their reporting.

The data load performance goals should clearly state when data is supposed to be available for the end user's reporting. You should have a comprehensive checklist to verify that your data loading is optimally designed, as in Table 3.5.

Focus Area	Checklist
ABAP (Start Routine, End Routine, Expert Routine)	▶ TYPE command is used instead of LIKE while declaring data element. ▶ Internal tables are defined with "TYPE STANDARD TABLE OF." Do not create work area with header. ▶ In SELECT statement, only required fields are selected in the same order as they reside in the table. ▶ Use "SELECT INTO TABLE" rather than "SELECT INTO CORRESPONDING FIELDS OF TABLE." ▶ Always specify as many primary keys as possible in WHERE clause to make the Select efficient. ▶ Check SORT inside if a LOOP is not used.

Table 3.5 Data Loading Performance Checklist

Focus Area	Checklist
	▶ Check SELECT statement inside if a LOOP is not used.
	▶ Sort internal table by fields in the correct order, which are used in a READ TABLE statement using BINARY SEARCH. If the order of sorting is invalid, the BINARY SEARCH will never work.
	▶ Use FIELD-SYMBOLS while processing internal tables with WHILE loop.
	▶ You can put many more checklists; however, you must put above points in your checklist.
Aggregates	▶ Check that there are no missing aggregates.
	▶ Attribute change run must be performed when master data changed.
DataSource Initialization	▶ Check DataSource initialization selection is covering all of your changed documents.
Dimension Table	▶ In a single dimension, characteristics have 1:N relationship.
Index	▶ Make sure indexes are removed before data loading and created after data loading. This procedure can be integrated in the process chain easily.

Table 3.5 Data Loading Performance Checklist (Cont.)

Query Performance Goals

Query performance is one of the most important factors for users. They expect queries to return their desired data as quickly as possible. The problem is that many times the users are unaware of the data volume in SAP NetWeaver BW and don't understand how the way they query this data can affect performance.

Part of any query-performance goal in SAP NetWeaver BW is training the users to go after the data in the most efficient manner. Users who drill a report down to the most detailed level might feel that the report is performing poorly, when, in-fact, they might be better off looking that the data at a more aggregated level and only drilling into the data that is relevant for their analysis. This should be considered an important part of SAP NetWeaver BW training.

The developer should keep in mind the following points while creating a query.

▶ Remove exclusion selection criteria in SAP NetWeaver BW queries. Query will not read data from aggregates or from BI Accelerator if you use selection criteria.

▶ If queries are built on MultiProvider, make sure to add selection criteria for InfoProvider in Filter area.

- If possible, avoid cell editor.
- Make sure query is re-generated in RSRT transaction.
- User Exit variables are efficiently coded.
- If currency conversion is used, make sure they are working well.
- If possible, try to move selection criteria in Filter area.

The previous points are partial, though important to run queries efficiently. You can add many other points in your checklist.

3.10.2 Measure Against the Performance Goals via Statistics InfoCubes

SAP NetWeaver BW has effective tools for monitoring performance. The most important of these tools are the statistics InfoCubes. These InfoCubes allow for reporting on load performance, query performance, and use of the SAP NetWeaver BW system.

> **Tip**
>
> Monitoring of the statistics InfoCubes is the single best way to make sure that you can be proactive rather than reactive in your performance efforts.

There really is no other way to address, determine severity, and set the priorities of issues without the statistics InfoCubes.

3.10.3 Establish a Performance Sub-Team

Several project teams have created a performance sub-team to track performance issues in SAP NetWeaver BW. This sub-team needs to be made up of representatives from the Basis team, the database team, the applications team, and business users. The team can work together to look at the statistics information to determine which queries and data loads are the most important and how to rank and discuss performance issues.

This would not be the full-time job of the performance sub-team members. The members act as a committee to solve performance problems and give some visibility to SAP NetWeaver BW performance tracking and issue resolution. It is important to have representatives from Basis, database, applications, and the business operations to make sure that the issues are addressed together.

Sometimes, because these groups represent different parts of the organization, they don't formally work together on performance issues, and problems linger while one group points to another in defining the root of the issue.

By using the statistics InfoCubes for this analysis, the team can quantify a performance issue. If a query is running slowly but that query is only run a few times per month, there is very little payoff from tuning that query for performance. However, having the business as part of the performance team can help, especially if the business users determine that the few such queries run each month are for the CIO. Suddenly, this query becomes much more important to tune.

3.10.4 Keep Up-to-Date on Support Packages

One of the most important ways of keeping performance optimal in SAP NetWeaver BW is to stay current with support packages. SAP adds significant performance-enhancement modifications to each support package and can minimize various bottlenecks in loading and query performance.

3.10.5 Data Model for Performance

Entire books have been written on data modeling, so this topic is quite vast. However, one of the important factors in establishing a data model is to clearly understand how the decision making in SAP NetWeaver BW affects the overall performance of the data model. Poor performance can manifest itself in both load performance and query performance. Thus, understanding the effects of the data model on performance is crucial to making sure that the data model is optimal.

Data Granularity

One critical decision that is made early in SAP NetWeaver BW development is the granularity of the data stored in SAP NetWeaver BW. The granularity of data refers to the lowest level of data that is stored in SAP NetWeaver BW.

For example, when loading sales orders into SAP NetWeaver BW, there are many choices of granularity. Data can be loaded at the most-detailed sales-order schedule line level, showing each release of the sales order. It could also be loaded into SAP NetWeaver BW and aggregated monthly without the document detail at all. The granularity of the data is determined based on the keys of data in the DSO structure or the combination of the characteristics in an InfoCube. The characteristics are the data fields used to analyze the Key Figure values in an InfoCube.

If you include the sales-order schedule line, line item, and header information in every sales order that you load into SAP NetWeaver BW, you increase the volume exponentially over the same data that is aggregated monthly. This increase in volume typically leads to inferior performance in SAP NetWeaver BW simply because the system must look through a larger data set to perform analysis.

To make sure that performance is considered when looking at data in SAP NetWeaver BW, you must understand the granularity of the data and thus the size of the data that is being loaded into SAP NetWeaver BW. When evaluating SAP NetWeaver BW designs for a project, one of the first things you should ask is: "What is the data volume that you expect in this InfoCube/DSO?"

Decreasing the granularity does not automatically improve the performance, but it goes a long way toward aiding the performance and flexibility of the data model.

Of course, there is a price to pay for decreasing the granularity. The flexibility of the analysis is also dictated by the granularity of the data. If the lowest level of granularity for your sales data is monthly, you cannot analyze sales by day or week. In SAP NetWeaver BW, it is difficult to serve both needs. You must take into account the needs of the users and balance this against the performance needs of the users.

The way that most projects handle this concern is to pull the detailed data into the DSO in SAP NetWeaver BW, and aggregate the data up into the InfoCubes. Whenever possible, the detailed data lies in the DSO and the less granular data is in the InfoCube.

Hybrid Approach to Granularity

There is also a hybrid approach that works rather well in many implementations. This is to have two or more InfoCubes with differing levels of granularity. For example, there may be many people in the organization that look at sales data at a monthly level. These people make up the majority of the user base.

However, there are a few users who require this same sales data at a lower level of granularity, weekly, or even daily. To satisfy the users with the lowest level of granularity, you could create one sales InfoCube and have the time characteristic of 0CALDAY and/or 0CALWEEK. By adding and populating these time characteristics, the data is automatically at a daily or weekly level of granularity. This increases the volume of data exponentially, and load performance and query performance suffer as a result.

Why should the majority of the user base suffer the performance burdens for the few users who desire the data at a granular level? The answer is that in many cases they shouldn't. How can you give them their data at a much summarized level while also providing the data at a granular level for the other users?

The answer is to create two InfoCubes and queries that are exactly the same except for the time characteristics. One InfoCube would include the time characteristics of 0CALDAY or 0CALWEEK. The other would only include the 0CALMONTH and neither 0CALDAY nor 0CALWEEK. This makes sure that the level of granularity in one InfoCube is at the day or week level and the other is at the monthly level.

The users who desire the monthly reporting could be pointed to the monthly query and thus would have significantly better performance because of the reduced volume of data queried.

Train the Query Developers Properly

Some of the worst query performance issues projects face are because of the design of the queries. SAP NetWeaver BW allows users to bring back a great deal of data in one pass. This flexibility allows users to take poor advantage of SAP NetWeaver BW's query power.

Some users create queries that bring back huge volumes of data in the first pass. This happens because users are accustomed to working with several long reports. Having acquired huge volumes of data, the user can then look at these multiple-page reports and find information on any issue or question that he has.

SAP NetWeaver BW works best in an interactive, drill-down fashion. A query should take advantage of this approach. The first view of a sales query should not typically show the sales data by customer and material at a very detailed level that stretches on for many pages. Instead, the report should be structured to show that same data at a higher level, perhaps sales by sales organization. The users can then use the interactivity and slicing technique to hone the overall sales data to the specific data they desire.

They might first drill down by sales organization, eliminating the sales organizations that are not relevant, and then select by distribution channel, division, etc. This drilling down reduces the granularity at each selection. By the time the user gets down to a detailed level, the volume of data returned is limited, and thus performance is better.

Sometimes, issues occur with SAP NetWeaver BW projects that are outside the control of the users or development teams. These technical issues not only slow a project, but depending on the level of understanding of the Basis team, can linger and cause many unnecessary delays. In the next section, we will discuss these issues.

3.11   Technical and Infrastructure Issues

There are many technical and infrastructure issues that can cause SAP NetWeaver BW implementations to fail or be delayed. Take the example of a large SAP

NetWeaver BW implementation that loaded large volumes of data into the system. When reporting on this data, the system occasionally queried the data so slowly that it would take several minutes to bring up a query that previously took several minutes. The issue was quickly reported to the Basis and database teams.

This issue was not addressed quickly because the Basis team attributed the issue to the resource constrained development and QA systems. The issue continued through unit testing and integration testing. It was only when the issue surfaced in the production environment that the Basis team reacted to the issue.

This was late in the implementation process, and what should have been a high priority issue early was left to fester until the issue became an emergency. These types of technical issues need to be recognized and addressed as soon as possible. Several of these issues are listed here:

▶ **Application Issues**
These issues are common on an SAP NetWeaver BW project. They are typically resolved either through an SAP Note application or a support package. An SAP NetWeaver BW support package is an interim patch from SAP that contains numerous fixes for the SAP NetWeaver BW system. These support packages are issued periodically by SAP and are listed in the SAP Service Marketplace. In between the support packages, SAP often issues SAP Notes to fix single issues. SAP encourages SAP NetWeaver BW application fixes to be implemented through a support package. This is to ensure that the fixes coordinate with each other. Thus, if a fix is not critical, it may make sense to wait until a support package is released to get the latest fix. If the fix is critical, the fix can be implemented via an SAP Note.

▶ **Database Issues**
SAP NetWeaver BW is a database-independent system. Thus, projects can choose any database system to use with SAP NetWeaver BW. However, some databases work better with SAP NetWeaver BW than others. This is because the more popular databases like Oracle are used by more projects and thus issues are discovered more quickly and can be resolved quickly. Most database issues are fixed via a patch from the database provider.

▶ **Network Infrastructure Issues**
Network issues can cause SAP NetWeaver BW issues both during data loading and query presentation. Network stability and size are vital to SAP NetWeaver BW's success. An improperly sized network infrastructure can cause data transfer to slow or even stop altogether.

▶ **System Issues**

These involve disk, memory, and similar aspects. Sizing of an SAP NetWeaver BW system is difficult because the sizing effort typically takes place before any SAP NetWeaver BW data is loaded and before the true scope of the project has been determined. Thus, periodically, the sizing effort should be reviewed to determine if the size of the SAP NetWeaver BW system is adequate for current demand and future growth.

▶ **Desktop Issues**

Users with various desktop configurations will access SAP NetWeaver BW. SAP NetWeaver BW integrates with Microsoft Excel and with the user's Internet browser. Keeping the desktops at a standard release and patch level of these products help to minimize some of the technical issues that can arise from older and more unstable versions of these products.

The technical issues can be quickly resolved through a clear testing and escalation process when issues occur. However, as with any team, the deeper the knowledge of those on the team, the more likely the team is to succeed. A strong team that understands the issues faced in SAP NetWeaver BW and works together to solve them is an asset to any project. When this team strength fails to occur, the opposite is true.

In the next section, we will discuss some common SAP NetWeaver BW team resource issues.

3.12   Resource Issues

Many potential resource issues can arise on an SAP NetWeaver BW project. Resource issues involve team members and the interaction among the different roles and personalities on the project. Because any SAP NetWeaver BW project requires a significant amount of communication between the various teams in the organization, the team dynamic of an SAP NetWeaver BW team is crucial to its success (see Figure 3.12).

3.12.1   Insist on the Best, Not Just the Most Available

For an SAP NetWeaver BW project to be successful, it is imperative that the SAP NetWeaver BW team has subject matter experts working on the project team from day to day. In the best projects, organizations have dedicated these people 100% to the SAP NetWeaver BW team and free them up from their other responsibilities.

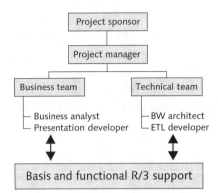

Figure 3.12 Typical Team Structure for Medium-Size SAP NetWeaver BW Implementation

It is through the constant interaction with the subject-matter experts that the SAP NetWeaver BW data warehouse can clearly represent the needs of the business. A good subject-matter expert can see a potential problem early in the process, allowing the project team to switch course in the design before too much time is wasted.

It is not always easy to get the most qualified subject-matter experts. Here is an example of a common struggle on an SAP NetWeaver BW project. There is an employee named Melanie who works as a sales department analyst. She is responsible for providing the various reports that the sales department needs to run their operation.

Melanie would be a perfect fit for the SAP NetWeaver BW project because of her vast knowledge of the reporting parameters. However, the business unit does not want to give Melanie up because she is too valuable to its organization. The organizations with the best projects understand that they need to provide this level of resource to the SAP NetWeaver BW team to make it successful.

3.12.2 The Consultant-Heavy Project

It is quite common for projects to fall into the trap of having the consultants do all the work, with few employees involved. This happens because it is much easier in many projects to defer the work to the experts. In this case, the experts are the consultants.

There have been certain instances where not a single employee has been assigned to the SAP NetWeaver BW project. A political discussion ensues when the consulting partner is asked why there isn't employee participation on the project.

Although an organization chart shows that there were employees on the project team, it was clear that the day-to-day configuration and project development work was solely done by consultants. Make sure that your day-to-day decision-making and configuration is provided, at least in part, by employees.

The quickest and easiest route is usually the one that is most often taken. In this case, the quickest and easiest is simply to have the consultants provide the configuration and completely lead and support the implementation.

Often, the largest SAP consulting partners are most guilty of this practice. This is because of a conflict in goals. The consulting partner is measured by its ability to bring a project live, on-time, and within budget. How can you do this if you are spending time keeping the employees up-to-speed? It is much easier doing the configuration, and then planning a handoff of the project configuration, after it is complete, in a knowledge-transfer process.

The consultants on the project must then be charged not only with implementing the project but also bringing the employees up to speed on the product and nuances of the SAP NetWeaver BW product. Unless there is a serious mandate to do this, it rarely happens in a project. It is the SAP NetWeaver BW project manager's responsibility to make sure that this occurs. If this is left up only to the consultants or the management of the consulting partner, it rarely happens.

You should rely on your consultants to provide the product and SAP NetWeaver BW configuration knowledge. However, make sure employees are in charge of each area of SAP NetWeaver BW and are performing the configuration. The consultants are there for issue management and implementation advice.

3.12.3   Insist on Interviewing All Candidates

To ensure that a consultant fits into the culture of an organization and is competent to do the work, conduct an interview. Use SAP NetWeaver BW knowledgeable consultants to determine the product knowledge, and take time to assess the interpersonal fit.

3.12.4   Transition Out Bad Consultants

Every project, sooner or later, ends up with a consultant that is not a good fit. Many projects let poor consultants continue working on the projects. You staff a project with consultants so that you can use their advice and later transition them off of the project. Therefore, it is difficult to understand why an organization might be hesitant to remove a non-productive resource.

On larger SAP NetWeaver BW projects, the staffing is done by the consulting partner. The situation can become quite political if you ask the consulting partner to provide you with resources, make the partner accountable for the project's success, and then tell his resources to go home. It is quite difficult for them to be successful if you do not allow them to staff with those they think would be a good fit.

However, if a consultant does not fit in with the organization culture, has communication issues, or does not have the skill set to complete the SAP NetWeaver BW tasks, then transition this consultant off of the project. A poor consultant not only does not help the process but slows the process because the rest of the team must slow down to keep him up to speed.

3.12.5 Avoid Conflict Between Consulting Partners, SAP, and Others

It's not uncommon for SAP NetWeaver BW projects to get political. This is because no matter how a project is staffed, there is a competition at the high level to secure the limited consulting spots.

> **Example**
>
> There was a project where the various consulting companies' project team members would not freely work together to resolve issues. They each felt that the delays on the project were the result of the others' incompetence. This caused the project to be delayed even more as issues lingered longer than needed.

It is frustrating when the various consulting firms are trying to cover their own mistakes and emphasize the mistakes of others for political gain with the client.

Sometimes, clients lose track of the big-picture goal of consulting firms. There are two goals of a consulting firm. The first is to keep the client happy through successful project management and consulting advice; the second is to improve the consulting firm's position at the client site.

The second goal can be counterproductive to the first goal. Various consulting firms attempt to gather more consulting seats on a project, and there are only two ways to do this: grow the project, or take existing seats. Sometimes, it seems easier for a consulting partner to spend his time casting doubt on various participants in the project in the hopes that he can gain more consulting seats than it would be to ensure quality work that could ultimately grow the business, which in turn would expand the SAP NetWeaver BW project.

Thus, we have worked on projects where we were forced to spend a great deal of time justifying the various goals and methodology when that time could have been spent on the configuration and tuning of the SAP NetWeaver BW system.

Although a certain amount of verification is good to ensure that the methodology is sound, this can get out of control if it severely interferes with accomplishing the goals of the project.

This problem is ultimately a result of the culture of the organization and cannot be tolerated. In the best-run projects, the consulting firm is irrelevant. The project goals are the ultimate goals. Watch for this in your project and make every effort to stop this counterproductive behavior.

3.12.6 SAP R/3 or SAP ECC Basis Experience is Not SAP NetWeaver BW Experience

A Basis team refers to the technical team in any organization that performs the technical system operations such as installation, support package upgrades, or backup and recovery.

SAP NetWeaver BW is a different implementation than SAP R/3 or SAP ECC systems. The SAP NetWeaver BW application team typically has much more interaction with the Basis team than any other does. Making sure that the Basis resources are knowledgeable in the product helps to make sure that all teams function at their best.

Sometimes, in order to fill a Basis role, an SAP ECC or SAP R/3 Basis resource will be used to fill the SAP NetWeaver BW Basis role. SAP NetWeaver BW has many fundamental Basis tasks that are unique to its environment. Therefore, an SAP ECC or SAP R/3 Basis team member accustomed to dealing with transactional data in the relational database structure of SAP ECC or SAP R/3 often has an unexpected learning curve when dealing with the unique star schema design of SAP NetWeaver BW and a data warehouse environment. Thus, it is necessary that the Basis resources have sound Basis skills, in supporting and maintaining the SAP NetWeaver *BW* environment.

3.12.7 Keep the Project Team Physically Together

It is amazing how many issues are solved by simply sitting in close proximity. Often, a seemingly insignificant, overheard conversation can evolve into a design session that solves some of the most challenging project issues. If the team members are physically separate in different buildings, or even separate countries, this dynamic thinking is much more difficult.

It also helps to try to avoid some of the political issues that can occur on any SAP NetWeaver BW project. These issues often involve collaboration within the team and between the team and its management and other management in the business. In the next section, we'll discuss common political issues.

3.13 Political Issues

Any SAP NetWeaver BW project has its political issues. Sometimes, these are the result of the priorities of the SAP NetWeaver BW project; other times, they are a direct result of the project manager. For instance, a consultant was bought into a company to help assess the SAP NetWeaver BW project to pinpoint why the project was slow to achieve results. He was first introduced to the project manager, who gave him a background of the project and the time line. After watching the interaction of the project manager and the business organization for a short time, it was clear that there was animosity between the two teams.

The reason for the animosity involved two different personalities in SAP NetWeaver BW project management and one area of the business. Because these two managers could not get along, they worked to make sure the other was not successful. This caused the SAP NetWeaver BW project to suffer and eventually caused it to be cancelled.

Understanding and avoiding these kinds of political conflicts can help an otherwise doomed SAP NetWeaver BW project succeed. SAP NetWeaver BW projects have the potential to be quite political. This is the result of the flow of information in the organization. It is inevitable that in the process of setting priorities for the subject matter to implement and defining the implementation strategy that the project will become quite political.

The best way to overcome most political issues is with open communication and a project management organization that is willing to step in and resolve political issues when they arise.

Another common issue that can occur is when a project team attempts to change the system drastically via customization. In the next section, we'll discuss some of the common issues with over-customization.

3.14 Over-Customization

It is easy to fall into the trap of over-customization. Typically, this occurs when, rather than changing the process, companies opt to change the software or look to a third-party vendor to provide functionality. This adds much more risk and complexity to a project.

These risks are difficult to quantify because the customizations that are required have never been done, so there is no template for scope. Applications that are not customized can be benchmarked against similar projects. The dangers of over-customization include:

▶ The more customized a solution, the fewer people are in the know about the solution, making support more difficult.

▶ Testing is more complex.

▶ Integration with other products is more challenging.

▶ Upgrades are more complex.

How can you avoid the trap of over-customizing your SAP NetWeaver BW solution? The next subsections give some insight on this issue.

3.14.1 Determine If the Customization Can Take Place Outside of SAP NetWeaver BW

There are many organizations that opt to severely customize SAP NetWeaver BW and transform data. This is usually to harmonize data from an outside source to an SAP source of data. For example, if there are internal orders that are processed in an external system, you might want to extract the data from the internal orders legacy system and combine these internal orders with the other orders existing in the SAP R/3 or SAP ECC system. How can you do that?

You need to perform some significant transformation of data to make sure that the material numbers, customer numbers, order types, etc., are populated with consistent values so the orders can be analyzed together.

To extract the order data from the legacy system, a program is usually written to extract the data. In many cases, you can eliminate a cumbersome transformation of data in SAP NetWeaver BW and centralize the development and transformation issues if you make the transformation of the data part of the legacy extraction program. This provides a single point of failure with the extraction and allows for easier testing in SAP NetWeaver BW.

This approach often is better for performance because SAP NetWeaver BW simply loads the file directly rather than provide the transformation and loading. In most environments, changing and testing of the extraction program can be less cumbersome than changing and testing of the SAP NetWeaver BW transformation. This is because SAP NetWeaver BW requires transports, reloads, etc., while the transformation program would only require a change to the program.

3.14.2 Develop a "Why not SAP?" Approach

The next step to reduce customization in SAP NetWeaver BW is to reduce or eliminate third-party software solutions in the landscape. The best way of doing this is to develop a "Why not SAP?" approach to customization tools.

This philosophy is simple. Any time that a non-SAP product is used, there are always complexities that arise. This occurs no matter how integrated the product appears to be. Many projects employ third-party systems for use with SAP NetWeaver BW. It's rare to find a seamless integration between the tool and SAP NetWeaver BW.

There are usually connection and integration issues. These issues can take a long time to resolve because there are typically few people who understand both the third-party system and SAP NetWeaver BW.

The best way to avoid these kinds of issues is to push back hard on any requirement that requires the use of any third-party solution. That's not to say that third-party systems should never be used with SAP NetWeaver BW. However, it's recommended that these be avoided whenever possible. This simplifies the environment and centralizes the issues on one product.

> **Tip**
>
> In most projects, there are enough issues simply getting SAP R/3 or SAP ECC data cleanly into SAP NetWeaver BW without the added complexity of a third-party tool. Don't use third-party tools unless absolutely necessary.

3.14.3 Know Where Many SAP NetWeaver BW Projects Use Third-Party Tools

There are some circumstances where the business process cannot be redesigned or the requirements that are needed are not possible in the SAP environment. The next sections describe the common third-party tools and the typical reasons for employing them.

Extracting, Transformation, and Loading (ETL) Tool

An Extraction, Transformation, and Loading (ETL) tool is used to centrally alter or change data that is loaded from one or many sources of data. This tool is usually required in companies that have multiple sources or external data and they need significant harmonization of this data prior to loading the data into SAP NetWeaver BW. The ETL tool can analyze, synchronize, or homogenize the data.

The tool makes sure that this analysis and transformation is done in one central place in the environment.

Figure 3.12 shows a typical ETL environment. An ETL tool is needed because there are multiple legacy systems and the data needs to be transformed centrally. Although this data could be transformed directly in SAP NetWeaver BW, if there are other destinations, the data either would have to be fed out of SAP NetWeaver BW or transformed again.

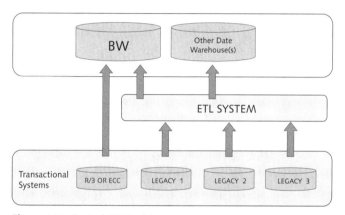

Figure 3.13 Typical ETL Architecture

Some companies prefer that this transformation takes place in a central place, with a central tool set. The ETL acts as a hub. All feeds come into the ETL tool, and then ETL sends the feeds to the various destination systems.

> **Tip**
>
> An ETL tool should not be used between the SAP R/3 or SAP ECC system and SAP NetWeaver BW.

SAP R/3 or SAP ECC data should be loaded directly from those systems' Data-Sources into SAP NetWeaver BW. Don't plan on having an ETL between SAP R/3 or SAP ECC and SAP NetWeaver BW. An ETL would cause a significant level of complexity and managing deltas; tracking loads, etc., would be much more difficult, if not impossible.

This is because one of the major strengths of SAP NetWeaver BW as an integrated tool is the delivered extractors (in SAP NetWeaver BW these are DataSources) that are part of the SAP ECC or SAP R/3 systems. The DataSources can be extracted from one table or a complex program that pulls data from many different source tables to provide data to SAP NetWeaver BW. Typically, projects do not use an ETL tool between SAP R/3 or SAP ECC and SAP NetWeaver BW because the ETL tool cannot take advantage of these DataSources and would require significant work before it could implement them.

This is also true of other SAP data. CRM, APO, ICH, etc. also have DataSources that are delivered or can be created via a function in the system. This allows for an easier extraction of data than would be required if the extractor programs needed to be created in these systems.

Thus, for most implementations, using an ETL tool only as part of the non-SAP data is the norm. This allows the ETL tool to provide benefits without the effort of recreating the DataSources on the SAP source system.

OLAP Tools

There are various OLAP tools on the market that can be used with SAP NetWeaver BW. OLAP tools serve as a presentation layer for delivering SAP NetWeaver BW data to the end user. Most projects use the SAP-provided Business Explorer (BEx) and Web tools to present SAP NetWeaver BW data. However, there are some projects that opt for a third-party (non-SAP) OLAP toolset.

To gather data, the OLAP tools take advantage of SAP's Business Application Programming Interfaces (BAPIs). These are standard interfaces used to access data in SAP NetWeaver BW. Major OLAP vendors are Crystal Reports, Cognos, SAS, Microstrategy, and SAP BusinessObjects. When project teams turn to an OLAP tool, it is usually because:

▶ Users are already familiar with an OLAP tool, so using it with SAP NetWeaver BW leverages this knowledge.

▶ The OLAP tool provides some functionality that SAP NetWeaver BW does not, typically formatted reporting.

Tip
As a general rule, it is recommended that projects don't use a third-party OLAP tool.

There are usually unexpected complexities with the tool. No matter how seamlessly vendors claim that their products interact with the SAP data, this is typically not the case.

Example
A project was implementing a third-party OLAP tool, and continued to have performance support help desk and data access issues for many months. When these issues occurred, they were often stuck between the third-party OLAP support vendor, their database vendor, and SAP's support.

When analyzing issues, it was extremely difficult to understand where the problem was occurring. The third-party OLAP support group told them that the SAP NetWeaver BW application was causing the issue. When they reported this to SAP, SAP claimed that it was not an application issue, and advised to push the issue back to the third-party OLAP provider support. Sometimes, the database application was also blamed. They had trouble establishing who actually owned the issues, so they lingered in limbo.

The good news is that SAP, in version NW 2004s, added significant functionality for formatted reporting and enhanced reporting capabilities, with many more features planned in future releases. Thus, the functionality gap between the BEx and Web reporting tools and third-party vendors is shrinking.

Projects sometimes fall into the trap of planning to use a third-party OLAP tool in the early stages of the project. This is even before their users have seen and worked with the BEx tool. When implementing SAP NetWeaver BW, hold off on any third-party OLAP tool decision until after you fully see the OLAP tools of SAP NetWeaver BW. Although third-party OLAP tools provide some features, the complexities of these tools usually make them much more difficult to implement and add significant time to the project time line.

Projects should plan their first rollout of SAP NetWeaver BW with the tools provided in SAP NetWeaver BW. This allows you to use these tools and get familiar with them. It is common that pushing off the third-party OLAP tool for reporting to another phase of the project allows this requirement to be eliminated altogether, because project organizations are quite satisfied with the power of the BEx and Web tools in SAP NetWeaver BW.

Scheduling Tools

SAP NetWeaver BW requires a significant effort in loading data. This typically occurs in the evening hours in the batch process. When SAP NetWeaver BW is live, there is a process for getting the batch-loading schedule correct. This is because data typically is being extracted from multiple source systems at various times and loaded into SAP NetWeaver BW. Issues can arise when data can only be loaded after a specific event has occurred in a legacy system.

Example

A company using a legacy system to track freight payments needs to load these payments into SAP NetWeaver BW. However, SAP NetWeaver BW should pull the day's freight payments only after the freight payment posting process is run on the legacy system. This is once each evening but at different times depending on the activity of the day. How can you make sure that SAP NetWeaver BW only pulls the data after the posting process is complete?

You do not want SAP NetWeaver BW to pull the data too early, before the process is complete. You could build a long delay into the data loading process and not pull into late in the evening to make sure you get the data. This might not be possible, though, if there is a tight batch window with many dependent jobs on the freight payments load.

You need to make sure that SAP NetWeaver BW can pull the data immediately after the posting process is complete. Because this process occurs outside of the SAP NetWeaver BW and SAP environment, it can be difficult to raise an event when this occurs. Thus, a third-party scheduler outside of SAP NetWeaver BW can be used to schedule the freight payments loading and then, once loading is successfully scheduled, kick off a process chain in SAP NetWeaver BW to load this data.

This can also be used for any other non-SAP scheduling as well. If certain other legacy processes need to take place before data should be pulled, the scheduler can ensure that this occurs.

Some popular third-party schedulers are Maestro and Control M. SAP also has a partnership with Redwood software's Cronacle scheduling software. This product may be preferred over Maestro and Control M because SAP supports the product; any issues with the product can be handled through the normal SAP help desk process. This may prevent the project team from being caught between the third-party vendor and SAP when issues occur.

3.14.4 Validation Tools

SAP NetWeaver BW does not provide validation tools out of the box to easily determine that the data from the SAP source systems matches the data that gets loaded into SAP NetWeaver BW. SAP has done little to address needs in this area. In many cases, the only way to validate the data in the SAP NetWeaver BW system and match this with the related SAP system is to build an application.

There are few non-SAP vendors with solutions in this area. One solution in particular, ValiData from ValiData LLC, provides extremely good and thorough validation between SAP and SAP NetWeaver BW. This helps to find issues quickly before the users find them. The interesting thing about the product is that it can be used in both the implementation and production support phases of development. It thus provides both the project team and the production support teams with tools to check their data against the source to make sure this data is consistent. Chapter 8 describes many of the common practices used for reconciling and validating data from its source.

3.15   Meeting and Decision Paralysis

Many projects fall into meeting and/or decision paralysis. This occurs when a decision is either too difficult or too politically dangerous to make. This can occur in any implementation project. However, because SAP NetWeaver BW projects typically shadow the transactional system implementation, the SAP NetWeaver BW team can often be victimized by the lack of decision making elsewhere.

3.15.1   Slow Decision Making

One large multi-national company was in the process of determining how its product hierarchy should be structured in source systems. This involved a complex series of decisions and had a wide-reaching effect on the organization because the grouping of products also defined departments and the organization as a whole.

This decision making did not directly involve the members of the SAP NetWeaver BW team. The decisions needed to be made by the organization as a whole. However, once decided on, the SAP NetWeaver BW team would be called on to make sure that the product structure that was determined could be reflected in the reporting.

As this decision process dragged on, the SAP NetWeaver BW project was delayed while waiting for the crucial information to complete their design. Once the decision was made, the transactional systems design followed, and SAP NetWeaver BW, as usual, followed that. The SAP ECC and SAP R/3 teams made the needed changes and implemented them in time for the scheduled go-live.

However, this did not allow enough time for the SAP NetWeaver BW team to reflect these changes in their design and test with the transactional team. Thus, the SAP NetWeaver BW team was not ready for their scheduled go-live. Frustration ensued because the project manager told the organization that the project was not ready to go live because the SAP NetWeaver BW team was not ready.

The SAP NetWeaver BW team was not the problem in this circumstance, but because the time line of the entire project slipped and SAP NetWeaver BW is at the end of that process, the SAP NetWeaver BW team got the blame for not being ready with the rest of the teams.

3.15.2   The Lonely SAP NetWeaver BW Team

Other projects face a different issue. Sometimes, the SAP NetWeaver BW team is not connected with the transactional teams. Thus, when critical decisions are made, the SAP NetWeaver BW team is not aware of them. This occurs quite often on projects.

Simply put, the attitude of some on the project could be summed up in one sentence: "Let's not invite the SAP NetWeaver BW team; they will just slow us down."

The transactional teams want to keep their meetings short and prevent their own meeting paralysis. Often, the best way to do this is to keep the number of participants to a few. This can cause issues because the SAP NetWeaver BW team is not informed of critical decisions.

For example, one project's implementation team changed the pricing structure in their SAP R/3 system. This severely affected the way the pricing data appeared in the SAP NetWeaver BW reports. Because the SAP NetWeaver BW team was not told of these changes, they were not added to the design. The SAP NetWeaver BW reports did not correspond with the SAP R/3 reports.

Fixing the issue to make SAP NetWeaver BW consistent with the SAP R/3 system was so complex that the SAP R/3 team ended up backing out all of their changes and going back to their original approach. This cost the time and testing resources that would not have been needed if the SAP NetWeaver BW team had been informed of the changes.

3.15.3 The Popular SAP NetWeaver BW Team

There is a flip side to the problem stated above. There have been other SAP NetWeaver BW projects where the SAP NetWeaver BW team is the most popular team in the project. The attitude of the groups could be summed up as: "We never know when a reporting decision will come up; invite the SAP NetWeaver BW team just in case."

This approach is just as counter-productive as the previous one. While the SAP NetWeaver BW team needs to be aware of the transactional team's approach and changes to design, it is easy to get so involved in meeting with the transactional groups that the SAP NetWeaver BW team cannot get its own work done.

3.15.4 What Can be Done?

The SAP NetWeaver BW team should plan meetings with the transactional process teams on a regular basis with strict rules. These meetings should be done sparingly, with a clear agenda to go over the issues and design changes that have recently occurred.

Keeping the transactional and process teams in sync with the associated SAP NetWeaver BW team is never an easy task on a project. Entire books have been written on collaborative teams and synergy, and these strategies can be employed to help the teams work together.

The most important thing to understand in an SAP NetWeaver BW project is that the SAP NetWeaver BW team can often take the blame for slow decision making simply because their processes are at the end of the time line. Any structures or plans that can be put in place can help the SAP NetWeaver BW team meet its goals.

The other key lesson is that all teams understand that when SAP NetWeaver BW is implemented in conjunction with the transactional system, the SAP NetWeaver BW team is at the end of the project time line. It is tempting for any project manager to seize this seemingly large chunk of time at the end of a project dedicated to SAP NetWeaver BW testing and use this as the project contingency time.

Thus, the upstream efforts that missed their planned dates are accommodated by simply collapsing the SAP NetWeaver BW time line, or by reducing or eliminating testing of SAP NetWeaver BW. Unfortunately, all too often the SAP NetWeaver BW production support team suffers while trying to solve issues post go-live that should have been caught in the pre-go-live testing.

Another challenge faced by many organizations is to clearly communicate the various change issues that come with implementation. The next section gives an overview of some frequent challenges.

3.16   Change Control and Change Management

Change control and change management are two different things and should be dealt with as such. Some SAP NetWeaver BW project organizations believe these two efforts are interchangeable; however, a separate strategy should be planned for each.

Understanding clearly who can make changes and allowing these users the access to make the changes is necessary in keeping the SAP NetWeaver BW project on track. If there are severe obstacles to make necessary changes, the momentum of an SAP NetWeaver BW project can be slowed.

It is also necessary to clearly understand how these changes are moved from one system to another. This knowledge ensures that the process is clear to all developers and changes can occur efficiently.

Communication of the change to the organization is the final step in the process, and a strategy must be developed for this to occur in a clear and efficient manner.

3.16.1 Change Control

Change control refers to the process of understanding how changes can occur in the system and the processes of an organization. A sound change control process ensures that when SAP NetWeaver BW changes occur, they are carried out by the right group, in the right fashion.

The SAP NetWeaver BW change control process involves transports, security, and documentation processes for the intended change. A clear change control process is important to a project because it makes sure that the intended person or group can make the changes needed and the processes are in place for them to do so.

Change Control Security

Setting the process team change control security in an SAP NetWeaver BW project is not always an easy task. Project management is often torn between two extremes: giving too much access and allowing a lot of flexibility for the developers and thus a bigger potential for unintended changes, and locking down the system so tightly that each change takes an extreme effort to implement.

You're likely to find yourself working in both environments. Organizations with a rigid security strategy slow development and you may find yourself waiting while you secure a development key or access to a transaction. You may also find yourself on projects where the system is so unsecure that people who are inexperienced (and unqualified) are making changes in various parts of the system.

Small global changes can have severe consequences, and troubleshooting these issues can be time consuming. Thus, there needs to be a compromise between a system that allows little change without authorization and a system that is wide open for anyone to make changes.

The correct strategy for most companies comes as the result of time. Once developers have been working for a while, it is easy to assess the access needed by each individual. To keep the development process going when a change process is needed but access is not granted, the most successful organizations usually allow someone in the SAP NetWeaver BW team to have far-reaching access. This is usually given to the SAP NetWeaver BW data architect role or a similar position. This person or group of people can make more severe changes to system settings.

Each developer is not able to make changes to such things as permitted characters, overall aggregate settings, packet size, load balancing, etc. At least one member of the SAP NetWeaver BW team, however, is able to change these settings, thus allowing the change process to occur without severely slowing the project.

Change Control Documentation

Any change control process needs clear governance on the change process and clear documentation of those changes. SAP NetWeaver BW is no exception. However, there is a fine line in an implementation between writing documentation for documentation's sake and writing documentation to truly track and record changes in the system.

To keep the documentation from severely slowing development, proper thought and refinement is needed to assess the documentation that is useful and the documentation that is not. Here is a simple rule to follow for documentation in SAP NetWeaver BW: The SAP NetWeaver BW system has limited self-documentation through the metadata repository. Thus, any documentation that duplicates the system's documentation process is redundant and often unnecessary.

In other words, the SAP NetWeaver BW metadata repository shows the structures of many elements of the system. This documentation area of the system shows the InfoCube, DSO, and the flow of data in and out of these InfoProviders. Thus, it should be assumed that documentation that repeats all the InfoObjects that are in an InfoCube or DSO is redundant.

Take the example of a project where you're forced to painstakingly go to each Info-Cube and DSO and copy each InfoObject to an InfoCube document. This serves no purpose because the document is not used for any future questions on the Info-Cubes or DSO. The metadata repository took care of this for you. The documents became redundant and slowed development without any added benefit.

However, documenting why a process occurred or where transformation of data occurs is vital to any SAP NetWeaver BW implementation, and a majority of the effort in the documentation should go to these types of documents. Most implementations that need to reference a document are much more interested in why a change was needed, who requested the change, and how the change was implemented than in the makeup and setup of the InfoProvider structures of SAP NetWeaver BW. For more information on the documentation of SAP NetWeaver BW, refer to Chapter 4.

SAP NetWeaver BW Transport Strategy

Another important area vital to any project is a clear transport strategy. This strategy is defined by determining how the changes flow from one system to another and the tracking and administration of these changes.

A transport is the process that any SAP system uses to move the changes across the landscape. Because all development is performed in the development system and the QA and production systems are not open for any development, the transport process moves the configuration to the QA and production systems from the development system.

> **Tip**
>
> SAP NetWeaver BW transports are notoriously difficult, so plan for this to be a difficult process in any SAP NetWeaver BW implementation.

Transports are difficult to manage in any project. SAP NetWeaver BW transports are even more so because of the nature of SAP NetWeaver BW; things in SAP NetWeaver BW build on one another. For instance, to create an InfoCube, the first step is to create or reference multiple InfoObjects. These InfoObjects act as the fields of data in the InfoCube.

If the InfoObjects are not present in a system, the InfoCube cannot be present either. Thus, if an InfoCube is transported to a system before all InfoObjects in the InfoCube are transported, the transport will fail and must be performed again.

Projects often face challenges when they do not clearly document and track the transports. Thus, a clear transport strategy must be developed before any transport is sent from the SAP NetWeaver BW development environment. This will ensure that the transports, although challenging, are processed as cleanly as possible.

For more details on developing an SAP NetWeaver BW transport and change control strategy, see Chapter 7.

Change Management

Change management provides the user base with understanding of the changes that have occurred. The earlier that this process occurs and the more ownership the business takes in this change management process, the smoother this process typically occurs (see Figure 3.14). There are several steps in creating a change management strategy:

▶ **Establish Clear Communication Path**
   This can be done via lunch and learn sessions, websites, newsletters, etc. The

goal is to make the end users aware of the changes that will be coming as soon as possible.

▶ **Keep Communication Consistent**
As much as possible, keep a common consistent message to the end users. Conflicting messages allow for confusion.

▶ **Develop Robust Training Material**
Develop as good a training program as possible. Have the training delivered by the power users with a clear understanding of the business goals and objectives, and not by the consultants, if possible.

▶ **Keep an Open-Door Policy**
Allow the end users to ask questions and keep them informed whenever possible.

▶ **Have a Good Help Desk**
Staff a well-equipped help desk with clearly informed power users to help resolve post go-live issues quickly.

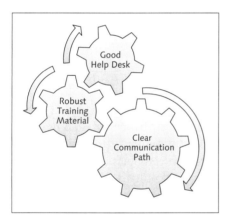

Figure 3.14 Driving Factors for Effective Change Management

3.17 Analyze Organization User Groups Using Different Reporting Tools

One of the most complicated parts of any SAP NetWeaver BW implementation is to make users adopt to the different SAP NetWeaver BW tools. Implementing SAP NetWeaver BW does not mean to force users to use SAP NetWeaver BW reporting tools only; rather, reporting tools should conform to the way users want to work. It would be a big mistake if you distribute a single type of reporting tool and then expect success of the SAP NetWeaver BW project. Different types of users (executives, managers, power users, frontline staff, customers, and so on) use information in different ways; tools presenting this information should be different.

As shown in Figure 3.15, organizations should segment users into categories based on information analysis habits and requirements.

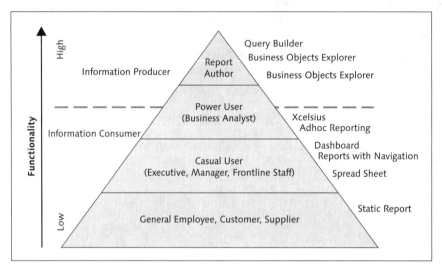

Figure 3.15 SAP NetWeaver BW Reporting User Segmentation

Maximum information consumers are normal business partners who do not have much technical knowledge. Information broadcasting with a spreadsheet is the best option for this kind of user. View and interact with reports on a regular basis but not intensively. A Web-based dashboard created through Xcelsius is a perfect medium for delivering information in a way that matches most users' requirements. There should be one group of power users who will have access to create SAP NetWeaver BW queries.

3.18 Conclusion

Simply working with an SAP NetWeaver BW project team that understands the key challenges can often allow a project to avoid many of the most common mistakes. This can pay dividends in quicker implementation time and a more sound SAP NetWeaver BW strategy. Where possible, it helps to clearly watch for the common mistakes others have made, and use these mistakes as a learning tool for the project. Let's discuss the points briefly that you learned in this chapter.

▶ Scope is the most important document during whole project lifecycle and you should never forget to implement scope during the change control process.

▶ Always set milestones for your projects.

▶ While estimating the time line, be realistic and never forget to add time to prepare user documentations and training materials.

▶ You learned various ways to align master data and transactional data coming from various source systems.

▶ You also learned how the Remodeling Toolbox can help reduce the pain of adding, replacing, and deleting InfoObjects or Key Figures in an InfoProvider.

▶ We discussed SAP NetWeaver BW team-building mistakes and how to get rid of those mistakes.

Let's now proceed to Chapter 4, where we will discuss project planning.

Understanding the scoping and process lifecycle can enable a project team to have the right expectations when delivering SAP NetWeaver BW.

4   Project Planning in SAP NetWeaver BW

Understanding and planning an SAP NetWeaver BW implementation involves many different challenges. Often, the diverse nature of the audience for SAP NetWeaver BW reports adds to this complexity. It is important to understand the typical lifecycle of an SAP NetWeaver BW project, and some of the common challenges faced when planning a new SAP NetWeaver BW project or upgrading to a new release of SAP NetWeaver BW. This chapter will help in the overall planning and aid in understanding the typical makeup of the project team.

To begin either an upgrade project or a new implementation of SAP NetWeaver BW, there are several things to understand about its implementation cycle. In many cases, the lifecycle of SAP NetWeaver BW is similar to implementation of a transactional system. However, because projects in SAP NetWeaver BW typically bring data from many different source systems and subject areas, rather than one source as with transactional systems, SAP NetWeaver BW requires additional design iterations.

In other words, SAP NetWeaver BW projects typically require more prototyping and rebuilding based on the lessons learned from harmonizing data from multiple sources. This iterative design should be considered a normal and vital part of the SAP NetWeaver BW implementation process. There are two main types of SAP NetWeaver BW projects: the new SAP NetWeaver BW project or the upgrade SAP NetWeaver BW project.

The new SAP NetWeaver BW project typically follows the data warehouse lifecycle shown in Figure 4.1. The upgrade lifecycle is different. It requires analysis of the new release and new features and their impact on the existing design. We'll discuss both lifecycles in detail.

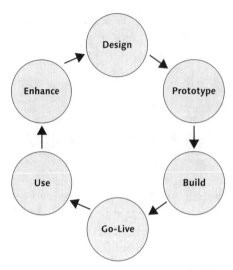

Figure 4.1 Typical Data Warehouse Lifecycle

4.1   The Data Warehouse Lifecycle

The first thing to consider about SAP NetWeaver BW is that it is a data warehouse. Thus, many theoretical data warehouse implementation strategies apply well to SAP NetWeaver BW.

▸ **Design**
This stage involves seeking out the various decision makers in the organization and determining the information they need to make decisions. The SAP NetWeaver BW system can be structured to match both current information needs, and to look to the future to make sure that the data warehouse takes into account those requirements in the upcoming months and even years.

▸ **Prototype**
The prototype phase is needed to show a select group of users or super users the various design features and the overall scope and data model of the SAP NetWeaver BW system prior to deployment. Prototyping a design allows the stakeholders to influence the deployment and suggest changes to make sure that the design reflects the true needs of the organization.

▸ **Deploy**
This is the formal rollout of the SAP NetWeaver BW system to the end users and the process of putting the SAP NetWeaver BW system into regular use. It is during this phase of the implementation that the change control process transi-

tions the SAP NetWeaver BW system to the end users and trains them in its use.

- ▶ **Operate**
  Operation is the day-to-day use of the SAP NetWeaver BW system, including data loads, query processing, etc.
- ▶ **Enhance**
  Typically, the implementation of SAP NetWeaver BW is an ongoing task. Based on the changing needs of the organization and the source system, the SAP NetWeaver BW system should be constantly evaluated to determine if it is still meeting the needs of the users. This includes the information delivery, performance, and technical environment.

Because SAP NetWeaver BW is an SAP data warehouse, its use and its scope often reflect the same overall goals as those of the SAP transactional systems; however, both systems retain their distinctive cycles of development.

SAP NetWeaver BW will constantly change, and redesigns of the existing environment should not only be expected but also welcomed. SAP NetWeaver BW is not like most transactional systems, which remain relatively constant to handle core transactional activities. The SAP NetWeaver BW model and configuration should be expected to change with the mission and goals of the company. Thus, models that are quite useful today could be replaced by others tomorrow.

Figure 4.2 shows iterative approach of building an SAP NetWeaver BW application where two-phased iteration is required before the final go-live. In the first phase, designing and prototype building should happen iteratively. When the first prototype is reviewed by the customer, new revision points should be included in the prototype. This way a final version of prototype is developed and the project is ready to go in the Build phase. Here comes the second phase of iteration where due to technical limitations prototype may need to be re-built again. After having several iterations, you get the final build version of the SAP NetWeaver BW application. This robust method of developing the SAP NetWeaver BW application ensures that change control is managed effectively.

SAP periodically comes out with new releases of SAP NetWeaver BW. These should not be confused with support packages and stacks that are fixes to the existing product. The new releases of SAP NetWeaver BW have significant functionality changes to the software and require extensive regression testing to implement. There are some differences in the lifecycle of an upgrade that differs from a new implementation of SAP NetWeaver BW. In the next section, we highlight some of the features of this lifecycle.

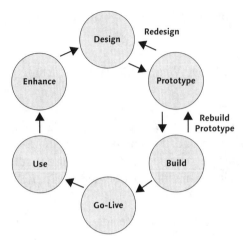

Figure 4.2 Enhanced Data Warehouse Lifecycle Model

4.2 The Upgrade Lifecycle

In the upgrade lifecycle, you take the existing configuration and bring that configuration and software to the newest release of SAP NetWeaver BW. This differs from a new implementation, which is focused on creating new functionality and models in the existing SAP NetWeaver BW environment.

The upgrade lifecycle is similar to the data warehouse lifecycle but with clearly different goals (see Figure 4.3). Most upgrade projects are planned to simply provide a technical upgrade. The technical upgrade is not designed to take advantage of any new features of the software but is only designed to get the software up to the newest release as quickly as possible.

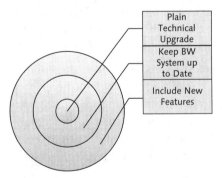

Figure 4.3 SAP NetWeaver BW Upgrade Goals

Most projects opt for a technical upgrade because this has the quickest lifecycle and also provides the best opportunity for success. No new features or functionality other than those required for the upgrade are used in the technical upgrade. Thus, in the example of an organization upgrading from SAP NetWeaver BW version 3.x to the version NW 2004s, an organization would simply take the software to the newest release but would not take advantage of the new features of NW 2004s, such as the new transformation logic or unit of measure conversion. These features would be added later as separate releases.

Those organizations that do not opt for the technical upgrade may opt for a features upgrade. This upgrade involves taking the software to the newest release and using many new features during the initial rollout. This is typically done by companies that require new functionality to run their businesses or when a feature offers a large time or performance savings.

The fundamental reason that many opt for a technical upgrade rather than a features upgrade is simply to minimize the risk. It is much harder to fully regression test an intact environment than an environment that now has changed and uses new functionality.

To perform a technical upgrade, the Basis or technical teams take the development system's software release and upgrade this development environment to the newest release so that unit testing can begin. This poses a problem in many organizations because most organizations have only one development system. If this is upgraded to the newest release, it is difficult to also provide production support to existing users during the rollout and unit testing of the new release.

This problem arises because the development system is the root of all system changes. If no transports can occur from the development system, there can be no production support changes during the upgrade process because there is no root system to make the changes. SAP does not recommend transports between two unlike releases, and in most cases this is technically impossible. In most environments, the development system is upgraded first. Later, the QA system is upgraded and tested, and finally the production system is upgraded.

4.2.1 What's New in NW 2004s SAP NetWeaver BW System?

Before upgrading an old SAP NetWeaver BW 3.x application to a NW 2004s SAP NetWeaver BW system, you should be aware of the new features available in the newer version. Table 4.1 describes the most important new features included in NW 2004s SAP NetWeaver BW system.

Changed Terminology	▶ Administrator Workbench is renamed as Data Warehousing Workbench. ▶ Former ODS (Operational Data Store) is renamed as DSO (Data Store Object) ▶ Transactional ODS is renamed as Direct Update Data Store. ▶ Transactional InfoCube is called as Real-Time InfoCube ▶ Remote Cube, SAP Remote Cube, Virtual InfoCube with Services is referred to as Virtual Providers.
Modeling	▶ Remodeling Toolbox InfoCubes can be changed without rebuilding them from scratch. New InfoObjects and Key Figures can be changed, added, or deleted with rich conversion methods. ▶ Write Optimized DSO ▶ Write Optimized DSO does not contain any Change Log and Activation Queue table. Data is directly written in Active table. This object is the foundation of the EDW concept in NW2004s SAP NetWeaver BW. ▶ Enhanced InfoSet Now you can integrate InfoCubes with master data to design queries like slow moving items. ▶ Transformations Former Update Rules and Transformation Rules are now replaced with Transformations only. Performance and UI is greatly enhanced with this change. ▶ Data Transfer Process (DTP) Earlier, InfoPackages were responsible to load data from source systems to data targets. But now, InfoPackages load data up to PSA level. Data from PSA to Data Target is transferred through Data Transfer Process (DTP). Many new features like Semantic Key, Filtering, and Error handling are incorporated in DTP. ▶ Improved Process Chain Conditional logic can be included in the process chain so that execution can take place with particular path.
Presentation	▶ BEx Tools The Query Designer and Report Designer tools were completely rewritten in VB.NET and support many new features like Drag and Drop, Wizards, etc. ▶ BEx Analyzer Integration with Microsoft Excel greatly improved with many tools to format Microsoft Excel sheets, giving it a dazzling corporate look. ▶ PDF Integration Any BEx Web query or Web applications can be converted to Adobe PDF form.

Table 4.1 New Features of NW 2004s SAP NetWeaver BW

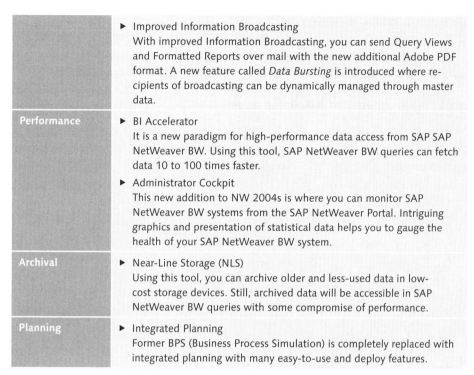

	▶ Improved Information Broadcasting With improved Information Broadcasting, you can send Query Views and Formatted Reports over mail with the new additional Adobe PDF format. A new feature called *Data Bursting* is introduced where recipients of broadcasting can be dynamically managed through master data.
Performance	▶ BI Accelerator It is a new paradigm for high-performance data access from SAP SAP NetWeaver BW. Using this tool, SAP NetWeaver BW queries can fetch data 10 to 100 times faster. ▶ Administrator Cockpit This new addition to NW 2004s is where you can monitor SAP NetWeaver BW systems from the SAP NetWeaver Portal. Intriguing graphics and presentation of statistical data helps you to gauge the health of your SAP NetWeaver BW system.
Archival	▶ Near-Line Storage (NLS) Using this tool, you can archive older and less-used data in low-cost storage devices. Still, archived data will be accessible in SAP NetWeaver BW queries with some compromise of performance.
Planning	▶ Integrated Planning Former BPS (Business Process Simulation) is completely replaced with integrated planning with many easy-to-use and deploy features.

Table 4.1 New Features of NW 2004s SAP NetWeaver BW (Cont.)

4.2.2 Upgrading on the Existing SAP NetWeaver BW Landscape

There are several options for upgrading the SAP NetWeaver BW landscape. In a stable and smaller SAP NetWeaver BW environment, some project teams opt to upgrade the existing SAP NetWeaver BW system landscape in place without adding new systems to the SAP NetWeaver BW landscape. This involves halting all production support fixes during the time of upgrade.

Once development is upgraded, the development and QA systems are now running different releases of the software. Transports must now be halted between the development, QA, and production systems. This means no production support fixes can be sent from development to QA, and then into production, during the upgrade.

This is a risk, because any mission-critical fixes cannot be implemented during the upgrade unless the systems are opened up for direct configuration and the normal migration path is not used. This scenario works best for small SAP NetWeaver BW implementations and those that are extremely mature with few production support risks.

In many cases, this is not realistic. The risk of halting all transports during the upgrade process presents too many complexities and opens the SAP NetWeaver BW team up to too much risk. In this case, many organizations opt to create a new stand-alone development environment created to support the upgrade.

4.2.3 Dedicated Upgrade Landscape

Many companies prefer to use the model pictured in Figure 4.4. This is similar to the two-release landscape strategy described in Chapter 2. A new development system is created (in this case, labelled DEV2).

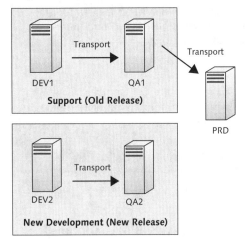

Figure 4.4 Typical Upgrade Landscape

Prior to the upgrade, the applications development team should create clear test scripts for walking through the functionality in the existing environment (see Figure 4.5). These test scripts should detail the transactional feeds into SAP NetWeaver BW and the full functionality in the form of unit test scripts. These scripts will be used to prove out the new release.

The first step in performing this upgrade is to take the DEV2 system and make a system copy of the production system. The Basis team takes this new development system (which is a copy of the production system) and upgrades it to the new release with the most recent SAP support-package levels. This now establishes a new development system that is identical to production but upgraded to the new release.

If the production system is too large to replicate on the smaller development system, the development system is upgraded in place without copying the production system. If this is done, however, more care will be needed during the testing phase because the data needed for testing must come from a non-production environment. This may not mirror the data in the production system.

1	• Make a system copy of production to DEV2 system
2	• Upgrade DEV2 system with latest release
3	• Create a transport connection with QA system
4	• Upgrade QA2 environment with latest release
5	• Change BW objects to adapt functionalities of new release. Pay special attention to custom objects and ABAP Programs
6	• Transport changed settings to QA environment
7	• Start regression testing to make sure all functionalities are working fine.

Figure 4.5 Typical SAP NetWeaver BW Upgrade Steps

The upgraded system is now typically connected to the QA transactional systems or a copy of the productive transactional systems, to test batch loading of data. Most organizations do not opt to connect the upgraded SAP NetWeaver BW development environment to the production transactional systems for fear of causing issues in those production systems.

The Basis team then *hands off* this system to the upgrade development team. The upgrade development team takes this system and uses it for unit testing on the newest release with the production or development data. The goal is to perform many tests reflecting the current system in production to determine how the new release affects the existing implementation.

Special attention should be paid to the custom transformation. This involves specific testing of all user exits, modifications, and transformations that involve ABAP code. These are the features most prone to failure during upgrade, because some of the features and functionality needed to make the code work may have been changed by SAP.

Special attention should also be given to the batch loading of data. Because of the complexity of batch loading and the timing involved, process chains should be run as if in production. This allows the timing and loading to be checked against the benchmark of the production system to determine if any new issues arise based on the new release. Most organizations opt to start the production process chains immediately and keep them running each night to see how the process chains act after many iterations.

Queries should also be tested in detail. This can be a difficult task because of the large volume of queries that typically accumulate in an SAP NetWeaver BW system. To make sure that the queries are taken in proper order, the SAP NetWeaver BW statistics InfoCubes can be used to determine the queries that are the most popular, so that emphasis can be placed on these queries.

4.2.4 Production Support During Upgrade Testing

To perform production support during the upgrade testing, the DEV1 and QA1 systems are used, as in Figure 4.4. Because the DEV1 and QA1 systems stay at the newest release, any production support fixes can be developed in the DEV1 system and migrated via transport to the QA1 system, and then onto production. This ensures that any fix can be sent to production.

This approach allows or ensures that this fix will be in the new upgraded environment. This must be analyzed and implemented manually in the new upgraded development environment (DEV2 and QA2) as seen in Figure 4.4. The fix may not be relevant in the new environment or might need to be developed differently.

If these fixes to the production environment need to be put into the new upgraded environment, a manual process is used. The fix is checked and evaluated with the new environment and then implemented manually in the DEV1 system. This manual fix is necessary because no transports can be used to move the fix from the DEV1 to the DEV2 systems, given the differing releases.

Because the fix cannot be transported and the fix needs to be evaluated based on the new release, make sure the fixes that are done to the production support system during the upgrade phase are manually tracked and manually inputted into the upgraded environment. These would then be migrated through the environment from the DEV2 to the QA2, and then onto the productive system, when the cutover occurs.

4.2.5 Obsolete Queries

Many organizations also use the upgrade time to make an assessment of their queries in the production system. Projects that have been live for a long time can end up with hundreds and even thousands of queries. Many of these queries may be obsolete. Thus, we recommend a periodic *housecleaning* of the queries (see Figure 4.6). To identify these queries, the statistics InfoCubes can show those queries that have not been used in a long time. These provide a potential query-removal list.

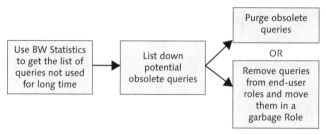

Figure 4.6 Steps to Obsolete Unused SAP NetWeaver BW Queries

This query list of potentially obsolete queries can be posted or distributed to users. If they do not act on the list, the queries can be removed from the end user roles. Because these queries might be needed again, it is important that the queries are not deleted; they should simply be placed in an obsolete query role for an extended period of time. This role would not be assigned to any end users.

Most organizations find it rare that an old query is needed again, but if a query in the obsolete role is needed, it can be placed back in the active role. Once the queries have been in the obsolete role for a period of time, these queries could be evaluated for purging from the system.

4.2.6 Upgrade Cutover

Once the testing is complete in the development system, the same testing should occur in the QA system. The QA testing allows the testing of the environment with a different set of data.

After the QA testing is complete, the upgraded system is ready for cutover, as shown in Figure 4.7. The DEV1 and QA1 systems are retired and the upgraded DEV2 and QA2 systems become the new development and production support systems, as seen in Figure 4.7. The Basis team shuts the users off the production system for a period of time and performs the upgrade on the production system. The team makes sure that the production system gets the same support-pack level and SAP patches (i.e., SAP Notes) that the DEV2 and QA2 systems received and that the production system mirrors the DEV2 and QA2 systems.

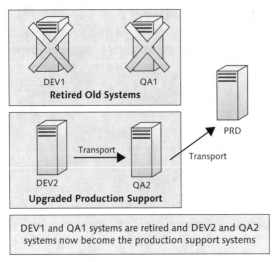

Figure 4.7 Typical Cutover Landscape

In most cases, there are transports that have been created in the upgraded system that are needed in production. These could include the following:

▶ New functionality

▶ SAP Notes (SAP help desk fixes) to patch system issues

▶ Workarounds or changes to existing flows

▶ Production support fixes, originated in the DEV1 environment, and manually done in the DEV2 system.

More testing should be performed at this time to make sure that the production system is ready for users. If possible, several nights should be used to completely test and watch the process chains loading into SAP NetWeaver BW to ensure that the batch is still working properly.

Once the process chains have been run and testing is complete, the system is ready to be opened up for users.

4.2.7 How Long Will This Take?

The timing of an upgrade project is difficult to estimate. This is because there are many factors that go into the upgrade project. The factors include but are not limited to the following:

▶ **Complexity of Release**
The SAP NetWeaver BW releases between 3.0 and 3.5 were minimal and took little time in the testing. This was because these two releases had few funda-

mental functionality changes, and there was less risk in the upgrade. The opposite is true of the NW 2004s upgrade that is quite a bit more complex.

▶ **Features Implemented**
The more new features implemented, the riskier a project becomes and thus the more time is needed for testing of these features.

▶ **Size of System**
Size can play a large role in the upgrade of systems. The bigger the size, the more time it takes to do the technical upgrades. More volume means more time dedicated to testing because of elevated performance concerns in query processing and data loading.

▶ **Quality and Maturity of Release**
SAP, like all software, gets better as more people use it. The longer the wait for the upgrade, the more software issues that will be discovered by others and fixed by SAP. An upgrade to the software in the early stages of the release typically takes longer because of the software issues encountered.

▶ **Resources**
It takes time for consultants to get up to speed on the features of new releases. To make matters more difficult, it can be hard to get organization resources to help on the testing needed for the upgrade project. This can add significantly to the time line, as the consulting resources learn the new release and the testing resources are secured and deployed to perform the upgrade.

In the early phases of a new release, the best way to estimate upgrades is to have SAP assess the environment, compare this project to other upgrade projects based on the above factors, and provide a time line estimate. SAP is in a better position to make such an estimate than many of the other software partners simply because it has worked with more organizations on upgrades and has better benchmarks.

Often, partners (non-SAP consulting companies) will perform one or two upgrades and use these for benchmarking, while SAP will benchmark 10 times that number or more. This usually gives a more accurate estimate of the upgrade.

> **Tip**
> If an upgrade is being performed in the early stages of its release, it's highly recommended to have at least one SAP consultant (a consultant employed by SAP, not a consulting partner) working on the project during the upgrade.

This is vital because the experience of the SAP consultant in the new software often makes him more proficient. This is due to the available resources and training within SAP and also because of the issues that often arise during an early stage upgrade. An SAP consultant can help to expedite and really prod the SAP Service Marketplace (formerly called OSS, for Online Support Service) to resolve issues quicker than non-SAP partners. This allows for a quicker resolution, and thus a more efficient upgrade.

However, once the product has been released and has been in general availability for more than six months, many other third-party vendors have performed upgrades. Some project teams might use non-SAP resources after doing their own research.

4.2.8 When Should I Upgrade?

SAP, unlike other software vendors, has a select group of users that work with the SAP NetWeaver BW product in its early stages to work through the various issues and challenges of integrating a new release of such a large software package. SAP works closely with these organizations to help them with their implementation issues.

In return for their efforts and inconvenience, the organizations get some added advantages. They get the new software first and some on-site expertise to help in the implementation process. They also have the power to influence the decision making and features planning of the product in return for their efforts.

There are some organizations that have gone through this process with SAP and others that have evaluated the process. It's usually recommended that organizations avoid being part of the *first customer ship* or *ramp-up process* of the SAP NetWeaver BW software. Organizations that do this typically spend a great deal of time chasing issues and working through various problems with the system. This can add a bit of time to the implementation and can frustrate even the most patient project managers.

Thus, unless there are features in the new release that are vital to the business or the timing does not allow an upgrade at a later phase, it does not make sense to be one of the first with new SAP SAP NetWeaver BW software. It is best to wait until the software is much more mature. As a general rule, this usually happens six months after the software has been available for general release.

After about six months, the software is usually at a state where upgrade issues are fewer and the stability of the software makes it more acceptable to upgrade. Organizations are urged never to rush to the new release. Instead, let others find the potential issues with the software; this allows for a quicker and cleaner upgrade path in the future.

4.3   Project Charter

A Project Charter is an important and dynamic document that is continuously updated throughout the lifecycle of the project. This document should be changed at the end of every phase of the project lifecycle. The changes should include outcomes from quality review, user review, etc.

Figure 4.8 shows how to develop your initial project charter document. After creating the initial project charter, don't forget to get reviewed and signed off by your customer. Any SAP NetWeaver BW project, small or big, will benefit from this preliminary planning.

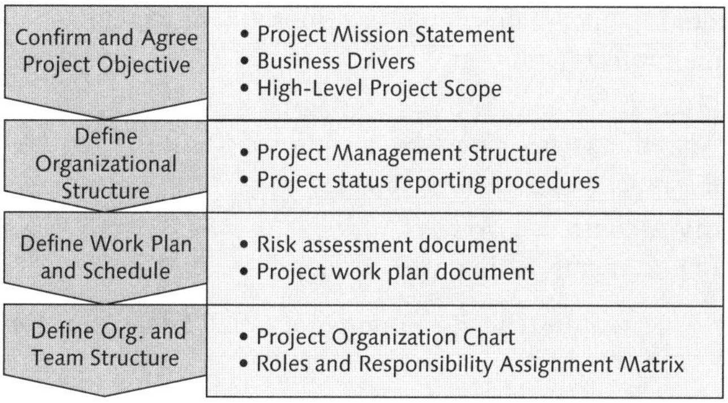

Confirm and Agree Project Objective	• Project Mission Statement • Business Drivers • High-Level Project Scope
Define Organizational Structure	• Project Management Structure • Project status reporting procedures
Define Work Plan and Schedule	• Risk assessment document • Project work plan document
Define Org. and Team Structure	• Project Organization Chart • Roles and Responsibility Assignment Matrix

Figure 4.8 Typical Process to Prepare Project Charter

▶ **Mission Statement**
A mission statement defines the overall objective of the project. It should be clear, concise, and motivational to the team. Mission statements should convey the vision to top management about the implementation of the SAP NetWeaver BW project.

▶ **Business Drivers**
In this section of your project charter document, mention the underlying business reasons to implement the SAP NetWeaver BW project.   This   step should be completed after interviewing with senior management.

▶ **High-Level Scope**
This section should define summarized scope such as OLTP systems, SAP or non-SAP systems, level of harmonization, presentation of reports, etc.

▶ **Project Management Structure**
In this step, identify key users and development staff required to carry out various project development and management activities.

- **Project Status Reporting Procedure**
  From the customer side, identify a person or a user group who will be responsible for reviewing and performing UAT (User Acceptance Test). This section should contain procedures for escalation of any issues arising during whole project lifecycle.

- **Risk Assessment Document**
  Identify the key risks to the SAP NetWeaver BW implementation. Potential risks to any SAP NetWeaver BW implementation could be budget, resource, adaptability, politics, etc.

- **Project Work Plan Document**
  In this section, define activities to be completed to cover the project scope. Initially, a high-level schedule should be developed and subsequently you need to update this section as the project moves on.

- **Project Organization Chart**
  Here, identify staff requirements to undertake the project, training requirements, and all logistical arrangements to be performed.

- **Roles and Responsibility Assignment Matrix**
  After identifying staff requirements, assign roles to them.

The next logical step is to determine and document the detail scope requirements.

4.4 Detail Scope Documentation

There are several important documents that need to be part of every SAP NetWeaver BW project. Each project has many internal and external parties or organizations. Understanding these stakeholders helps to ensure project success. Thus, after completing the scope document, the next vital document is the one that formally identifies the stakeholders in the SAP NetWeaver BW project.

4.4.1 What Is a Stakeholder?

A stakeholder is an individual or group who has a vested interest in a project and can gather resources to affect its outcome. Project stakeholders usually include the project manager, business users, and team members on the project. However, there are other stakeholders in any SAP NetWeaver BW project.

When thinking about stakeholders, you must include those stakeholders who can affect the attention and resources committed to the project, both now and in the future. These stakeholders typically have individual agendas that may differ from those of other stakeholders.

Failure to meet the needs of one powerful stakeholder at a critical time can have significant adverse affects on a project. Thus, proper documentation of stakeholders' interests and expectations is critical to understanding and communicating with these individuals or organizations.

4.4.2 Stakeholder Document

The stakeholder document should include all organizations and individuals expected to use SAP NetWeaver BW, along with all those affected by its use. The challenge with the stakeholder document is to understand the influence and importance of each of the stakeholders and their individual impacts on the project.

Of course, it is important to recognize that stakeholders change, as do their interests and impact on the project. This is a living document and can be updated as the various roles in the organization change and evolve.

The stakeholder document serves as a vital input to the communication plan because the communication plan can be tailored to keep the various stakeholders informed of the project and its progress.

4.4.3 Communication Plan Document

Developing a strong communication plan is vital to any SAP NetWeaver BW project. The communication plan should include all plans and steps to keep the various stakeholders informed of the project. Some common elements included in the communication plan are:

- ▶ Project website
- ▶ Issue tracking lists
- ▶ Meeting minutes template
- ▶ Position paper template
- ▶ Status report template
- ▶ Training plan and templates.

4.4.4 Integrated Project Plan

All SAP NetWeaver BW projects require a project plan to track the different tasks involved. A sample project plan provided by SAP can be used as a template for starting a project. This plan is part of the ASAP methodology and can be found on the SAP Service Marketplace website.

This sample plan is useful for tracking the tasks needed to complete a successful SAP NetWeaver BW project. Remember, however, that because of the many project integration points between an SAP NetWeaver BW project and other simultaneous implementations, an integrated project plan is necessary. This would include but is not limited to the following:

▶ Integration and timing with the technical group for the installation and delivery of systems

▶ Coordination with the process teams for completion of configuration and sample master and transactional data

▶ Coordination with any outside source system dependency

▶ Integrated testing plan in coordination with the transaction systems

▶ Integrated cutover planning.

4.4.5 Naming Standards Document

Naming standards are vital to identifying custom objects and SAP-developed objects, and to ensure consistency in finding and recognizing objects in the SAP NetWeaver BW system. When a project starts, it is easy to do without a naming standards document. This is a mistake, because it is hard to rename objects after go-live to get them in line with new standards.

Thus, the best approach for any SAP NetWeaver BW project is to make sure that a sound naming convention document is in place before any development occurs. These naming conventions are only necessary for objects that are created in the development system and intended for transport to the production system.

It is not necessary to use and enforce the naming standards on the sandbox system because this system is designed for ad-hoc testing. Any sandbox prototype should be redeveloped in the development system using the naming convention document. The use of standard naming conventions will provide key benefits:

▶ Enhancing the usability of the system by providing a logical grouping of objects

▶ Providing a framework to develop appropriate security and authorization models (if needed)

▶ Ensuring consistency for all the layers of SAP NetWeaver BW instances, thus making future developments more consistent

Adherence to these standards allows for tracking of modifications and transformations of data, which leads to faster troubleshooting of issues.

The naming standards document addresses the following areas of SAP NetWeaver BW:

- InfoAreas
- InfoCubes
- DataStore objects and DSOs
- InfoObjects
- InfoSources and DataSources
- InfoPackages
- Process chains
- BEx queries
- Other objects such as custom tables, variables, etc.

The naming structure for each SAP NetWeaver BW object is based on a series of logical codes, which can have a number of permitted entries. SAP by default begins all delivered objects with the number 0. This quickly separates the SAP objects from the project-created objects. Projects cannot develop objects starting with 0.

The naming standards document is only intended for those objects that are custom developed. When SAP standard objects are used, the naming standards document does not apply, and the standard object names should be used.

The naming standards document should be considered a living document that can be changed as new object types are added or as different releases of SAP NetWeaver BW are implemented. A sample naming document is found in Appendix E.

4.4.6 SAP NetWeaver BW Development Standards Document

The development standards document is used to document the various strategies that will be used on a project regarding the SAP NetWeaver BW implementation. This may be one document or a series of documents that can help new project team members understand the implementation standards of the project. These contain many of the following standards:

- **Data Strategies**
  How should an ODS or InfoCube be used to provide reporting? What features and functionality should be used during the loading process?
- **Source System Strategies**
  How can you determine when an external source of data should be loaded into SAP NetWeaver BW? What is the process for transforming that data? Should it occur in SAP NetWeaver BW or in the external system?

▶ **Loading/ETL Strategies**
When should transformation occur? At what level should this occur? Should data go into an ODS first or to an InfoCube?

▶ **Query Strategies**
Should users plan to create queries in the production environment? Should there be many smaller queries or fewer large queries?

▶ **Performance Strategies**
How should performance be evaluated and tested? What should be implemented in the data model to ensure that performance is optimal?

▶ **Transport Strategies**
How will transports be collected and handled? What is the process to send transports?

Who will prepare all this documentation and who is responsible for the various tasks in the project? The next section describes the typical roles in an SAP NetWeaver BW project.

4.4.7 Other Documents

The following documents are also important in detailed scope documents. However, this information may not be available during preparation of the initial scope document, but you should update these after several interviews with customer. Table 4.2 lists all of these points.

Source Systems	Define all kinds of SAP and non-SAP source systems in the scope document.
Harmonization	How data will be harmonized (e.g. concatenate method or compound method).
Report Presentation	Determine how end users will prefer to view reports.
Quality Plan	Define how unit and integration testing will be performed.
Information Lifecycle	Determine how old data will be kept in the SAP NetWeaver BW system for reporting and how data will be archived.

Table 4.2 Other Informations Required in Scope Document

4.5 Planning for Information Lifecycle Management

Planning of Information Lifecycle Management (ILM) before go-live helps you understand the overall system requirements. It is important to adopt sound ILM policy to align the value of your information with storage cost and facilitate compliance with regulations.

ILM in SAP NetWeaver BW has several methods for optimal data retention and history backup. ILM tools in SAP NetWeaver BW help reduce the volume of less-used data, thus improving system performance to a great extent.

You can choose various data archival options based on your business requirements.

▶ **Archive Based on ADK**
This type of archival is recommended when the archived data is no longer required for analysis but must be stored due to legal regulations or emergency purposes.

▶ **Near-Line Storage (NLS)**
Near-line storage (NLS) is recommended where data is sufficiently old and less used. Storing historical data in near-line storage reduces the data volume of InfoProviders; however, the data is still available for BEx queries.

▶ **ADK and NLS Combined**
This type of archiving is recommended if you want an extra backup of your data in addition to near-line storage. Some third-party tools for near-line storage must also be connected to the ADK to allow the data to be stored.

Figure 4.9 shows basic points that need to be defined to have an efficient ILM planning document.

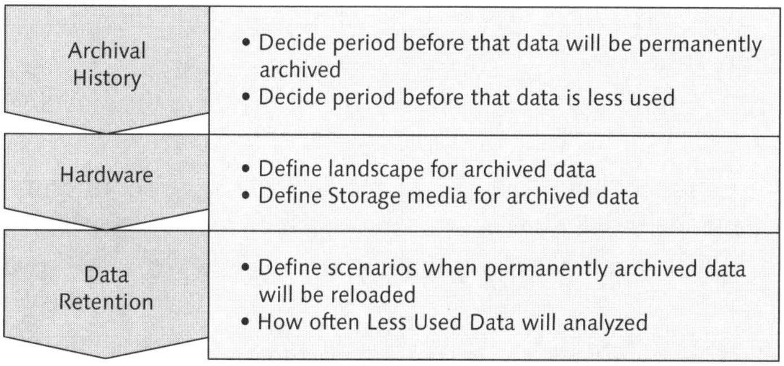

Archival History	• Decide period before that data will be permanently archived • Decide period before that data is less used
Hardware	• Define landscape for archived data • Define Storage media for archived data
Data Retention	• Define scenarios when permanently archived data will be reloaded • How often Less Used Data will analyzed

Figure 4.9 Planning for Information Lifecycle Management

4.6 Typical Roles Needed for an SAP NetWeaver BW Project

There are several roles needed for a typical SAP NetWeaver BW project. These roles are not always held by separate individuals. Often, several of these roles can be performed by the same person. This section is designed as a guide to help understand the skill sets involved in a typical SAP NetWeaver BW project.

4.6.1 SAP NetWeaver BW Project Manager

The SAP NetWeaver BW project manager has the ultimate decision-making power on the SAP NetWeaver BW project. He is responsible for every aspect in the SAP NetWeaver BW implementation. This includes development, testing, troubleshooting, implementing SAP NetWeaver BW, and even the transition of the system to a production support environment. The project manager's responsibilities include the following:

- ▶ Coordinate and centralize responsibility and accountability for the design, development, release, and maintenance of the SAP NetWeaver BW system.
- ▶ Work closely with business users, sponsors, and other stakeholders to identify and maximize opportunities for SAP NetWeaver BW.
- ▶ Ensure cost-effective SAP NetWeaver BW design, development, and integration with other systems.
- ▶ Oversee maintenance and coordination of the integrated SAP NetWeaver BW project plan.
- ▶ Oversee the SAP NetWeaver BW implementation, testing, and maintenance in support of business and information objectives and requirements.
- ▶ Provide SAP NetWeaver BW technical and financial direction, by developing controls, budgets, and measurements to monitor progress.
- ▶ Approve resources and staff SAP NetWeaver BW project internally, and, if required, with external resources.
- ▶ Provide overall responsibility for the quality and performance of the SAP NetWeaver BW system.
- ▶ Coordinate communication between all key IT groups, the user community, and SAP NetWeaver BW team members.
- ▶ Facilitate adoption and change management of the SAP NetWeaver BW system.
- ▶ Develop cutover plans and activities and coordinate resources for go-live.
- ▶ Develop and maintain a production support strategy.
- ▶ Provide support and transition the SAP NetWeaver BW system from development to production support.
- ▶ Coordinate and assign priorities for new development in the SAP NetWeaver BW system with production support activities.

▶ The time commitment of the SAP NetWeaver BW project manager is full time during all phases of the project. All decision making and responsibility for the implantation of SAP NetWeaver BW ultimately falls to the SAP NetWeaver BW project manager (see Figure 4.10). Chapter 1 describes the qualities of a good SAP NetWeaver BW project manager.

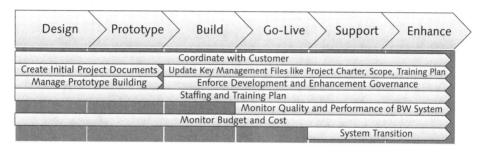

Figure 4.10   Important Responsibilities of a Project Manager

4.6.2   SAP NetWeaver BW Business Subject Matter Expert

The business Subject Matter Expert (SME) acts as the conduit between the business organization and the SAP NetWeaver BW development team. The main responsibilities of the SME are to understand the reporting requirements of the business and incorporate these requirements into the design for SAP NetWeaver BW.

The SME provides a voice of the business in each of the decisions in SAP NetWeaver BW. Typically, there are multiple SMEs on any SAP NetWeaver BW project, providing expertise in different functional areas of the system. The typical responsibilities for this role include the following:

▶ Understand the needs of the business and future direction of the business analysis needs.

▶ Coordinate communication between the SAP NetWeaver BW project and the end user community.

▶ Aid in generating functional specifications for matching the business requirements to the design of SAP NetWeaver BW.

▶ Provide escalation of business issues and facilitate decision making.

▶ Aid in the testing of SAP NetWeaver BW to ensure that it matches requirements.

▶ Work with the training and change management team to communicate the new business processes as a result of the SAP NetWeaver BW implementation.

▶ Act as first contact for aid in resolution of issues.

▶ Aid in transition to SAP NetWeaver BW and away from the current processes.

In a best-case scenario, the SME role is a full-time position on the SAP NetWeaver BW team. This makes sure that SMEs are always available to make the decisions needed to keep the project momentum going.

In many projects, it is difficult to secure qualified SMEs. To be useful, the SME must be involved in the day-to-day business operation and must be able to understand and communicate the issues that arise in normal business operation (see Figure 4.11). Such people are thus already useful in their current positions.

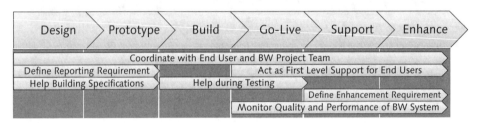

Figure 4.11 Important Responsibilities of a Business Subject Matter Expert

To keep the SMEs focused on the SAP NetWeaver BW project as their priority, it's recommended that they leave their existing business role completely and become part of the SAP NetWeaver BW implementation team full time. This allows them to focus on the project without the distraction and needs of the day-to-day business process.

4.6.3 SAP NetWeaver BW Data Architect

The SAP NetWeaver BW data architect is the most important person on the SAP NetWeaver BW project, from the SAP NetWeaver BW product standpoint. The SAP NetWeaver BW data architect plays a critical role matching the business requirements to the SAP NetWeaver BW implementation that will satisfy these requirements (see Figure 4.12).

This person must be experienced in the implementation of SAP NetWeaver BW and works with the SAP NetWeaver BW project manager to make implementation decisions on the design of SAP NetWeaver BW. Because the data design and model must be strong in order for the project to succeed, this role is critical for the current and future success of the project.

In larger projects, the SAP NetWeaver BW data architect is either a single role or a role filled by a group of individuals. They map out the design of the SAP NetWeaver BW project from a product standpoint to ensure that the data model and decision making reflect the best use of the SAP NetWeaver BW system.

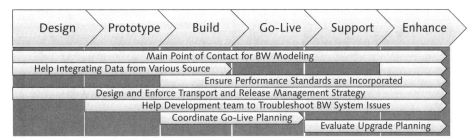

Figure 4.12 Important Responsibilities of a Data Architect

In smaller projects, this task is typically performed by the various application consultants who are implementing their specific areas of SAP NetWeaver BW. Because consultants have differing levels of skills and experience, this can sometimes lead to conflict. An SAP NetWeaver BW data architect helps to steer the project and sets an overall SAP NetWeaver BW strategy. If application consultants who are focused on their own deliverables are asked to take on this role, often not enough thought is given to the overall strategy and future direction of SAP NetWeaver BW.

Take the example of a company that was going through an implementing several years ago and did not have a data architect overseeing its SAP NetWeaver BW design. One consultancy was implementing a finance InfoCube. These consultants had several reports that they were focused on delivering as part of their project. They worked diligently to make sure that these reports were delivered.

However, if those consultants had understood the overall direction of the company was toward more finance visibility and more detailed financial data, they would have adjusted the SAP NetWeaver BW data model accordingly. Because they were unaware of the multi-generational plan for SAP NetWeaver BW, they did not bring this level of detail into SAP NetWeaver BW. Thus, once these new requirements were due, much of the finance work that was done had to be redesigned.

If the project had a data architect role from the start, this person could have steered the current requirements toward a future goal and accomplish both at the same time. The data architect's responsibilities include the following:

▶ Act as the main point of contact for all data model and system design decisions.
▶ Have a clear understanding of the SAP NetWeaver BW product and functionality.
▶ Be the primary contact for SAP NetWeaver BW decision making and functionality decisions.
▶ Ensure the development of corporate standards for data warehousing.
▶ Assemble and coordinate the multi-generational data plan and steer the SAP NetWeaver BW design to this plan.

▶ Develop and provide a clear understanding of the SAP NetWeaver BW data model and strategies for data modeling.

▶ Work to avoid rework, reload, and restatement of SAP NetWeaver BW transactional data.

▶ Help to incorporate performance standards into the design of SAP NetWeaver BW.

▶ Understand the end user requirements and the data that makes up these requirements.

▶ Recognize the integration points of the data in the various systems in the SAP NetWeaver BW landscape and bring this data together in a logical fashion to deliver reporting needs.

▶ Recommend an SAP NetWeaver BW landscape strategy and coordinate transports across the landscape.

▶ Aid in troubleshooting the SAP NetWeaver BW system issues.

▶ Possess excellent communication skills to understand and articulate the overall vision of SAP NetWeaver BW to the project community.

▶ Evaluate the timing and need for upgrades.

▶ Coordinate and plan the system tasks for go-live.

4.6.4 SAP NetWeaver BW Applications Developer

The SAP NetWeaver BW applications developer uses the implementation strategy and data modeling decisions of the data architect to implement the various business requirements in the SAP NetWeaver BW system. This involves creating the various SAP NetWeaver BW InfoObjects, ODS or DataStore Objects, InfoCubes, etc. The applications developer's responsibilities are as follows and in Figure 4.13:

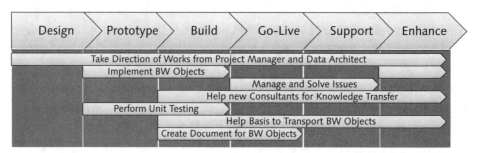

Figure 4.13 Important Responsibilities of an Application Developer

▸ Use strong SAP NetWeaver BW product skills to implement business requirements of SAP NetWeaver BW.

▸ Work with the user community to verify that the SAP NetWeaver BW data model captures the SAP NetWeaver BW requirements.

▸ Take direction and work effectively in a team environment.

▸ Use strong communication skills to communicate and understand scope and requirements.

▸ Track, troubleshoot, and escalate product issues.

▸ Offer knowledge transfer about the product and design.

▸ Document design, both from a functional and a technical standpoint.

▸ Determine the transformation of data needed and provide that transformation in the SAP NetWeaver BW system.

▸ Code or coordinate coding of ABAP to complete design where necessary.

▸ Work with the other consultants and team members to establish a batch load strategy.

▸ Verify data quality and ensure that SAP NetWeaver BW is in sync with source systems.

▸ Unit-test SAP NetWeaver BW system, and work with the various parties involved to achieve a sound integration test.

▸ Aid in transports and cutover to production environment.

▸ Transition to production support team.

4.6.5 SAP NetWeaver BW Presentation Developer

The SAP NetWeaver BW presentation developer is responsible for creating the presentation layer of the SAP NetWeaver BW system. This includes, but is not limited to, SAP NetWeaver BW queries, workbooks, dashboards, formatted reports, Web queries, etc. This role covers all portions of SAP NetWeaver BW that the user sees. In many projects, this role is covered by the SAP NetWeaver BW applications consultant. However, in larger projects this could be a separate role. The SAP NetWeaver BW presentation developer's responsibilities include the following and in Figure 4.14:

▸ Understand the presentation needs of the project.

▸ Plan the presentation of the SAP NetWeaver BW data in the most effective way to fulfill user needs.

▸ Communicate with the applications developers to understand the sources of data.

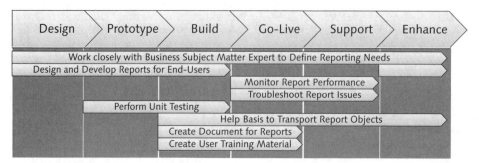

Figure 4.14 Important Responsibilities of a Presentation Developer

▶ Keep presentation of information in SAP NetWeaver BW consistent using common templates, query strategies, etc.
▶ Work with the business users and business SMEs to refine the presentation of data.
▶ Troubleshoot and track presentation issues.
▶ Aid in transports and cutover to production environment.
▶ Transition to production support team.

4.6.6 SAP NetWeaver BW Basis Developer

The Basis developer is responsible for all technical and system areas of SAP NetWeaver BW. This includes the setup of the system, administration of transports, patch application, etc. The SAP NetWeaver BW applications consultants, presentation developers, and SAP NetWeaver BW architects typically work closely with the SAP NetWeaver BW Basis developer.

Because the SAP NetWeaver BW environment is usually a dynamic environment, the SAP NetWeaver BW Basis developer is usually kept busy monitoring the SAP NetWeaver BW system and troubleshooting issues. Because the SAP NetWeaver BW system has many tables being loaded and reloaded, there are many opportunities for Basis support.

Many SAP NetWeaver BW projects make the mistake of trying to have one Basis resource to cover SAP NetWeaver BW and the same resource to cover the SAP R/3 or SAP ECC systems. This is a mistake. The Basis SAP NetWeaver BW role is unique and has different tasks and expectations that are not the same as the SAP R/3 or SAP ECC systems. The SAP NetWeaver BW Basis resource spends much of his time working on connecting systems, troubleshooting loads and query performance, etc. This is a different role than the SAP R/3 or SAP ECC Basis resource (see Figure 4.15).

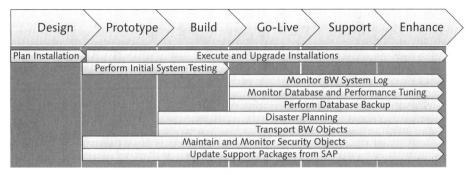

Figure 4.15 Important Responsibilities of a BASIS Consultant

Because the teams work so often together, it is important that the teams meet regularly to go over the various open issues and prioritize the open tasks. The Basis developer is responsible for the following:

▶ Plan and execute new installations, upgrades, and maintenance of the SAP SAP NetWeaver BW system.

▶ Perform initial testing of SAP maintenance applications and ongoing SAP SAP NetWeaver BW log monitoring.

▶ Aid SAP SAP NetWeaver BW system performance monitoring and tuning in conjunction with the SAP NetWeaver BW application teams.

▶ Provide database-performance tuning and log monitoring and issue resolution.

▶ Perform connection creation and maintenance between systems setup and monitoring.

▶ Plan and execute SAP NetWeaver BW copies between systems.

▶ Implement SAP NetWeaver BW system backups and disaster recovery contingency planning.

▶ Perform transports between systems execution and aid in transport issue resolution.

▶ Maintain and monitor security in the SAP NetWeaver BW system.

▶ Document basis procedures and policies.

4.6.7 ABAP Developer

Most SAP NetWeaver BW projects require some ABAP coding. ABAP is the source-code language of SAP and the source-code language of SAP NetWeaver BW. When data needs to be transformed, ABAP coding is often needed to perform this transformation. For example, a legacy system's orders need to be loaded into the SAP

NetWeaver BW system. These need to be combined with the orders that have been entered into the SAP ECC or SAP R/3 system. To make the different company numbers and material numbers match, transformation is needed to change the source data into a common customer and material number. This transformation is done using ABAP.

Many SAP NetWeaver BW applications consultants code their own ABAP transformations, and for this reason, this role can be avoided or reduced on many projects. However, if the applications consultants are not proficient in ABAP or there is complex transformation of data, a separate ABAP developer may be needed, at least temporarily. This is typically not a full-time role in any SAP NetWeaver BW project because the ABAP coding needed in most SAP NetWeaver BW projects is usually limited. The ABAP developer's responsibilities include the following and in Figure 4.16:

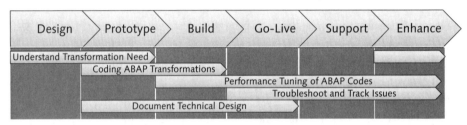

Figure 4.16 Important Responsibilities of an ABAP Developer

▶ Understand the transformation needs of the project.
▶ Understand ABAP coding strategies and possess development language skills.
▶ Plan the ABAP transformation of the SAP NetWeaver BW data in the most effective way to fulfill user needs.
▶ Communicate with the applications developers to understand the sources of data.
▶ Keep ABAP coding consistent, using ABAP development strategies.
▶ Troubleshoot and track coding issues.
▶ Document technical design.

4.6.8   SAP Portal Consultant

An SAP portal consultant is necessary in many SAP NetWeaver BW projects, especially those that use Release NW 2004s and later. This is because the portal is a mandatory part of the landscape. The role of the portal consultant can be limited or intensive, depending on the planned use of the SAP portal. Thus, the various responsibilities vary. However, it is important to include some portal consulting in any SAP NetWeaver BW project.

The goal of the SAP portal is to allow all users one place to enter the various SAP systems and give a common look and feel to all applications. Thus, SAP NetWeaver BW queries would be housed on the portal, and the portal would be used to present these to the end user.

In most SAP NetWeaver BW projects, the SAP NetWeaver BW developers are responsible for gathering up the data from the source system and creating the presentation of that data, usually in the form of SAP NetWeaver BW queries. After the queries are complete, these are passed to the portal consultant for inclusion in the portal. Typically, the SAP NetWeaver BW team is not responsible for the portal.

In many projects, the portal consultant is not part of the SAP NetWeaver BW organization. Because this role creates the launch pad for all applications, it is often part of a shared services group, reporting to the Basis organization.

How do you find all these individuals? Understanding the staffing models and needs helps in filling the roles.

4.7 Staffing a SAP NetWeaver BW Project

Staffing a SAP NetWeaver BW project can be a difficult task because historically the demand for SAP NetWeaver BW resources has been much higher than the supply of strong resources. In addition, there are many candidates who have strong resumes but really do not possess the skills that their resumes would seem to indicate.

Several times, when asked about details on their resumes, these candidates are unable or unwilling to give details about past projects and the tasks they actually performed at those projects. This often indicates that they were not active participants in this part of the implementation, and thus do not have a clear understanding of the functionality.

> **Tip**
>
> The first step in staffing any SAP NetWeaver BW project is to ensure that you have adequate internal resources.

Many projects are staffed entirely or almost entirely by external resources. This is a mistake for many reasons. There simply is no incentive to transition the consultants out of the project, and the effort to transfer knowledge is much too great after the implementation has been ongoing for a long time.

The best projects are those where organizations make sure that there is adequate exposure of both internal and external resources. Each functional area of the project should have an internal resource that is responsible for the implementation. For example, a project that is implementing sales, purchasing, and financial reporting should have internal resources who are ultimately responsible for each of those functional areas. The resource would be charged with making the day-to-day decisions that affect this data model and the report delivery in that area.

4.7.1 Small SAP NetWeaver BW Project

A small SAP NetWeaver BW project organizational chart often looks much like the one in Figure 4.17. A typical small SAP NetWeaver BW project has the following:

▶ Very few sources of data (often just SAP SAP R/3 or SAP ECC)—often fewer than 10 specific sources

▶ Few queries needed—typically fewer than 40

▶ Few end users—often fewer than 100

▶ A low volume of data

▶ Little transformation or harmonization

▶ Few subject areas of data (often only one), such as sales reporting or financial analysis

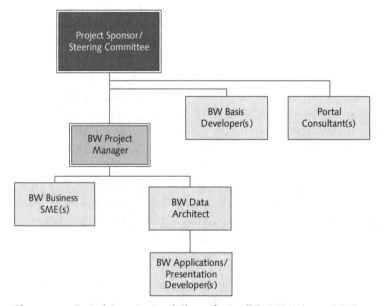

Figure 4.17 Typical Organizational Chart of a Small SAP NetWeaver BW Project

▶ Many large SAP NetWeaver BW projects start as small projects as a proof of concept to the organization or to determine the acceptance and viability of product as a whole.

▶ Smaller projects are best staffed with many resources wearing many hats because of the work needed and the resources allocated to smaller projects.

In a smaller SAP NetWeaver BW project, as with any project, the project sponsor is the resource providing the requirements, scope, and budget. In many cases, this is one person or a small group in the organization with a business point of pain or area of risk that SAP NetWeaver BW is being looked on to resolve.

The project manager coordinates the implementation. In many smaller projects, the project manager is not only handling issues and coordinating resources, but also aiding on the configuration and implementation of the product. A dedicated SAP NetWeaver BW Basis consultant is needed, even in a small project, to keep the SAP NetWeaver BW system running from a technical standpoint.

> **Note**
>
> It should not be assumed that in a smaller project the SAP NetWeaver BW Basis consultant can be a part-time resource primarily dedicated to the SAP R/3 or SAP ECC environment. Each SAP NetWeaver BW project, no matter how small, needs to have a dedicated Basis or technical resource to handle the technical and security tasks.

A portal developer is also needed if SAP or another portal is within scope. This is typically not a full-time position in the SAP NetWeaver BW project because the portal is simply used to house the SAP NetWeaver BW queries and present them to the end user. The portal consultant or portal resource works with both the SAP NetWeaver BW team and the transactional teams to provide the launch pad for transactional and reporting processes.

If the portals resource is part of a larger portal implementation, the resource should have some time dedicated to the SAP NetWeaver BW team. If SAP's or another vendor's portal software is only being implemented to provide a portal for SAP NetWeaver BW reporting, this resource can be staffed for a short time during the latter part of the query development to provide a way for the queries to be published and launched.

In small SAP NetWeaver BW projects, it is important to have capable business representation in the form of business SMEs to communicate the business needs and requirements of the project. These resources may or may not work full time on the project, but they must be available to the team to help scope and refine the SAP NetWeaver BW data model. These resources are the first point of contact to the business users. They help to roll the end result functionality out to the end user community.

The developers and/or data architect roles work with the business SME or SMEs to provide the solution. The number of data developers or data architects depends on the resources and amount of functionality needed. Often in smaller projects, a dedicated data architect is not needed because the developers perform the data-modeling tasks.

4.7.2   Medium-Sized SAP NetWeaver BW Project

Figure 4.18 shows the organizational chart of a typical medium-sized SAP NetWeaver BW project. This would be a project that had moderate scope and some of the following characteristics:

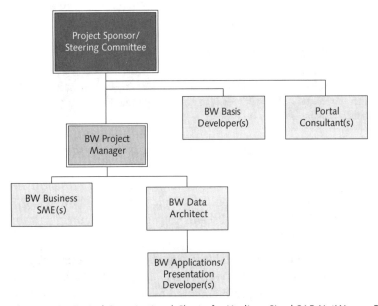

Figure 4.18 Typical Organizational Chart of a Medium-Sized SAP NetWeaver BW Project

- ▶ Several sources of data (often more than SAP SAP R/3 or SAP ECC)
- ▶ Several queries needed—typically 50 to 100
- ▶ Moderate number of end users—often 100 to 300
- ▶ Moderate volume of data
- ▶ Some transformation or harmonization of data
- ▶ Multiple subject areas of data such as sales reporting and financial analysis.

In the medium-sized project, there is usually a dedicated SAP NetWeaver BW data architect to oversee all development in the SAP NetWeaver BW system. This person would make sure that all the data models are in sync and are following standards and work with the various developers on the common master data and data strategy. Typically, this architect is also doing some of the development. The developers work with the architect to deliver the requirements in SAP NetWeaver BW.

In some cases, depending on the presentation complexity, there may be dedicated developers working on the presentation of the data. These are separate from the applications development team and would work on extracting the data from the source, transforming and harmonizing the data, and loading the data in the SAP NetWeaver BW system. However, in many medium-sized projects, the presentation development is handled by the SAP NetWeaver BW applications development team, and there is no separate resource to handle the presentation.

Depending on the source of external data, there may also be another role, which is not shown in Figure 4.18. This role would be the extraction or ETL resource from the source system. This role is responsible for gathering the data from the external source system and presenting it in a format that can be read by SAP NetWeaver BW.

For example, a project needs to report on data from a legacy transactional purchasing system. To be loaded into SAP NetWeaver BW, data must first be extracted from the source system. If it cannot be extracted by existing extractors, appropriate views created to directly map SAP NetWeaver BW via a database link such as SAP DBConnect or SAP UDConnect. These tools allow for a direct link between SAP NetWeaver BW systems and eliminate the need for data to be extracted to a file and then loaded into SAP NetWeaver BW.

To source this data, these systems must have the views or extraction programs written to gather the data. This role is usually considered outside the SAP NetWeaver BW team because it is done on the legacy system. This role is typically filled by someone familiar with the legacy system.

4.7.3 Large SAP NetWeaver BW Project

A large SAP NetWeaver BW project typically has many of the following characteristics:

▶ Multiple sources of data, often in many subject areas with harmonization required between data

▶ Multiple presentation means, including dashboards, formatted reports, etc.

- Many end users, often more than 200
- Large or high volume of data
- Transformation or harmonization of data
- Multiple subject areas of data.

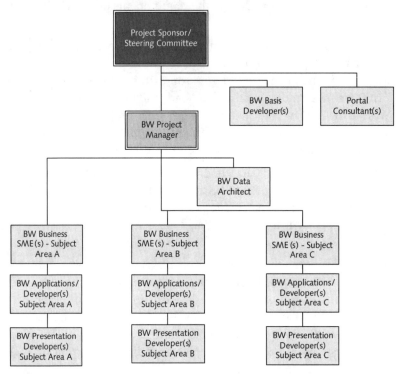

Figure 4.19 Typical Organizational Chart of a Large SAP NetWeaver BW Project

A large SAP NetWeaver BW project typically has several distinct and separate subject areas with a complex scope, as seen in Figure 4.19. This requires dedicated SAP NetWeaver BW business resources and dedicated subject-area developers. In small and medium projects, developers can work on multiple subject areas at one time, but in larger projects developers are focused on one subject area.

For example, one subject area might be purchase order analysis. The developers in that area work on the extraction of the purchase orders from one or many source systems, often including SAP ECC or SAP R/3 and external systems. They would then either develop the purchase order presentation queries, workbooks, etc., or work with presentation developers to develop the presentation of the purchasing data.

In a larger implementation, the large data volume and the higher complexity mean that more dedicated resources are needed to understand the data and make sure that the data is being transformed properly to meet the business requirements.

In a large project, the business SMEs are also dedicated project team members because understanding the reporting needs requires constant communication between the business and the development group. The developers work on prototypes that are refined by the business SMEs in a back-and-forth fashion until the data model is complete.

The data architect role brings all the groups together to make sure that the design standards are followed and that the models make the most efficient use of the system.

As in any SAP NetWeaver BW project, there are dedicated SAP NetWeaver BW Basis developers to handle the technical and security tasks. In many larger projects, there are multiple Basis resources, and a dedicated database administrator to handle database-specific tasks.

4.7.4   Large Global SAP NetWeaver BW Project

A large global SAP NetWeaver BW project typically has the following characteristics:

- Multiple sources of data
- Multiple presentation means
- Many end users
- Large or high volume of data
- Transformation or harmonization of data
- Multiple subject areas of data
- Global reach with one or many SAP NetWeaver BW or data-warehouse environments
- One or many languages
- Regional requirements and global requirements.

In global SAP NetWeaver BW projects, there is much more complexity, and thus the organization is typically much larger than other non-global projects. Most global projects have one or many SAP NetWeaver BW or other data warehouse environments.

Global SAP NetWeaver BW projects are typically complex because they usually have both regional and global requirements. These projects usually involve many different companies or affiliates, each working with some autonomy from the global parent. In this case, the parent company needs some data from the regional groups for global reporting. This may or may not be the same data requirement that the regional groups need for themselves.

In this case, a global template is typically built by a global organization or global Center of Excellence (COE). The COE is responsible for developing a global strategy for reporting across the organization and making sure that the regional groups follow the global strategy. This can be a difficult and often political task, because the regional groups also require flexibility to deliver regional reporting requirements in the same environment.

This global template spells out in detail the data that is needed from the regional groups and how the data is to be rolled up into a global view. The regional teams can utilize the global template to pass data to this global group, thus providing analysis across the regional groups.

This global template must allow for both flexibility of regional standards and needs and the rigor of enforced standards to make sure that the global reporting requirements can be met.

As seen in Figure 4.20, this involves separate SAP NetWeaver BW groups. There are regional groups, each working on their specific regional subject matter. A global COE group with global SAP NetWeaver BW developers helps to gather data from the various groups and stage and transform this data as required for presentation to the global users.

In this environment, there may be multiple SAP NetWeaver BW data architects and often multiple SAP NetWeaver BW teams. Communication between the teams is vital to ensure that the data model is consistent and that the delivery of the data and implementation of the global and regional templates meet standards and can be aggregated successfully.

How can these needs be met? Many projects look to outsourcing to find resources but with limited success.

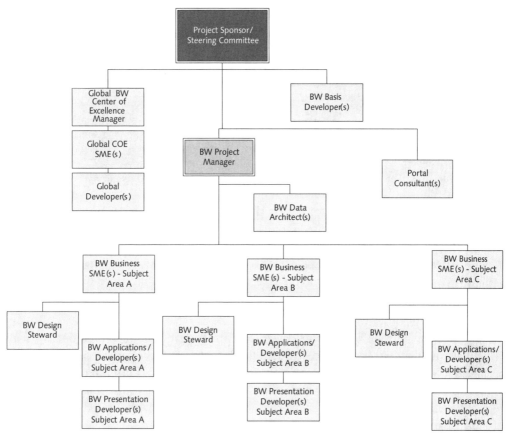

Figure 4.20 Typical Organizational Chart of a Large Global SAP NetWeaver BW Project

4.8 Outsourcing and SAP NetWeaver BW

Many project organizations that look to outsourcing as a quick answer to hasten development and ensure a less costly implementation. These projects typically gather the requirements and provide documentation to offshore resources that take the documentation and convert it into a data model and working SAP NetWeaver BW system.

While this sounds like a tempting strategy, experience tells us that outsourcing the development of SAP NetWeaver BW is of limited usefulness, in most instances and in most projects (see Figure 4.21).

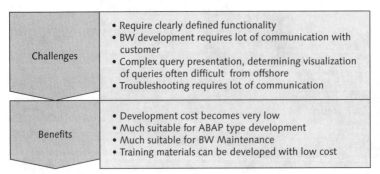

Figure 4.21 Benefits and Challenges of SAP NetWeaver BW Project Outsourcing

Outsourcing works well for clearly defined functionality with limited reach. This is because if there is a limited scope and the scope can be clearly documented, the process can be communicated, developed, tested, and transitioned. For example, many projects use outsourced resources to handle ABAP or coding work. This is because the work is of limited scope, and once the specifications have been written, for the most part, there is limited interaction between the requirements and the delivery of the code.

Thus, if the specifications are clear, the project can save development costs by having outsourced resources to handle this custom coding work. However, SAP NetWeaver BW development rarely has limited scope and often requires a bit of interaction between the business and the developer. Handing off a written set of instructions and waiting for the development to occur with limited interaction is usually challenging.

The SAP NetWeaver BW environment usually requires multiple sources of data as well as many harmonization and transformation points. This makes it difficult to troubleshoot without a lot of communication. Adding to the challenges are issues with data integrity. In addition, business users often have complex query-presentation needs; these are often difficult to communicate. These challenges can make for a complex environment to outsource.

Often, it is also difficult to enforce development standards to a group that is outsourced. In many cases, it's challenging to get a non-outsourced group to obey development and data-modeling standards. This becomes complex, if not impossible, with an outsourced group.

Many organizations find that in most cases it's too difficult to document all the standards, requirements, and test cases, while also conveying an understanding of business needs and integrity issues in a small communication window.

Finding qualified outsourcing resources is also challenging. This is because SAP NetWeaver BW has a steep learning curve and outsourcing firms are often competing for a small high-quality group of resources. Thus, turnover is often high and quality resources can be scarce.

4.8.1 When Does Outsourcing Work?

There are times that outsourcing SAP NetWeaver BW work can be successful. If there is involved transformation of data requiring some complex ABAP, some organizations turn to outsourced resources.

Take the example of a company that needed to extract data from a legacy transactional system and transform much of this data to an SAP-friendly format. The coding became complex to check the data against existing source data tables and check various values for consistency.

This company looked to outside resources to deliver this functionality and was successful. This was because they could clearly communicate the tables needed for the transformation and validation and could provide clear test cases to check this data. This made the project easy to hand off to outsourced resources.

Outsourcing this kind of development work is often successful. This is because the scope of the transformation can usually be limited to a small area; it has limited scope and can be communicated and tested easily.

Projects that look to outsourced resources to handle more localized requirements often find that the outsourced resources often succeed at delivering these types of application areas. The project saves some money over using internal or local resources to perform the development.

As previously stated, the interview process in SAP NetWeaver BW is necessary to help select a qualified candidate, whether this candidate is part of an outsourcing group or in-house on the development team. Often, when you are new to SAP NetWeaver BW and SAP NetWeaver BW consulting, having a few sample questions can help to choose the best candidate. The next section gives some common interview questions and some answers to expect.

4.9 SAP NetWeaver BW Interview Process

It is often difficult to find the most qualified SAP NetWeaver BW consultants and internal resources to staff an SAP NetWeaver BW project. SAP does have an SAP NetWeaver BW certification process. This is a test that is administered by SAP to determine some level of proficiency in the product.

In general, it is not helpful to use the certification process to determine the level of the consulting resource during the interview process. Certification does not prove whether a consultant is any more qualified to implement SAP NetWeaver BW. In some cases, the certified consultant resources were knowledgeable in the terminology but not in the processes and implementation strategies. Therefore, do not assume that a certified consultant is any more qualified than one that is not certified.

The lack of knowledge in the process and implementation during interviews is likely the result of the many test questions and books available to help people pass the test and become SAP NetWeaver BW certified. Thus, it is not recommended that you look at these criteria alone when determining whether a consultant is qualified to implement SAP NetWeaver BW. It does help to highlight those consultants with a basic understanding of the SAP NetWeaver BW product but not necessarily those who would be a great resource on your project.

To find the best resources, conduct a detailed interview of the candidate. This will allow you to understand not only his product knowledge but also his communication skills. Because both are equally important, ask a lot of open-ended questions to try to get the interviewee talking about his specific experiences in one area of SAP NetWeaver BW implementation (see Figure 4.22).

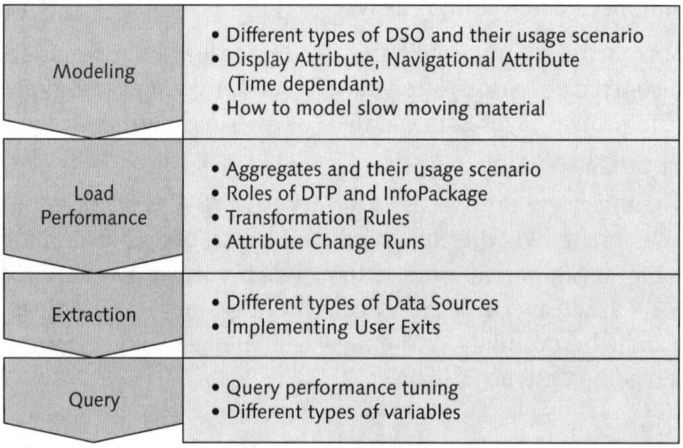

Modeling	• Different types of DSO and their usage scenario • Display Attribute, Navigational Attribute (Time dependant) • How to model slow moving material
Load Performance	• Aggregates and their usage scenario • Roles of DTP and InfoPackage • Transformation Rules • Attribute Change Runs
Extraction	• Different types of Data Sources • Implementing User Exits
Query	• Query performance tuning • Different types of variables

Figure 4.22 Interview Topics for Interviewees

Interviewing SAP NetWeaver BW candidates is not easy, especially if you are new to the product. We have included some interview questions that can be used to evaluate a SAP NetWeaver BW consultant:

1. **What is the difference between a DSO (also called DataStore Objects) and InfoCubes and why is this difference important?**

   This question is intended to make sure the candidate understands the basic architecture of SAP NetWeaver BW. This is a basic question with serious ramifications if the candidate does not understand the use of each of the structures. The answer should clearly indicate that the InfoCube is the primary reporting repository for SAP NetWeaver BW data, although the DSO can be used for reporting in some circumstances. The database structure of the InfoCube and DSO are completely different.

   The DSO is a relational database structure with a user-determined key and can have additive or overwrite capabilities. The InfoCube is a star schema design. The key is made up of a combination of the various characteristics in the dimension tables that establish dimension IDs used in the two central fact tables for reporting. The InfoCubes is only additive; there is no overwrite capability in the InfoCube.

2. **What kinds of things can be used to determine query performance bottlenecks?**

   Performance management is one of the more difficult tasks in SAP NetWeaver BW. This is because if you understand what performance issues can occur, you clearly understand the underlying design of the SAP NetWeaver BW system. The more a candidate understands performance in SAP NetWeaver BW, the more he seems to understand the product and its interworkings, and thus the stronger applicant he is. Thus, it's good practice to ask many different performance-related questions to determine if the interviewee understands performance management in SAP NetWeaver BW.

   This also makes sure that if candidates understand it, they will incorporate this into their data structures in SAP NetWeaver BW, which is clearly an important overall goal of any implementation. In this answer, the candidate should mention something about SAP NetWeaver BW statistics and an ongoing process to monitor these statistics. There are also some various other performance tools, such as Transaction RSRV. But for the most part, determining performance bottlenecks should come from the statistics InfoCubes.

3. **What are some things that can be used to fix query bottlenecks?**

   This question is trying to get to the root of the performance questions to see how the candidates would actually apply their knowledge to a performance issue. Because there are many reasons for performance issues, it's best not to let a candidate give just one answer. Look for several of the following answers:

   ▶ Adjust the query, adding filter values to reduce the data retrieved.

▸ Check the query to see if the filter logic is using exclusive logic.

▸ Check the data model. If the query is going after an InfoProvider with massive amounts of data, reduce the volume by segregating the InfoProviders into smaller individual ones, and use a multi-provider or adjust the data model appropriately.

▸ Check to see if the query is running from an ODS/DSO. This is not the preferred InfoProvider for query performance; switch to an InfoCube. This is because queries typically run faster from InfoCubes, and more performance-enhancing tools are available on InfoCubes. If the query is running from an ODS/DSO, the candidate should mention adding indices to the ODS/DSO.

▸ Check to see if the query is coming from a virtual InfoProvider.

▸ Implement SAP NetWeaver BW Aggregates.

▸ Turn on/adjust OLAP Cache settings.

▸ Implement the BI Accelerator (available only in NW 2004s and above).

▸ Implement partitioning.

▸ Implement compression.

4. **What is a navigational attribute and why would one use this in the SAP NetWeaver BW design?**

This question is posed to ensure that the interviewee knows about the concept of data being read from either the transactional data or the attributes of master data. A navigational attribute is a master data field that is a related field of master data that can be used for reporting. For example, transactional data is loaded into SAP NetWeaver BW with the customer and a net sales value. The customer master data record has an attribute "country" that is populated on the customer master data but not in the transactional data. Although the transactional data does not have the country field, the data can be reported by country because the master data table for the customer does have the country.

This allows the SAP NetWeaver BW report to show net sales by country without having this field in the transactional data. They need to fully understand that data read and accessed from the navigational attributes is stored in the master data and is dynamic. It changes with the master data. This provides an automatic restatement of the data each time the master data is reloaded.

In this question, you're trying to make sure that they understand the concept of using master data in their design. There are several ways of delivering reports in SAP NetWeaver BW. If all the data comes from the InfoCube directly, all reports are sourced in the transactional data.This can be fine if the users are only concerned about a snapshot of the transactional data at the time that the transaction occurred.

However, understanding that the user can also view the data as a reflection of the current master data attributes gives them a more dynamic approach to the data, allowing transactional data to be restated based on the current view of the master data attributes. A navigational attribute is a master data field that is an related field of master data that can be used for reporting. For example, transactional data is loaded into SAP NetWeaver BW with the customer and a net sales value.

The customer master data record has an attribute "country" that is populated on the customer master data but not in the transactional data. Although the transactional data does not have the country field, the data can be reported by country because the master data table for the customer does have the country. This allows the SAP NetWeaver BW report to show net sales by country without having this field in the transactional data.

5. **What is the delta initialization process and why is it important? Is there a way to resend a failed delta? How?**
This question is intended to make sure that the candidate has actually loaded data into SAP NetWeaver BW on an ongoing basis. Sooner or later, a delta will fail for various reasons including data issues, space issues, etc. The interviewee should understand that the initialization of the delta process establishes the delta queue in the source system. This delta queue is used to store and track the changing delta records.

If a delta fails, it is possible to resend this delta by simply backing out the failed delta on the SAP NetWeaver BW system and using the delta-processing transactions in the source system, including Transaction RSA7, to resend a failed delta.

6. **What is the change run? (It is also called the apply hierarchy change)**
Understanding the change-run job shows that the interviewee has done some work managing the batch processes of SAP NetWeaver BW. Master data comes into SAP NetWeaver BW in an inactive state. Changes to master data are not immediately reflected in the master data values. This job simply takes the new master data values and moves them to the active status. This allows the changes in master data to be reflected.

The job also has one other important role. It adjusts any SAP NetWeaver BW aggregates that have navigational attributes to the new master data value. Simply put, it does for the aggregates the same thing that it does for the master data. Consultants who understand both of these parts of the change run have usually worked hands-on with aggregates, batch, and master data. This is a good sign that they understand the most important aspects of the SAP NetWeaver BW design.

7. **Explain the methodology you have used for transitioning a project from the development stage to the production support phase.**

   This question is especially telling. Many candidates list multiple go-lives on their resume but cannot explain how the project was transitioned to the production support phase. Understanding this transition means understanding how knowledge was passed on to that group, how the help desk was staffed and transitioned, etc. This process is usually not clearly understood or articulated without being a large part of the process. Usually, if candidates cannot answer this question, they were part of a small piece of a project but were not there through the go-live and into the production support phase. If possible, it's preferable to use those consultants who have been through this transition process. They usually understand what needs to be done to bring a project live.

The next step after choosing a team is to make sure the team is fully educated on the SAP NetWeaver BW product. Understanding the typical training requirements help to make sure that the project plan reflects the typical training time needed.

4.10 Training Requirements

Product training is important for SAP NetWeaver BW project managers and SAP NetWeaver BW applications or presentation developers. However, typical SAP classes take several weeks and are popular. Thus, it can be difficult to book a class at the time and location required. It is important to make sure that the training be planned as early as possible to ensure that the training is completed in time for the design and build processes.

SAP R/3 or SAP ECC skills are not easily transferable to SAP NetWeaver BW skills. SAP NetWeaver BW has its own skill sets and one should not expect someone from an SAP R/3 or SAP ECC background to easily understand SAP NetWeaver BW. SAP NetWeaver BW takes some hands-on time to understand (see Figure 4.23).

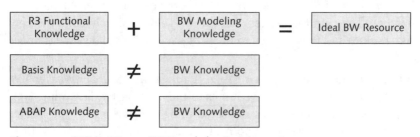

Figure 4.23 SAP NetWeaver BW Knowledge Requirement

Most SAP NetWeaver BW project scope includes bringing data from various parts of the SAP ECC or SAP R/3 system. For example, to successfully bring in sales orders into SAP NetWeaver BW, you should understand the sales-order process. It helps even more if the SAP NetWeaver BW developer can enter and change his sales orders in the development system.

It is likely to be necessary that the SAP NetWeaver BW team either completes some training in the core area that they will be extracting or schedule time with the process team to educate the SAP NetWeaver BW team on the basic workings and scope of that area. What works well in many projects is for the various process teams to schedule lunch and learn activities. This means each of the process teams, once a week or more, gives an informal presentation on the functionality and plans for their areas of expertise.

For example, in a project that is bringing in data from SAP ECC for APO and planning information from APO for reporting, the APO team could give a presentation on the entire planning process at a high level. This allows the SAP NetWeaver BW team to ask questions and clearly understand the various parts of that process so they can effectively ask the right questions during the implementation process. The more the SAP NetWeaver BW team is aware of the scope and needs of the process teams, the better the implementation meets those needs.

These sessions should be planned to take advantage of the various process teams' expertise. Typically, during the early phases of the project, the resources on-site are most aware and can devote more time to educating the SAP NetWeaver BW team because they are not yet under extreme deadlines. This is the time to make sure the SAP NetWeaver BW team is on their calendars for training.

4.11   Conclusion

Understanding the scoping and process lifecycle can enable a project team to have the right expectations when delivering SAP NetWeaver BW. In this chapter, you learned about the SAP NetWeaver BW development lifecycle model and its variant to accommodate change controls during design and prototyping phase.

You learned new features of NW2004s SAP NetWeaver BW and different aspects for migration such as the cutover process and time estimation, etc.

The project charter and detailed scope document is the most important and live document throughout the project lifecycle.

As with any team, selecting the right team members is vital to success. Using the typical team structure noted in this chapter helps to plan for all roles in the project and to help staff the project.

In Chapter 5, we'll explore the process needed to gather requirements from the end users. This process involves working with them to understand their vision and analysis needs and help them articulate these into a clear document with which to begin work.

Developing sound requirements is vital to any project. By using the functional model document and Key Figure or KPI matrix, you build scope agreement with which to begin making decisions.

5   Gathering and Analyzing SAP NetWeaver BW Requirements

In the most efficiently run SAP NetWeaver BW projects, team members work to clearly understand in as much detail as possible the end user requirements for analysis. These requirements not only include the information needed but other aspects such as the format and security requirements. Gathering these requirements in the detail required to implement in SAP NetWeaver BW can be a challenge.

Take the example of one company that wanted to provide purchasing analysis. This involved taking data from two outside source systems and analyzing that data with the existing SAP ECC purchasing data. The requirements that were given appeared to be detailed. They clearly understood which data needed to be extracted. They understood the SAP data that was needed. They even had mock-ups of the queries that were expected.

The business users agreed with the approach and the intended data model in SAP NetWeaver BW, so they started to build the solution. Only then did they understand that the external data was at many different levels of granularly and detail. It also did not always contain key fields that were needed for comparison.

To match the data, extensive transformations of data were needed to compare values and determine measurement values. It took a lot of time to analyze the data and prototype new solutions.

Because they spent a great deal of time trying to work around the source data, they were late delivering the solution. However, if they had understood the issues and challenges with this data and the difficulty of harmonizing the data with other data, they would have allowed more time to analyze and implement.

For the business requirements to be clearly understood by all involved, you need a clear methodology for gathering and understanding the SAP NetWeaver BW requirements. In the next section, we'll discuss some methods for gathering these requirements.

5.1   Requirements Gathering

Analyzing SAP NetWeaver BW data and requirements can be a difficult task. It requires not only an understanding of the SAP NetWeaver BW software but also some level of understanding of the source systems and their functionality. This allows the data to be extracted and combined in a meaningful way to provide the necessary reporting.

The first stages of SAP NetWeaver BW requirement-gathering are typically performed by the overall project-management organization, the SAP NetWeaver BW project management, the SAP NetWeaver BW data architect(s), and the business SMEs. Usually, the business SMEs present and fully communicate their business analysis needs and help determine where SAP NetWeaver BW might help to meet these needs.

Once the overall project management organization and the SAP NetWeaver BW project managers agree that requirements should be included in the SAP NetWeaver BW scope, the SAP NetWeaver BW data architect and SAP NetWeaver BW project management then make a high-level assessment of the level of effort and timeline needed to implement those requirements in SAP NetWeaver BW.

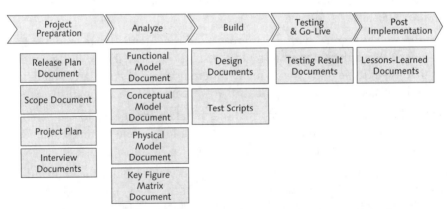

Figure 5.1   Important Document Deliverables During the SAP NetWeaver BW Project

Figure 5.1 shows some of the documents that are needed at each stage in the SAP NetWeaver BW project. It is through the completion of these documents that the scope of the SAP NetWeaver BW project is established, agreed on, implemented, and documented for handoff to the production support organization for post-implementation support. Samples of several of these documents are found in Appendix C.

Figure 5.2 shows the steps required to gather all necessary information before building the SAP NetWeaver BW application.

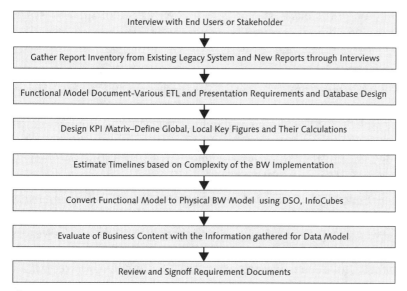

Figure 5.2 SAP NetWeaver BW Requirement Gathering Steps

To begin to start understanding the end user requirements, the most logical place to begin is with these end users. The most common way to begin to gather requirements is through the interview process.

5.1.1   Interviews

The first step in any SAP NetWeaver BW requirement gathering and analysis is to recognize the various stakeholders and interview these stakeholders to determine the reporting requirements and sources of data. The next step is to establish ongoing communication between the shareholders and the SAP NetWeaver BW team to articulate the needs and business analysis pain in the organization.

As shown in Figure 5.3, the interview process allows the SAP NetWeaver BW functional team and the business process teams to review their requirements and set the scope for the project. These interviews allow the SAP NetWeaver BW team to ask focused questions of the process team members to determine where their analysis pains are felt.

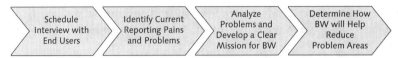

Figure 5.3 Typical Interview Process for SAP NetWeaver BW Requirement Gathering

The main goals of the interview process are to gain agreement with the stakeholders on the definition of the business questions and the causes of analysis issues. The interview should identify constraints to current analysis and create a clear mission for the SAP NetWeaver BW project.

It may be helpful to have a business-modelling session to articulate more complex business problems and allow both parties to clearly understand the business issues. The next step in the process is to analyze the business requirements that have surfaced and determine how the requirement should be realized. This requires knowledge in where SAP NetWeaver BW excels, and what SAP NetWeaver BW does not do as well. This is a good time to determine whether the reporting requirement should be met in SAP NetWeaver BW at all.

Once the business owners and intended users are interviewed, the requirements for analysis become clearer. This is an important time in the SAP NetWeaver BW lifecycle. This is where you are confronted with the basic question: SAP NetWeaver BW or not SAP NetWeaver BW? Often, the SAP NetWeaver BW team assumes that because the analysis requirement was initially slated to become an SAP NetWeaver BW requirement its ultimate delivery must be in SAP NetWeaver BW.

This should not be assumed. After the interview process, when the requirements are fairly well known, the SAP NetWeaver BW team should assess the requirements to determine where the analysis is best delivered. Sometimes, SAP NetWeaver BW is the best solution. At other times, the analysis requirement is best fulfilled in another area of the system, or even outside of the system.

Some SAP NetWeaver BW projects fail for the simple reason that they attempt to use SAP NetWeaver BW for something that it is not intended to do. So, in the early stages of the requirement gathering, a scoping session should be planned. This often occurs after the interview sessions but before any functional specifications are written. The goal of these sessions is to determine if SAP NetWeaver BW is the right tool to deliver the analysis requirements that are needed.

It is best to do this early in requirements gathering because then you will not waste a lot of time writing specifications that are intended to be in the SAP NetWeaver BW scope but that are better served in another SAP application or even outside the system. The following subsections tackle the basic questions that should be asked.

5.1.2   Is All Data in SAP ECC or SAP R/3 or in Multiple Systems?

If *all* data is coming from the SAP ECC or SAP R/3 system, the source data should be evaluated to determine if there are standard reports or standard list functions in the SAP ECC system to provide the analysis needed. This analysis is typically done by the process team that is implementing or has implemented the affected area of the system.

Example

An analysis report is requested that will show all customers with open credit balances in accounts receivable. There are several standard reports that can show this information in the SAP ECC or SAP R/3 system. Thus, a representative from the finance team should evaluate the reporting requirement to see if there are already reports in this area that satisfy the reporting need. Although this seems a rather obvious step, there have been several SAP projects where companies spent a great deal of time implementing reporting that already exists on the transactional system.

5.1.3   Is Intra-Day or Real-Time Reporting Needed?

SAP NetWeaver BW is not primarily designed to provide real-time data. Although there is functionality to provide some real-time reporting, this is not something that is often implemented in SAP NetWeaver BW. Thus, intra-day reporting, or analysis reports that require data to be loaded multiple times per day, can become a challenge in SAP NetWeaver BW. This type of reporting requirement is typically a red flag that the reporting requirement *might* be better served in the transactional system.

SAP NetWeaver BW can provide intra-day reporting; data can be loaded multiple times a day into SAP NetWeaver BW. Several project teams have this requirement and successfully provide this type of reporting to their end users. However, often when reporting requirements need to have the most up-to-date data as part of their analysis, this is a sign that you need to learn more about the requirement.

After analyzing these types of requirements, it is often found that either the most up-to-date information is not needed, or that the report needs to truly be real time and the analysis might be better achieved in the source system.

Once data is loaded multiple times per day into SAP NetWeaver BW or even set up to provide real-time reporting in SAP NetWeaver BW, this often causes more issues. This is because users have a single point in time that the data is static for analysis. This can make analysis much more difficult, because data is constantly being updated in the SAP NetWeaver BW environment.

5.1.4   What Else Do You Know About the Requirement?

There are several questions that should be asked to determine more about the requirement. It helps if you know the answers to these questions:

1. **Is the data analysis using high volumes of data?**
   This question is important because SAP NetWeaver BW handles high-volume reporting well. On the contrary, SAP ECC and SAP R/3 typically do not. When reports require analysis on a higher-volume data set, this is often a flag that the reporting should take place in SAP NetWeaver BW and not the SAP ECC or SAP R/3 source system.

2. **Does the analysis need to serve many users?**
   The number of users is important because often SAP NetWeaver BW can be quickly rolled out to a large user base with less effort than can a solution on the SAP ECC or SAP R/3 system. This is because the SAP ECC or SAP R/3 reports usually require a graphical user interface client to be loaded on the user's machine and training on the transactions in SAP ECC to find and run the report.

   In SAP NetWeaver BW, adding more users is often easier because the reports can run as a Web link or iView on a portal. Many reports can be rolled out to users more quickly because the link, login, and security access only need to be established for analysis to begin.

3. **Is the analysis interactive? Does the user need to drill down in order to provide the information required?**
   Often, this is a red flag that a reporting requirement might be a good match for SAP NetWeaver BW. Because SAP NetWeaver BW provides interactivity and drilling down, often the reporting requirements that require this should be developed in SAP NetWeaver BW. Drilling down is often limited in SAP ECC or SAP R/3–developed reports.

4. **Is the data integrated from multiple sources?**
   SAP NetWeaver BW excels at integrating data from multiple sources, where the SAP ECC system usually reports data from one functional area. Once data needs to be integrated or harmonized from several source systems or several modules of SAP ECC or SAP R/3, the report often is best in the SAP NetWeaver BW system.

These types of questions are used to determine if the analysis requirements that are needed play to SAP NetWeaver BW's strengths. If the questions are answered affirmatively, this typically means that the reporting requirements are often best in the SAP NetWeaver BW system rather than the associated transactional systems.

Some project organizations opt to create a report-determination matrix to allow some of the evaluation of the reporting method to be performed by process team members rather than the SAP NetWeaver BW team. For example, as the organization starts to grow and the analysis needs become more mature, new reporting requirements often surface. Sometimes, each of these reporting requirements end up in a rather long list that is evaluated by the SAP NetWeaver BW team for inclusion in the SAP NetWeaver BW scope.

Often, to keep the process of determining new SAP NetWeaver BW scope more efficient, the process teams that are supporting or implementing the various modules of SAP ECC can help with this effort. For example, if a finance report is requested, the finance team should first evaluate and prioritize these requests and then provide them to the SAP NetWeaver BW team, rather than having the list of these requests given to the SAP NetWeaver BW team immediately.

In order for the finance team to help in this evaluation, they often need a report-determination matrix to allow the finance team members to look at the requested inventory of reports and triage them into the area that they are best suited. Figure 5.4 shows an example of a report-determination matrix that could be used by the process teams to help determine which reporting system should be used to provide the analysis to the end users.

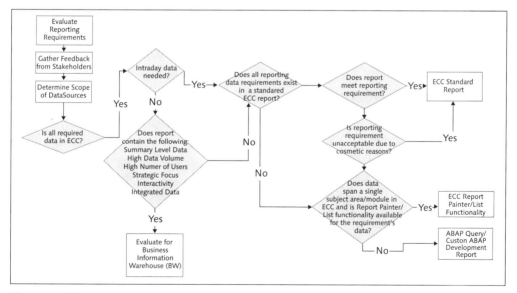

Figure 5.4 Report Determination Matrix

Typically, a dialog is needed between the SAP NetWeaver BW team and the process teams to complete the SAP NetWeaver BW scope. This allows the process teams to begin questioning the business users requesting the new reporting functionality to make sure that this can be evaluated most efficiently.

Often, the next step in any project is to gather up all the existing reports and proceed to plan how these can be duplicated in the SAP NetWeaver BW system. Projects frequently create a full report inventory to track the current reports and map them to new SAP NetWeaver BW reports. Let's look at this approach now.

5.2 Information Request Form

Interviewing end users may not be feasible all the time due to their global presence in a multi-region SAP NetWeaver BW implementation. For this reason, you may need to create a simple information request form that will ask all the necessary information related to SAP NetWeaver BW requirements. This should include at least the following fields:

- Contact information of the requester
- Department
- Name of the report
- Purpose of the report
- Description of the report
- Number of users expected to use this report
- Type of users
- Frequency of the report
- Required fields
- Optional fields
- Security requirements
- Comments.

Generally, these kinds of forms are created in Microsoft Word or Excel and posted in an intranet where end-users will have easy access to this form.

5.3 Gathering a Report Inventory

While determining reporting requirements in new implementation of a subject area in SAP NetWeaver BW, process teams often spend a great deal of time gathering up existing report inventories. For example, a company that is replacing a legacy system with the SAP R/3 or SAP ECC equivalent gets a large binder of sample reports from the legacy system. This is supposed to be used to track existing reports so they can eventually be mapped into the SAP NetWeaver BW system.

In most cases, this effort does not yield many useful results. This is because typically there cannot be a one-to-one correspondence between the legacy reporting system and the new SAP NetWeaver BW system. Typically, the new system and the legacy system track and record data in different ways, so the data analysis needs are different.

Trying to map the legacy reports to new SAP NetWeaver BW reports often leaves the process teams frustrated. Sometimes, it keeps them thinking in the legacy system's terms and analysis needs. For example, suppose a company is moving its inventory distribution functions from a legacy system to a new SAP ECC system. The analysis from the SAP ECC system will be performed in the SAP NetWeaver BW system.

The legacy system measured inventory obsolescence by determining orders and stock movements on inventory. If the user of this legacy system is to measure the same obsolescence in SAP NetWeaver BW from a new SAP SAP ECC transactional source, he might look to the same formula to determine obsolete items.

Thus, the business SME might ask for an obsolescence report with the same formula. This would not take into account some of the new functionality in SAP to track missed sales and other functions for planning, and inventory analysis. Because SAP ECC has other tools for measuring and tracking obsolescence, the old factors may no longer be valid, or may be enhanced with new features from SAP ECC. Often, if a report inventory is used, the business limits its thinking on those reports to an exact or close match of the reports without proper analysis of the functionality of SAP ECC.

In some cases, this works fine, while in others, it may not be as effective. Often, it is more advantageous to track the analysis requirements and not match these requirements one-for-one with the report inventory. This allows the analysis needs to be driven by the reporting requirements and not the reporting inventory. This can yield new thinking on the new transactional data and often gives more meaningful reporting requirements than trying to map to existing reports.

> **Note**
>
> ▶ Avoid creating full inventory of all reports in the organization. The top five (most used) reports from each department should cover most of the requirement.
>
> ▶ A single SAP NetWeaver BW report can satisfy dozens of legacy static reports. So, never directly map legacy reports with SAP NetWeaver BW reports.

Once these requirements have been established, the next step is to get more detail behind each of these requirements. It is not always easy to get all the answers needed to begin developing in SAP NetWeaver BW. A document is needed that gathers all the requirements from the end user and matches them with some expertise from the SAP NetWeaver BW team to develop and agree on the scope of each subject area that will be analyzed.

The best way to get more details about the scope and to come to agreement on what needs to be delivered is via a functional model document. Let's explore this document and how it can be used to help gather and organize the requirements.

5.4   Functional Model Document

Once the business needs have been clearly established during the interview process, and the reporting functionality is determined to be in scope for SAP NetWeaver BW, the next step in developing an understanding and agreement of scope is to develop a *functional model document*. This document serves as a template of the initial scope of what will be delivered in SAP NetWeaver BW. A sample of this document can be found in Appendix C.

> **Note**
>
> The functional model document is a vital step in the SAP NetWeaver BW requirements gathering process. The better the effort up front getting this document as robust as possible, the better and more efficient the implantation process.

In most cases, there are two groups that need to agree on scope. One is the business process teams that are providing the business needs and asking that these business needs be represented in SAP NetWeaver BW. The other party involved is the actual SAP NetWeaver BW team that would provide and implement the need in the SAP NetWeaver BW product. Getting clear agreement between these two teams is vital to a successful project.

> **Note**
>
> The most common reason for an SAP NetWeaver BW project to fail is lack of agreement on the scope and lack of understanding of the requirements between the SAP NetWeaver BW team and the process teams providing the requirements.

There are several reasons why the process of getting the scope agreement is difficult. Usually, there is a combination of the following factors:

- Process teams have not completely decided on their own needs.
- Communicating needs of the process team is difficult.
- The process teams do not understand the SAP NetWeaver BW tool.
- SAP NetWeaver BW team does not understand the process team's analysis or transactional needs.
- Neither team understands one or many legacy systems needed to provide the analysis.

From my experience, the best way to get the business process teams to help the SAP NetWeaver BW teams and business process teams to agree on their scope is to work together to develop a functional model document. Basically, this document acts as a template for the process teams to communicate their needs and the SAP NetWeaver BW team to ask questions to refine those needs. This functional model document process works no matter what subject matter data is being brought into SAP NetWeaver BW and regardless of source.

> **Tip**
>
> The functional model document should be considered the responsibility of the process teams to complete.

This document should be listed and tracked as a deliverable of the process team. The reason this is considered a process-team deliverable and not a SAP NetWeaver BW team deliverable is because you want to shift the analysis gathering and ownership to the process teams. This gives them the incentive to gather and own the functional model document, because without a completed functional model document, no development can take place in the SAP NetWeaver BW system. This gives the process teams some ownership of the requirement.

In one of my projects, the project manager referred to the functional model document as the process team's ante. Like a player *ante-ing up* in a poker game, the process teams are forced to bring something to the table before anything other than preliminary analysis is done on the requirements.

Often, the process teams will scrutinize their analysis needs and set priorities better if they are forced to write a functional model document for the reporting requirements that are needed.

Without this ante, the process teams often gather up reporting requirements in a spreadsheet list and present this to the SAP NetWeaver BW team and ask the SAP NetWeaver BW team to fill in the details of the scope. This is not only an inefficient use of the SAP NetWeaver BW team's time; it often leads to conflict later because the needs are not clearly understood and therefore not clearly met in the design.

Even though the functional model document is primarily owned by the process teams, it should not be considered a document that is solely developed by the process teams. The document requires a lot of back and forth from the SAP NetWeaver BW team to complete all the sections.

Understanding the security requirements and functionality of SAP NetWeaver BW is often a complex task. The functional model document needs to clearly state the security requirements, but the SAP NetWeaver BW team should help to steer the security requirements dialog to represent what eventually will be possible in the SAP NetWeaver BW system.

The functional model document is designed to be a blueprint to begin creating a SAP NetWeaver BW physical data model. However, during the process of creating, refining, and completing the functional model document, there should be no talk of InfoCubes, DSO structures, or any physical SAP NetWeaver BW tables.

Once the functional model document is complete and the needs are better known, the SAP NetWeaver BW team takes it and uses it to create a physical model, including InfoCubes, DSOs, etc.

5.4.1 How Many Functional Model Documents are Needed?

In most SAP NetWeaver BW projects, multiple functional model documents need to be developed. One functional model document should be implemented for each *subject area*. A subject area can include many different interpretations. The subject area is not always designed only to reflect one actual business area, such as sales and distribution, or purchasing. This is because there are many SAP NetWeaver BW teams who track their scope at a more granular level than simply by business area.

To determine the subject areas in an SAP NetWeaver BW project, the scope should be examined to determine where different sub-groups of the SAP NetWeaver BW team would be used to implement the functionality needed.

For example, in some SAP NetWeaver BW teams, procurement would be considered a subject area. The SAP NetWeaver BW team would scope, staff, and deliver the procurement needs as a group deliverable. In this case, the procurement area would be one subject area, and one functional model document would be produced for purchasing.

In other projects, procurement is much more complex and would be delivered as more than one sub-group. For example, there may be one sub-group that delivers the purchasing, another that does vendor performance, and another that might deliver the receipt tracking.

If these sub-groups require significant work, involve significant scope, and answer different business questions, they require individual functional model documents to track and deliver their scope.

The functional model document can be time consuming to create if there are many sections that need to be completed. Too many subject areas require a great deal of time from the process teams. This should be weighed against the business needs. If multiple business needs can be clearly captured in one functional model document, it is fine to combine the business needs into one document; however, each need should be clearly understood and documented.

5.4.2 Sections of the Functional Model Document

Figure 5.5 shows several sections to the functional model document. Each section needs collaboration between the SAP NetWeaver BW team and the process teams to complete. Each section allows as many of the requirements to be understood and documented. This is the template for all future development.

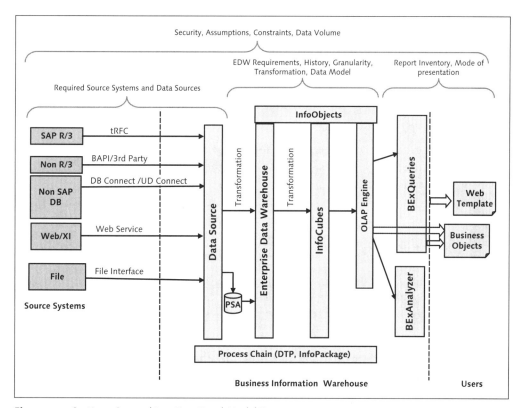

Figure 5.5 Sections Covered in a Functional Model Document

Subject Area

Each functional model should cover one subject area. The definition of subject area can vary by project and scope, but the subject area represents one area of SAP NetWeaver BW implementation that can be tracked and staffed as one unit of work.

Business Questions Asked and Answered

This section of the functional model document gives an overall understanding of the business pains and the questions that this functional model should answer once implemented. Although this appears to be an easy section to complete, it is often the one that process teams have trouble completing fully. The business questions detailed in this section are used for several things, which include the following:

▸ To help to make sure that the SAP NetWeaver BW team understands the business pain and the business analysis needs

▸ To allow the physical SAP NetWeaver BW model to be developed with specific needs in mind

▸ To help when questions arise that there is a foundation for the business analysis needs.

These business questions will also be used as a foundation for the test cases in the future, to make sure that the physical model, once implemented, answers the questions posed in this section.

These questions should be in bullet format, be listed with specific measurements, and include time horizons. In most cases, there are several of these questions posed for each functional model. Examples include:

▸ To measure and track vendor performance to determine on-time delivery based on purchase order expected dates and actual receipt dates across months

▸ To track inventory turns based on stock items across fiscal periods to determine stock availability levels

▸ To manage and track the voluntary turnover of a division in the calendar year based on the employee headcount.

History Requirements of Information

The history requirements help to define the information and source of data for the solution. If history is required, it is important to understand what history and how much history are required to complete the model. This is most important to understand when legacy systems are involved.

> **Example**
>
> A new SAP ECC implementation with sales and distribution data requires some reporting from the SAP NetWeaver BW system. To provide that, the assumption is that the data needed for the reporting would come out of SAP ECC as its sole DataSource. However, unless history is being loaded into SAP ECC and converted to SAP ECC SD orders, there will be little meaningful data to support reporting.

Many projects need to have the legacy data loaded into the SAP NetWeaver BW system and require that this data be harmonized with the SAP ECC data so they can compare and provide analysis. It can be time consuming to map the legacy fields, master data, etc., to the SAP ECC data. Understanding these requirements early helps to define and understand the scope of the reporting needs.

DataSources Required to Complete the Model

DataSources are the places where data is stored currently and the scope of data to be loaded into the model. This section of the functional model typically requires input from the SAP NetWeaver BW team. The goal of this section is to see what data is needed to satisfy the reporting requirements and where it is found. This section should concentrate on the transactional DataSources. It may require, in some cases, to analyze the specific fields of data. You will probably need to compare the fields to the existing standard content DataSources.

For example, this section should state if data is to come from an external system, SAP ECC or SAP R/3 systems, Advanced Planning and Optimization (APO), etc. It should clearly state the specific area of the system from which data is to be extracted. If the data is to come from a legacy purchasing system, this section should clearly state the system name, the tables, or files that are needed to load this data into SAP NetWeaver BW, and some information about this data.

If the data is to come from the SAP ECC or SAP R/3 system, the SAP NetWeaver BW team should work with the process team to analyze standard delivered Business Content DataSource extractors to determine which of these matches the data that is to be extracted. This helps to establish the scope and number of DataSources that will be needed to satisfy the reporting requirements.

Volume, System, Frequency

Understanding the volume of data that is required helps to set the eventual data model. If data volume is substantial, the data needs to be partitioned into multiple

ODS/DSO structures or multiple InfoCubes when eventually loading the data into SAP NetWeaver BW. Understanding this volume helps plan and scope out any potential performance issues that could bottleneck loading or query processing.

It is also helpful to know the frequency with which data is required for analysis. This helps to spot possible needs for intra-day loads or real-time analysis. Typically, if real-time analysis of data is needed, this involves a much more significant effort during the SAP NetWeaver BW implementation. Often, real-time analysis is better handled in the source system. The functional model can help to show these requirements so they can be managed.

> **Example**
>
> If sales-order data is to be extracted from a legacy system, this section might state that the sales orders will be extracted on a daily basis once a day, after midnight, with the approximate volume of 2,000 orders a day with approximately five lines on each order.

Dependencies, Constraints, Assumptions

Sometimes, data cannot be loaded until after a certain procedure or load is run on either the SAP ECC or legacy system. It is helpful to know about any constraints or dependencies so that you can plan the data model accordingly. It also helps to spell out the assumptions regarding the data at an early phase to make sure that these assumptions are shared by the SAP NetWeaver BW and the process teams.

> **Tip**
>
> A billing document should only be extracted after the billing run is complete. It should be noted when the billing run typically completes and what other dependencies are needed as a result. This allows for the SAP NetWeaver BW team to plan the data loads around these constraints.

This section is also good to clarify any assumptions that have been made on the SAP NetWeaver BW data. If the data needs to be verified or checked against other tables to ensure that the data is valid, this can be stated in this section.

Transformation of Data Required

Often, some type of transformation of data is required to meet a business need. This transformation can often require significant time from the SAP NetWeaver BW development team. It is difficult to determine all transformations of data until the data is loaded. However, those transformations of data that are recognized early should be clearly spelled out in the functional model document.

For instance, legacy data often needs to have its master data objects transformed into SAP objects. If legacy sales data is being extracted and will be compared with the SAP R/3 or SAP ECC data, this data must be shown to the user using a common customer and material. Often, the legacy system has its own master data values.

To get the data harmonized, the data needs to be transformed in SAP NetWeaver BW into the SAP master data objects. The customer data would need to read a cross-reference table, and the SAP customer would replace the legacy customer number. The same process would be needed for material, vendor, etc.

The transformation needs that are identified early can then be planned as part of the SAP NetWeaver BW project plan. In the previous example, the SAP NetWeaver BW team would need to make sure that they also populated the cross-reference tables to map the legacy customer to the SAP customer. This data would need to be tracked and stored in a logical format and a methodology created to keep these tables up-to-date. A process would also have to be designed to determine what would happen if a customer is in the legacy extract and there is no entry in the cross-reference table.

Understanding the transformations needed enables you to properly plan and organize the data needs to ensure that a process is in place to develop the transformations and deliver the infrastructure needed.

Functional Model Diagram to Show Flow and Data Model

Often, a diagram of the functional model is helpful to see all the data and the sources feeding this data. This diagram can be used later when the model is being evaluated to determine if it meets the needs of the organization.

This diagram represents the different dependencies and the flow of the data into the SAP NetWeaver BW system. This is often helpful in understanding that the feed of the data might come from SAP, but that the data may have originated in a legacy system first, and then was fed to SAP ECC and then onto SAP NetWeaver BW. Understanding the flow of the data through the organization allows for a clearer understanding of the dependencies involved.

Presentation Requirements

The presentation requirements refer to the actual queries, dashboards, etc., that will be used to show the data in SAP NetWeaver BW to the end users.

When the functional model document is being developed, the presentation needs should be understood, but the main focus of the functional model document should be on understanding the information that is needed to deliver the model.

This section should spell out the presentation needs, but it is typically not necessary to list all queries or analysis needs in detail. There is a basic understanding that as long as the DataSources are clearly spelled out, that data is being loaded into SAP NetWeaver BW. The presentation needs can be flexible and based on the needs of the organization. Thus, in this section, only the most vital presentation needs should be listed, with an understanding that the presentation layer of SAP NetWeaver BW can be flexible to provide many different forms of analysis, as long as the source of data for the analysis is in SAP NetWeaver BW.

This section should also list the audience and the form of distribution for the presentation. It is helpful to understand the roles of the SAP NetWeaver BW users and how they will be accessing the presentation to understand and plan its delivery. This section should state whether Web or portal access is required and if Microsoft Excel functionality will be used in reporting.

Security Requirements

Understanding and implementing security requirements are often left until the end of the SAP NetWeaver BW build process. This can be a mistake. If the security requirements are known from the beginning, the model can be planned and presentation of data developed using the security requirements. If the security needs to be retrofitted into an existing complete model, some rework may be needed to complete the security requirements.

This section should state if the security is not needed at all. If it is needed, how should the security be implemented? Is the security by query? Are there certain key figure values in the data that are sensitive and thus should be protected? Are there certain characteristics that should be secured? For example, if several divisions of sales data are being loaded into SAP NetWeaver BW, should all divisions be allowed to see each other's sales? Is there a restriction on any other characteristic of the data?

This section should be filled out and verified before any modeling can begin. However, often this section should also be reviewed multiple times during the implementation.

There was one finance SAP NetWeaver BW project where the idea of security needs was repeatedly rejected. The process teams clearly stated that all data could be seen by anyone who could access any of the finance queries. The model was based on these requirements.

Later, as the implementation was getting ready for integration testing, the testers saw that there were research divisions whose queries should not be shown to other finance users. Otherwise, users could see budgets and planning of research that was considered confidential in the company.

The finance team was unaware of this restriction, and we were forced to retrofit the security in a design that was already complete. Had they known about this requirement, they may have designed the data model to exclude queries to exclude this data. They were forced to add the security after the fact, and it challenged their time line for implementation and rollout.

Sign-Off

To make sure that all groups are in agreement on the functional model document, a signoff process should be established. This way, any changes to the functional model can be discussed as a scope-change process. No development or planning on the SAP NetWeaver BW physical model should commence until the functional model document receives signoff.

Once the functional model has been completed, the next step is to get more detail and uniformity around some of the measures that are requested in the functional model document(s). The best method to provide some uniformity and structure is with a key figure matrix or KPI matrix. Let's look at this document next.

5.5   SAP NetWeaver BW Key Figure or KPI Matrix

After the functional model document is complete, many project teams find that there are several key figure or key performance indicator (KPI) values that are used universally in the organization. Often, these are used so commonly in the organization that few stop to ask what calculation was used to arrive at the value.

Common KPI values are Mean Absolute Deviation (MAD) and Mean Absolute Percentage Error (MAPE). These totals need to be universal in the organization to provide meaningful measurement and tracking.

Often, while implementing an SAP NetWeaver BW project, it becomes clear that different organizations might calculate the MAD or MAPE differently. This can lead to conflict when trying to implement SAP NetWeaver BW. Unless the business organizations settle on one measurement for the KPI values, the SAP NetWeaver BW team cannot implement these KPIs.

To proactively manage and encourage decision-making based on these values, it is helpful to make sure that the organization has one common list of their KPIs, with the calculations of these values clearly spelled out. This can often become a political discussion, as the organization settles on national and even global standards. However, it is vital before implementation to make sure that these discussions do not affect the SAP NetWeaver BW time line. If a KPI matrix is developed and signed off by the organization, the SAP NetWeaver BW team can work from this document to make sure that all KPIs reflect the calculation agreements of the organization.

5.6 Steps to Obtain SAP NetWeaver BW Star Schema Model from the KPI Matrix

After determining your SAP NetWeaver BW key figures or KPI matrix, the next step is to determine the SAP NetWeaver BW star schema model in detail. One way to achieve this is to create an Entity Relationship Model diagram, which provides a good base for building multidimensional modeling. However, most customers refuse this approach because of the underlying complexity. In the following subsection, we'll design the SAP NetWeaver BW star schema model using Microsoft Excel.

5.6.1 Step 1: Determine Business Subjects

In general, business subjects are known as Characteristics with Master Data in SAP NetWeaver BW terminology. An organization may have many business subjects like Customer, Business Unit, and Product etc. In this step, you'll determine all the business subjects and their attributes. Attributes of a business subject should have a 1:N relationship. In Figure 5.6, a customer can have a customer group, country, and address as its attribute with a 1:N relationship so you can model these attributes together with "Product" business subject. There may be some scenario like a customer being assigned with multiple business units. Here, the relationship is N:M. In this case, colors cannot be added with "Customer" master data.

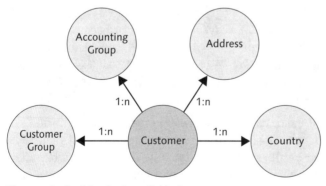

Figure 5.6 Deriving Business Subjects

5.6.2 Step 2: Assign Business Subjects to Key Figure

In this step, you'll determine key figures for different business subjects. For example, a sales volume key figure can be described with a sales organization, product, customer, site, etc. In Microsoft Excel, you can put these assignments as shown in Figure 5.7.

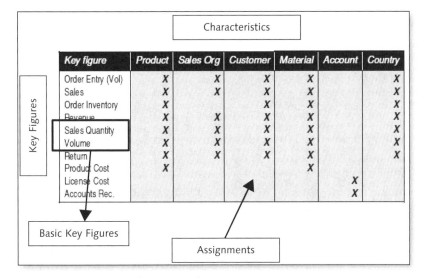

Key figure	Product	Sales Org	Customer	Material	Account	Country
Order Entry (Vol)	X	X	X	X		X
Sales	X	X	X	X		X
Order Inventory	X		X	X		X
Revenue	X	X	X	X		X
Sales Quantity	X	X	X	X		X
Volume	X	X	X	X		X
Return	X	X	X	X		X
Product Cost	X			X		
License Cost					X	
Accounts Rec.					X	

Characteristics

Key Figures

Basic Key Figures

Assignments

Figure 5.7   Assignments of Business Subjects to Various Key Figures

5.6.3 Step 3: Determine Strong Entities and Granularity

In this step, you design your model with time dimensions. Granularity of the data depends on the time dimension. So, get an agreement from the customer before defining this. There are other entities that are strongly tied with key figures but have N:M relationships with other business subjects. Document Number is a good example of this. It's always advisable to put this kind of entity in a different dimension.

5.6.4 Step 4: Join Similar Key Figures

As shown in Figure 5.8, you will integrate sales quantity and volume in same Info-Cube because they have the same business subject assignments. Other key figures like sales and revenue can be determined from basic key figures in the query.

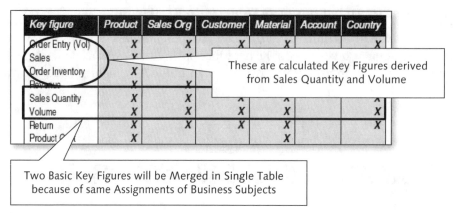

Key figure	Product	Sales Org	Customer	Material	Account	Country
Order Entry (Vol)	X	X	X	X		X
Sales	X	X				
Order Inventory	X					
Revenue	X	X				
Sales Quantity	X	X	X	X		X
Volume	X	X	X	X		X
Return	X	X	X	X		X
Product	X			X		

These are calculated Key Figures derived from Sales Quantity and Volume

Two Basic Key Figures will be Merged in Single Table because of same Assignments of Business Subjects

Figure 5.8 Joining Similar Key Figures

In a real world scenario, obtaining and documenting an SAP NetWeaver BW star schema model is a tedious and time-consuming process. It is always advisable to create prototype applications in parallel with work shop sessions with end users. Simultaneous interaction with end users and building prototype will help you to model a robust SAP NetWeaver BW data model.

5.7 Budgeting or Estimating SAP NetWeaver BW Time Lines

It is challenging in any project to estimate the time line and therefore the budget needed for the project. There are many factors involved the calculation, and many of these factors are unknown or outside of the control of the project. This is typically the reason that estimates can be inaccurate.

However, to set an initial budget, a time line needs to be determined. The only way to determine the number of days for a project is to break down the days into the primary tasks that need to be completed and assign a level of effort and number of days for each. The aggregate of the days, multiplied by the complexity becomes the estimated number of days. These days can then be multiplied by a rate per day to determine the budget.

There are several steps to budgeting and estimating the SAP NetWeaver BW time line, which are examined here:

▶ **Size SAP NetWeaver BW Effort Based on Scope Presented**
This allows a clear understanding of what is requested for implementation. This is typically done as part of the functional model document.

▶ **Prioritize**
Set priorities based on the functional models to determine the time lines needed for each.

▶ **Plan Delivery**
Often, there are organizational constraints on when functionality can be rolled out. These factors need to be weighed in budgeting steps.

▶ **Plan Resources**
Based on the effort, scope, and delivery schedule, the resource plan can be developed.

Developing a clear formula to estimate time lines and budgets is difficult in any project. This becomes even more difficult in SAP NetWeaver BW projects because so many factors are involved in the calculation. We will describe factors that are used and a basic formula that can determine the time line needed for the SAP NetWeaver BW implementation. This can then be applied to the resource plan to determine the budget and cost of the project.

The following subsections explain the factors involved in estimating the time and therefore the budget needed to deliver the SAP NetWeaver BW solution. A time estimate should be given to each factor based on the resource plan. Let's look at these now.

Complexity Factor (1 to 5)

The first step in estimating the time line for an SAP NetWeaver BW project is to understand the complexity factor involved in the project. This complexity factor is used in the time line calculation as a multiplier, as seen here:

▶ **Complexity Factor One**
A project complexity factor of one is the least complex project. These projects typically involve all Business Content and are usually straightforward in design. Most of the project time is spent evaluating the Business Content and ensuring that the content matches the requirements. There is usually some development work on the queries; however, little development work is required to get the data extracted from the source and get this data loaded into SAP NetWeaver BW. These projects always involve only one source, SAP R/3 or SAP ECC.

▶ **Complexity Factor Two**
These projects usually involve a small amount of development effort on the loading of SAP NetWeaver BW and some simple transformations of data into the SAP NetWeaver BW system. There is usually some query development, and the data is typically coming from only one source.

▶ **Complexity Factor Three**

These projects often involve more than one source system, but the source data is not complex. The source data often resides in legacy systems that do not require a significant amount of transformation. This is then harmonized with the SAP or SAP ECC data to provide reporting to the end user. These projects often involve some significant query design.

▶ **Complexity Factor Four**

These projects often involve multiple modules of SAP R/3 or SAP ECC or multiple source systems. The data requires some transformation in many areas. These projects also require some significant query design efforts.

▶ **Complexity Factor Five**

These are the most complex projects and usually involve multiple source systems and multiple subject areas to be loaded into SAP NetWeaver BW. Little standard Business Content is to be used to realize the solution, other than the standard DataSources in the SAP ECC or SAP R/3 system. Often, these projects involve significant transformation and harmonization efforts to bring the data from multiple source systems into one system and report the data as if it came from one source.

Often, projects that are implementing the SAP APO system fall into complexity factor five. These types of projects typically bring data from multiple source systems, and then pass this data over to the APO system. They often also bring dates from the APO system into SAP NetWeaver BW for reporting of planning vs. actual data.

Once the complexity factor is established, the next step is to establish a time estimate of the most time-consuming tasks of the project. These tasks will later be multiplied by the complexity factor to come up with a project time estimate.

Project Management Time

This is the time dedicated to the early analysis of the solution, gathering the resources needed to understand the solution and set the infrastructure needed to implement the SAP NetWeaver BW system. If this is a new implementation, allow much more time to establish review standards, naming standards, etc.

Education

This time estimate depends on the knowledge level of the people who will be implementing the product. The time needed should not only include the time in training to understand and grasp the SAP NetWeaver BW product but also some ramp-up time to build on the knowledge in the SAP NetWeaver BW solution. If an upgrade is planned, some time should be allowed for understanding the new upgrade and the new features in that release.

The education day estimate should also include the number of days that will be used understanding and getting any developers or consultants to understand the business aspects of the solution being implemented. This often involves several workshops or interview sessions to understand the business environment.

Interviews

The interview time estimate is a prediction of the time needed for conducting interviews with the process teams and the business SMEs to understand the business analysis needs and solutions requested. These interview sessions estimates should not only include the actual interview time but also the time needed to prepare for the interviews and the time needed to document the results and follow-up from the interviews.

Modeling Workshops

The modeling workshop time approximation represents the time needed to meet with the SMEs and business process representatives to understand their business issues and needs for analysis. This is typically not a great deal of time but should be provided for in the overall time estimate.

Functional Model Development

The functional model development usually takes most of the time of the analysis phase. The time to complete this is often one of the longest time allocations of the project, other than the realization and the testing. This time estimate needs to take into account the time it takes to understand the business needs and fill out the entire functional model document. This also should include some time to review and ask for revisions to the document.

Business Content Review

This often takes a few days to review the content and understand how the content can match the business requirements. Often, some of this time in any project is because almost all projects that extract data from the SAP ECC or SAP R/3 system use Business Content DataSources to extract data from the SAP ECC or SAP R/3 system.

Physical Design

The physical design estimate is the time that it takes to fully design the solution on paper. This involves reading over the functional model document, reviewing the Business Content to make sure that the design can be realized in the SAP NetWeaver BW system, and understanding how the design will be implemented. This often takes less than half of the time that it takes to develop the functional model document.

Design Realization (Build)

The design realization phase is often the second-longest time allocation in the project (the longest is typically the testing phase). This phase expands with new releases and new functionality.

Tuning

The tuning phase occurs at varying stages of the project and involves Basis tuning, database tuning, and tuning of the application. This time estimate should be much higher if you are implementing a new release of SAP NetWeaver BW in the earlier stages of release. There is often much time spent applying SAP Notes and working through software issues.

Testing

Testing is often one of the most significant time estimates in the project because it not only involves several phases of unit, string, and integration testing but also involves issue tracking and resolution. This should be given the largest time estimate in the project.

Security

Security is dependent on the complexity of the authorization strategy and the amount of roles required to implement the solution. This should also include the time for setting up the users in the various systems.

Transports

Transports in SAP NetWeaver BW are much more complex than in the SAP ECC or SAP R/3 environments, and thus significantly more time should be allowed for this process. It can often take four days to move a solution up to another environment. This time is dependent on the number of transports that are associated with the design. If a design is kept in the development environment longer, the number of transports decreases, and the time for transporting decreases as well.

Rollout

The rollout timeline involves turning on the solution to the various users and the training of the power users on the solution. This depends on the logistics of the power users, their ability, and the timing of the training. This should also include time for training development.

Change Management

Change management timing involves the time it takes to make the solution available to the end users. This often involves end user training, job aids, website development, deployment plans, etc. The change management effort can vary widely depending on the new job functions created as a result of the implementation.

Post-Implementation

The post-implementation time estimate should include the time it takes to transition the solution to the production support organization. It should also allow time for a post-implementation review of the solution and a lessons-learned session. This time can significantly be reduced based on the quality of the documentation and the knowledge of the production support organization of the SAP NetWeaver BW product.

> **Note: Formula**
>
> SAP NetWeaver BW Implementation Timeline = (Project Management Time + Education + Interview Time + Modeling Workshops + Functional Model Development Business Content Review + Physical Design + Design Realization + Tuning + Testing + Security + Transports + Rollout + Change Management + Post Implementation) × (Complexity Factor).

Although this formula seems complex, it can be broken down into estimates in a spreadsheet and used for preliminary budgeting and time line purposes. Because the formula takes into account many of the most time-consuming tasks and also allows for a complexity factor, it provides a basic estimate of the time line of the project. In many cases, this estimate is not too far off what is eventually realized.

In most cases where the formula result differs from the actual time line, this is because the complexity factor is set too low. Often, a model that is assumed to be easy turns out to be more complex as more is known; this pushes all the pieces of the calculation off, and the entire project estimate is not valid.

Once the functional model, KPI or key figure matrix, and budget/time estimate is complete, it is now time to begin to take the requirements and determine how this model should exist in the SAP NetWeaver BW system. This becomes the SAP NetWeaver BW physical model. Let's explore this next.

5.8 SAP NetWeaver BW Physical Model

Once the functional model and star schema models are complete, the next step is to create a SAP NetWeaver BW physical model document. This document shows the various DataSources, InfoCubes, DSOs, etc. It should clearly flow out all the data being loaded into the model and should clearly state the volume of data that will be loaded from each source.

Creating the physical model requires understanding of the functionality and development process of the SAP NetWeaver BW system. This task is typically performed by a group familiar with the SAP NetWeaver BW system and also someone well versed in the business requirements and analysis needs of the organization. In most projects, this is the data architect.

The first step in developing the physical model is to gather the requirements from the functional model document and break the requirements down into data requirements. This allows the team to understand where the data is to come from and how this data is to be presented to the end user. Understanding this helps to know what data needs to be transformed and what data needs to be harmonized with other data.

In understanding the harmonizing needs of the organization, the physical model can be established to make sure that the data that needs to be combined together is linked properly. For example, if the organization needs to track vendor performance, it may need to track purchases, good receipts, and even accounts payable information. To develop a physical model, these different areas must have a common link at least with the vendor that links the data.

The various InfoCubes and DSO structures can be planned based on the analysis needs. In many cases, the data volume also is a big factor in determining the physical data model. As a general rule, it is better to have many smaller InfoCubes or DSO structures with different slices of the data than it is to have one large structure. This is because performance during loading and query analysis typically suffers if one large structure is used.

In my experience, the best way to start this process it to look at all the requirements and begin to *whiteboard* the model and flow of data through the SAP NetWeaver BW system. This allows the requirements to be seen by the interested members of the SAP NetWeaver BW team and also allows them to measure the SAP NetWeaver

BW physical model against the requirements that have been established in the functional model document.

This whiteboard physical model is then used as a template for refinements and eventually the model that is realized in the SAP NetWeaver BW system. These whiteboard sessions allow a starting point and avoid paralysis in analyzing and re-analyzing the requirements. It gives the team something to build from. This task is usually performed by the data architect in the presence of various SAP NetWeaver BW team members.

The data architect and SAP NetWeaver BW team members should use best practices when developing the physical model. To make sure that the standards are known and that all parties are using the same set of standards, let's explore some common standards.

Many organizations have documented physical modeling standards to make sure that any data model that is developed is consistent and can work with other data models that are developed.

The Standard Data Model shown in Figure 5.9 is described below in detail. These are common standards and are not absolute rules. There are many legitimate cases where the standards are not valid based on the needs of the organization or implantation or system constraints:

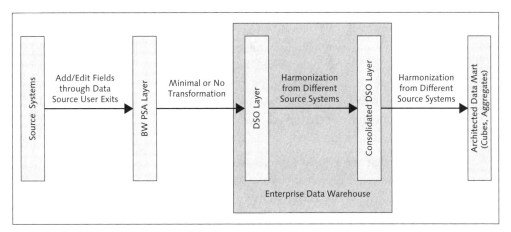

Figure 5.9 Standard Physical DWH Modeling

▶ All SAP NetWeaver BW structures built should follow clear standards developed by the SAP NetWeaver BW data architect. These include best practices on development, naming standards, security, presentation, etc.

- ▶ All data should first load into a DSO structure and not directly into an InfoCube. This allows for the raw data to be available in SAP NetWeaver BW without aggregation to other DSO or InfoCubes.
- ▶ All data should be loaded to the first level DSO with minimal or no transformation. This allows for this data to be used elsewhere in SAP NetWeaver BW without having to untransform the data. It also allows for easier reconciliation reporting.
- ▶ A consolidation layer DSO should be established whenever possible to allow for data from various sources to be harmonized and reported together.
- ▶ Few changes should be made to standard InfoObjects in SAP NetWeaver BW. For example, changing the standard customer InfoObject 0CUSTOMER to ZCUSTOMER precludes this from being combined and reported with any future analysis that includes 0CUSTOMER.
- ▶ Appending new fields onto existing master data or transactional InfoObjects, InfoCubes, and DSO structures should be encouraged. For example, a new field that has been added to the customer table in SAP ECC can easily be appended to the SAP NetWeaver BW master data 0CUSTOMER object and mapped via a change to the DataSource on the SAP ECC system. This is the preferred method for modifying existing structures.
- ▶ Think globally when developing the model. If the existing physical model is not designed for global reporting, it should allow for extraction to other sources that can consolidate the data into a global model.
- ▶ The model should be constantly checked to prevent future reloads and restatements of data. This can be prevented by leveraging master data or making sure re-stateable fields are read from navigational or display attributes of existing master data values rather than write the values into the transactional data.
- ▶ All ABAP code transformations should be reviewed for consistency and to make sure they are following good coding standards.

To make sure that the physical model is sound, it is best to analyze the volume, presentation, and harmonization needs to make sure that the physical model can deliver the analysis to the end user.

Often, the best place to start with the physical data model is with the Business Content. This allows a clear flow and understanding of a predelivered solution as a springboard to help the development process. Let's look at the Business Content next.

5.9   Business Content Evaluation

SAP Business Content is a series of predelivered DataSource extractors, InfoCubes, ODS or DataStore Objects, InfoObjects, queries, and workbooks, etc. These can be either used exactly as they are delivered or may be modified to allow these objects to be tailored to individual company requirements.

SAP developed the Business Content by analyzing the business needs of customers who have used SAP NetWeaver BW in the past and tracking future trends for analysis in the industry. The goal of Business Content is to allow a company to use some of SAP's expertise and other customer's analysis needs to structure its own analysis environment.

The main goal of the Business Content is speed. It can be activated and filled quickly, often in a matter of days. This allows the SAP NetWeaver BW system to have some productive analysis without a lot of time configuring and analyzing the SAP NetWeaver BW and SAP R/3 or SAP ECC environments. Simply put, the SAP NetWeaver BW Business Content allows SAP NetWeaver BW to be implemented much quicker than a project that had to be completely developed.

Business Content can be powerful for several reasons. If the Business Content fits well with the business requirements, it can be activated, transported, and used in a production environment. It can even be combined with existing structures in a data model, so a SAP NetWeaver BW system can exist with Business Content as well as with custom objects in the same environment.

Business Content can be used during Information Gathering, during building logical data model, and should be used when building physical data model. There are two approaches you can adopt for comparison with your model: Top Down or Key Figure approach and the Bottom Up or DataSource approach.

5.9.1   Key Figure (Top Down) Approach

In this approach, we focus on Key Figures and find corresponding SAP NetWeaver BW objects for comparison. It is important to understand the business behind every model; otherwise, you won't get 100% result only searching by technical names. There may be cases where you may not find some of the Key Figures; these Key Figures may exist as calculated key figures in an SAP NetWeaver BW query. Figure 5.10 shows the steps to be performed for a Top Down comparison approach.

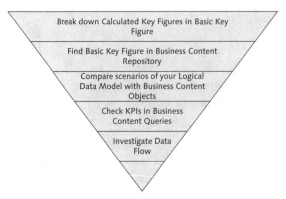

Figure 5.10 Steps for Comparing Business Content in Key Figure–Based Approach

5.9.2 Data Source (Bottom Up) Approach

It is recommended to adopt the Bottom Up approach if you are running SAP R/3 system as your source of data. Once you find your data source, you can search relevant SAP NetWeaver BW objects like InfoObjects, InfoCubes, Transformation Rules, and SAP NetWeaver BW Queries. Figure 5.11 shows the steps to be performed for the Bottom Up approach.

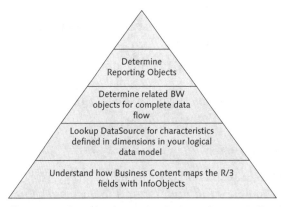

Figure 5.11 Steps for Comparing Business Content in DataSource–Based Approach

5.9.3 Business Content as a Learning Tool

One popular use of the Business Content is as a learning tool. One of the analogies often used is this: It is difficult to build a house if you have never seen one. This is often the case with SAP NetWeaver BW Projects. Customers who are ready to start an SAP NetWeaver BW project often have a difficult time explaining the use of the SAP NetWeaver BW tool.

The Business Content allows them to quickly activate and fill the Business Content DSOs and Cubes and run the predelivered SAP NetWeaver BW queries based on any existing data from the SAP ECC or SAP R/3 systems. This allows the project team and the business users a place to see some queries of *real* data to help them understand the use of the SAP NetWeaver BW tool.

Although this practice can lead to these Business Content structures being used in the production environment, it can just as easily be used as a springboard for a discussion of the existing environment and the various ways that SAP NetWeaver BW can store and present data.

> **Tip**
>
> Although the Business Content is a useful tool, it is not recommended that all Business Content be activated.

Activating a large amount of Business Content takes a great deal of time and would cause many needless InfoCubes, DSO structures, and queries to be activated without the corresponding transactional data to fill them. Thus, only the Business Content that is relevant should be activated to ensure that there is a manageable amount of the content in SAP NetWeaver BW at one time.

Business Content Benefits

There are many benefits to Business Content:

▶ Quick access to extracted information
▶ Ready-to-use reports, data models, extractors, and transformations
▶ Significant reduction of implementation time and costs
▶ Easily extendable to allow modification
▶ Validated and comparable information
▶ Rich set of standard KPIs

Business Content

Business Content can be used as the following:

▶ A complete or partial solution for data analysis needs
▶ A repository of standard requirements and modeling ideas (examples and templates)
▶ A guideline during the implementation of a solution
▶ Powerful learning tool

5.9.4   Evaluating Business Content for Your Needs

The process of evaluating the business requirements involves looking at the reporting inventory, KPI matrix, and any other reporting requirements documentation to determine exactly what reporting demands exist in the organization. To quickly provide value and to leverage what has already been analyzed by SAP, you can look to the Business Content to determine if there is any opportunity to leverage the content DataSources, InfoCubes, DSO structures, queries, or workbooks.

The DataSource represents the extraction method on the SAP R/3 source system. In almost every case, you will look to leverage the DataSource because this will allow you to use the standard extractors in the SAP R/3 system. Almost all standard transaction and master data have existing DataSouces with which to extract data. The following are contained in Business Content:

- Global views and workbooks
- Queries and web templates
- InfoProviders
- Extractors and InfoSources.

The following steps are used to evaluate the Business Content and determine its usefulness for meeting the reporting requirements:

1. **Gather reporting requirements**
   Use the documents from the process teams such as their KPI templates, report templates, and other reporting requirements to determine what the process teams require for reporting. This allows you to understand what Business Content is relevant for activation.

2. **Group reporting requirements**
   Group the reporting requirements so you can determine what requirements are similar, both from a role standpoint and from a data-requirements standpoint. This lets you make sure that you know the organizational roles of those running the reports and what information they are seeking. One way the Business Content is organized is by role, so it helps to know the role of the users running the reports.

3. **Walk through Business Content to determine leveraging opportunities**
   There are various ways to search the Business Content. All Business Content is listed in the help area of SAP NetWeaver BW. The metadata repository is also used to store and present all available and activated Business Content. It is best to search this content either by the DataSource on the SAP ECC or SAP R/3 system or by user role. The role will show those InfoCubes, queries, and/or DSO

objects that are used as part of the role. You can then determine that all or some of the relevant content should be activated.

4. **Activate SAP NetWeaver BW content as necessary**

   If you have determined that the Business Content is relevant for training and/ or possible productive use, you must activate the content. Business Content is activated in the Business Content area of SAP NetWeaver BW.

5. **Activate SAP R/3 or SAP ECC DataSources, if necessary**

   If there are associated DataSources from the SAP R/3 or SAP ECC system that are needed to load the Business Content, you must also activate these in the transactional system. To determine which DataSources are necessary from SAP R/3, you can look at the sources used to feed the needed Business Content, for example, the InfoSource used to load the purchasing data line information is 2LIS_02_SCL. This DataSource would need to be activated in SAP R/3 to load the purchase line item data from SAP R/3 into SAP NetWeaver BW.

6. **Replicate DataSources**

   Replication of the DataSouces matches the DataSources from the SAP R/3 or SAP ECC system with the SAP NetWeaver BW system. This must be done after activation of new DataSources on the SAP R/3 or SAP ECC system to use the DataSource in the SAP NetWeaver BW system. To replicate DataSources, choose transaction RSA1—Administration Workbench. Choose the Source Systems tab and go to the SAP R/3 or SAP ECC system and right click, and then select the Replicate DataSources option.

7. **Load data**

   Use the InfoSource(s) in SAP NetWeaver BW to load the data into the newly activated DSO, InfoCube, or master data records. This process involves following the data flows established as part of the overall SAP NetWeaver BW Business Content design and loading data from the project SAP ECC or SAP R/3 systems into SAP NetWeaver BW to see what the Business Content model looks like with *real* data. This assumes that the data exists on the SAP ECC or SAP R/3 source systems. If the data has not been created, typically this means that the SAP NetWeaver BW team needs to urge the process teams to configure and load the source data.

8. **Analyze Business Content for gaps**

   Evaluate the Business Content to determine how it fits with the requirements. This process includes looking at the various parts of a Business Content section and at the existing requirements to see where the gaps exist. Usually, the best place to start this evaluation is with the delivered queries in the activated Business Content. Once you attempt to match the queries to the business requirements, it is easier to eliminate or include some of the underlying data in the overall assessment to see if it matches the user requirements.

9. **Supplement as necessary**
   If there is a gap between the activated Business Content and the requirements, this content can either be altered directly or can be copied and the new objects changed. If it is a standard master data object such as 0MATERIAL, changes should be made in the standard master data InfoObject. If there are changes needed to DSO or InfoCube structures, these should be copied to new custom InfoCubes or DSO structures using the naming standard document and changes performed directly in the new DSO or InfoCube.

There are two different versions of Business Content:

▶ Content version
▶ Active version.

The content version refers to the delivered content InfoCubes, Queries, etc., of the standard content from SAP. So, this version of the Business Content is configured by SAP and cannot be changed. The active version represents the version that has been activated on an SAP NetWeaver BW system. After activation, the content can be loaded and customized to fit business needs.

When Business Content is activated, it is moved from the content version to the active version. This allows the content version to be upgraded. An upgrade of the Business Content does not affect the active objects used in production. This is because SAP NetWeaver BW only updates the content version of the Business Content and not the active version. If there is new functionality in the content version that is needed, the Business Content must be reactivated to use it.

Thus, modification of SAP SAP NetWeaver BW Business Content does not influence the ability to update in the future. After analyzing the Business Content requirements, the next steps are as follows:

1. **Demo/Present to process teams**
   Once the Business Content is loaded, this can be demonstrated to the process teams to determine the fit with the business requirements.

2. **Perform custom development**
   For those requirements that do not match to Business Content or are radically different from the existing content, custom objects must be created. These could include custom InfoObjects, InfoCubes, or DSO structures.

5.9.5 Using a Subset of the Business Content

In most projects, all of the Business Content is not used. Often, a subset of the content is used. Most projects take advantage of the SAP ECC or SAP R/3 DataSources to extract data from the SAP ECC or SAP R/3 systems. However, as the Business Content data proceeds through its model, less and less of the Business Content is used in organizations.

> **Example**
>
> Suppose that sales order data is loaded from the 2LIS_02_ITM DataSource into a Business Content DSO, and then into a Business Content InfoCube. Queries can be activated to present data from the InfoCube. Many customers use the DataSource, fewer use the DSO, even fewer the InfoCube, and even fewer than that use the queries.

The reason for the scenario taken in this example is that as the model gets more specific, the less chance there is that it matches the needs of the organization, and thus fewer customers choose to use it. This is expected when leveraging the Business Content.

Once the SAP NetWeaver BW design is complete, whether using the Business Content, a completely custom design, or a combination, the design needs to be checked to ensure that it follows project standards. In the next section, we'll walk through the design review process.

5.10 Design Reviews

To complete the design, several design reviews should be anticipated as part of the overall project plan. These design reviews should be considered mandatory and allow for the overall SAP NetWeaver BW data architect and SAP NetWeaver BW project manager to go over the planned designs to make sure that they are logical and conform to the standards established as part of the project.

Usually, the design reviews are conducted at specific stages of the design. The project manager and the SAP NetWeaver BW data architect lead the discussions with the developer and SAP NetWeaver BW process leaders representing the design in their various areas. For example, in a functional design review of the procurement area, the SAP NetWeaver BW project manager, SAP NetWeaver BW data architect, the SAP NetWeaver BW process owner for procurement, and/or any SAP NetWeaver BW developers should be present.

The project management should develop a checklist for each of the following reviews to make sure that at each stage of the review it is clear what is expected and how the review is to be conducted. The review process needs to be non-confrontational and should act as a learning tool for all parties involved. This process helps the project manager and data architect understand all aspects of the design and to speak about each one in a formal setting that allows comment from the developers.

Figure 5.12 shows the most common design reviews recommended as part of the SAP NetWeaver BW implementation strategy. These occur at different stages of the project and allow for a formal check of the process and design. A signoff document and results document should be published after each review to make sure that the results of the review are formally communicated.

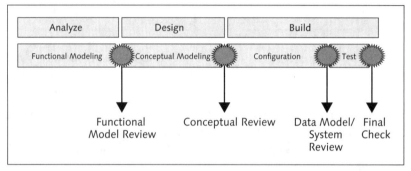

Figure 5.12   SAP NetWeaver BW Design Review Process

5.10.1   Functional Model Review

The functional model review makes sure that the functional model document has all sections filled out clearly and that the functional requirements are clearly understood by the SAP NetWeaver BW team. This review takes place during the analysis phase after the functional model document is complete but before signoff has taken place.

This review allows the SAP NetWeaver BW team to make sure that the scope of the design is clearly understood and that all information is known to make a sound SAP NetWeaver BW physical model from the functional model document.

After signoff of the functional model review, the SAP NetWeaver BW team can begin to develop the physical model. This is simply an SAP NetWeaver BW model on paper, and no system configuration can take place. The physical model document represents what will be delivered in the SAP NetWeaver BW system as a result of the functional model.

5.10.2 Conceptual and Physical Model Review

The conceptual model review covers the physical model documents and design to make sure that the model appears to match the requirements that were laid out in the functional model document. It also ensures that the physical model adheres to sound data modeling design standards.

This review takes place after the physical design is complete on paper but before any building has occurred in the system on that model (other than some prototyping). The goal of the conceptual model is to catch any issues with the design before the full amount of time is invested in building a solution that might not be sound or may not provide the answers to the business questions raised in the functional model document.

After signoff of the conceptual model review, the configuration of the solution can begin. This configuration takes place in the development environment, using the development data.

5.10.3 Data Model and System Review

The data model and system review allows the data architect and the SAP NetWeaver BW project manager to look over the design in the system to make sure that all SAP NetWeaver BW design standards have been followed and that all documentation is complete. This review checks naming standards, design standards, data standards, etc.

This review takes place after the build but before any transports from the development system. The goal is to make sure that any design deficiencies are caught by the SAP NetWeaver BW team before the design is released to the QA environment and the solution is formally tested. This design typically takes place after the unit test of the design is complete, but this is not mandatory.

Some project organizations opt to perform this review after configuration but before the unit test is complete. That way, any changes that are recommended as a result of the review can be incorporated into the design and formally tested during the unit test in the development environment.

After signoff of the data model and system review, the configuration can be transported to the QA system and string and integration testing can then be performed on the model in that environment.

5.10.4 Final Check

The final check occurs in the QA environment and allows the SAP NetWeaver BW team one more review of the solution before the solution is moved to the production environment. Many project teams opt for several of these checks, one after each phase of the integration testing. For example, if there are to be three rounds of integration testing, they would perform a review at the end of each round to determine what issues occurred, why, what adjustments are needed in the SAP NetWeaver BW data model, or what has been done to prevent the issue from occurring again.

After the final check, the solution is ready to move to the production environment. After transport and loading in the production environment, there typically is another final check to make sure that the data is sound and the solution is ready for users. This is more of a validation check against the data than a check of the design, because the design should be complete by then.

5.11 Conclusion

Developing sound requirements is vital to any project. However, finding a method that can generate the requirements and have them agreed on by the various parties involved is not an easy task. By using the functional model document and Key Figure or KPI matrix, you should be able to get some scope agreement with which to begin making decisions. These will allow you to either develop the reporting requirement outside or in SAP NetWeaver BW.

It is easy to take short cuts on the functional model document and some of the other documents listed. If these documents are not fully filled out with a significant level of detail, it is likely that the end product will not completely match the user expectations. This can cause delays in the project as different areas are re-done to fill the requirements.

It is much better to spend more time from the beginning working on getting these requirements to a significant level of detail than it is to re-do the work in SAP NetWeaver BW. As a general rule, if you feel that the functional model document has any unanswered questions, this document should not be signed off, and no physical modeling in SAP NetWeaver BW should commence. This will allow the issues to get the visibility they need and encourage all parties to agree on the scope and analysis requirements.

In Chapter 6, we'll discuss how these requirements are developed in the SAP NetWeaver BW system. We will point out some common pitfalls and things to be aware of when developing in SAP NetWeaver BW.

By understanding the way data flows through the system and the methods that are typically used to transform the data, it's easier to anticipate the various issues that might occur.

6   Sound SAP NetWeaver BW Development Strategies

The actual configuration and build of the SAP NetWeaver BW solution is typically performed by the SAP NetWeaver BW development team under guidance from the SAP NetWeaver BW data architect and the SAP NetWeaver BW project manager. In most projects, the SAP NetWeaver BW data architect helps to make sure that the design remains sound and the project manager helps to refine and enforce scope, while also helping to escalate and solve business and technical issues.

The development of SAP NetWeaver BW can become complex, depending on the scope and nature of the various analysis requirements that are presented to the team. Explaining all aspects of the SAP NetWeaver BW build process is much too lengthy a task for one chapter, but we will gain some understanding of the flow of data in the SAP NetWeaver BW solution.

Once the flow of data is understood, we can then explore some of the most common issues that might arise during implementation. Understanding these challenges will help ensure that the project manager can be more proactive in solving them and thus avoid unnecessary delays on the project.

Understanding all aspects of the development cycle and typical issues presented by any SAP NetWeaver BW project takes a great deal of hands-on experience with the product. However, a clear understanding of the product and its typical challenges will help to prepare your project management for usual challenges.

During the build phase, all of the decisions and planning during the design phase are realized in a physical SAP NetWeaver BW data model. This data model is the combination of the various DataSources operational data store and Data-Store object (ODS/DSO) structures, InfoCubes, and the transformation of the data between these objects. The build phase also includes the presentation of the data to the end user.

There is no replacement for actual product experience, and each project presents many different issues with the product. Still, reading the chapters will help you understand the main functionality of the SAP NetWeaver BW product, challenges that are typically faced, and ways to meet these challenges using the SAP NetWeaver BW product.

One of the first things to examine in the development process is the extraction of the data from its source. This requires a thoughtful analysis of the source system data, its quality, and some of the common methods for extracting data. Let's explore this topic further.

6.1 Extracting and Loading Data from SAP Source Systems

The best place to start on the development cycle is with the extraction of data from the various source systems and the methods of gathering the data from these systems. The better the methods are understood, the better able the project team can be at choosing the best method to extract this data, and therefore can provide the most efficient path of this data into SAP NetWeaver BW.

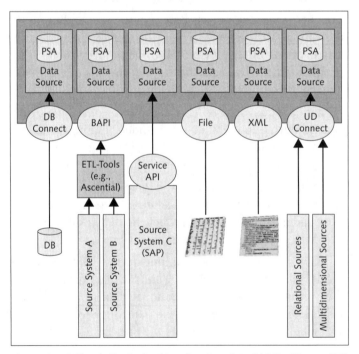

Figure 6.1 Different Methods of Loading Data into SAP NetWeaver BW

There are many different ways to extract data from source systems to be loaded into the SAP NetWeaver BW system, as seen in Figure 6.1. This data could be sourced from either SAP systems or externally, from other legacy or third-party systems. In most cases, the key to choosing a method to extract the data lies in the source system.

Because most SAP NetWeaver BW implementations gather data from multiple source systems, each system should be evaluated individually to determine the best method of loading this data into SAP NetWeaver BW. In choosing the method of loading, consider the following factors:

▶ **Source of Data**
This could be SAP R/3 or SAP ECC or an external source. SAP data being loaded from SAP systems typically follows and uses the standard delivered Service API DataSources (see Section 6.1.1, Service API DataSources for details).

▶ **Volume of Data**
The more data that is being loaded into SAP NetWeaver BW, the more this data becomes a concern during the load process. There are several load methods that work fine when the data volume is low but are not efficient at higher volumes of data. The volume is only relevant with non-SAP data, given that the Service API DataSources should be used with data extracted from SAP sources.

▶ **Transformation of Data Required**
Often, data being loaded into SAP NetWeaver BW requires some level of transformation. If possible, the loading should require minimal transformation. This increases the load speed and reduces the points of failure on loads. Thus, it is often recommended that any transformation of data from a non-SAP source occur on the source system prior to extraction.

This allows for faster and less complicated data loads but enables faster and easier reconciliation of data from the external source system to SAP NetWeaver BW. As an example, consider a project that is loading data from an external freight tracking system into SAP NetWeaver BW. If possible, this data should be transformed into a SAP NetWeaver BW–friendly flat file prior to extracting this data, to make the loading process less complicated.

6.1.1   Service API DataSources

Service Application Programming Interfaces (Service API) DataSource refers to the multitude of pre-delivered extractors provided by SAP. In SAP R/3 and SAP ECC Version 5.0, these were delivered as part of a software plug-in that is loaded onto the SAP ECC or SAP R/3 systems. The plug-in contains all of the DataSources that are available for that system. In SAP ECC 6.0, the plug-in was included as part of the software release, and any changes to the DataSources are planned so as to be delivered via software patches.

If data is being delivered from any SAP system, including SAP R/3, SAP ECC, APO, CRM, or SEM, the system has some Service API DataSources, so these should be the first place to look in order to extract data from these systems. In many cases, these DataSources may deliver much more data than required. This is expected. Often, one DataSource is used to pull large data sets so that DataSource can be used for many tasks.

To see the list of the available DataSources, use Transaction SBIW. They are also shown in Table RSDS (SAP NetWeaver BW 3.x ROOSOURCE). Use Transaction SE16 to look at all DataSources in this table.

Figure 6.2 shows the partial view of RSDS table in a SAP NetWeaver BW system. Interpretation of different Delta type can be seen in RODELTAM using Transaction SE16.

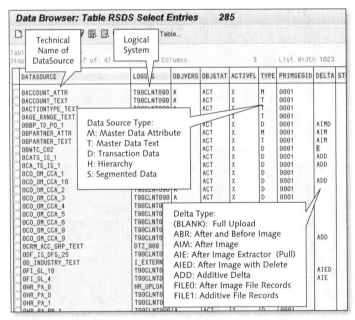

Figure 6.2   Partial View of RSDS Table in NW2004S SAP NetWeaver BW System

When a DataSource is delivered in a system, it is delivered inactive. To use the DataSource, it must first be activated. This is done in Transaction RSA5. Once the Business Content DataSources are activated, the system then makes them available for use.

When extracting data from the SAP ECC or SAP R/3 system, the best way to determine which DataSources to activate in Transaction RSA5 is to look at the Business Content. The Business Content in SAP NetWeaver BW shows the various delivered InfoCubes, ODS/DSO, queries, and DataSources that can be activated, if needed.

To see the available content, go to the SAP NetWeaver BW help page at *www.help.sap.com.* Once in the help page, you will find the *BI Content* area within the SAP NetWeaver BW section. Typically, the best way to determine which Business Content to activate is to look at the content and determine which InfoCubes, DSO/ODS, or queries match the business needs most thoroughly, and then activate the DataSources that correspond with that area.

After the DataSources have been activated on the SAP source system, SAP NetWeaver BW needs to be aware of the newly activated content. To make sure that SAP NetWeaver BW knows about these new DataSources, a *replicate DataSources* or *replicate metadata* step should be performed to allow SAP NetWeaver BW to use the new DataSources. Figure 6.3 shows standard steps to be performed to set up extraction from an SAP source system.

1	• Transfer DataSource using RSA5
2	• Maintain Extraction Structure
3	• Maintain/Generate DataSource
4	• Replicate DataSource
5	• Maintain Transformation between DataSource and Data Target
6	• Create Data Transfer Process
7	• Activate Extraction Structure (LO)
8	• Perform setup extraction (LO)
9	• Select update method (LO)
10	• Create InfoPackage for delta initialization
11	• Create InfoPackage for delta extraction

Figure 6.3 Typical Steps for Data Extraction from an SAP Source System

The advantages of the standard Business Content API DataSources are:

▸ There are vast numbers of these DataSources and many more come with each release of the software. These DataSources represent a large percentage of the data in SAP. Almost every standard transactional data table and master data table already has a standard DataSource that can be activated and used.

▸ These cover both transactional and master data, thus preventing the SAP NetWeaver BW developer from developing a DataSource. This lowers the development costs of the SAP NetWeaver BW system.

▸ Most are delta ready. This means that SAP has determined how to flag those records that are changed to ensure that only the changed or added records are loaded to SAP NetWeaver BW, not the entire table.

▸ They are ready to be used immediately. The only thing that is required is to activate the DataSource and replicate the DataSource or replicate metadata to the SAP NetWeaver BW system.

6.1.2 Generated DataSources

Some SAP R/3 and SAP ECC applications do not use fixed data structures for extraction but rather generated ones. This occurs when an application has an open-ended mechanism for configuring and generating data. For example, the CO-PA module in SAP ECC allows for an open-ended configuration based on cost and profitability analysis. SAP cannot pre-deliver an extractor for this module because each project team can configure its CO-PA differently, based on business-analysis needs.

Because organizations need to be able to gather this data and extract it to SAP NetWeaver BW, SAP delivers programs that can be run to generate the DataSources to extract this data. These programs can be found in Transaction SBIW. Other examples of programs to generate DataSources deal with operating concerns, classifications master data, Special Ledger, and the Logistics Information System (LIS).

6.1.3 Generic DataSources

The generic extractor is intended to generate extractions specifically for data not covered by Business Content DataSources. Generic extractors can capture data from database views, database tables, ABAP reports, ABAP queries, or ABAP Function Modules. Typically, the generic extractor captures custom "Z" tables that have been customized in the SAP transactional system but are also commonly used for those standard SAP ECC tables that are not covered by Business Content DataSources.

The generic extraction tool can be accessed via Transaction RSO2. It should only be used in the absence of a standard DataSource. This is because the standard API

DataSources delivered by SAP typically are more efficient than a generic Data-Source. Figure 6.4 shows the screen capture to create a Generic DataSource.

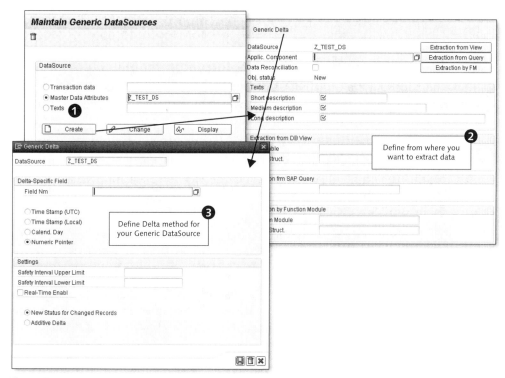

Figure 6.4 Creating Generic DataSource

A generic DataSource is best used when there are custom-created tables on the transactional system that need to be loaded to SAP NetWeaver BW. For example, a custom table might be created on the SAP ECC system to house some custom cross-reference values. This is a custom "Z" table on the SAP ECC system; there would be no standard extractor to gather this data to load to SAP NetWeaver BW. The generic DataSource can be generated from this table and, in turn, loaded into SAP NetWeaver BW.

In some cases, it is even possible to use delta functionality to bring over custom data. The system needs a date field to determine delta values. Thus, it is recommended that whenever there is a custom table with a large number of records, that a *last created date* be added to the table to be used for a generic DataSource delta. In the absence of this field, the entire table must be loaded on each extraction.

> **Note**
>
> Many projects require you to create complex custom data sources. This can be accomplished by creating a generic data source based on a function module. You can use the Function Module RSAX_BIW_GET_DATA_SIMPLE to create a generic data source based on a function module.

6.1.4   Custom ABAP DataSources

It is possible to write a custom ABAP report, extracting data from some dictionary tables and downloading those to a file, which then could be uploaded as a flat file feed into SAP NetWeaver BW.

This would be considered the absolute last resort for extraction from an integration and administration point of view. This is only recommended in extreme cases where the data cannot be extracted via the service API DataSources or via generic extractors.

This is because understanding the complex table structure and extracting data from a combination of the transactional tables can be time consuming, given that we have to make sure that all fields and tables are being accessed and extracted properly.

It's rare to have the need to create a custom ABAP DataSource to a flat file at any project. Although there are projects and implementations that do require this method, they are rare because of the maintenance and overhead of managing the program and flat file interface.

Any changes to the source systems via support packages or upgrades would require full regression testing of the custom ABAP DataSource. It is because of this type of overhead that this always should be the last option when considering how data should be extracted from the SAP ECC or SAP R/3 source system.

6.1.5   Filling In Missing Data in Extractions

In many cases, projects run into issues because an SAP-delivered DataSource has most of the fields that are needed, but some are missing. For example, a DataSource might have all the sales-related fields that are shown on the SAP ECC system except for some custom fields that have been appended onto the sales order-entry screen and tables by the project teams implementing the sales and distribution area of SAP ECC. These missing fields will not automatically show in the DataSources.

If a DataSource provides most but not all data needed for extraction, it is possible to append fields to the extractor and fill these fields via ABAP code. This is a popular way to enhance the existing extractors that might provide most but not all data needed for a requirement. This method also can provide some custom data fields that have been configured and included in the transactional system design but are not in the delivered DataSources.

For example, a new field is needed to track and store the material color code. The transactional implementation could not find a field to store the color code and thus appended a custom field to the existing master data fields to store the color code. If the color code is needed in SAP NetWeaver BW, this field will not automatically be extracted when loading the material data.

As shown in Figure 6.5, to get this data into BWSAP NetWeaver BW, several steps are needed. First, the new field must be added to the extractor; this is done in Transaction SBIW or Transaction RSA6. In some cases, the system can automatically map the new custom field to the appended field in the extractor.

1	• Use Transaction code RSA6 to maintain Append structure of the DataSource • Activate the modified Append Structure
2	• Use Transaction code CMOD to open your enhancement project • Implement RSAP0001
3	• Use EXIT_SAPLRSAP_001 (Transaction Data), EXIT_SAPLRSAP_002 (Master Data Attribute), EXIT_SAPLRSAP_003 (Master Data Text), EXIT_SAPLRSAP_004 (Master Data Hierarchy)
4	• Use ZXRSAU0# include program to add your code. In this code you have write logic with CASE-WHEN for your datasource
5	• Test your data source using RSA3

Figure 6.5 Typical DataSource Enhancement Steps

If the field that is appended to the DataSource has the same field name as in the stored custom master data table, the system can sometimes map the field automatically to the new DataSource. Simply appending the new field to the DataSource will allow the field to be filled.

In other cases, the newly added field is not automatically filled by the system. It is also possible that some logic is needed to determine the value of the field, perhaps reading from multiple tables to fill the new field in the DataSources. In these cases, this field must then be filled via the extractor customization performed in Transaction CMOD. The extractor customization functionality and capability is detailed in Transaction SBIW.

Customization of the extractor can range from mapping a simple field to performing a calculation from multiple table sources. Because ABAP is used in this method, the flexibility to fill any added field is virtually limitless.

This code is considered a user exit, not a modification to the core code of SAP. Thus, this code is not affected directly by upgrades to the system. The code does need to be checked to make sure that the code still functions properly after any upgrade or patch, but the code will not be replaced by an upgrade or patch. This code is written into a reserved area of SAP designed specifically for user exits. Be aware that because this custom coding occurs on the source system, not on the SAP NetWeaver BW system. The code is added to the SAP ECC or SAP R/3 system, not to the SAP NetWeaver BW system.

Additional fields can be added to DataSources for transaction data, master data, text, and hierarchies. For more information on adding custom fields to DataSources and filling them via these user exits, Transaction SBIW has detailed instructions along with sample code that can be implemented.

As with any custom code, this code must be tested thoroughly. This often means testing with full loads, delta loads, and also testing for performance to ensure that the code added does not significantly affect the performance of the DataSource.

The user exit is designed to fill appended fields; it's not recommended that this user exit be used to attempt to change values in an extractor. For example, suppose that a sales organization on a sales order is showing as "1000." The process teams have determined that a select number of sales orders have incorrect sales organization data.

Rather than fix the source, the SAP NetWeaver BW team has been asked to change selected sales orders from "1000" to the correct sales organization "2000." In cases like this, it is not recommended that the user exit be used to fix values in the extractor. This user exit should be used mainly to fill appended fields that are not included in the extractor.

A common issue with this user exit is that a newly added field is not automatically flagged for deltas, and this should be tested in detail. For example, the material master data table noted above is being extracted in delta mode and only the custom field *material color code* is changed. Because this is a custom field, the system does not flag this as a delta change and the change could be lost. More custom coding or configuration might be needed to make sure that a delta record is generated when only a custom field is changed. This can also be avoided by bringing in full loads of the master data for each extraction, but this might not be possible in some cases depending on the volume of the data.

Because many SAP NetWeaver BW projects gather data from non-SAP sources, it is also important to understand and develop ways to extract and load data from non-SAP sources. These are listed and explained in the next section.

6.1.6   Testing the DataSources

There is a handy tool used to test the DataSources to make sure that they provide the needed fields. Transaction RSA3 allows for a test extraction to be performed in the transactional data system. This allows for data to be extracted without actually sending the data to the SAP NetWeaver BW system. It can help test and troubleshoot the DataSources and ensure that all fields that are needed are coming through the DataSource. This transaction can also be used to help troubleshoot any user exits that are used on the SAP R/3 or SAP ECC system, to populate fields that are missing on the DataSource.

Figure 6.6 shows the extraction checker screen (RSA3). After entering the technical name of the DataSource, selection criteria fields will be populated and you can check the DataSource with your desired selection criteria.

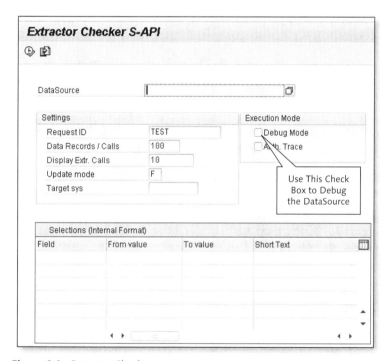

Figure 6.6 Extractor Checker

Tip for Debugging User Exits

If you run the DataSource with debug mode, the source code debug screen appears. In this screen, go to menu path BREAKPOINTS • BREAKPOINT AT • FUNCTION MODULE (Shift F7). In the popup screen, enter any user exit function module such as EXIT_SAPLRSAP_001 for Transaction data, EXIT_SAPLRSAP_002 for Master Data Attribute, EXIT_SAPLRSAP_003 for Master Data Text, and EXIT_SAPLRSAP_004 for Master Data Hierarchy. After this, press F8. Control directly goes to the user exit.

6.2   Loading Data from Non-SAP Source Systems

There are several common formats and methods for loading data for later processing and loading into the SAP NetWeaver BW solution. The most common are listed below in order of popularity. These are common methods for loading non-SAP data.

These methods are employed where there is external or outside data that needs to be loaded into SAP NetWeaver BW. These methods would not typically by employed when SAP data is being loaded into SAP NetWeaver BW because the SAP data typically has standard API DataSources that can extract and load data into SAP NetWeaver BW.

6.2.1   Flat File Interfaces

SAP SAP NetWeaver BW supports the transfer of data from flat files. A flat file consists of data that is saved into a file with either a fixed record length or with separators or delimiters between the various fields in the file. This file can then be loaded directly into the SAP NetWeaver BW system (see Figure 6.7).

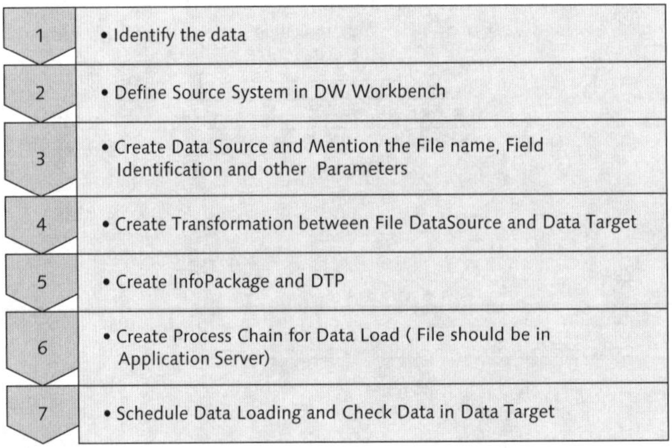

Figure 6.7   Steps to Implement Flat File Interface

SAP NetWeaver BW can accept files in ASCII fixed-length format or CSV format with a predefined delimiter to separate the data fields. The CSV format simply refers to the extension of the file typically added. A CSV file is a file with a specific delimiter between the records. The flat file interface is the most common way of loading external data into SAP NetWeaver BW. This is because it is the easiest to set up and the quickest to implement.

Generation of the flat file must take place on the third-party or legacy source system, and the file must be saved to a location that can be read by the SAP NetWeaver BW system. If the data file is sensitive in nature, limit authorization to the file location.

SAP NetWeaver BW must be configured for the file to be loaded. One benefit of SAP NetWeaver BW is the ability to preview the data and available metadata to allow for a test of the load into SAP NetWeaver BW. From the preview, you can then run a simulation of the data-loading process.

In most cases, some transformation of the external data is needed to combine this non-SAP data with SAP data. This can be done via transformation logic when loading into the ODS or InfoCubes in SAP NetWeaver BW.

> **Note**
>
> The more transformation that can occur in the source system, the better. Thus, if possible, the flat file should be generated in a format that is ready to be loaded into SAP NetWeaver BW with minimal transformation on the SAP NetWeaver BW system.

There are several reasons for keeping transformation in the source system. By allowing the source system to generate the flat file in a format already friendly to SAP NetWeaver BW, the performance of the flat file load is increased because the overhead of transformation is reduced. This also reduces the points of failure. The more frequently the data is transformed, the harder the troubleshooting of the loads.

In my experience, if the flat files can be loaded with minimal transformation, troubleshooting of the loads is minimized because the data simply needs to be reconciled back to the flat file. Otherwise, the data needs to be reconciled back to the flat file and the transformation logic applied manually to reconcile. This is much more labor intensive.

Because the flat file interface of SAP NetWeaver BW allows for both a CSV (comma-delimited file) and a fixed file length, you must decide which of the two approaches should be used when generating the flat file for loading into the SAP NetWeaver BW system. A comparison of these different file formats follows.

CSV Files

CSV files are commonly referred to as *comma-delimited files*. This means that between each field in the file, the data is separated by a separator (or delimiter), typically a comma. At the end of each record, there is also a designator to show the end of the record. Any data delimiter can be used with flat files. Many projects opt for a delimiter other than a comma because a comma can usually come in many data feeds. This can cause the file to fail because the comma is read as a delimiter, not as the data set. For example, if a data feed has text values and the text contains a comma, the system would think that the comma represents the end of the text. This typically causes the load to fail because the data does not load properly.

Fixed-Length Files

Fixed-length files are flat files where each field represents a full record length. For example, if there are 5 fields in a file, each set for 20 characters, the file will be padded with spaces to fill each of the fields, even those that are less than 20 characters long. This preserves the fixed length of the records. Thus, in the example above, each full record in the file would have a total length of 100 characters, comprising the five 20-character fields. These fixed length files are typically processed much faster than CSV files when loading higher volumes of data into SAP NetWeaver BW. This is because the system does not need to look for the data separator to differentiate the fields and records. As a general rule, higher volumes of data should be loaded using fixed-length files if performance is an important factor, and also when there is limited time to load the files.

Pseudo Delta

While utilizing flat file DataSource, to avoid duplicate loading in the new file, utilize the pseudo delta mechanism for flat file naming convention. Suppose an InfoPackage runs monthly to load sales data of an organization and upstream application creates the file with name SALES_DATA.csv. After loading this data, in the next run, the InfoPackage has no way to identify the file as new or old. To resolve this issue, you can write a routine in the InfoPackage of the file type data source to derive a file name with month as the suffix or prefix.

6.2.2 DBConnect

SAP NetWeaver BW allows extraction of data from non-SAP systems through a tool known as *DBConnect*. This tool allows you to create and keep *live* automated connections to these non-SAP systems that regularly feed data into your SAP

NetWeaver BW data warehouse. Although flat files are the most common method of loading source data into SAP NetWeaver BW, DBConnect is a distant second.

In essence SAP NetWeaver BW creates DataSources in the source system(s). DBConnect reads and references the views and tables on the external database system. SAP NetWeaver BW calls these tables and views and allows the SAP NetWeaver BW developer to extract these tables and views via a DataSource in SAP NetWeaver BW.

This approach allows for the reduction of overhead generating, storing, and loading flat file data. The DataSource in SAP NetWeaver BW reads directly from the database views and database tables on the source system through a live connection. This connection does require some set-up work in SAP NetWeaver BW and in the source system. The source system requires a login for the SAP NetWeaver BW system to gather the data. Proper authorizations must be granted to the user, and the views and tables must be maintained to house the data needed for SAP NetWeaver BW.

There are many white papers and help resources on setting up and maintaining DBConnect for SAP NetWeaver BW. These can be found in the SAP Service MarketPlace. DBConnect can be set up between two like or even unlike database platforms. If your SAP NetWeaver BW system is built on Oracle and the data you wish to load into SAP NetWeaver BW is housed in a SQL Server database, these can be connected and data can be loaded directly between the two different database platforms.

The advantage of DBConnect over a flat file interface is that DBConnect allows for a live connection into SAP NetWeaver BW and less latency with gathering the data, saving the data, and loading into SAP NetWeaver BW than would occur with a flat file interface. However, DBConnect does require maintenance, keeping the connection active and maintaining the database tables and views on the source system side.

Often, the source system's transactional and master data tables and views can be used for extraction, but in some cases, these tables require filtering or transformation. For this reason, custom tables and views are sometimes needed on the source system to pull this data into SAP NetWeaver BW.

Because there is some overhead establishing connections and setting up the source system in SAP NetWeaver BW to gather data, use DBConnect for ongoing interfaces of data into SAP NetWeaver BW. It is not recommended that DBConnect be used for one-time loads because of the overhead required to establish the connections. In the case of one-time loads of data into SAP NetWeaver BW, the flat file interface should be used.

6.2.3 UDConnect

UDConnect is similar to DBConnect, but it uses Java connectors for different drivers, providers, and protocols (JDBC, OLE DB for OLAP). Thus, it offers connectivity to a wide range of relational (MS SQL Server, Oracle, etc.) and multi-dimensional sources.

Some customers have had success with UDConnect and virtual InfoProviders. These are InfoProviders in SAP NetWeaver BW that do not physically store data but instead map to an external system. For example, it is possible to connect to an external system via UDConnect and create a virtual InfoProvider to gather this data. The query runs off of the InfoProvider, and the data is stored outside of the SAP NetWeaver BW system. This allows the SAP NetWeaver BW system to be free of this data but also allows the data to be reported on within SAP NetWeaver BW queries.

UDConnect does not support higher-volume data loads without severe performance degradation. Thus, if you can set up a connection using DBConnect, this usually is far preferable to UDConnect. UDConnect can and should be used with smaller data sets that cannot be set up using DBConnect.

6.2.4 XML Interfaces

Third-party or legacy systems that can provide data in XML format can be loaded directly into SAP NetWeaver BW using the Simple Application Object Protocol (SOAP) service.

The transfer of XML files into SAP NetWeaver BW is suitable for regular SAP NetWeaver BW services with limited amounts of data for each call. An example would be the transfer of small amounts of transactional data. XML is currently not suited for large transfers of data because of the performance overhead associated with this type of loading. If large volumes of data need to be loaded into SAP NetWeaver BW, the XML interface is not recommended, and either the flat file interface or the DBConnect functionality should be used.

6.2.5 ETL Interfaces

There are some ETL systems that connect directly into SAP NetWeaver BW. These systems can connect to one or many legacy systems and then are provided as a one-stop system for loading data into SAP NetWeaver BW. The ETL system acts as a hub for the data, providing an intermediate staging and transformation area for SAP NetWeaver BW data.

6.3 Extracting Data From the SAP NetWeaver BW System

It is sometimes necessary to extract data from the SAP NetWeaver BW system and move it to an external outside system. This might be an external data mart, data warehouse, or even a transactional or analytical system.

The Open Hub Service enables you to distribute data from an SAP NetWeaver BW system into external systems. In essence, this creates a DataSource in SAP NetWeaver BW and this DataSource is used to feed the external systems.

When data is staged for an external system using the Open Hub Service, the data is extracted and the resulting data set is stored in a CSV table or a relational database table in the SAP NetWeaver BW database system. This table can then be used for reading or extraction to the external system, as seen in Figure 6.8.

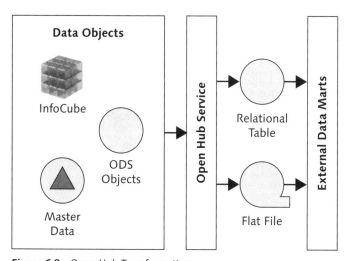

Figure 6.8 Open Hub Transformation

The Open Hub Service also allows for customization and transformation. Data from SAP NetWeaver BW often fills input requirements of a third-party system. For example, SAP NetWeaver BW data is needed to feed a third-party shipping transactional system. This system tracks and maintains manifests of orders on a monthly basis. This third-party package has specific requirements for data storage.

To extract the desired data out of SAP NetWeaver BW into this third-party shipping system, the Open Hub Service may be used. However, the service will extract data in its current form. In other words, it uses structures and values of the data that is stored in SAP NetWeaver BW.

Suppose the third-party system needs the material converted to another material number, or the division preceded by leading zeroes. This could be converted using the Open Hub transformation to change the data coming out of SAP NetWeaver BW.

The ABAP code in the Open Hub transformation user exit allows for a flexible ABAP solution to meet these specific data needs of the third-party package while allowing the data to be unchanged in the SAP NetWeaver BW system. The data is simply altered as it is extracted out of SAP NetWeaver BW via the Open Hub transformation. Open Hub transformation is not mandatory; it is only needed if the data coming out of an external source into SAP NetWeaver BW requires data to be changed or transformed.

Based on experience, the Open Hub Service is not a robust tool and does not provide extreme flexibility in the output files. When trying to generate flat files with a predefined format, it's difficult to make sure that the file is generated properly. If this is a requirement, give ample time to implementing the Open Hub functionality and devote sufficient time to the testing phase to make sure that the Open Hub file meets your specific requirements.

The next step is to understand the method and process for loading data into the SAP NetWeaver BW system. Let's explore the methods for loading and the common ways to transform the data once it is loaded into SAP NetWeaver BW.

> **Note**
>
> If you have complex transformation in Open Hub, then you have to implement BAdi OPEN-HUB_TRANSFORM (Transaction Code SE19). This BAdi includes a method TRANSFORM that is called in similar way to a function module.

6.4 Loading and Transforming Data into SAP NetWeaver BW

It is rare that data is extracted from a source system and loaded unchanged into the SAP NetWeaver BW system. Thus, in most projects, the majority of the build time is spent understanding the data that is being extracted and using the transformation tools of SAP NetWeaver BW to ensure that the data that is being extracted can be harmonized with other data in the SAP NetWeaver BW system.

In most projects, the data architect and the SAP NetWeaver BW developers demonstrate their value through the quality and consistency of the transformations of data into their SAP NetWeaver BW ODS/DSO structures or InfoCubes. Simply put, the more experienced developers and data architects are able to provide the best tools and methods to extract data consistently and accurately. They understand the interdependency of the data, and thus can help to make sure that the solution is consistent for end users.

It is vital to managing an SAP NetWeaver BW project tounderstand the different ways that data is loaded and extracted. Many of the most complex and far-reaching decisions about the project deal with what data should get transformed in SAP NetWeaver BW and what method should be used for this transformation.

There are many ways that data can be transformed once it has been loaded into the SAP NetWeaver BW system. SAP radically changed the transformation logic between the releases 3.x and NW 2004s.

Figures 6.9 and 6.10 show the different methods of transformation in the two releases.

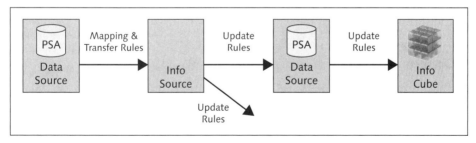

Figure 6.9 Version 3.x Data Loading

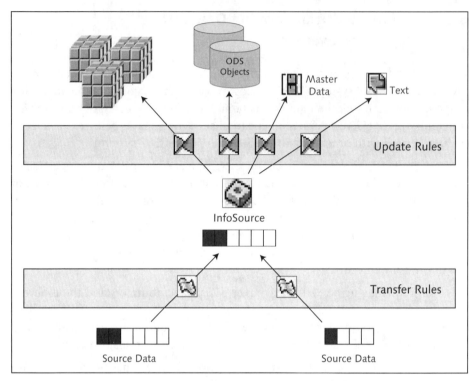

Figure 6.10 Typical Flow of Data in the 3.x Version of SAP NetWeaver BW

6.4.1 Transformation and Mapping of Data in SAP NetWeaver BW Version 3.x

In SAP NetWeaver BW Versions 3.0 through 3.5, SAP provided two main places to transform data:

- Transfer rules
- Update rules

The transfer rules and update rules are mandatory for transactional data being loaded into SAP NetWeaver BW InfoProviders such as InfoCubes or ODS structures. See Figure 6.10 for the typical flow of data in the 3.x release. The data starts at the PSA, goes through transfer rules to an InfoSource, through update rules to an ODS structure, and then through update rules again into an InfoCube that will be used for query processing.

Suppose, for example, that you wish to load sales data from the SAP R/3 or SAP ECC system into SAP NetWeaver BW. This data would use the standard Data-

Sources in the SAP R/3 or SAP ECC system. These extractors allow the data to be extracted out of the source system. When this data is loaded into SAP NetWeaver BW, one option is to have it first loaded into the Persistent Staging Area (PSA) of SAP NetWeaver BW.

In release 3.x, the PSA is an optional part of the data loading process, but it does allow a place for the data to be loaded into SAP NetWeaver BW without any possibility of transformation. Simply put, the PSA is SAP NetWeaver BW's *loading dock*. The data in the PSA represents exactly how the data came in from the source without any transformation occurring in this data. The system provides no possibility of transforming data when loading into the PSA. Thus, it is a good place to look at the data to determine if it has been loaded into SAP NetWeaver BW properly.

After the PSA is loaded, the sales data is typically loaded into an ODS structure. The ODS structure would store all the sales data at a transactional level and would be mapped and loaded from the source system via an InfoSource. This InfoSource has two main parts. One part is the communication structure that represents all the fields that will be loaded as part of the data. The other is the transfer rule.

Transfer Rules

The transfer rules provide two main functions. The first is to map all the fields coming into SAP NetWeaver BW InfoObjects. In other words, there are various fields coming in on the sales order feed: customer, material, sales volume, etc. Each of these fields represents data that is to be loaded into SAP NetWeaver BW. Thus, each of the fields needs to be mapped to a field in SAP NetWeaver BW. The fields in SAP NetWeaver BW are represented by InfoObjects.

In the transfer rules, the fields can be mapped to their corresponding InfoObject in SAP NetWeaver BW. Thus, in the sales field, the SAP KUNNR field represents the customer, this field can be mapped to the 0CUSTOMER InfoObject in the InfoSource, representing the customer field in the data load. Each of the relevant fields from the feeds would be mapped in this manner.

Transfer rules can also map constant values into fields when loading into SAP NetWeaver BW. For example, suppose all sales data is not mapped with the sales organization, but the sales organization is always 1000. The sales organization could be mapped with a constant of 1000 in the transfer rules to allow that value to always appear as 1000 in SAP NetWeaver BW.

The transfer rules are not only used to map fields directly to InfoObjects or as a constant. It is also possible to provide some transformation of data in the transfer rules. Thus, ABAP routines can be created to provide custom transformation of the data in the transfer rules. This transformation of data can be limited to one field or spread across multiple fields depending on the data that needs to be altered to load into SAP NetWeaver BW.

Transformation of data is needed if the source data does not match the reporting requirements or if data needs to be changed or transformed to harmonize with other sources.

In the example above, the materials and customers need to be translated into a common customer number or material number to ensure that the data can be aggregated and analyzed together. This transformation of the material or customer number can occur in the transfer rules.

There is a great deal of flexibility provided in the system for transformation because the system allows for custom ABAP routines to be developed. This allows for an almost limitless range of possibilities for transformation and validation of data when loading into SAP NetWeaver BW.

Typical transfer rules have logic to determine the values of data that will be filled or read out to other tables within SAP NetWeaver BW to determine the values that should be filled into a specific field. In the example above, where a common customer number is to be determined, often a cross-reference table would be built in SAP NetWeaver BW between the customer numbers in one system and the customer numbers in another. This table can be read while the data is loaded to determine the customer number that should be loaded into SAP NetWeaver BW.

Thus, the transfer rules might register the customer number that is coming in, compare it to the cross-reference table, and determine a new customer number. It can then replace the old customer number with the new customer number in the transfer rules when the data is loaded.

Not all fields that come in from a DataSource need to be mapped to fields in the InfoSource. For example, there might be 300 fields that come in from the sales DataSource. If there are only 100 that are relevant for SAP NetWeaver BW, you only place InfoObjects for the 100 fields in the communication structure, and only those 100 fields are mapped. The other unmapped field values are lost when the data is loaded. This allows for a larger DataSource to be loaded and a subset of data to be used from this DataSource.

It is common that multiple fields from a DataSource are not mapped, especially when loading data from the SAP ECC or SAP R/3 system. This is because the SAP ECC and SAP R/3 systems often have fields that are relevant for modules that might not be implemented. If there are no plans to implement the CRM system, the fields from CRM need not be mapped because many of these would have initial values and would not be valuable for SAP NetWeaver BW query analysis. Thus, only the relevant fields need to be mapped when loading data; the rest of the fields can remain unmapped.

Update Rules

Update rules are similar to transfer rules. However, update rules allow for data to be transformed later in the data loading process. As seen in Figure 6.10, the update rules happen after the transfer rules have been processed. The update rules map and/or transform data when loading data into the InfoProvider; this is typically an InfoCube or an ODS structure.

Like the transfer rules, the update rules are also mandatory in the data model because the update rules are needed to map the various InfoObjects into the corresponding fields in the ODS or InfoCube.

In many cases, the update rules simply map the data directly into the InfoProvider; however, the update rules also allow for transformation and/or constant selection to transform the data.

As with transfer rules, not all fields coming from the source need to be mapped to the destination. For example, there might be 200-characteristic fields in the ODS and 50-characteristic fields in an InfoCube fed from the ODS. The fields that are not required in the InfoCube are simply not mapped into the InfoCubes update rules from the ODS.

Transformation Library Formulas

SAP has made every effort to try to reduce the amount of ABAP coding required in any SAP NetWeaver BW implementation. Many of the most common update rules and transfer rules can be accomplished via transformation library formulas. Using these makes it possible to configure transformations of data without custom ABAP coding.

A transformation library formula is a group of common transformations that are included as part of the transfer rules and update rules in SAP NetWeaver BW. Because these are already pre-coded, there is no need to write ABAP code to use them to transform data.

The transformation library has many functions, including mathematical and character value. There is also the ability for projects to create their own customized functions to be added to the transformation library. In many cases, this is not used by many SAP NetWeaver BW implementations. This is because custom transformations that are to be used multiple times usually are handled via custom routines and SAP custom ABAP function modules that can be called from various routines in the system.

Determining When to Use Update Rules vs. Transfer Rules

When to use transfer rules or update rules depends on which InfoProviders need the transformed data. Because update rules happen further in the process and within individual InfoCubes and/or ODS structures, the rules should be used when there are individual InfoCubes or ODS structures that require the data to be transformed. If all InfoCubes and/or ODS structures need the data to be transformed, data is typically transformed in the transfer rules.

> **Example**
>
> If one InfoSource is used to load the sales data into SAP NetWeaver BW, the data goes through one InfoSource and thus one set of transfer rules. It then is loaded into several ODS structures and several InfoCubes for sales analysis.

To determine if the data should be transformed using the transfer rules or the update rules, you first must look at the InfoProviders and determine if the data needs to be transformed in all the ODS and all the InfoCubes. If so, the data most likely should be transformed in the transfer rules because this would only require configuration to occur in one place.

If the transformation is only required for a subset of the ODS structure or InfoCubes, the data should be transformed only into those InfoProviders. Thus, the update rules should be used for this transformation. This allows for the InfoProviders that require the transformation to have the update rule transformation and those that do not require the transformation to have update rules without any transformation.

6.4.2 Transformation and Mapping of Data in NW 2004s

The transformation logic in the NW 2004s system, as seen in Figure 6.11, is different. Instead of the update rules and transfer rules that were available in the 3.x versions of SAP NetWeaver BW, SAP introduced the concept of the transformation area.

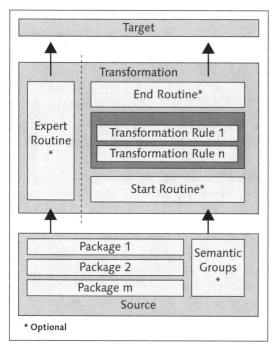

Figure 6.11 NW 2004s Method of Loading and Transforming Data

SAP also makes the PSA a mandatory part of the data model. All data that is loaded into the system must first be loaded (un-transformed) into the PSA. It can then be loaded into InfoProviders in the SAP NetWeaver BW system.

This transformation area acts much like the update rules and transfer rules in version 3.x. It allows for direct mapping of fields, constant values, and data transformation of data via ABAP. SAP just simplified the terminology and methods for transforming data into one. Thus, when data needs to be transformed, this can be done only in the transformation area.

Data that comes from the PSA into a DSO goes through the transformation area, as does the data from the DSO to the InfoCube. These transformation areas are separate and distinct depending on their source and destination of the data. Thus, there are separate transformation areas that need to be created when loading from one DSO to multiple InfoCubes.

6.4.3 Start Routines

Start routines are placed in the transformation that can be used for a mass transformation or filtering of data. The start routine is the first thing that is run during a transformation. This optional area allows you to place complex filtering and transformation for multiple fields in one place, in order for many fields and or complex logic to be performed all at once. The start routines are available in both the NW 2004s transformation areas and the update and transfer rules of the 3.x versions.

Start routines are often used if there are data values that need to be filtered out of data that is loaded, but these filters cannot be easily applied in the InfoPackage load. For example, each record that is loaded into an InfoCube should be checked to make sure that it is one of the valid divisions and that the dollar value is above a certain amount. The start routine could loop through all the data that is coming in and determine which data should be filtered and take this data out of the data set. The remainder of the data can then be loaded.

Often, the start routines are used when a great deal of custom logic is needed to transform data. For example, sometimes there are many fields that need to be transformed; it can be cumbersome to look at each field to troubleshoot the transformation logic. If all the transformation logic is placed in the start routine, it often is much easier to troubleshoot because all the code for the transformation is in one place.

Thus, as data is loaded, it first completes the start routine, and the code in the start routine loops through the values and transforms those that need to be transformed based on the business rules. Once the data set has been completely transformed, all data is loaded into the destination. The start routine allows for one place for this transformation and filtering logic.

Usage Scenario
- Deletion of records that are not required for updating in data targets.
- Buffering master data tables in memory that can be used in transformation rules for lookup. If we don't buffer the tables in internal memory, database tables will be read for each record from source.

6.4.4 End Routines

End routines were introduced in the NW 2004s version of SAP NetWeaver BW. These end routines run after the start routine and after all fields have been mapped and data is ready for commit to the destination area. These end routines allow for the data to be verified, checked, or transformed one final time.

This is useful if there is complex transformation logic and verification of data is necessary. It is also useful for checking data against a source to make sure that all data was properly loaded.

End routines can be useful but are not as popular as start routines in most project implementations. In most implementations, the start routines are used to perform most of the complex transformations; the end routines are only used if some verification of data needs to be performed.

> **Usage Scenario**
>
> ▶ End routines should be implemented for deletion of the records after transformations that are not required for updating in data targets.
>
> ▶ Validate the field contents after transformation.

6.4.5 Expert Routines

Expert routines were also introduced in the NW 2004s version of SAP NetWeaver BW. These special routines bypass all normal mapping, start routines, and end routines, to allow a complete custom coding of all mapping and transformation of data. These are rare and would require special circumstances to be implemented. Most often, the transformation area of the NW 2004s, in conjunction with the start routines or end routines, provides enough functionality to transform data as needed.

In the future, these expert routines might be also used by third-party vendors to populate InfoProviders in a specific application running on the SAP NetWeaver BW system.

> **Usage Scenario**
>
> ▶ If application logic is well known and transformation requires reading a lot of database tables, use Expert Routine.
>
> ▶ Using Expert Routine, you can easily transpose wide data records into several smaller records. This feature is called *pivoting*.

6.4.6 Implementing Transformations

In most SAP NetWeaver BW projects, it is expected that transformation of data will need to be implemented. This is because transformation data from different sources can be harmonized and joined to allow for homogenized analysis. Typically, these transformations are performed either in the SAP NetWeaver BW system or in the SAP ECC or SAP R/3 source systems. They are most often implemented by the SAP NetWeaver BW team members.

This means that an SAP NetWeaver BW team should have at least one member who is proficient in ABAP. This ABAP is typically small, often less than 10 lines of coding. Often, it is a simple change of a characteristic value from one to another, or a lookup of a table to determine a new value.

As a general rule, the SAP NetWeaver BW team members who implement the ABAP routines for transformations are not ABAP coders as their primary jobs. Sometimes, the ABAP code implemented is not as efficient as possible. This can cause issues in large data loads because a small performance issue in a routine is made exponentially worse by multiple iterations reading and running the inefficient code.

A good SAP NetWeaver BW practice is to include an ABAP audit of all custom routines before this code is transported from the development system to the QA system. This allows the code that will be called during higher-volume loads to be checked for efficiency.

6.4.7 Auditing Transformations for Efficiency

There are many ways to check code for efficiency. One of the most popular is to run a trace on the code while a load is running. Typically, this is done via Transaction SE30 in the SAP NetWeaver BW, SAP ECC, and/or SAP R/3 systems. This trace is typically performed only on custom-extracted data, not on the standard DataSources or data in SAP NetWeaver BW that is using standard mapping without custom ABAP transformations.

The standard transformations are already tuned by SAP and should be assumed to be efficient. If there are issues with efficiency using standard delivered DataSources, these are typically handled via support messages to SAP via the SAP help desk support.

The Transaction SE30 trace can be run in the SAP ECC or SAP R/3 transactional systems if there are user exits transforming the data on the source system. These transformations are typically implemented in either the user exit RSAP0001 or the BADI RSU5_SAPI_BADI.

It can also be run in the SAP NetWeaver BW system when loading data through custom transformation code. This code is usually implemented in transformations in the NW 2004s release or in transfer and update rules in the SAP NetWeaver BW 3.x release.

6.4.8 Converting from Version 3.x to NW 2004s Transformations

Because the new transformation logic is used only with the NW 2004s release of SAP NetWeaver BW, you may need to migrate the transformations from update rules or transfer rules to NW 2004s transformations after upgrade.

When you create the transformation, the system retains the update rules, Version 3.x InfoSources, and transfer rules. However, it will use the new transformations that are created to map the various sources to their destinations. Instead of the load using the update and transfer rules, transformation logic is used.

NW 2004s and SAP NetWeaver BW 3.x versions differ substantially on the method to transform data in ABAP code. Thus, in order for any existing 3.x ABAP transformations to work in the NW 2004s system, the coding must be changed to the new type of coding.

NW 2004s uses ABAP OO (ABAP Objects) coding and SAP NetWeaver BW 3.x versions use ABAP coding. There are many similarities in the coding techniques, but there are also some substantial differences. For this reason, SAP has changed the format and variables needed to use 3.x code in NW 2004s; no custom coding that has been developed in version 3.x will work in the NW 2004s version.

When converting from the 3.x update, transfer rules, routines, and custom ABAP code are not automatically transformed. This code must be evaluated and created again manually.

The way that routines can be implemented changes when the programming language for routines is converted from ABAP to ABAP OO. Table 6.1 provides an overview of the special features regarding ABAP form routines for the update and transfer rules compared to the routines in the transformation.

Form Routine for Update/Transfer Rule	Routine for Transformation
Parameter COMM_STRUCTURE	SOURCE_FIELDS
Parameter ABORT <> 0	RAISE EXCEPTION TYPE CX_RSROUT_ABORT.
Parameter RETURNCODE <> 0	RAISE EXCEPTION TYPE CX_RSROUT_SKIP_RECORD or RAISE EXCEPTION TYPE CX_RSROUT_SKIP_VALUE
Sub-programs are included in the global part of the routine using an INCLUDE	You cannot use INCLUDES. You can convert these sub-programs in order to: ▶ Convert the subprograms into global, static methods ▶ Create a sub-routine pool in the ABAP editor and execute these sub-programs using PERFORM SUB-ROUTINE ▶ Define a function module that has the logic of the sub-program ▶ Call function modules, methods, or external sub-programs in the local part of the routine

Table 6.1 Methods for Changing ABAP to ABAP OO

Form Routine for Update/Transfer Rule	Routine for Transformation
STATICS statement	The STATICS statement is not permitted in instance methods. Declared static attributes of the class can be used with CLASS DATA instead.
Addition OCCURS when the internal table is created	► The OCCURS addition is not permitted. ► You use the DATA statement to declare a standard table instead.
Internal table with header row	► You cannot use an internal table with a header row. ► You create an explicit work area with the LINE OF addition of statements TYPES, DATA and to replace the header row.
Direct operations such as INSERT itab, APPEND itab on internal tables	You have to use a work area for statements of this type.

Table 6.1 Methods for Changing ABAP to ABAP OO (Cont.)

Table 6.1 shows you some of the differences in ABAP OO and 3.x transfer and update-rule coding. You can use this table to help manually change the existing update and transfer rules to the new coding technique.

Auditing a DataSource in SAP R/3 or SAP ECC for Performance

Performance is always a concern whenever custom logic is used for transformation, because one small bottleneck in the transformation can cause a significant performance bottleneck when large volumes of data are being extracted. Thus, SAP has provided several tools to audit the extraction process to determine if there are any performance bottlenecks and eliminate these bottlenecks by adding indices, redefining the ABAP code, etc.

To audit a DataSource for efficiency in the SAP R/3 or SAP ECC system, the first step is to run Transaction RSA3. This allows for a test extraction of the data from a DataSource. This transaction also runs through any existing user exits in RSAP0001 or the BADI RSU5_SAPI_BADI. Any custom transformations can also be tested using a test extraction in the source SAP ECC or SAP R/3 system.

While the RSA3 test extraction is running, start another session and start the Transaction SE30. This transaction allows tracing of the loads while in progress. Thus, the trace can be run on the RSA3 test load while in progress to determine what part of the extraction process contains the most resource-intensive statements.

The statements that are the most resource intensive will have the highest net percentage in the output of the trace. To see the most costly statements, the output should be sorted by the *net percentage* field. The ABAP can then be changed, indices added, etc., to help tune the ABAP to make the process most efficient.

Auditing Custom Transformation Logic in SAP NetWeaver BW for Performance

Transaction SE30 can also be used on SAP NetWeaver BW transformations. To apply the SE30 tool to the transformations in SAP NetWeaver BW, the transformation should be started, and while in process, Transaction SE30 should be run in another session of SAP NetWeaver BW. This will allow any transformations that are inefficient to be audited for performance.

Often, part of the transformation process will require appending or adding to existing SAP NetWeaver BW objects. Now, we'll discuss the method for performing this function.

6.4.9 InfoSource

In NW2004s, InfoSource is an optional object in dataflow from Source to Target. However, you may need an InfoSource to consolidate more than one DatasSource in one data target. In NW2004s, InfoSource architecture is based on flat InfoObject-based structure.

As shown in Figure 6.12, an InfoSource can be used as a uniform source for several data targets and as target from different sources.

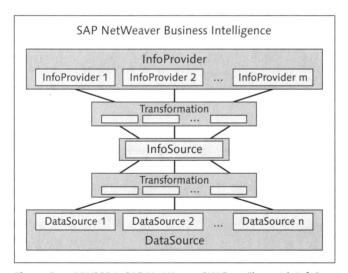

Figure 6.12 NW2004s SAP NetWeaver BW Data Flow with InfoSource

6.5 Appending or Changing Standard SAP NetWeaver BW Objects

There is a serious misconception about appending objects in SAP NetWeaver BW. Many project managers and developers are first introduced to SAP via the SAP ECC or SAP R/3 transactional systems. In the SAP ECC or SAP R/3 system, whenever you use an SAP-delivered object, you do not change the standard objects. If any new configuration changes are needed to a standard object, it is copied and the copied object is changed.

For example, users configuring the sales order area of an SAP ECC system might need their own custom order types. The recommended approach in the SAP ECC system is to take the standard delivered order-type table value and copy it to a new value and configure only this new order type.

This approach differs from the configuration of SAP NetWeaver BW. This is because SAP has designed the standard objects to be used, changed, and appended to if needed. Thus, suppose there is a new custom field that needs to be added to the material master data table for reporting. The recommended approach is simply to append this field to the standard 0MATERIAL InfoObject. Sometimes, this is difficult, especially for those who are accustomed to copying objects. The reason why it works in SAP NetWeaver BW lies in the design of the standard content.

The SAP NetWeaver BW standard content is a series of InfoCubes, InfoObjects, DSO structures, queries, etc. To use any of these structures, they must be activated in SAP NetWeaver BW.

In any SAP NetWeaver BW system, there are two types of Business Content. There is an active version and a delivered version. When Business Content is activated, the system takes the delivered version of the Business Content and converts this to the active version.

This provides a distinct advantage. The active version of the ODS and InfoCubes can be used for loading, reporting, etc. in SAP NetWeaver BW. It can also be appended to and modified to meet user needs. Because there is still a delivered version of each object in the SAP NetWeaver BW system, it is always possible to get back to the delivered version of the objects if needed.

When SAP does an upgrade, the only version of the Business Content objects that is affected is the delivered version. Thus, if several business-content versions of InfoCubes or ODS structures are implemented, these are not affected by the upgrade.

The upgrade only affects the delivered version of the content. You must be careful not to reactivate the Business Content once an object has already been activated. This is because if an ODS or InfoCube has been modified and content is reactivated, this will write over the existing ODS or InfoCube and the changes will be removed.

The system provides a warning before the content is overwritten, and this warning must be obeyed or existing structures can be destroyed, along with the data that was stored in these tables.

Essentially, the SAP NetWeaver BW content is designed to be activated and modified if needed. There is no need to copy the content to another object to perform modifications. The system does not affect any changed content during upgrade because only the delivered version of the objects is changed in the upgrade process.

Once the data has been readied for extraction, the next step is to establish a stable place to house the data in the SAP NetWeaver BW environment. This process is called data modeling. The next section explores strategies for data modeling in SAP NetWeaver BW.

6.6   Data Modeling

The general concept of establishing and maintaining a data model in SAP NetWeaver BW is complex, and the rules for determining how the model should function are just as complex. It is not easy to make sweeping generalizations. However, there are many data modeling tips that can help to make the general reporting more complete.

6.6.1   Loading into an DSO or ODS

The NW 2004s version of SAP NetWeaver BW refers to the ODS as a DSO, and the 3.x version of SAP NetWeaver BW simply refers to them as ODS. In this section, we describe them together because, even though the NW 2004s DSO has additional functionality beyond the 3.x ODS version, the underlying purpose of the structure is the same.

One of the most important rules for working with DSO/ODS structures is to, whenever possible, make sure that data that is loaded into SAP NetWeaver BW is loaded into a DSO/ODS first with minimal transformation.

It is a mistake to load data into SAP NetWeaver BW and make sweeping transformations of that data as it is loaded immediately into SAP NetWeaver BW. An example is extracting and loading data from SAP ECC for sales orders into a sales order DSO/ODS and adding significant transformation to that data into the first DSO/ODS.

If these significant transformations are incorrect, the data must be dumped and reloaded from the source. Because initial loading of data often requires downtime in SAP NetWeaver BW, this can be a difficult task.

To avoid this, we recommend that the first time data is loaded into SAP NetWeaver BW, it is loaded into one DSO/ODS and kept as close to the source system as possible. If transformation is needed, this should be done into a second level or secondary DSO/ODS layer. If any transformations are incorrect or inconsistent, they can simply be reloaded in the SAP NetWeaver BW environment without involving any source system resources or downtime. This also ensures that if the transformation requirements change, only SAP NetWeaver BW is affected. The dump and reload only occurs in the secondary DSO/ODS.

In the example above, data could be loaded verbatim (or with minimal transformation) into one DSO, then transformed into a secondary DSO, and then loaded onto any InfoCubes for reporting. Although this requires more processing and more batch time, it does allow for a cleaner audit of data and easier dump and reload of data, if needed.

To ensure that data is not lost in the first level DSO/ODS, the level of granularity for the first level DSO/ODS should match the level of granularity of the DataSource that extracts the data. For instance, if the DataSource is extracting data at a sales-order line item level, the first level DSO should also store this data at a sales-order line item level to ensure that there is a one-for-one match between the data that is being extracted and the data that is being loaded into the first level DSO/ODS in SAP NetWeaver BW.

6.6.2   Create a Consolidation Layer for Data

In general, business-content data is set to load in silos. For this reason, there is a Business Content DSO for order header and order line, delivery header, and delivery line data. However, reporting is often needed that consolidates data (Figure 6.13). In this case, often data is needed that would provide an order lifecycle analysis. For example, a user might want to see the order data and its associated deliveries and invoices spanning the lifecycle of the order. This lifecycle analysis is a consolidation of data.

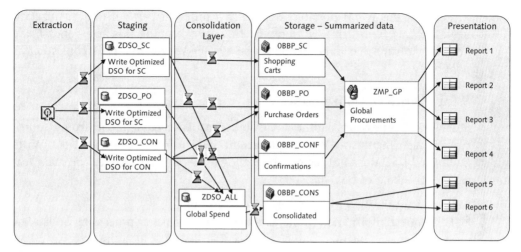

Figure 6.13 Consolidation Layer Example

For the most part, the standard Business Content does not provide a good consolidation layer of data. This is because it is difficult for SAP to determine what data would need to be consolidated and what data would be measured in consolidated form.

This consolidated layer of the data model can then be used as an information hub to provide data to various InfoCubes or for other analysis needs in the organization.

6.6.3 Extract Once, Use Many Times

As a general rule, it does not make sense to extract the same data multiple times from a source system. This allows for different data marts from within the SAP NetWeaver BW system to develop and consequently can allow reporting of the same data to be reported differently, even though it is coming from the same source.

For example, suppose that sales data was extracted from the SAP ECC system and loaded into two separate DSO structures, and then onto two separate InfoCubes. Each InfoCube could have different transformation rules that are being applied to the data as it is loaded into the InfoCube.

The end result would be sales data that is redundant but also data that is loaded into two different InfoCubes with different transformation logic applied. The reporting off this data might then be inconsistent. Whenever possible, all data should be extracted once and used many times.

Sometimes, this is not possible, especially if different parts of the organization need the data transformed differently. However, keeping this as a general rule helps make sure that data loaded into SAP NetWeaver BW is as consistent as possible.

6.6.4 Write Optimized DSO

SAP NW2004s provides additional flexibility to load document data from a source system faster than using Write Optimized DSO. Unlike normal ODS/DSO, Write Optimized DSO does not have a change log and activation queue. The main features of this kind of DSO are:

▶ Data can be written into DSO without activation.

▶ The request information of the data load enables further processing of data.

▶ Missing change log does not allow delta determination of multiple records with same key.

▶ This type of DSO is optimized for data loading in bulk, so that source system can be released faster.

As shown in Figure 6.14, you can switch the standard DSO into Write Optimized DSO.

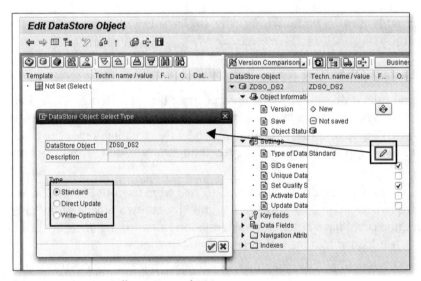

Figure 6.14 Creating Different Types of DSO

6.6.5 Use the Right Object for the Job

There are two main providers and storage facilities for data in SAP NetWeaver BW: the DSO/ODS structure and the InfoCube. Understanding the differences in these two main InfoProviders allows the data model to be most efficient and stable. Often, projects have data modeling issues because they are using the wrong tool for the job. The following discusses the two InfoProviders and highlights each of their strengths.

DataStore Objects (DSO) and Operational Data Store (ODS)

▶ **Consolidates Data**
The DSO/ODS is primarily designed as the main storage area for data in SAP NetWeaver BW. This is typically where the largest volume of SAP NetWeaver BW data resides. This is also a good place to consolidate data from multiple subjects or DataSources into one harmonized data set. Many projects use different layers of ODS/DSO structures to provide this type of consolidation. For example, sales data might be loaded from the SAP ECC system into one first level ODS/DSO structure. This data is typically not transformed in any way. The data is then loaded from the ODS/DSO into a secondary ODS/DSO. The data is transformed and harmonized with other data into the secondary DSO. This consolidation layer of data can then load into one or many InfoCubes for reporting by the end user.

▶ **Transactional or Document-Level Data**
Typically, the DSO/ODS contains detailed level data, often at the document level. In most cases, the DSO/ODS stores many detailed fields from the transactional data. These transactional data fields are typically stored in the DSO/ODS and later aggregated into one or many associated InfoCubes. For example, a typical sales order DSO would contain almost all fields for the transactional order information. Often, only a subset of these fields may actually be loaded into a related InfoCube. The other fields are there either for more detailed reporting or for any future analysis needs.

▶ **Overwrite or Addition Enabled**
The DSO/ODS can be enabled either to be overwritten or added to. This allows each key figure value to aggregate or overwrite the values that are loaded into the DSO/ODS. For example, if a value for sales is $10,000, and a new value of $100 comes in from the source, should the new number be $100.00 or $10,100? This depends on the source and the data presented from the source. When loading the DSO or ODS, the overwrite or additive option can be chosen individually for each key figure value. It is possible to have one key figure overwrite and

another additive in one DSO or ODS. This allows for a great deal of flexibility with the data as it loads.

▸ **Relational Database Structure**
The ODS or DSO is a relational database structure; the data is stored in various tables and linked by this key structure, much like the SAP ECC or SAP R/3 system. This differs from the InfoCube that uses a star-schema methodology.

▸ **High Level of Granularity**
Typically, the ODS or DSO has a high level of granularity because the data is often detailed and at an individual transactional level. The data in the ODS or DSO is detailed and granular.

InfoCubes

▸ **Aggregates Data for Multi-dimensional Reporting**
The InfoCube aggregates or gathers up data and adds these values into one central area for reporting. The InfoCube is the most common repository for reporting in the SAP NetWeaver BW data model.

▸ **Used for Analytic and Strategic Reporting**
Most often, the InfoCube data is used for strategic reporting because the data is often aggregated and not presented at a transactional level of granularity.

▸ **No Overwrite Allowed — Only Additive**
Contrary to the ODS or DSO, the InfoCube does not allow for individual Info-Cubes to be loaded with an overwrite option. This is because the data always aggregates into the InfoCube.

▸ **Extended Star-Schema Design**
The InfoCube has a star-schema database design with one central fact table and multiple dimension tables surrounding this central fact table.

The different attributes of the DSO/ODS and the InfoCube designs allow the two different InfoProviders to be used to exploit their strengths. The InfoCube is primarily designed for providing reporting of many aggregated values. The DSO/ODS is designed to store large amounts of data and pass this data onto existing InfoCubes for analysis.

Strong projects do a good job at tracking and resolving issues. The next section covers some common methods to track and resolve issues that occur in SAP NetWeaver BW.

6.7 Designing Process Chains

Designing a robust process chain is another key reason for efficient implementation of SAP NetWeaver BW. Poor process chain design can lead to overall performance degradation of data loads in SAP NetWeaver BW, and at the same time, SAP NetWeaver BW reports will not reflect updated data within a scheduled time.

Figure 6.15 shows an alternative approach to build process chains by incorporating all equivalent process chains into one instead of running process chains in individual time points. The main process chain will contain all dependant process chains and will have one time point. Scheduling time will be maintained efficiently and you can also set dependency of lower process chains.

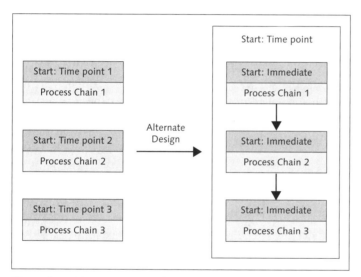

Figure 6.15 Alternate Process Chain Design

6.8 Issue Resolution and Issue Tracking

One of the most important processes in any project is the tracking of the issues. Projects often create elaborate means to track and measure the issues on the project. The most important thing is to make sure that each issue is tracked with a priority, date, and the responsible person or owner of the issue.

In many cases, make sure that the person who is responsible for each issue is an employee, not a consultant. This provides some ownership by the project team of the issue lists and also keeps the issues in the hands of the employees and not the consulting organization.

6.8.1 Reporting Issues via SAP's Service Marketplace

SAP Service Marketplace, formerly called On-line Support System (OSS), is SAP's method for tracking and reporting software issues. Understanding how to report issues properly and—more important—how to search for and use issues that have already been reported and solved help ensure that projects can quickly overcome software issues that are inevitable with any SAP project.

SAP Service Marketplace should be used to report any software issue or anomaly to SAP. A user can search through the existing SAP help desk tickets to see all the reported fixes by SAP. These fixes are called SAP Notes. SAP provides SAP Notes that can be applied to a project system to fix various issues. Periodically, SAP batches up a large number of these notes and puts out a support package. The support package contains all the note fixes from one support package to the next.

When a problem arises with the software, an SAP message is created. This is a project trouble ticket that has been reported to SAP. SAP takes the message and may respond by recommending one or many SAP Notes be applied to a customer system to fix a software issue.

6.8.2 Response Delays

A number of factors can delay having messages responded to by SAP. Here are some tips to get an SAP message responded to quickly with a quality answer:

► Before any message is answered, spend time researching the existing SAP Notes. More often than not, the same problem that you have has already been reported and solved.

► If you cannot find any SAP Notes that reference the software issue that you encountered, enter a detailed SAP message. Many SAP messages fail to give the proper detail and thus produce days of back-and-forth between support personnel and the customer, delaying resolution of issues.

► The SAP message should include a full description of the issue, the steps to reproduce the problem, and any background information needed to understand why and how the problem is occurring.

► Often, SAP help desk representatives will log in to a customer system to reproduce the problem. Expect that this will happen with any SAP message that is created. Make sure that all messages have clear login instructions with user ID and password specified.

▶ Proper care should also be taken to assure that the user ID provided to SAP has security to troubleshoot the issue.

▶ For SAP to log in to a customer system, the SAP connection must be opened. It is typically a Basis task to open the line of communication from SAP to the customer system. Make sure that this connection is open before any SAP message is created. This confirms that if SAP needs to log in to the system, the connection to log in is open.

▶ Use the proper priority on SAP messages. Many projects enter many, if not all, their SAP messages with a high priority. They are often quick to complain that SAP takes a long time to respond to their messages. It helps SAP to be able to prioritize messages if the correct priority is assigned.

▶ Some of the more common issues that occur in SAP NetWeaver BW involve performance. The next section will help you understand some of the tools that can be used to solve performance issues.

6.9   Query Performance Analysis in SAP NetWeaver BW

The most important thing to understand about performance in SAP NetWeaver BW is that the data model needs to be designed from the beginning with performance in mind. Performance, both in query analysis and the load performance, often cannot be retrofitted. Therefore, proper care should always be given to ensure that performance is one of the utmost concerns in any SAP NetWeaver BW implementation.

The following subsections cover some of the most important performance data modeling tools and issues and some information on how to overcome performance problems in the SAP NetWeaver BW implementation.

6.9.1   Data Model Does Not Fit the Data Volume

Often, projects fall into the trap of trying to do too many things or store too much data in one SAP NetWeaver BW object. If one InfoCube contains 100 million rows of data, performance will always be a concern. Thus, understanding and planning for data volume becomes an important task in any project.

Before any InfoCubes or ODS/DSO structures are built in the system, the data volume that will be loaded should be clearly understood. This means that not only should the initial volume of data be analyzed, but each data load that will end up in the model should also be tabulated to make sure that the true data volume is understood.

This data volume helps determine how to create InfoCubes and ODS/DSO structures. SAP provides an easy method to help performance of high-volume data loads. The single best approach to handling high volume is to break up this volume into multiple identical structures. Rather than having one InfoCube or one ODS/DSO structure with 50 million rows, separate this out into four separate but identical ODS/DSO structures or four separate InfoCube structures.

This allows the system to use parallelism for data loads or query access. The end user will never be aware that the data that is being queried comes from multiple InfoCubes. He will, however, get the benefit of faster performance when the database can use parallelism to read the large volume of data in smaller sets because the data is physically separated. This process is known as logical partitioning of data.

To join the various InfoCubes or ODS/DSO structures for reporting, a MultiProvider can be used to provide this join. Any number of InfoCubes and/or ODS/DSO structures can be added to the MultiProvider to provide parallel query processing.

This method should be used any time that volume of data is a concern. It is used to a large extent with projects that have many terabytes of data in their SAP NetWeaver BW systems. It does add to development time, and any changes have to be repeated to all the destination structures; however, the benefit can be pronounced.

6.9.2 Poor Query Definition

Another common concern in SAP NetWeaver BW projects is poor performance with queries. One of the most common reasons for poor query performance lies in the way that queries are constructed.

Queries in SAP NetWeaver BW should take advantage of the tools to slice and dice data in SAP NetWeaver BW. This means that, instead of bringing back large quantities of data on the initial view of a query in SAP NetWeaver BW, the project should instead be designed to provide a small amount of data at a much aggregated level. This will allow for a quicker response time for the query.

If a user is looking for a more detailed set of data, he can then choose the specific characteristics of the desired data. Users should be trained to filter the data as much as possible to limit the data that is shown.

Another way to make sure that a query is defined well is to make sure that it has mandatory variables. Variables are the parameter screen that can first appear when any query is run in SAP NetWeaver BW. The variable screen allows the user to first choose the data filters that will be used on the query.

> **Tip**
>
> It is recommended that all queries have at least one mandatory variable.

These mandatory variables serve several purposes. They provide a filter of data and thus make for better performance. However, they often help performance even more in other ways. If there are no mandatory variables on a query, users typically run the query without filter values in the variables. In other words, they run the query on all data in the system.

This can be a strain on the system, if all users are constantly running queries in this manner. When a user is presented with a mandatory variable, this causes them to reflect on the data that they actually need in the query. This forces them to limit the data, thus helping performance for them. This also helps other users who now have freed-up system resources to run their queries.

Often, the most effective mandatory variables in queries are the date fields. This is because there are few queries that are run in the SAP NetWeaver BW system that do not involve date criteria. If these date fields are used as mandatory variables, the filters can help to make queries run much faster for the users.

6.9.3 Lack of Aggregates

Understanding the tools to improve performance helps to make sure that any performance bottlenecks can be mitigated. If most of the performance slowdown involves gathering the data from the InfoCube, the best way to speed this query performance is via aggregates.

> **Note**
>
> Aggregates, as the name implies, aggregate or pre-group the data during the data load process to greatly speed up the data-retrieval process.

In other words, if a user has developed a query to see the sales for the entire country by sales division, there are two ways of gathering this data. It can either be gathered up at the time that the query is run, or pre-summarized into SAP NetWeaver BW aggregates so the data is read off the aggregates rather than the larger InfoCube. Typical aggregate sizes are less than 10 percent of the size of associated InfoCube fact tables.

For example, an InfoCube might exist with 50 characteristic values. However, 80 percent of all queries use the same six characteristics. This is typical in many SAP NetWeaver BW implementations. Thus, an aggregate or series of aggregates can be created to pre-summarize the data for these six oft-used characteristics.

When a query is run, the system automatically checks to see if there is an available aggregate that can be used to report this data. If one exists, the system uses the aggregate rather than the InfoCube fact table. This results in better query performance.

There is, however, a cost for this better performance. The cost lies in the loading process. Whenever aggregates are created, time data for each is loaded into an InfoCube (aggregates are not currently available on ODS or DSO structures), and a step must be performed to *roll up* that data into the associated aggregates. This roll-up step slows the load time, causing the loading to take much longer than it would without the roll-up step.

This allows for the aggregates to be populated with the most current data. This extra step does slow the load process, but the extra time added to the load process can allow for much faster query performance.

Aggregates can also be used on navigational attributes. These are attributes of master data characteristics in the InfoCube. For example, if there is a division on the material master that is needed for many reports, the division on the material navigational attribute can be added to the aggregates.

This allows for much faster access to navigational attributes, which by nature are slower than the characteristics that exist directly in the InfoCube.

There is one more process that is slowed by navigational attributes in aggregates. The attribute change run job is scheduled after each load to activate the master data object values. It also has another task. If there are aggregates that exist that contain navigational attributes, the change run populates these aggregates with any new data values.

This can cause this change run process to run longer during the batch load window. It does, however, typically allow for much better query performance because the queries only need to look to the aggregates, rather than the fact table and the attribute table, to get the data.

Aggregate Maintenance

Assume that aggregates are not a one-time task. All aggregates should be analyzed to evaluate their usefulness. The best way to see the usefulness of the aggregates is to look at the aggregate maintenance screen. This allows a view of which aggregates are used and which are not. It is typical that many iterations of aggregates are tried until a good set of aggregates is chosen.

Aggregates should be created in the development system and transported to the production system, and then filled in the production system. Any adjustment of the aggregate would also be done via transport.

Any aggregates that are not being used often should be deleted because of the extra overhead that they are costing the system during the data load process.

6.9.4   OLAP Cache

OLAP cache was first introduced in SAP NetWeaver BW Version 20B. Caching is a means of improving query performance. As with most performance-improvement techniques, there are costs as well as benefits to caching.

Caching takes a snapshot of the query results and saves them. When a user has a scenario that requires the same result set, the cache can be read rather than the system re-running the query from the database.

The cost with OLAP cache lies in the organizing and retention of data in the cache. The cache data can be held in the main memory or distributed to an application server or a network. In general, good candidates for caching are complex, popular queries that are run on a data set that is not often refreshed.

The query cache mode determines if and how the system caches the results of the query. It can be set as a default by InfoCube and also individually by query. The cache mode can be set up per query, because it allows the query author to determine if cache would be advantageous for the query.

Example
If a query is created that will be run by a small group of users who never run the same query variables twice, the users would not benefit from cache because there is no repeated query data set to be read from cache. Thus, it would make more sense to turn off cache via the cache-mode setting for this query. Otherwise, the system would incur the overhead of filling cache that would be rarely, if ever, used. Thus, it is up to the query author to evaluate each query to determine if there are multiple users who would run the same query for the same results. If this is the case, the query should be set to cache.

The cache setting by query is in the Query Monitor (via Transaction RSRT). The cache mode determines if cache is used at all. If the cache mode is 0, no cache is used and the query will not benefit from cache. The other options for setting up cache are explained below. There are five different modes of query cache in SAP NetWeaver BW.

- ▶ **0: Cache is Inactive**
  Queries are not set up for cache at all.

- ▶ **1: Main Memory Cache Without Swapping**

  Queries save cache entries into shared memory but do not permit swapping. Swapping is the act of moving the cache from main memory to a file or cluster table when the memory cache is full. Therefore, if the memory cache is full, no cache is saved.

- ▶ **2: Main Memory Cache with Swapping**

  Queries cache entries into shared memory, but allow "swapping" or saving overflow values to disk.

- ▶ **3: Persistent Cluster/Flat File Cache for Each Application Server**

  Queries save cache entries into a cluster or flat file on each application server. In a multi-server environment, the cache is saved on each application server.

- ▶ **4: Persistent Cluster/Flat File Cache Across Each Application Server**

  Queries save cache entries into a cluster or flat file to be shared by all application servers. This setting is preferred when multiple application servers are used in an SAP NetWeaver BW landscape.

The cache settings specify how cache is to be saved. It can be in memory cache or persistent cache. Main memory cache saves query results in shared memory. Memory cache uses main memory to store result sets, thereby taking this memory from other SAP NetWeaver BW processes. In an active SAP NetWeaver BW environment, typically persistent cache is used. This allows the cache to be saved either to a flat file, cluster table, or binary large object (BLOB) table. As a general rule, use a persistent cache using cluster table or BLOB table across the applications server. This allows main memory to be avoided while also enabling users who access queries via different application servers to take advantage of OLAP cache.

The query results can even read subsets of the OLAP cache. If one query was run early in the day for all divisions of the company, each division is shown in the result set. If the identical query is run later in the day for one division, the system can read the division subset of the cache to get results for only one division. This can be a significant feature of OLAP cache.

Some projects use their reporting agent and/or the information-broadcasting feature of SAP NetWeaver BW to schedule high-volume queries to be run in batch. When these queries are run, the data is saved to cache. This allows many users who run the report throughout the workday to take advantage of the cache, and thus provide better query performance on this query.

It should be noted that because cache is set and stored per query, it works well in environments where few queries are run by multiple groups of users. In organizations where many queries are run by few people, the cache is less effective because there is little redundancy to help the performance.

To recap, the OLAP cache allows for saving of query result sets so future queries can take advantage of queries run previously. The data in the cache is automatically made invalid after a query is regenerated or a data load takes place. The cache is therefore typically good for only one day in an environment where data is refreshed daily. However, it is easy to implement and can provide significant performance benefits.

Compression Not Run

One frequent reason for poor query performance is that the compression jobs have not been run on high-volume data sets in SAP NetWeaver BW. This compression job is important for reducing the data volume, thus providing better loading and query performance. It is important to understand compression and the consequences of compressing data in SAP NetWeaver BW.

The goal of compression is, as the name implies, to compress or reduce the amount of data that is stored in an InfoCube. Compression is only possible on an InfoCube, not with ODS or DSO structures. Every InfoCube has two fact tables for storing data. These are the F fact table and the • fact table.

Initial data loaded into an InfoCube is first loaded into the F fact table. The system assigns a unique request identifier to each data package that has been loaded into the InfoProvider. This is set as part of the key of the data load package. The reason for the request identifier is to designate and separate the different data requests that have been loaded into the InfoCube.

Once a request has been compressed, the system flags the request as compressed in the Manage screen of the InfoPackage. Thus, there can be multiple requests in an InfoCube, some compressed and some not compressed. Those that are compressed are stored in the • fact table; those that are not are stored in the F fact table.

If an InfoProvider has not been compressed, the system keeps the request identifier as part of the key structure of data. This causes tremendous inefficiencies when reporting, because the same data can appear multiple times in the uncompressed InfoProvider.

For example, an order InfoCube is created with the characteristics customer, material, calendar month and year, and order quantity. If data is loaded daily into the InfoProvider and one transaction record's order quantity has been changed in the source system five times on five different days, the corresponding data that is loaded into the InfoCube will appear five separate times in the F fact table of an uncompressed InfoCube.

The system keeps the key of the request identifier in the data each time that the data is loaded. Because there were five different loads of that same order, there are five different request identifiers and thus five different records in the F fact table. A query that is created on this order data would be forced to aggregate the five requests at query runtime. This adds significant performance overhead to the query processing.

If this order InfoCube is compressed, the system physically moves the data from the F fact table that is keyed by the request identifier to the • fact table that is not keyed by the request identifier. This compresses the data because the request identifier is eliminated, and the five records noted above exist as one record in the compressed • fact table of the InfoCube.

The system combines and aggregates all records with the same master data keys. Typically, this results in a 20% to 30% percent reduction in the amount of data. The percentage varies based on data, but query performance on compressed data is usually much faster than performance on the uncompressed data because of the reduced data volume.

Compression runs sequentially on each data package. Thus, if many data packages need to be compressed, this could take a long time because each request is compressed in order and no compression parallelization is possible.

InfoCube compression is completely transparent to the end user. There is no evidence that compression has been performed other than improved query performance due to the reduction of data. Data is automatically kept consistent after compression.

Disadvantages of Compression

There is a distinct disadvantage to compression, one that stops many people from compressing data. Once data packages have been compressed, there is no way to back out, or remove individual compressed packages from the InfoProvider. For example, data that has been loaded into an uncompressed InfoCube can simply be deleted by package.

Once an InfoCube has been compressed, it is impossible to remove one individual request. The system has eliminated the request identifier from the key once the compression job has been run. Because the request identifier is gone, you cannot delete one request. Thus, the only way to remove the data from InfoCube is to selectively delete InfoCube data based on other keys. This can be difficult in some circumstances.

It is possible to have some compressed and some uncompressed data in an Info-Cube. The system will aggregate the compressed data in the • fact table with the uncompressed data in the F fact table automatically. To compensate for this disadvantage, many projects keep a few data loads uncompressed. This allows them to have the flexibility to back out recent loads if needed while keeping most of the data compressed in the InfoProvider.

Compression with Zero Elimination

Zero elimination is another performance-enhancing function that can be performed by the system during compression. Depending on the data model and source system data, records can be loaded into an InfoCube with characteristics populated but zero values in all key figures. This is inefficient because these records provide no reporting value and slow the overall reporting performance.

To eliminate these records, the option for zero elimination during compression can be chosen. If this option is checked, the system will remove any records with all key figure values equal to zero during compression. This reduces the data volume and thus provides better query performance. The zero elimination flag should be set whenever compression is run to ensure that the zero records are eliminated from the InfoCube. The only exception is if zero values are valuable for reporting. This is common in planning functions, where a zero plan is used for reporting.

To achieve the optimal query performance, InfoProviders should be compressed as quickly and as often as possible. Compression can greatly improve query performance by reducing the amount of data that is accessed at query runtime. However, this benefit needs to be weighed against the inability of backing out data from the InfoCube.

6.9.5   Partitioning Not Set

Partitioning is a performance-enhancing technique that separates the InfoCube into multiple transparent database tables to enable parallelization and provide better query performance. This occurs because each partition contains a series of the data and queries that can gather data in parallel, thus improving performance. Partitioning can be set in the InfoCube on the InfoObjects calendar month or the fiscal period.

It should be noted that only the InfoCube • fact table is partitioned when the partitioning option is set. Thus, if data has not been compressed and moved from the F fact table into the • fact table, the data is not partitioned. Simply put, if compression is not run, there is no partitioning of data in the InfoCube, even if the partitioning option is set.

To achieve optimal reporting performance and enable parallel processing of queries across partitions, InfoCubes should be compressed. This will ensure that the system is partitioning the data in the InfoCube.

6.9.6 Database Statistics Not Up-to-Date

Database statistics are used by the underlying database platform to optimize query results. The more up-to-date the statistics, the better view the database has on the size of the tables and the better the database optimizer can suggest a join or a path to gather the data.

Every effort should be made to keep these database statistics up-to-date. The best way of doing this is by running the statistics job after the batch loads have been complete. Sometimes, in a system where the batch window for loading data is not long, these statistics are run weekly rather than daily.

The database statistics should not be confused with the SAP NetWeaver BW statistics. The SAP NetWeaver BW statistics are tables and InfoCubes in SAP NetWeaver BW meant to report the speed of processing in the SAP NetWeaver BW system. The database statistics report the table sizes and lengths of the data to the database optimizer.

6.9.7 Virtual Characteristics and Key Figures

Virtual characteristics and virtual key figures determine values at runtime by reading out to other values in SAP NetWeaver BW or even outside systems to show values in a report. These use a virtual key figure or virtual characteristic because they are created during the building of the InfoCube and/or ODS or DSO structure but not actually filled using transformations. They are filled using ABAP code in SAP enhancement RSR00002 or BAdI RSR_OLAP_BADI.

There are several reasons for using a virtual characteristic or virtual key figure. For instance, a sales organization may determine the salesperson's assignment based on the volume of sales to a series of customers. If the sales go over a certain dollar amount, a different salesperson is determined.

Typically, the salesperson is assigned during the time of loading. For example, a sales organization may wish to assign the responsible salesperson who gets commission for sales based on the volume of sales made to a series of customers. In the example above, the salesperson cannot easily be determined at the time of data load because the salesperson is determined based on volumes of sales for groups of products. Only after the entire InfoCube has been loaded can you determine which salesperson should be determined.

In this case, it is not easy to load the salesperson data on each record in the Info-Cube. The other way of determining the salesperson is during the time the query is run. When the data is shown, based on the specific values of the data, the salesperson data is displayed on the report and not stored in the InfoCube data at all.

The virtual characteristic makes the most sense in this example because the only time the salesperson can be determined is after the volume of sales has been aggregated. Unless the InfoCube or ODS/DSO is loaded completely each day, the salesperson cannot be determined on each load but rather by using the query.

Thus, the virtual characteristic is added for the salesperson. If the volume is over a threshold, stored in a custom table in SAP NetWeaver BW, the salesperson is determined from the volume of the sale and the custom table gives the salesperson value. The code determines the salesperson's value.

This approach works well to determine this value, but because of the value being determined at runtime, there is often no way to use aggregates or OLAP cache on the report. This can slow the reporting dramatically. Thus, to stay away from slower reporting, virtual characteristics, and virtual key figures should be avoided if possible or limited to few queries to help query performance.

6.9.8   Time-Dependent Master Data

Time-dependent master data allows for the display of master data snapshots for a specific time or in its present state. This can be a useful feature if multiple views of master data are part of the reporting requirements. However, there is a cost for storing these snapshots of master data. This cost should be weighed against the reporting benefits.

The need for time-dependent master data arises because of the nature of master data. Each loaded record either creates a new record or replaces the attributes of the old master data record. After loading, the former master data view is lost. Any reporting analysis of past data (i.e., sales) reflects the sales using the current view of the attributes and hierarchies of master data, not the view of these at the time of the transaction.

For example, you might need to see sales reports that show the material division of the past month before reorganization was done. The master data will not allow this to occur because it only shows the data as it currently is stored. Master data is replaced each time that the master data is loaded.

This can be frustrating if reporting analysis is desired, showing the master data as it existed in the past. This is especially frustrating if there are frequent realignments of master data. If you analyze prior sales using current master data, you could come to incorrect assumptions on this data. Seeing the master data as it was in the past or when the transaction occurred makes for a more complete view of the data.

Time dependency can be set on InfoObject attributes, hierarchies, and texts. The time dependency is established on the configuration screen for the InfoObject.

Performance is an important factor in determining when and how to add time dependency to the data model. The addition of the new key to the master data increases volume, and often adversely affects query performance.

> **Tip**
>
> All efforts should be made to avoid time dependency in any SAP NetWeaver BW data model.

Once time dependency has been introduced into a data model, it is often difficult to remove it. Once implemented, the increased data volume that is generated often adversely affects query performance. Time-dependent master data does provide a useful process that allows for queries from snapshots of master data. On the other hand, the performance concerns should be weighed against the potential benefit of this SAP NetWeaver BW feature.

There are some ways to speed up the reporting of time-dependent data, including adding time-dependent aggregates. This allows data to be aggregated using a certain key date. This data is set in the aggregate and all data is summarized by this date. As long as the queries are processing based on that date, the aggregate is available for use. This often helps to speed up the time-dependent query performance.

Another way to speed up the query performance is to limit the time dependency to only those attributes that require it. For example, if there are only two fields that are needed for time dependency, only these two attributes should be turned on for time dependency. Many developers make the mistake of turning on all or most attributes for time dependency when only a few are needed.

Yet another way of preventing the time dependency from adversely affecting reporting is to have a shadow attribute that is non–time dependent for each time-dependent attribute. For example, you can require the division on the material master data to be time dependent. You can set the division field to time dependent but also have another division attribute that is non–time dependent.

Typically, most queries do not require the time dependency, so those queries should use the non–time-dependent attribute to show the division. Only the queries that need the time dependency should use the time-dependent attribute of division.

This limits the impact of the time dependency to those queries that require it, thus limiting the impact of the time dependency in the data model.

6.9.9 Complex Authorizations

Adding complex security authorization checks to a data model can often slow the query processing. This occurs because the system must check the authorization objects in the 3.x version and/or authorization analysis in the NW 2004s version of SAP NetWeaver BW. The more complex the authorization strategy, the more this has a potential to slow the query results.

To avoid authorizations slowing the query processing, a clear strategy for security with an eye toward performance should be considered. Often, the security requirements are non-negotiable. For example, if one division of a company cannot see another division's budget numbers, this should be considered as a requirement in SAP NetWeaver BW. The strategy needs to include these requirements.

If the data model involves lower volumes of data, this is not a concern. But, as the system is required to access many millions of rows of data and check security on each one, this can cause query processing to slow. Authorizations can be implemented and secured on the following:

- Query level
- InfoProvider level (ODS/DSO InfoCube)
- Characteristic level
- Characteristic value level
- Key figure level
- Hierarchy node level

The list above is sorted by the least resource intensive to the most resource intensive security strategy. If the security requirements can be fulfilled using a security strategy that is broad rather than more detailed and system intensive, performance can be better.

In this example, security requirements are established to allow for one division not to see the other division's budget information. This can be handled by setting security at a characteristic value level, in this case at the division level. In a high-volume data environment, this can slow the query processing as the system checks each division and compares that with the role of the user running the query.

With some data modeling, this can be handled at a higher level. For example, the division can be secured at an InfoProvider level if the data is segregated into like InfoCubes by InfoProvider. This would allow for a parallel processing of the data and provide only one check at the InfoCube level rather than at the characteristic value level.

The system keeps statistics on the time used for authorization checks. So, to pilot several methods of security, each can be evaluated to determine its load on the overall query performance. Often, this is difficult to judge in the development system, but at least, you can estimate the cost of authorizations.

There are many different circumstances for security implementations, and thus each needs to be evaluated individually. Performance should be one consideration when developing a security strategy.

6.9.10 NW 2004s BW Accelerator

There has been a lot of discussion and excitement over the BW Accelerator appliance that has been announced and rolled out by SAP. This allows for Google-type indexing of data in the data model. Running in place of aggregates, this accelerator can index data and provide startling query performance.

The basic issue with the BW Accelerator is the cost. There are limited lists of hardware vendors that build this appliance. They have created a custom chip to run the appliance. To make implementation profitable, the price is steep for many projects.

At the current time, this does appear to be an exciting performance-enhancing tool. However, it may be outside of the budget of many projects. Even with the appliance in place, sound data modeling practices should be followed to ensure that, even in the absence of this hardware, the model will perform well.

6.10 Conclusion

Although the actual building and configuring of the SAP NetWeaver BW system can become complex, it is important to understand the way that data flows through the system and the methods that are typically used to transform data. By understanding these tools, it is easier to anticipate the various issues that might occur with these tools. This will help the project manager be more proactive in problem solving.

Because the SAP NetWeaver BW product itself is robust, a project manager would have a difficult time managing the project while also providing substantial configuration. This reduces some of the effectiveness of the project management staff because they find themselves limited in their configuration experience of the product. This is typical in any SAP NetWeaver BW project.

The most experienced project managers rely on an experienced data architects and SAP NetWeaver BW developers to keep the solution and design intact but also to keep a close eye on the requirements. If the project management staff understands the requirements fully, it can keep the team focused on what the solution should deliver.

This allows the project managers to assert themselves during the design phase and then again even more strongly on early unit tests. If the unit tests do not appear to match the known requirements, the project management staff can step and redirect the design to better match those requirements. This does not require significant configuration strength but rather requires one eye on the business and the other eye on development.

In Chapter 7, we will discuss some of the challenges associated with a project after the configuration is complete. Planning for the rollout of SAP NetWeaver BW during the build phase helps to allow for a smooth transition to go-live.

The cutover tasks associated with go-live are often stressful, but proper planning should help to relieve some of the stress by providing the right resources and escalation in the event of issues.

7 Preparing for Go-Live and the Go-Live Process

After the configuration of SAP NetWeaver BW is complete, the SAP NetWeaver BW team has not finished work. Typically, the next logical step in the process is to do a review of the entire model to ensure that it follows the naming standards, design standards, etc. Once this is complete, the SAP NetWeaver BW configuration can be transported to the QA environment for testing.

After this testing is complete and all issues resolved, the SAP NetWeaver BW configuration can then be transported to the production system. In this chapter, we will explore the various challenges presented during the process of actuating the data model in the production system. This involves setting a clear strategy for publishing queries to the portal for end user processing.

Figure 7.1 outlines the activities to be performed for SAP NetWeaver BW go-live preparation. The main objective in this phase is to test and review the different SAP NetWeaver BW objects and configurations. This phase may also include execution of any additional explanation or training for information users. There are generally hundreds of different tasks that must be completed before go-live; it is mandatory that a critical path-based checklist is prepared, discussed, agreed, and followed to ensure a successful and smooth go-live.

In Figure 7.1, we outlined the steps and you will learn in-depth procedures about each step in subsequent sections.

Review	• Make sure there is no functional gap in data model • All BW objects adhere the naming standards • All security strategy is implemented as per plan • All BW objects are well documented
Transport Management	• Make sure all BW objects are included in transports • Prepare an extensive plan for Transport failure • All Transports should be well documented to go-live without much problems
Test	• Develop test scripts for testing the BW objects • Different kind of tests (Unit test, Integration test and Stress test) should be performed to ensure smooth and expected behavior of BW objects in production system
Change Management	• Plan for end • Develop proper training materials • If necessary plan for some hands
Go-Live Checklist	• All Defects are fixed • Resources in the production server are installed properly • Technical parameters are set properly
Initialize Production	• After transporting BW objects, perform the initialization loads • Schedule jobs in ECC system • Schedule process chains

Figure 7.1 Overview Steps for the Go-Live Process

7.1 Data Model and System Review

As mentioned in Chapter 5, the data model and system review is vital for consistency and should be performed after the SAP NetWeaver BW development configuration is complete. The SAP NetWeaver BW data model design review walks through an existing data model in SAP NetWeaver BW prior to transport to QA, or other systems, to make sure that the design is sound. As project teams grow, it is often hard to make sure that each design being populated into an SAP NetWeaver BW system is stable and conforms to standards.

This is because new team members are not always aware of the design and naming standards of the project. We recommend that as new team members join, part of their orientation includes a walk though a design-standards document. It should also be clear to all team members that design reviews will be conducted to keep the designs consistent.

The data model design review process includes formal evaluation to determine if standards have been followed and if the model seems sound from both a business and technical standpoint. This is designed as a two-part working session. One of the reviews occurs in the analysis phase but before the build; the other occurs after the build but before any transports are released. This allows all data models in SAP NetWeaver BW to be formally checked to make sure that they follow development standards.

This design review should be a formality in most projects, because the data architect or design lead should be reviewing the design throughout the project. However, the review allows for a more formal check covering several aspects. A full formal checklist of each is found in Appendix B. The following team members need to be present during the design review:

▶ Business team representative or SME
▶ Data architect or design lead
▶ SAP NetWeaver BW project manager
▶ SAP NetWeaver BW developers for the model

It is important that this session not be seen as a group evaluation of the design work and should not be performed in a confrontational environment. It should be seen as a collaboration to confirm and verify the design. The design review team works together to make sure that the data model conforms to the following:

▶ Naming standards followed
▶ Security requirements understood
▶ SAP NetWeaver BW design standards followed
▶ Business expectations and requirements understood
▶ Documentation complete

The overall goal is to make sure that there are no design issues with the model. Making sure that the model adheres to SAP NetWeaver BW best practices helps to avoid restatements and dumps and reloads of data later.

Making sure that all documentation is complete is a vital part of any review process. Understanding and enforcing adequate documentation can make the transition of any SAP NetWeaver BW project from the SAP NetWeaver BW development team to a SAP Center of Excellence (COE) or production support organization much easier.

Let's explore some of the most common configuration documentation and its main sections and goals.

7.2   Documenting SAP NetWeaver BW Configuration

Documenting of the SAP NetWeaver BW data model should occur throughout the SAP NetWeaver BW data modeling and development process. However, the data model review is a good time to make sure that this documentation is up-to-date and matches the system configuration.

There are four main documents that we recommend to describe the configuration design in SAP NetWeaver BW. Each project typically has its own documentation standards and templates; some have more documents, and some have fewer documents. These are as follows:

- Functional Model Document
- DSO/ODS Technical Design Document
- InfoCube Technical Design Document
- ETL Technical Design Document

Samples of these documents are in Appendix C.

These documents are usually used to bring new developers on board in such a way that they understand the current development environment. It can also be used to transition the development to the COE or production support organization. In some cases, these documents show the data models at a high level to the project management organization.

Let's now explore the most common ways of documenting SAP NetWeaver BW configuration.

7.2.1   SAP NetWeaver BW Functional Model Document

This document, described in Chapter 5, gives an overall understanding of the business and organizational needs for the SAP NetWeaver BW model. This serves as the functional design document for an entire subject area. This document should answer the following questions: Why did we do this? What needs were we trying to fill? What was the goal of this model?

7.2.2   DataStore Object/Operational Data Store (DSO/ODS) Technical Design Document

This document provides the business use for a DSO or ODS. NW 2004s uses the term DSO, while the SAP NetWeaver BW 3.x release uses the term ODS, but the purpose of both structures are similar. The same document can be used for both. This document should clearly define and document the type of data in the DSO/

ODS and the overall part that the DSO or ODS plays in loading the data model. For example, when loading purchasing data, the data might first load into one DSO, and then to another DSO, where it is transformed to meet specific reporting requirements. In this case, there would be two DSO documents, each explaining the role of its DSO, its use, transformation logic, and how the data flows between each object.

This document is also designed to provide a profile of the data that is loaded. The overall goal of this document is to answer the following questions: Why did we create this DSO/ODS? What is its purpose in the data model? What kind of data is stored in this DSO/ODS? What data flows in and out of this DSO/ODS? How is data transformed before or after this DSO/ODS, and why?

7.2.3   InfoCube Technical Design Document

The InfoCube technical design document is designed to document the InfoCube, its contents, and its use. This document contains information on how data is being fed into the InfoCube. It also details the type of data, its volume, and whether there are any historical data that has been loaded into the InfoCube at the time of go-live.

This document also has information on the partitioning settings of the InfoCube and any aggregate designs associated with the InfoCube to provide faster reporting to the end user. If InfoSets are used, these are also documented using this template. InfoSets are another kind of InfoProvider used to present data to the end user.

7.2.4   Extraction, Transformation, and Loading (ETL) Technical Design Document

The ETL technical design document is helpful in a complex SAP NetWeaver BW environment. There often are many different InfoCubes and DSO/ODS structures in an SAP NetWeaver BW model that are used for many different purposes. The data flows through the various structures for use in analysis reporting, and one DSO/ODS may be used for many different tasks. Therefore, when looking at the overall flow of data in the organization, it is often difficult to understand which DSO/ODS structures feed which InfoCubes, etc.

Transformation introduces further complexities. Sometimes, because transformation occurs between a DSO/ODS and an InfoCube, it becomes difficult to fully describe the transformation. This is because you do not know where the transformation should be documented, or whether it should be documented with the source or the destination structure.

The ETL document prevents any debate over where the documentation should reside for the complete flow and transformation of data in the data model. By creating one ETL document for each subject area, the ETL documents can be used to follow the data through the SAP NetWeaver BW system from DataSource all the way to query analysis.

By using these four main documents, the data model in SAP NetWeaver BW can be fully documented. In many cases, a signoff is added to each document to formally finalize it.

As shown in Figure 7.2, a document needs to be completed at a particular phase in the project. That is, there are specific times that each document needs to be created and delivered. Samples of each document are in Appendix C.

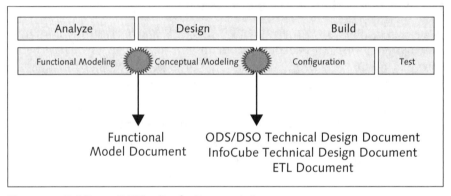

Figure 7.2 NetWeaver BW Timeline for Documentation

One of the other documentation features of SAP NetWeaver BW is in the Metadata Repository. This is a function that can be run either from within SAP NetWeaver BW or as a Web frontend that shows the different structures in a data model. Let's see how this can be useful in a SAP NetWeaver BW project.

7.2.5 The MetaData Repository

One of the more useful features of SAP NetWeaver BW is in its ability to self-document. The MetaData Repository can be used to show all the different structures that have been activated and loaded in the SAP NetWeaver BW environment. The MetaData Repository also shows those structures that have not been activated. These represent the business content that is available for activation in the SAP NetWeaver BW system. See Figure 7.3 for a screenshot of the MetaData Repository.

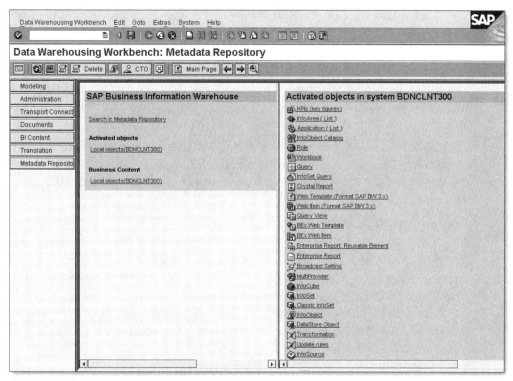

Figure 7.3 The MetaData Repository

The MetaData Repository also shows the full flow of data through the data model. This will allow the viewer to see the different DSO/ODS structures that are being loaded as part of a data model. If multiple structures are being loaded from one source, the MetaData Repository has this information.

One of the mistakes that some project organizations make is not taking advantage of the Metadata Repository to help document the SAP NetWeaver BW solution. They create their own design documents that painstakingly map out each InfoObject for each structure in the design documents. This not only is a tedious process but is unnecessary because of the MetaData Repository.

Rather than spending a lot of time cutting and pasting the various InfoObjects that make up the InfoCubes and DSO/ODS structures in SAP NetWeaver BW, it makes much more sense to leverage the MetaData Repository for this type of documentation. The focus of the InfoCube, ODS/DSO, and ETL documents is not to show every InfoObject and field associated with each structure in SAP NetWeaver BW. The goal is to understand the flow, transformation, and purpose of data to provide the analysis for the end users.

The documentation should not be used to track and document each and every InfoObject that makes up an SAP NetWeaver BW structure. This not only requires a major effort in creating the initial document, it also makes it more difficult to keep the documentation up-to-date as new fields get added to the structures.

The MetaData Repository allows a user to look at the configuration and fields for each InfoCube, DSO/ODS, and query in the system and enables a greater understanding of each structure as data flows through the organization.

The MetaData Repository provides the fields and flow of data through SAP NetWeaver BW. This tool does not show the business questions that the model represents and the various reasons for transformation, field supplementation, etc. Thus, the documentation should reflect this information.

The MetaData Repository can also be exported to the Web to be used as a portal link so the entire organization can see the existing data model. This makes the MetaData Repository more useful because it opens it up to more users.

Another popular tool for documenting configuration is SAP Solution Manager. This allows documents to be posted to one central documentation area that is open to all users. In the next section, we'll explore what works well in SAP NetWeaver BW for SAP Solution Manager and what areas need improvement.

7.3 SAP NetWeaver BW Document Management Tool

SAP NetWeaver BW has built-in tools to create, store, and display the documents for different SAP NetWeaver BW objects. This document management tool can be accessed from RSA1- • Document Tab. Figure 7.4 shows the document management tool available within SAP NetWeaver BW.

Main functionalities of this tool include:

▶ You can add documents for metadata, master data, and InfoProvider data.
▶ You can write the documents in different formats like RTF, Text/HTML, and Microsoft Word, etc.
▶ You can maintain documents in different languages.
▶ You can set links between the documents using hyperlink.
▶ Documents can be accessible from different SAP NetWeaver BW tools like BEx analyzer, Web Applications, etc.

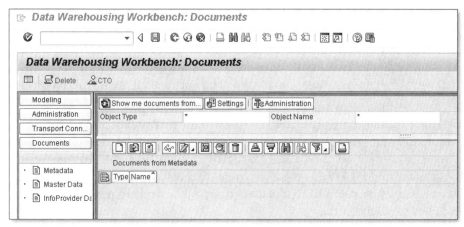

Figure 7.4 SAP NetWeaver BW Document Management Tool

7.4 SAP Solution Manager

SAP Solution Manager is a standalone SAP product designed to serve as a document repository and also provide documentation of configuration steps used in an SAP system. The product is designed mainly to centralize the place that the process teams go to complete their configuration. Instead of performing the configuration steps in the actual system itself, the developer would log on to SAP Solution Manager to enter the configuration and record documentation with each step.

Many projects use SAP Solution Manager to keep the process teams organized around the use of one tool to document and perform all configuration tasks. For this reason, SAP Solution Manager is a useful product when used by the SAP ECC and SAP R/3 environments because much if not all the configuration is done in the Implementation Guide (IMG) section of the product.

The IMG is a series of tables and settings that are used to tune, add features, and set up the SAP ECC and SAP R/3 systems. In the SAP R/3 and SAP ECC systems, the users would log on to SAP Solution Manager and perform their configuration steps in the SAP Solution Manager environment and this would set the configuration in the associated SAP ECC or SAP R/3 systems.

Because the SAP NetWeaver BW system also has an IMG that is used for some central settings, some project managers believe that they can use the features of SAP Solution Manager to provide in the SAP NetWeaver BW environment the same kind of central configuration and documentation available in SAP ECC and SAP R/3.

Unfortunately, this is not currently advisable. Although the SAP NetWeaver BW system does have an IMG, it is used rarely. Of all the configurations done on the SAP NetWeaver BW system, fewer than 5% are actually done in the IMG. Because SAP Solution Manager currently only documents the configuration in the IMG, it is not useful for configuration centralization and documentation in SAP NetWeaver BW.

Therefore, for those project teams that plan to use SAP Solution Manager, don't use Solution Manager to provide centralized configuration documentation. There is, however, a common use for SAP Manager in conjunction with SAP NetWeaver BW. It is as an SAP NetWeaver BW document repository. SAP Solution Manager does a good job at centralizing document management, help desk tracking, and document version control.

SAP Solution Manager can provide a place for all in-process and completed SAP NetWeaver BW configuration documentation. SAP Solution Manager typically keeps documents better organized and with better version control than you could achieve by keeping the equivalent data in a shared drive. It allows documents to be locked while editing, thus providing a convenient way to publish documentation that can be reviewed by the project team.

Some projects also use some of the features of SAP Solution Manager for issues tracking in SAP NetWeaver BW. The SAP Solution Manager is evolving as a product and does allow for some useful features for document management, but in its current form, it is not useful for centralizing the configuration management in SAP NetWeaver BW.

Another challenging area in SAP NetWeaver BW is transport management. Transport management moves configuration from one SAP NetWeaver BW system to another. Let's explore some of the challenges that this presents.

7.5   Transport Management in SAP NetWeaver BW

The SAP NetWeaver BW Transport Management System (TMS) allows you to transport or move your work from one system to another. For example, an InfoCube that was created in the development environment can be moved to the QA environment via the TMS. Configuration, objects, roles, and Business Exchange (BEx) objects (queries) can and should be transported from the development system to the QA system, and then onto the production system.

As shown in Figure 7.5, the transport path in SAP NetWeaver BW—as with any SAP system—originates in the development system. All transports move from the development system to their intended destination system. To move configuration, a transport is created.

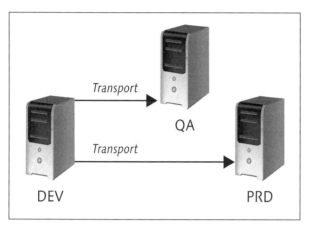

Figure 7.5 Typical Transport Path in SAP NetWeaver BW

A transport in SAP NetWeaver BW can contain one or many configurable items that need to be moved from one system to another. Each transport is automatically numbered by the system in a sequential manner with a prefix of the source system. Let's take the example of BDN900010. This transport number will track the status of the transport as it moves from one system to another. If there are issues with the transport, the transport number serves as a tracking tool to find the issue and view the failure log for the transport.

Typically, the SAP NetWeaver BW transport is first moved to the QA environment, tested fully, and then the same transport is moved to the production environment. If the tests fail, another transport is usually created to fix any issue; this transport is sent to the QA environment again and re-tested. If it passes, both transports are usually sent to the production environment. The first transport establishes the configuration and the second transport fixes the issue, keeping the configuration in the QA environment in sync with the production environment.

The most popular way to create transports in the SAP NetWeaver BW system is to go into the Transport Connection screen in SAP NetWeaver BW; this is found as a menu item from Transaction RSA1. Figure 7.6 shows a detailed screen shot of the Transport Connection in SAP NetWeaver BW. This transaction is found as a menu option on the bottom of the Transaction RSA1 screen.

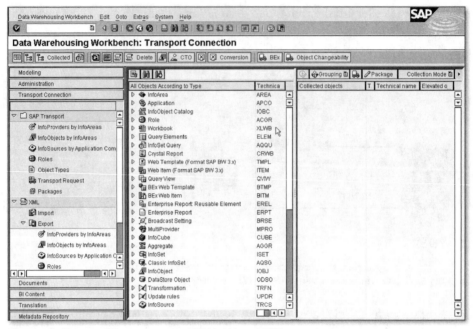

Figure 7.6 Transport Management in SAP NetWeaver BW

The Transport Connection also does a good job pointing out any prerequisite objects that need to be activated before other objects. This allows the user to avoid some of the common errors that are associated with the SAP NetWeaver BW transport process. There are several tips to remember when using the SAP NetWeaver BW transport system. These are noted in the subsections that follow.

7.5.1 SAP NetWeaver BW Transport Management System Tips

SAP NetWeaver BW is known for transport issues. The typical issues involve transport failures when transports are being sent into a destination system. This is the nature of the SAP NetWeaver BW system, because much of what is done in SAP NetWeaver BW is leveraged from previous work. For example, when creating an InfoCube, various InfoObjects need to be either activated or created.

If the InfoCube is transported before the related InfoObjects, the transport will fail. The only way to fix the transport is to create another transport with the missing InfoObject and send the original transport again. There is no way to append the missing InfoObject onto the original transport because the original transport has already been released. SAP does not allow appending to transports that have been released.

Many project teams make the mistake of allowing little time for the SAP NetWeaver BW transport process. Often, it takes several days to get the entire SAP NetWeaver BW configuration from one environment to another. Because SAP NetWeaver BW transports are challenging, the expectation should be set immediately that SAP NetWeaver BW transports can and will fail. There are people who are accustomed to working with SAP ECC and/or SAP R/3 transports, and they are amazed at the difficulty of SAP NetWeaver BW transports and the expertise and effort needed for troubleshooting.

If possible, it helps to have a developer or data architect who is familiar with the SAP NetWeaver BW transport process to help guide the transports and troubleshoot their failures.

7.5.2   General SAP NetWeaver BW Transport Tips

The following are some general tips for SAP NetWeaver BW transports:

▶ To avoid multiple transports, do not begin transporting until development is complete and stable.

▶ Wait until as long as possible to transport.

▶ Do prototyping and playing in the sandbox and try to keep the *junk* out of development. Delete any unneeded objects to prevent them from being included in a transport accidentally.

▶ Be mindful of the transport order. The sequence in which transports are sent to the QA system is the same in which they should be sent to the PRD (production) system.

▶ Do not try to create one large SAP NetWeaver BW transport. Instead, separate the SAP NetWeaver BW transports into smaller transports grouped by object type.

7.5.3   Separate SAP NetWeaver BW Transports into Logical Groups

Errors and transport failures can be reduced if, instead of trying to group all SAP NetWeaver BW objects into one transport, you add the SAP NetWeaver BW objects to transports based on their object types.

Although there is no functional reason that transports cannot be grouped together with unlike objects in one transport, it is not a best SAP NetWeaver BW practice. For example, the system would allow an InfoObject and InfoCube to be placed together in one transport and sent to the QA system. The issue that can sometimes be encountered is that an InfoObject is needed for another InfoCube that is in a different transport; these transports are dependent and must be sent in the proper order.

If unlike objects are stored together in different transports, it is difficult or impossible to determine what transport order should be used. Thus, if all InfoObjects are kept in one transport, they can be sent first, allowing all InfoObjects to be generated in the QA system first before any InfoCubes are sent. The following is a list of the object types and the order in which the transports should be sent to the destination system:

1. SAP ECC and/or SAP R/3 DataSources and structures (replicate after transporting)
2. Application components/InfoAreas
3. InfoObjects
4. DSO or ODS structures
5. InfoCubes/InfoSets
6. Security authorization objects (if applicable)
7. Stand alone Ztables and ABAP (if applicable)
8. Transfer rules (3.x logic)
9. Update Rules (3.x logic)
10. Transformations (NW 2004s)
11. MultiProviders
12. Aggregates
13. Web templates
14. Variables from BEx
15. BEx Web queries
16. Portal objects

The transports can be released in any order; however, the transports should only be imported and executed in the order above. Thus, if there is one subject area with multiple DSO/ODS, InfoCubes, and queries, the objects should be split up into transports based on their type. All DataSources are sent first, followed by all InfoObjects, etc.

After any SAP ECC or SAP R/3 DataSource activation or DataSource transports, a manual step of replication should be included to make sure that the new Data-Sources are available in the destination system.

7.5.4   Keep Careful Watch of Transports — Take Good Notes

Because of the tendency of SAP NetWeaver BW transports to fail, keep a careful log of each transport and its status and order. The order of the transports in the QA system should be exactly the same order as the transports into the production system.

Some projects opt to keep this order intact for each system. If transport into the QA system fails, they track and document the failure. During cutover, they send the same transports in the same order and allow those that fail in the QA environment to fail again on the way to the production system.

> **Example**
>
> Suppose the order in Transport A fails, Transport B succeeds, and Transport A is sent again. This should be exactly the same order in which the transports are sent to the production system, to ensure that the system stays in sync.

Some project organizations opt to reorder the transports slightly between the systems. For example, when building the QA environment, Transport A is sent first and fails because it is missing a dependent InfoObject 0PLANT. Transport B is created to transport 0PLANT. Transport B is sent to the QA environment, and then transport A is re-sent. Transport A succeeds the second time because 0PLANT now exists in the system from Transport B.

Some project organizations opt to reorder these transports when sending them to the production environment. Rather than letting Transport A fail, they reorder the transports: sending Transport B first, then sending Transport A, and allowing them both to move successfully into production.

Both processes work. The decision of which to use depends on how strict the project team wants to be in sending the transports to production in the exact order in which they were sent to the QA environment.

7.5.5   Never Leave a Transport Behind

It is a best practice to make sure that all transports that are released and imported are tried again and again until they are transported successfully. It is not recommended that a new transport be created each time a transport fails.

For example, Transport A is created with two InfoCubes inside it. The transport has been released, and the Basis team has attempted to import and execute it into the destination system. The transport fails because of a missing InfoObject. This missing InfoObject can be included on a new transport, released, imported, and executed in the destination system. Now the original transport should be executed again. This ensures that everything in the transport exists in the new system.

If a new transport is created each time a transport fails, it is difficult to trouble-shoot and track the transports to make sure that all objects are transported. If any-thing is missed on subsequent transports, the systems can become out of sync. It is recommended that, each time a transport is released, every effort be made to make sure that the transport is imported and executed successfully in the destina-tion system.

7.5.6 Final Cutover Recapture of Transports

Typically, transports are sent into subsequent systems in exactly the same order. Sometimes, there are issues with this process. In the case of SAP NetWeaver BW transports, sometimes it is not advisable to follow this procedure. This happens when the same objects have been sent from development to QA many times. For example, one InfoCube, if changed many times, might have been captured in a transport several times. If all these transports are sent, the InfoCube will be cre-ated over and over. This increases the time that it takes for the transports to be sent to production.

This can mean that when it is time for cutover to production prior to go-live that there are many hundreds, if not thousands, of SAP NetWeaver BW transports for each iteration of the design. Sending each transport into production in the exact order that it went to QA can take a great deal of time and effort.

Some projects decide to re-gather these transports into a brand new grouping and resend them rather than use the existing transports to send to the production sys-tem. For example, in the process of developing an InfoCube, this InfoCube could be sent to the QA system 10 times, 15 times, or even more, depending on how many changes happen to the InfoCube in the lifecycle of the development.

If the transports are sent in the same order from QA to production, this InfoCube is regenerated 10 or 15 times. Often, the cutover to production occurs on a weekend shutdown, and time is of the essence. If the same InfoCube is created and recre-ated, this can take up a great deal of time.

It may be advisable to recapture the transports for cutover. This process involves gathering up all the objects from the development environment into new trans-ports. These transports will be sent in place of the large volume of cutover trans-ports noted above.

This allows the transport process to complete more quickly and smoothly. Every effort needs to be made to make sure that no objects are missed. After going live, the production system can then be copied to QA to keep these two systems in sync.

7.5.7 The Mock Cutover

Some customers opt to have a mock cutover. This involves creating a new server that would mimic production. Sending all transports over to the new mock cutover system ensures that the actual cutover will go smoothly. This mock cutover is often the best way to ensure that the actual cutover goes smoothly and without issue.

Typically, the mock cutover is performed after all transports are sent to QA. The list of transports is now intact, and the mock cutover can be performed to send all transports from the development environment to another non-production box as a dress rehearsal for sending the transports to the production system.

This allows the project to estimate the timeline of the transports and make sure that any issues during the actual cutover are minimized. This is often performed in projects where there is limited time for cutover to production. Most often, the cutover to production takes place when the production system is down.

If the downtime has a short window, there is little allowance for errors and issues with the transports. The mock cutover allows these issues to be understood and fixed without the time constraints of the typical production transport downtime. After the cutover has occurred, the data must then be loaded into the SAP NetWeaver BW environment.

After the data is loaded, it can then be verified and reconciled against its associated source system data. In the next section, we will walk through a common testing scenario for SAP NetWeaver BW.

7.6 Testing in SAP NetWeaver BW

After the transports have been loaded into SAP NetWeaver BW, the next step is to populate the data in the various systems and measure this data against the desired data model. There are several different processes that can be established to reconcile and test the data in SAP NetWeaver BW to ensure accuracy.

7.6.1 Develop at SAP NetWeaver BW Test Plan

The first step in testing SAP NetWeaver BW is to create a test plan based on the scope of the project and the functional requirements of the system. This should include the testing resources, testing goals, and timeline.

Several different types of tests are required in an SAP NetWeaver BW system. Each test is designed to test that the system is ready for production and that it meets the defined business, technical, and validation requirements. The following paragraphs describe different types of SAP NetWeaver BW testing:

▶ **Unit Test**
Ensures that development activities work in line with the functional and technical design documents.

▶ **Integration Test**
Ensures that development objects hand off data in a manner that is consistent and correct. It will also ensure that the SAP NetWeaver BW application design works end-to-end, including all applications with input to SAP NetWeaver BW and all applications receiving output from SAP NetWeaver BW.

▶ **Stress Test**
Ensures that the system and application components meet performance requirements. This is designed to make sure that the system can handle the intended volume.

▶ **Operational Readiness Test**
Ensures readiness of the organization to support the system in production. Test issues include error management, disaster recovery, and system availability.

7.6.2 Developing Test Scripts for SAP NetWeaver BW

The following guidelines should be followed while writing SAP NetWeaver BW test scripts and executing the test process. A sample integration test script is found in Appendix F. Every test script should have the following:

▶ Testing cycle
▶ Source system
▶ Created by
▶ Creation date
▶ Tested by
▶ Tested date
▶ Verified by (business person)
▶ Primary developer.

The test purpose should be clearly defined to explain the reason for the test and the expected outcomes. This should include the inputs and outputs to the process. Any setup requirements should be clearly spelled out in the test script. These setup requirements include all of the following:

- ▸ Business Information Warehouse setup
- ▸ Other source system setup (if applicable)
- ▸ Transactional data requirements
- ▸ Master data requirements

All SAP NetWeaver BW test scenarios should be developed to ensure that all mandatory and important requirements identified in the functional specification are tested thoroughly. The test scenarios should walk through all the steps of the process in detail. Assume that the executer of the test script is familiar with SAP NetWeaver BW and the processes of SAP NetWeaver BW.

All custom-developed objects should be tested in detail for all fields. Standard InfoObjects need not be tested in detail. Test script should list all the transformation routines that are used in the respective objects. The script should clearly list the expected results and the actual results. All test results should be saved together for future reference.

Someone other than the primary developer or test-script author should execute the test scripts. Thus, the test script should be detailed enough for others to run the test. In most cases, the test script will involve both SAP NetWeaver BW and legacy roles.

For example, a test script might be used to prove that the sales order data is loading properly into SAP NetWeaver BW. A new sales order should be created and this followed into the SAP NetWeaver BW system and verified against that SAP ECC or SAP R/3 transactional data to make sure that it matches. All order values should then be loaded to test that all orders are coming in properly. List functionality can be used on the SAP ECC system and compared with SAP NetWeaver BW queries to make sure that the total order quantity and order values match.

In all cases where delta loads are used, the full load of data should be tested along with the delta loads of data to make sure that the delta loads are working properly.

Query testing should include validating all relevant data values. Fields that are transformed may be validated before and after each transformation. Every effort should be made to get a sample of production data. For example, a process that works fine with a standard purchase orders may fail when drop-shipments are used. Every effort should be made to include as many data scenarios as possible. Screen captures of all steps should be included as documentation of the testing. These can be attached to the test script.

All issues that are encountered during the test script execution should be recorded on the test script and also using the project issue-tracking process. The scripts should be clearly denoted as PASS/FAIL, and those that fail should be designated for re-test.

Because query performance is a big consideration in SAP NetWeaver BW, the test scripts should also focus on performance. When possible the performance should be documented in the script. These can be used for benchmarking against what could be expected in the production landscape. It is not always possible to benchmark against the production environment, but every step possible to validate performance should be performed.

7.6.3 Automated Testing Tools

There are many automated testing tools on the market that can aid in the testing of transactional systems. These systems work well to simulate users entering values into the system. Typically, automated testing tools do not work well for SAP NetWeaver BW testing.

The problem with attempting to use an automated testing tool in SAP NetWeaver BW lies in the nature of SAP NetWeaver BW reporting. Unlike iterative processes like entering in sales orders or making journal entries, SAP NetWeaver BW is a more interactive process. Once live, users have many different ways of drilling into and filtering reports based on need.

Thus, because the uses of SAP NetWeaver BW vary so greatly, it often does not make sense to use an automated test tool to test SAP NetWeaver BW. An automated testing tool cannot reflect and show a series of users with many differing analysis patterns. SAP NetWeaver BW also needs to be checked against the source during the testing process. The automated testing tools often cannot perform these types of tests.

Thus, the most popular way of using automated testing tools in the SAP NetWeaver BW environment is to run a stress test on the system. The automated testing tools can often give an idea of how many users are capable of running analysis queries in the SAP NetWeaver BW system, thus gauging the potential workload.

Typically, most testing in SAP NetWeaver BW is done manually. The SAP NetWeaver BW testers often work closely with an SAP R/3 or SAP ECC counterpart to provide transactional data additions, changes, and deletions to test and reconcile the loaded data into SAP NetWeaver BW.

In some projects, the transactional processing teams teach the SAP NetWeaver BW team to enter, change, and delete transactions, and the SAP NetWeaver BW team performs the transactions and reconciles the data into SAP NetWeaver BW.

Now, let's proceed with understanding organizational change management in an SAP NetWeaver BW implementation.

7.7   Organizational Change Management

Many projects see training as a necessary evil of SAP NetWeaver BW implementation, and for this reason, they do not spend much time or energy on the training process development and execution. In reality, a sound training strategy can reduce both costs and user frustration by ensuring that work can be done right the first time.

7.7.1   Training

One of the biggest challenges in delivering SAP NetWeaver BW training is timing. Typically, many end users need to be trained on the SAP NetWeaver BW system in a short time. This can make it difficult to find enough trainers to handle the regular workload. To compensate for that, many project organizations opt to perform the training well in advance of go-live to ensure that all users can be trained. This presents challenges because it means that all configuration must be fairly complete to create the training material. Also, many users who are trained early need refresher training because so much time has passed since their training.

Another challenge to the training of SAP NetWeaver BW is the lack of good data to use for training. Often, the training group is forced to create data to show some valid data in the system. The configuration often changes during the training process, as issues are being uncovered and solved.

We recommend that project managers opt for a *train the trainer* approach. This involves picking a group of qualified people at each of the sites and training them on the system, and then having them train the end users. This serves two purposes: It gets more people training the system, and it develops super users who can help support the system during the production support phase. These super users become the first level support for any issues that occur after go-live.

7.7.2   A Separate Training System

Many project organizations opt for a separate training system. In most large organizations, this is vital because trying to train users using either the QA or development systems can create many issues. The development system changes frequently and often is much too unstable to bring in end users for testing.

Furthermore, development systems often are unsecured; a user could inadvertently change configuration, causing issues for the development team. The QA system is often too volatile for training. The testing of SAP NetWeaver BW often requires a lot of dumping of data and reloading. This cannot occur during the training process, so if training is going on, testing typically must stop.

To counteract these issues, many customers opt for a separate SAP NetWeaver BW training system. This guarantees a steady environment that can be locked down and used for training exercises. The biggest difficulty typically encountered with a training system is getting staff from the SAP NetWeaver BW development team to build this system and populate it with data.

Many projects opt to fill the QA system with data and then copy this QA system to another system and use that for the training system. This lessens the burden on the SAP NetWeaver BW team to populate the training system.

7.7.3 Do I Really Need Hands-On Training?

The value of a *hands-on* vs. a *hands-off* training is simple. Hands-on training provides a much more complete understanding by end users but requires a much more patient training team and a much more complete training environment.

However, it is difficult for users to really understand the functionality of the SAP NetWeaver BW system and the query-processing tools without hands-on time on the system. They can use this time to run queries, perform drill downs, etc.

The general rule with SAP NetWeaver BW end user training is to try to get some real or close to real transactional and master data loaded into a SAP NetWeaver BW system. Users typically respond better to data that approximates what they will be seeing after the go-live.

The training should be structured to first include an overview of the data that has been loaded into SAP NetWeaver BW, along with a multi-generational plan on the data that will later be in scope. Often, training focuses exclusively on the SAP NetWeaver BW tool set and ignores the more important questions related to data strategy.

7.7.4 Training Budget

Lack of funding is one of the biggest reasons that SAP SAP NetWeaver BW customers' training initiatives fall short of their goals. Most SAP NetWeaver BW projects begin with a plan and rather significant budget for training the end users. But as contingency needs arise, the training budget can often be raided to supplement shortfalls elsewhere.

It is the nature and timing of training that causes this to occur. At the end of the project, there is no other place to find contingency money, so training gets the deepest cuts.

Make sure that the SAP NetWeaver BW training budget is set from the beginning of the project and holds steady throughout so the training needs are not compromised by a lack of budget.

Let's continue proceeding in our path towards go-live by discussing cutover planning.

7.8   Cutover Planning

The next step in preparing for go-live is to create a cutover plan. This document is designed as a project plan for the go-live. A sample cutover plan and associated checklist are found in Appendix B. The document in this appendix serves as a list of all tasks the typically need to be performed.

The main purpose of the cutover plan is to make sure that each task is fully documented, so that when the go-live cutover occurs, there are no tasks that are missed.

In many cases, the cutover team is under a great deal of pressure to complete the tasks correctly and quickly to ensure the least downtime of the SAP NetWeaver BW and associated transactional systems. The more organized the team can become at communicating the various tasks and their responsibilities, the more smoothly the cutover will progress. Some of the most important tasks in the cutover plan are as follows:

▶ Activities and tasks that need to be performed in both the SAP NetWeaver BW and any source systems to prepare the systems and data for the go-live should be clearly listed. For example, if there are several flat files that need to be generated from a source system, this task should be scheduled and planned to make sure that the file is available when needed.

▶ All data loading requirements should be documented in detail with the approximate duration of each load process. Many projects have a dress rehearsal for the initial data loading procedure in either the production system or a copy of the production system to ensure that the initial data load procedure is sound.

▶ All data load jobs should be listed with a clear task list in the order that they should be performed. This is especially important because many SAP NetWeaver BW jobs have predecessor jobs. For example, to load the initial delivery data from the SAP ECC system, the delivery-creation job should be run to make sure that all deliveries in the system are being prepared for loading into SAP NetWeaver BW.

▶ Outages for any systems need to be clearly stated. In many initial loads from the SAP ECC or SAP R/3 transactional systems, it is required that no transactions occur while the initial loading programs are running. Ensuring that there is some quiet time planned for the transactional source systems is vital to cutover planning.

▶ Batch windows of loading time should be clearly stated. If the users are promised the system on Monday morning at 7 a.m. EST, this should be clearly understood by the cutover team to make sure data is loaded and verified before the users log on to the system.

▶ A reconciliation plan should be established to document how the initial loads into SAP NetWeaver BW are going to be matched with the equivalent data on the source system. This allows for the data to be verified and blessed by the business SMEs associated with the process.

▶ Assignment of a responsible person for each data load process is vital. This allows a clear understanding of who is responsible for the tasks and how escalation can occur if critical tasks are not complete in time.

▶ A communication plan of all tasks and their current status should be created. This allows the project management staff to clearly see each cutover step, its status, and state of the process.

▶ A security plan should be developed and included in the cutover plan. Often, when the cutover occurs, several jobs need to be run on the SAP ECC or SAP R/3 system to start data initialization. Team members performing these jobs need to have proper access to complete the jobs. The security plan should also cover any external systems needed for extraction or reconciliation along with the SAP NetWeaver BW system. Planning for these authorization issues can help to prevent issues and delays during the cutover.

▶ An escalation plan needs to be established to understand clearly how issues are to be documented and resolved. This plan should include escalation for application, Basis, database, and business-process issues.

▶ SAP should be informed of the go-live plans and timing. SAP keeps a list of those customers that are going live. This helps their support organization prepare and prioritize those issues that are reported to SAP.

▶ A data purging, cleansing, and cleanup procedure should be documented, if applicable. In some cases, during the cutover, some setup tables or data load tables need to be purged during or after the cutover. These tasks should be clearly listed in the cutover plan.

- Contact numbers and cutover schedules should be clearly documented and posted.

Once the cutover plan is established, the next step is to make sure that the system is prepared for this go-live. This involves making sure that all system settings are correct and the overall health of the system would support go-live. The best way of making sure that the system is ready for the go-live is via a go-live checklist.

7.9   Go-Live Checklist

Several things need to be checked in any system prior to getting it ready for a cutover. This checklist is typically called the go-live checklist. It differs from the cutover plan because it provides a list of all the things that are needed begin transporting. This list can and should be used for any new system that has been created or copied.

Here are some of the important activities that need to be performed or checked when a new SAP NetWeaver BW system is built:

- **SAP Notes Checked for High-Priority Fixes**
  When a new system is built, this is a good time to look at the SAP Notes for the current support package in the SAP Service MarketPlace to ensure that SAP has not released any high-priority fixes. Search on the support package number in the SAP Service MarketPlace.

- **Database/Kernel/Operating System Patches Applied**
  Often, the focus of SAP NetWeaver BW projects is simply on the application, but there are several underlying patches that should be checked to make sure that they are consistent with the QA environment. This is typically performed by the Basis or technical staff. It is a good idea to have these tasks on a new system checklist to make sure that these checks are performed whenever a new system is built.

- **Technical Infrastructure Checked**
  All users' systems should include whatever they need to access SAP NetWeaver BW including the proper GUI, portal links, etc. This involves checking the user setups and ensuring that their desktop and network access is optimal to access the system. Some of the more common issues are obsolete or outdated releases of Microsoft Excel or Microsoft Internet Explorer. These can sometimes cause issues with running BEx Analyzer or some of the Java tools.

- **Connections to Source Systems Established**
  Check that the connections to all source systems are sound and functioning

properly. This involves setting the connections to any external system including the SAP and non-SAP systems. If flat file data is to be loaded, a source system connection should be established to allow this data to be loaded into SAP NetWeaver BW.

▶ **Transfer of Global Settings Performed**
Each SAP R/3 or SAP ECC source systems should have their global settings transferred so the UOM, currency, and calendars populated in the SAP NetWeaver BW system.

▶ **Permitted Characters Checked**
Check the permitted characters setting in Transaction SPRO to make sure that the permitted characters match in QA and Production.

▶ **Default Packet Size Checked**
Check the settings in the SAP NetWeaver BW IMG to make sure that the default packet size is identical to the QA system. This is needed for loading data from SAP ECC or SAP R/3 into the SAP NetWeaver BW system.

▶ **Flat File Parameters Verified**
Check the flat file loading parameters to make sure the QA system matches with the production system. This setting is needed to load the flat file data into the SAP NetWeaver BW system.

▶ **All System Traces Switched Off**
If there are any system traces in Transaction ST01, these should be turned off. These traces can slow performance.

▶ **All User Logging Switched Off**
If user logging has been turned of in Transaction RSRTRACE, this should be turned off. These traces slow performance if not needed.

▶ **Security Checked**
One of the most popular help desk issues post go-live is security. Checking and rechecking of the roles can make the security issues less painful.

▶ **Transports Completed**
All transports complete and system setup matches the QA environment.

▶ **Process Chains Checked**
Check to ensure that the process chains have been migrated properly and run properly on the SAP NetWeaver BW system. Issues often occur because there are no valid connections or not enough processes or database log size to complete the process chain.

▶ **OLAP Cache Turned On**
Most OLAP cache settings are performed in each system. Check the cache set-

tings on all queries to make sure that they are correct and functioning properly.

▶ **Statistics Turned On**
The SAP NetWeaver BW statistics cubes can track the performance of the SAP NetWeaver BW system. The statistics need to be checked and turned on in each system. Verify the settings and ensure that there is a process chain to load the statistics cubes.

▶ **Aggregates Filled**
Any aggregates that are part of the data model need to be filled. Aggregates speed up the query performance.

▶ **DB Statistics Run**
Database statistics should be run on all InfoCubes and ODS tables to ensure that they are up-to-date. This allows the database to know the size of tables and makeup of their data to allow for faster query processing.

▶ **RSRV Checks Performed**
Transaction RSRV has many tools to check the system prior to go-live. Run the various checks to ensure that indexes are built and the table structures are sound.

▶ **Portal Content Checked**
Check to see that all portal links are working properly and that SAP NetWeaver BW queries exist and function properly on the portal.

▶ **SAP Go-live Check Performed**
SAP provides a service to check a system to determine if it is ready for go-live. These technical checks can give a sanity check to determine if the system is ready.

Once the testing has been completed, the data is ready to be loaded into the production environment.

In the next section, we will explain the loading process in SAP NetWeaver BW and some of the common issues with loading data.

7.10   Run Initial Loads in SAP NetWeaver BW

When the production transports are complete, the system is ready for loading. In most projects, the initial loads of data are performed manually in the production system. In the case of a delta load, the SAP NetWeaver BW system is loaded and delta queues are generated on the SAP ECC or SAP R/3 system. Once the delta queue is established, any new delta records will be added to the delta queue.

In the event of data where a delta is not possible, a full load is kicked off. These loads typically are performed manually as well. The SAP NetWeaver BW team should take proper care to monitor the data loads and reconcile the data back to the SAP ECC, SAP R/3, or legacy source system.

In some cases, setup programs must be run to initially fill the data queues in the SAP ECC or SAP R/3 system. These are common with those DataSources that involve the logistics extractors, for example, extractors that are configured in SAP ECC in the Transaction LBWE. Look at the documentation or configuration guide to determine the appropriate initial loading program needed for the specific DataSource used.

Most customers opt to have SAP NetWeaver BW live for a few weeks prior to inviting the users onto the system. This allows for SAP NetWeaver BW to be loaded and tested and the batch loads to run for a few weeks to work out any issues that might occur.

The initial loading of data is performed manually because the steps that are performed for the initial loading of data in SAP NetWeaver BW are usually only performed once. Once the initial load of data is complete, there is no reason to run it again unless there are major issues or a realignment of data for a reload of data. Thus, once the data is loaded for the first time manually, the next step is to establish process chains for the periodic loading process in SAP NetWeaver BW.

7.10.1 Create and Schedule Process Chains in SAP NetWeaver BW

The process chains schedule the data loads in SAP NetWeaver BW. To automate these loads, the various process chains to load both master data and transactional data must be configured and scheduled. These process chains allow the many different jobs to be scheduled, either in parallel or serially as part of the nightly batch window.

In a typical SAP NetWeaver BW implementation, there are hundreds of jobs that need to be run nightly. These jobs may include loading master data or transactional data, or running database statistics. The role of the process chain is to organize and kick off all these loads in a consistent manner.

It also allows for one place to monitor and watch the jobs for failures. The process chains have functionality to notify the administrator of any failures. This notification allows administrators to fix any job failures quickly before end users get on the system.

When loading data in SAP NetWeaver BW, all master data must be loaded first and then the transactional data. This allows the master data to be established so that when the related transactional data is loaded, it can leverage these entries.

In most projects, the process chains are administered and created by one individual or a small subset of the SAP NetWeaver BW team. This is because the complex web of jobs that need to be run nightly can become difficult for all the members of the team to understand.

In most projects, one steward should be in charge of all the process chains. This steward is responsible for gathering all the loading requirements from the process team members and assembling that into the process chains. This allows for a consistent organization of all new jobs and one person to contact when new jobs are needed.

The task of monitoring the nightly batch jobs for failures and acting on those failures is typically the responsibility of the production support team. However, until the production support team starts to support an environment, the SAP NetWeaver BW development team often monitors the data loads for a stabilization period. This role is usually shared by several members of the SAP NetWeaver BW team.

Because monitoring the batch loads takes place in the evening, and often this requires the team to work late into the night, the project manager should be careful about who monitors the data loads. For example, in one project, the team had some of their most qualified people monitoring the data loads at night, and these team members thus were not available to tackle other issues that occurred during the day.

As shown in Figure 7.7, all SAP ECC and/or SAP R/3 transactional loads should also be considered before scheduling the SAP NetWeaver BW process chains. For example, if a process chain is created to load invoice data, the process chain should only be scheduled to run after the invoices have been created in the SAP R/3 or SAP ECC systems. In many cases, the process chains are not scheduled until after midnight to make sure that all entries for the previous day have been processed and can be loaded into SAP NetWeaver BW.

Many times, dependent jobs need to run on the SAP ECC or SAP R/3 transactional system. These dependent jobs are needed before any SAP NetWeaver BW jobs can run. Let's explore some of the most popular SAP ECC jobs that are related to the SAP NetWeaver BW batch.

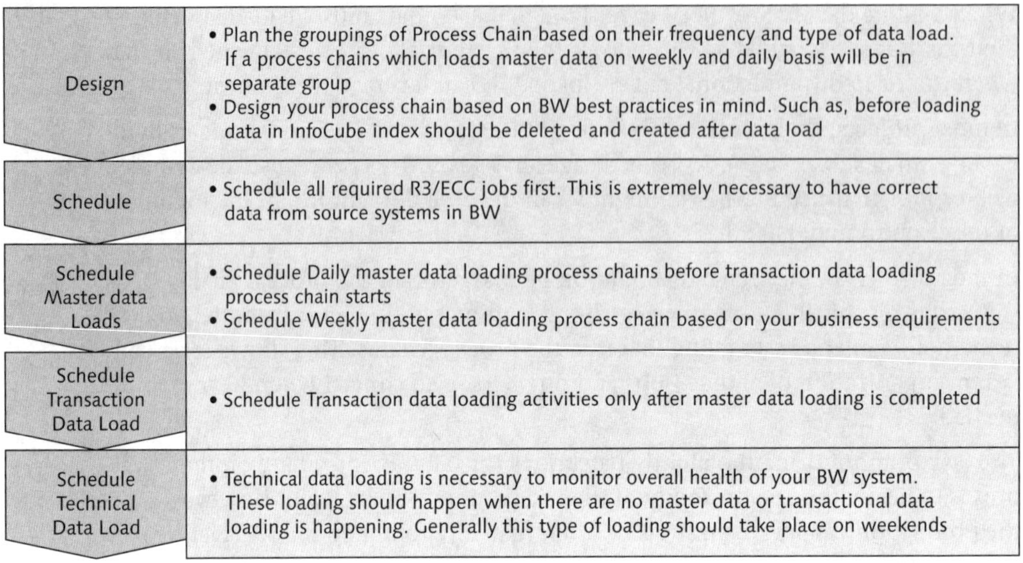

Design	• Plan the groupings of Process Chain based on their frequency and type of data load. If a process chains which loads master data on weekly and daily basis will be in separate group • Design your process chain based on BW best practices in mind. Such as, before loading data in InfoCube index should be deleted and created after data load
Schedule	• Schedule all required R3/ECC jobs first. This is extremely necessary to have correct data from source systems in BW
Schedule Master data Loads	• Schedule Daily master data loading process chains before transaction data loading process chain starts • Schedule Weekly master data loading process chain based on your business requirements
Schedule Transaction Data Load	• Schedule Transaction data loading activities only after master data loading is completed
Schedule Technical Data Load	• Technical data loading is necessary to monitor overall health of your BW system. These loading should happen when there are no master data or transactional data loading is happening. Generally this type of loading should take place on weekends

Figure 7.7 Recommended Scheduling of Process Chains

7.10.2 Schedule SAP ECC Jobs

In most SAP NetWeaver BW implementations, there are several SAP ECC or SAP R/3 jobs that must run on the transactional system. Some of these jobs are part of the normal transactional workday in the SAP ECC or SAP R/3 system. For example, for the system to be able to load the invoices into SAP NetWeaver BW, the billing generation program must be run in the SAP ECC or SAP R/3 transactional system. Only after this job has been run can the SAP NetWeaver BW system pull these billing documents.

There are several other transactional jobs that must be run on the SAP ECC system before the SAP NetWeaver BW system can load data. Often, these are the responsibility of the SAP ECC or SAP R/3 process team to schedule. The SAP NetWeaver BW team simply needs to know when these jobs will run to ensure that SAP NetWeaver BW does not try to load its data before these other jobs are complete. If the SAP NetWeaver BW system pulls data too early, it will not be available for the end users for that day.

For example, the billing documents are typically run at 11 p.m. each evening. If the SAP NetWeaver BW system pulls the billing documents at 10 p.m., they would only get the documents that have been run throughout the day since the last invoice run. However, the billing documents that are generated on the 11 p.m. run would only be available for the next day's load. SAP NetWeaver BW batch loads frequently do not even start until midnight to ensure that all the processing in the transactional systems is complete for the day. This gives the end user a complete picture of the day's transactions.

Another popular kind of job that is scheduled in most SAP NetWeaver BW implementation is known as the V3 job. These jobs gather up the recent changed logistics data and move this data into the logistic delta queues. For many of the common logistics transactional data loads, this process must be scheduled on the SAP ECC or SAP R/3 system each evening before the SAP NetWeaver BW system loads the data. In some cases, project teams opt to run the V3 job multiple times in the work day, depending on the volume; however, it must be run before the SAP NetWeaver BW system can pull that day's delta records.

The V3 jobs are only necessary if the logistics extractors are being used in SAP NetWeaver BW. The logistics extractors are set up and V3 jobs scheduled using Transaction LBWE on the SAP ECC system. Figure 7.8 provides a view of the V3 process in the transactional system.

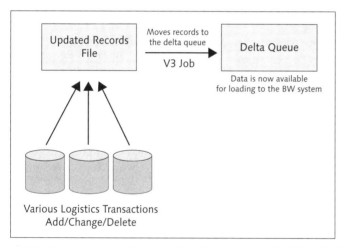

Figure 7.8 Description of the Logistics V3 Process in SAP ECC or SAP R/3

The V3 job moves the data from the updated records file to the delta queue. This delta queue is then used to load the data to the SAP NetWeaver BW system. If the V3 job has not been run for the day, there are no delta records in the delta queue; thus, the data load in the SAP NetWeaver BW system would load zero records.

The SAP NetWeaver BW team needs to coordinate with the SAP ECC or SAP R/3 teams to make sure that this job runs consistently during the evening before SAP NetWeaver BW loads data. This allows all the logistic delta records to be loaded into SAP NetWeaver BW.

Once the process chains have been created and scheduled, the data is now ready for reporting. The next step is to make sure that the queries are ready to provide this data to the end user. These queries are typically launched via the portal. The next section discusses the various strategies for the portal and publication of queries into the portal.

7.10.3 Portals and SAP NetWeaver BW

In general, a portal is the transactional launch pad for the user to run transactions and analysis, or to view data from multiple sources in one place. The need for a portal came about because as SAP and other vendors introduced more and more products, the users became increasingly frustrated with the need to log on to multiple systems to do their work.

To add to this frustration, the user also needed to go to several places to perform analysis in these systems. The need quickly arose to have one place that users could log on that would provide them access to multiple systems, links, documents, and transactions across the enterprise. Basically, the user wanted one place to go to do their job. Thus, the portal was born.

There are many different portal software solutions to choose from in the marketplace. The most common choice among SAP customers is the SAP Portal. This makes sense because the SAP Portal comes with the SAP NetWeaver products along with the SAP NetWeaver BW system. In fact, as part of all NW 2004s systems, an enterprise portal is loaded as part of the installation.

The SAP Portal, although designed to work and integrate with all SAP products, is not limited to only SAP products. This can be used to launch documents, reports, and analysis from virtually any Web-based solution. This provides users with a wide range of content that can be used for their portal.

The portal is an important part of the SAP NetWeaver BW environment because it is needed in order to present the analysis to the end user. Only after queries are complete can they be published to the portal, so this is typically the last step in the query-development process in an SAP NetWeaver BW implementation.

In the 3.x releases of SAP NetWeaver BW, the portal team and SAP NetWeaver BW team had limited interaction. In the cases where customers were using a portal, the SAP NetWeaver BW team typically developed their queries on their own and then passed these queries to the portal team via a uniform resource locator (URL) link or as an iView. The portal team placed this link on the portal, and the user could access the query.

In the NW 2004s environment, the SAP NetWeaver BW team and portal team are much more integrated. This is because all SAP NetWeaver BW reports are now published to the portal via a standard publishing process in the SAP NetWeaver BW report designer. When publishing queries, the SAP NetWeaver BW team needs to work with the portal team to develop a clear publishing strategy that allows the SAP NetWeaver BW content to be developed and presented to the end user in accordance with the portal strategy.

For example, suppose the SAP NetWeaver BW team develops several unrelated queries: one for sales, one for finance, and one for purchasing. The publishing strategy needs to ensure that the queries show up properly on each of the various portal views and that the queries have a consistent look and feel. They also need to be published in accordance with any security and authorization strategy developed by the portal team.

This requires clear communication between the SAP NetWeaver BW team and the portal team and a clear portal strategy.

7.10.4 Developing a Portal Strategy

To ensure that the various users have a consistent tool to perform their jobs, a portal strategy needs to be developed. This strategy mainly looks at the different audience of the portal and determines what is needed by each group and how this should be presented to the end user. This strategy also ensures that the users can access the various transactions and analysis in accordance with the security model.

It is recommended that any portal strategy be developed and owned by a portal resource, in conjunction with the business representatives and the change management team. Portal strategy decisions are not primarily performed by the SAP NetWeaver BW team. However, because the SAP NetWeaver BW queries are often launched via the portal, and the portal is the end user's first view of the SAP NetWeaver BW solution, it is vital that the SAP NetWeaver BW team be involved in the portal strategy.

Portal strategy should take into account any other systems that will be accessed by the end user and act as a launch pad for these applications as well. SAP NetWeaver BW can then leverage these roles and this strategy to make sure that the users not only have one common place for all transactions but that their reporting needs are also met in the same area. In general, a portal strategy has several goals:

▶ Provide one central point of entry to view, analyze, and transact data across multiple systems

▶ Expedite user logon and entry into systems

▶ Reduce the number of logons by using a single sign-on (SSO) process

▶ Centralize important documents and links and make these available to the user

▶ Provide one place to run all analysis regardless of the source system.

Another important aspect of the portal strategy is governance. This helps to determine and maintain the content that will be shown on the portal. Because the portal is a public place and gives the users their first and most common view of the organization, these portal governance decisions are important in preserving user confidence in the organization. This confidence often comes from a well-designed and useful-looking portal. These decisions come from portal governance. There are several goals for portal governance:

▶ Defining and understanding the portal users and key stakeholders

▶ Determining the content administrators

▶ Creating a governance model to develop portal content and provide this to the end user

▶ Integrating with any authorization or security strategy

▶ Communicating with the various systems owners about how to connect and where possible providing single sign-on (SSO) for the users

▶ Prioritizing and completing portal work.

A common place to start developing the analysis portion of the portal strategy is in the SAP NetWeaver BW landscape. If SAP NetWeaver BW reports are to be presented to the end user via the portal, there are two main approaches for providing these portal links. These two strategies are as seen here:

▶ **SAP NetWeaver BW Portal Display Strategy**
Because the SAP Enterprise Portal (EP) comes as part of the NW 2004s installation, this portal can be used as the SAP NetWeaver BW analysis launch pad. In this strategy, only the SAP NetWeaver BW portal as part of the NW 2004s system is used as a portal. No other portal systems are installed. This provides the user one basic method of providing a fully functional portal to the end user.

▶ **Federated Portal Strategy**
In a federated portal strategy, a completely separate portal environment is established that is separate but mirrors the SAP NetWeaver BW system with an EP development, EP QA, and production standalone systems. This standalone system is called the Federated Portal, and resembles the illustration seen in Figure 7.9.

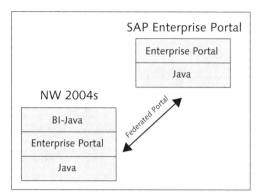

Figure 7.9 Portal Design in NW 2004s and SAP Enterprise Portal

In most cases, the federated portal strategy is preferred to using the SAP NetWeaver BW portal display strategy. In most cases, a standalone EP system should be used as the portal for the organization rather than relying on the SAP NetWeaver BW portal.

There are several reasons why the federated portal strategy makes sense. A project team may start to build its content into the SAP NetWeaver BW portal rather than a standalone EP implementation. If a project team opts to use the SAP NetWeaver BW portal and develops a great deal of content in that portal and then decides to use another SAP software product like CRM or APO, it may find that these products have limitations regarding the version of the portal that can be used. In some cases, there are severe limits on how these systems can be linked.

However, if the federated portal approach is used, the systems can be linked in the federated portal by each of their underlying EP products. For example, the SAP NetWeaver BW system can link to the federated portal via its EP, CRM can link via its EP, etc. This provides much more flexibility for linking systems.

So, why not begin using the SAP NetWeaver BW Portal for end user access, develop content and configuration on this system, and then convert to a federated portal later? The answer is that it takes a lot of effort to migrate to a federated portal from a SAP NetWeaver BW portal. Often, this means that once a federated portal is needed, the organization has to redevelop all the portal content on the federated portal.

Therefore, it is not advisable to begin using the SAP NetWeaver BW portal as the main portal for the end users. Instead, it makes sense to opt for the standalone EP implementation and use the central federated portal for content and access by the end users. This provides the flexibility for growth in the future.

7.11   SAP Safeguarding Service for SAP NetWeaver BW Go-Live

SAP provides a safeguarding service to reduce implementation or upgrade risk of an SAP NetWeaver BW project. This service may be useful for big multi-region implementation/upgrade projects where classic testing and validation of check-points are difficult. SAP uses proven tools and methodologies to identify and assess your SAP NetWeaver BW objects. At the end of this process, SAP provides a comprehensive report suggesting optimization of your SAP NetWeaver BW objects. This report contains the following points:

▸ **SAP NetWeaver BW Administration**
In this section, you receive comprehensive analysis on data distribution, Info-Providers, and aggregates.

▸ **SAP NetWeaver BW Reporting**
Here, the report analyzes the SAP NetWeaver BW Query definitions, OLAP cache, frontend servers, etc.

▸ **Application Checks**
Here, the report contains the analysis of different checks such as InfoCube, Report, Data load, ABAP codes, etc.

> **Note**
>
> SAP safeguarding information is available at *http://service.sap.com/safeguarding*.

7.12   Conclusion

Preparing for go-live involves many decisions and checks to ensure that the system is ready for users. Because the cutover tasks are often stressful, proper planning should help to relieve some of the stress by providing the right resources and escalation in the event of issues. Another important aspect of going live is developing a clear portal strategy to make sure that users have a consistent place to launch their transactions and analysis needs.

In Chapter 8, we'll discuss what is needed after the project goes live to ensure that any future SAP NetWeaver BW rollouts will be successful.

Understanding and providing a clear go-live strategy requires careful plan-ning before the go-live to make sure that the COE can provide definite value to the end user.

8   After SAP NetWeaver BW Go-Live

SAP NetWeaver BW projects like SAP R/3 or SAP ECC projects are not complete once they go live. There are many jobs that need to be done after the users start using the system. These include establishing periodic tasks to reconcile the data and keep the system healthy, and transitioning the solution to the production sup-port organization for ongoing maintenance.

This can be a challenge in many organizations because budget resources have not been adequately allocated to post go-live activities. Often, the budget that is allo-cated is used as a contingency for other activities that are over-budget. This makes post–go-live tasks even harder.

To add to the frustration, many of the project team members either leave to work on other projects or go back to their former jobs. Others may be burned out from the long hours spent during the implementation process and go-live. Keeping a core team motivated to help on the post–go-live activities requires planning prior to the go-live and coordination after the go-live.

To plan for these activities, you first need to understand the typical project responsi-bilities after go-live and the challenges faced in this phase of the project lifecycle.

When a project goes live, the SAP NetWeaver BW development team is often the first level of support for issues that occur. After the stabilization period is com-plete, the next step is to transition the solution to the production support group or Center of Excellence (COE). At the same time, SAP NetWeaver BW developers should analyze and review the SAP NetWeaver BW system in production.

8.1   Post-Implementation Review

For many SAP NetWeaver BW projects, a lot of information concerning how the application will be used may not really be known until after it has gone live. This activity is particularly important for SAP NetWeaver BW implementation, which can be modified later for better end user experience.

▶ Check that all transports are moved. There should not be any missed transports. In some complex implementation projects, even a missing transport can cause failure of complete data flow and debugging the issue takes a lot of time.

▶ It is extremely necessary to monitor the performance of data load and queries frequently in first few months of go-live. You may find that some configuration was working fine in QA and on the other hand performance is poor in production. This kind of issue occurred in almost all SAP NetWeaver BW projects because there was not enough data in QA to test the performance.

▶ Take complete feedback from end users. Ultimate success of your SAP NetWeaver BW implementation is dependent on the usage and efficiency of SAP NetWeaver BW reports.

▶ You may need to fine tune the timings of the data loading.

▶ Check the SAP NetWeaver BW statistical report for overall efficiency of the SAP NetWeaver BW objects.

▶ Check that authorizations are working as per design.

8.2 Building a Production Support Center of Excellence (COE)

A production support Center of Excellence (COE) is a central organization used for ongoing production support after go-live is complete. The COE should be seen as a long-term organization and reinforced with staffing and budget. All the ongoing support for the product should be coordinated and organized through the COE organization.

The COE has many different responsibilities, and once established, it should be considered a vital part of the organization. Figure 8.1 illustrates the lifecycle and the responsibilities of the COE. The typical COE has a core staff but relies on many extended team members to provide the support needed to keep the SAP NetWeaver BW system functioning properly. Some of the primary goals of the COE are shown in Table 8.1.

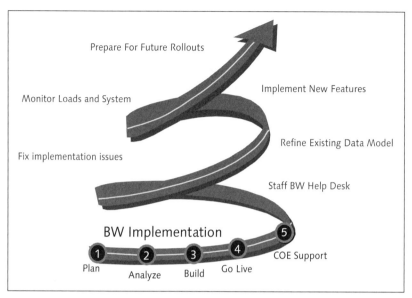

Figure 8.1 Lifecycle and Responsibilities of the COE

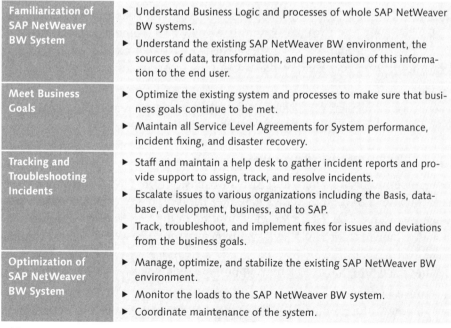

Familiarization of SAP NetWeaver BW System	▶ Understand Business Logic and processes of whole SAP NetWeaver BW systems. ▶ Understand the existing SAP NetWeaver BW environment, the sources of data, transformation, and presentation of this information to the end user.
Meet Business Goals	▶ Optimize the existing system and processes to make sure that business goals continue to be met. ▶ Maintain all Service Level Agreements for System performance, incident fixing, and disaster recovery.
Tracking and Troubleshooting Incidents	▶ Staff and maintain a help desk to gather incident reports and provide support to assign, track, and resolve incidents. ▶ Escalate issues to various organizations including the Basis, database, development, business, and to SAP. ▶ Track, troubleshoot, and implement fixes for issues and deviations from the business goals.
Optimization of SAP NetWeaver BW System	▶ Manage, optimize, and stabilize the existing SAP NetWeaver BW environment. ▶ Monitor the loads to the SAP NetWeaver BW system. ▶ Coordinate maintenance of the system.

Table 8.1 Primary Goals of an SAP NetWeaver BW COE

User Support and Trainings	► Coordinate maintenance of the system.
	► Provide a proactive approach to system issues to help find problems before the users do.
	► Provide ongoing user support and training for new users.
	► Act as a conduit for user feedback on desired features and functionality.

Table 8.1 Primary Goals of an SAP NetWeaver BW COE (Cont.)

The challenges in setting up a COE are to find the right resources and to transition the knowledge from the SAP NetWeaver BW development team that built the solution to the COE that will be maintaining the system.

To build a successful COE, there must be an organized and planned transition from the development team to the COE.

8.3   Transitioning from SAP NetWeaver BW Development to Production-Support COE

Transitioning from the development role to a production-support COE can be difficult. In most projects, the development team provides the production support on all new objects for several weeks until the new development is stabilized. After the stabilization period, the newly developed objects are transitioned to a production support team that handles the ongoing monitoring and maintenance of the solution.

Several tasks must be performed to have a successful hand-off from the SAP NetWeaver BW development group to the production-support COE.

8.3.1   Transition the Knowledge

A clear communication plan and plan for transition to production support can allow for a clean transfer of knowledge and a hand-off of the responsibilities of the design (see Figure 8.2). However, the transition of the SAP NetWeaver BW design often does not go smoothly. New development frequently suffers because the SAP NetWeaver BW development team spends a great deal of its time working with and supplementing the production support team on issues.

Thus, once the development build is completed, start the knowledge transfer of the solution to the production support team, keeping it engaged in the solution. The SAP NetWeaver BW development team members need to make themselves available to the production support team but not to the extent that they are unable to perform the new development required by the project.

Make sure that the COE staff is able to understand not only the technical configuration of the system but, more importantly, the business needs and goals of the organization. In many organizations, this means that the COE works closely with the business subject matter experts (SMEs) and business stakeholders to ensure ongoing communication.

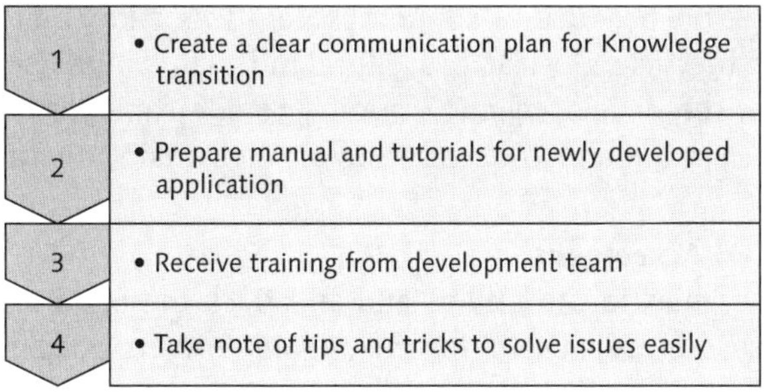

1	• Create a clear communication plan for Knowledge transition
2	• Prepare manual and tutorials for newly developed application
3	• Receive training from development team
4	• Take note of tips and tricks to solve issues easily

Figure 8.2 Knowledge Transition Process Overview

The best way to ensure a smooth transition of the business and development knowledge is to plan this well in advance of go-live. Many projects wait until late in the process to begin the transition to the production-support COE. This also occurs when the COE is not staffed until well after go-live. By then, many of the developers have either left or are busy working on other enhancements and it is difficult to get their time to aid in the support of the system.

8.3.2   Determine Measurement Criteria

Once the knowledge has been adequately transitioned to the production support team and they are comfortable about beginning to support the solution, a process must be developed to measure and track the success of the COE and its processes.

To provide adequate SAP NetWeaver BW support, some measurement criteria for the production-support COE are needed. This enables us to understand how well the COE is meeting the needs of the organization. Some of the measurements and processes that should be established and agreed on are as follows.

▶ **Service Level Agreement (SLA)**
  This is for query-processing performance, and is typically set as an average query response time across the organization. This can be tracked and measured in SAP NetWeaver BW via the statistics InfoCubes.

- ► **Issue Tracking Agreement**
  This helps in understanding how issues will be logged, prioritized, tracked, and resolved in a timely manner. This strategy will also include a strategy on how the COE will communicate the resolution of issues.

- ► **Roles and Responsibilities Agreement**
  These help the COE to draw a clear line between the support organization and the new-development organization. This allows each group to concentrate on its assigned tasks. In many organizations, the new development team is often called in by the COE to work on production support issues. This takes time away from the development lifecycle. A clear procedure and plan should be established to make sure that the development team can provide some background and expertise to issues while also concentrating on their main role of new development.

- ► **Total Cost of Ownership (TCO) Agreement**
  This calculation allows the organization to understand and track the ongoing cost for maintenance of the system. It is useful for the ongoing project budget and to benchmark the project against other projects.

Establish a Help Desk

Most often, issues are reported to the COE via the help desk. Help desks establish a phone line, email address, and/or website to track incidents reported by end users. These incidents are tracked, assigned, and prioritized by the SAP NetWeaver BW help desk (see Figure 8.3).

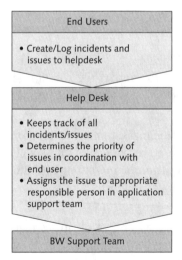

Figure 8.3 SAP NetWeaver BW Help Desk Functionalities

Typically, this requires software to track incidents, status, and resolution. Some companies use a basic Microsoft Access database; some opt for an off-the-shelf package for a more sophisticated tracking of incidents and help desk calls. Here are the most important things to understand about the SAP NetWeaver BW help desk:

- Understanding the source systems is vital to troubleshooting an SAP NetWeaver BW issue. This is often where you encounter the gap of knowledge in a help desk. Often, you find someone who is knowledgeable about the SAP NetWeaver BW environment but who is not as proficient in the SAP ECC or SAP R/3 system.

- Many of the issues will be the result of master data or transactional data in the source system. Many of the help desk tickets simply show that the data in the SAP NetWeaver BW system matches the data in the source system. Although this does not always solve the user's issue, it does provide the proof that SAP NetWeaver BW matches the source.

  This is then passed on to the COE for the associated SAP ECC or SAP R/3 system for repair. Suppose, for example, that a user runs a report and wonders why the sales for his division seem low. The SAP NetWeaver BW team matches the sales figures by division to the SAP ECC system, but some of the sales are from the wrong division. Although this appears to the user to be a SAP NetWeaver BW issue, the issue can only be resolved on the SAP ECC system by adjusting the sales divisions in the transactional data.

- Understanding the latency of the data in SAP NetWeaver BW is also vital. Because SAP NetWeaver BW data is typically loaded once a day, the data is not current with the source system. Often, users expect that the data in SAP NetWeaver BW is more current than it is. Many issues are resolved by making sure that users understand this latency.

- Knowing the flow of data through the SAP NetWeaver BW system will help in troubleshooting the issues quickly. Many help desk incidents are resolved by working backward through the data loads. For example, a user sees values that appear to be incorrect in the Net Sales key figure. To resolve this incident, the query is run to verify the data.

  The Multi-Provider is then examined to determine if the issue is in the joining of the data. Next, the InfoCube is studied, then the DSO/ODS structure, and then the PSA. Finally, the comparison to source data is next. This requires an understanding of the data and the flow of the data through the SAP NetWeaver BW system. It also requires a clear vision on how the data is transformed at each step in the process.

- Sometimes, the data in SAP NetWeaver BW will be mapped incorrectly. This may require a dump and reload of the SAP NetWeaver BW data. This occurs when transactional data has been loaded into an SAP NetWeaver BW InfoProvider incorrectly. These activities are a normal part of the production-support COE but obviously need to be avoided, if possible.

- Leveraging the organization's development resources from time to time is an effective way to resolve the more difficult issues. Although it is important not to go to the development team for most issues, it can be helpful to enlist the people who built the solution to help on some of the more difficult issues. Many projects schedule sessions with the development team weekly to deal with open issues. There should also be an escalation process for timely involvement of the development team in critical production issues.

- Turnover in the COE can be frustrating. Keeping a good COE staffer for a long time can be difficult, because many of these people move to other areas of the organization or into the development team. Keeping the team motivated is important.

One of the ways that a strong COE organization becomes more proactive to the end user's needs is to spot issues and fix them before the end user is even aware that the issue exists.

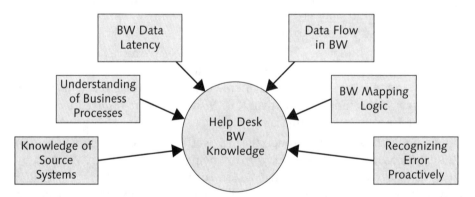

Figure 8.4 Knowledge Requirements for SAP NetWeaver BW Help Desk

This requires a process of reconciliation and validation. This process compares the data in the various systems to see if the data differs between systems or if other issues exist.

8.4 Ongoing SAP NetWeaver BW Reconciliation and Validation

To keep the COE working toward a proactive role in understanding and preventing issues, a process needs to be established to periodically reconcile the data in the SAP NetWeaver BW system with the SAP ECC or SAP R/3 system.

This process can be used to validate accuracy and ensure that all related data is being loaded into SAP NetWeaver BW. This process should be considered an ongoing and vital part of the SAP NetWeaver BW post-production tasks. Thus, it should occur on a scheduled periodic basis.

The mistake that many SAP NetWeaver BW project organizations make is to consider SAP NetWeaver BW reconciliation to be a one-time pre– and post–go-live activity. They verify that the initial loads of data correctly match the SAP R/3 or SAP ECC source, and then they assume that all future loads will follow suit. Because SAP NetWeaver BW is typically the reporting system for management decisions, it needs to be periodically reconciled.

The reconciliation allows the SAP NetWeaver BW team to proactively manage the SAP NetWeaver BW system to make sure that the data does indeed match with the SAP ECC or SAP R/3 system. This is not always an easy task. Often, the SAP R/3 or SAP ECC source data is not found in one table or one report. Thus, to match the data from the SAP NetWeaver BW or SAP ECC system, multiple sources of data may have to be read in the SAP ECC system and matched against the equivalent data in the SAP NetWeaver BW system.

Rarely is the process of reconciling data between SAP NetWeaver BW and the transactional source systems automated. Thus, most methods of reconciling data in the SAP ECC or SAP R/3 system to the SAP NetWeaver BW systems involve a manual process of running reports periodically in the SAP NetWeaver BW system and comparing the reports to equivalent data in the source system.

8.4.1 Develop a Reconciliation Strategy

There are several elements that go into the ongoing reconciliation strategy:

▸ **Sources**
All important and vital sources of data should be checked against the equivalent SAP NetWeaver BW data. Typically, this involves not only transactional data but also master data.

▸ **Granularity**
Transactional can exist at many levels of granularity. Typically, the strategy is to

check the data at a more detailed level and to spot check the transactional data. This is because it is not reasonable to assume that each transactional record can be verified with the source.

▶ **Scope**

In an SAP NetWeaver BW data model, there are many characteristics and key figure values that make up an SAP NetWeaver BW InfoProvider. Again, it is not usually practical to verify all data fields; the data fields should be prioritized to make sure that the reconciliation efforts are expended wisely.

▶ **Frequency**

The frequency of reconciliation depends on the granularity of the data and the frequency of the loads. For example, an InfoCube that is kept at a monthly level in an InfoCube is typically not reconciled more frequently than once a month.

▶ **Time**

The reconciliation needs to occur at an inactive or low-activity period to ensure that the systems are synchronized. This may not be easy in a dynamic environment. In some cases, it involves using data from the past and ignoring the recently changed data.

▶ **Testers**

Many environments use the SAP NetWeaver BW team to provide the testing of SAP NetWeaver BW. This process should be owned and executed by the business-process teams. This fosters ownership of the SAP NetWeaver BW reconciliation and data and ensures that those who use the data most and understand the information being presented best are checking that information for validity.

▶ **Steps**

The reconciliation steps need to be developed and documented. These steps depend on the data that is in SAP NetWeaver BW and also the availability of the data in the related source system. These steps cover the detailed procedure to reconcile the data in SAP NetWeaver BW with the data in the source system.

▶ **Prerequisites**

Often, reconciliation can only occur after specific jobs or tasks are complete on the SAP NetWeaver BW and/or source systems. These should be clearly understood.

▶ **Documentation/Signoff**

The reconciliation should have a clear documentation procedure and a signoff process to make sure that all parties agree on the reconciliation.

8.4.2 Reconciling the Data to SAP ECC or SAP R/3

A periodic and systematic verification of the data in the SAP NetWeaver BW system and its source data should be checked in either the SAP ECC or SAP R/3 system. This is to make sure that the data in SAP NetWeaver BW is valid and reflects the equivalent data in the SAP ECC or SAP R/3 transactional systems.

This effort should be proactive. Rather than waiting for users to report any issues with missing data, the team can run periodic checks to make sure that the characteristics and key figures match between the systems. The most frequently used methods of gathering data from the SAP ECC or SAP R/3 source systems include the following tools:

- SAP standard reports
- Report-painter/report-writer tools
- Virtual InfoProviders (remote InfoCubes)
- Transaction SE16 and/or manually inspecting SAP source tables
- Logistics Information System (LIS) reconciliation
- SAP Queries, which are queries run on the SAP system using the SAP Query functionality (this is not the SAP NetWeaver BW query functionality)
- Custom ABAP reports

Although there are multiple ways of reconciling data from SAP systems to the SAP NetWeaver BW system, many COE organizations rely on only few of the tools mentioned. The first place to check for a source of reconciliation is in SAP standard reports. There are many list-functionality reports that allow for totaling and comparison with SAP NetWeaver BW data. The report-writer and report-painter reports can also be used for this reconciliation. Typically, these reports are run and compared to specific SAP NetWeaver BW queries.

This is the most common way of reconciling and is the easiest because no development needs to take place to begin the reconciliation process. The issue that often occurs is that there are no SAP reports that match the data in SAP NetWeaver BW. This happens because the SAP NetWeaver BW data is often transformed or harmonized with other data in the SAP NetWeaver BW system. This makes reconciling the data from standard reporting difficult.

Another common way to reconcile data is to use Transaction SE16. This allows a user to inspect table contents in the SAP source system to look at various table contents. This output can sometimes be compared to the SAP NetWeaver BW transactional data to ensure that the data matches. This allows the totalling up of transactions for some key figure values, and these can be compared to the SAP

NetWeaver BW system to see if the totals match. Although this is not a perfect method of reconciliation, it does provide a way of checking against the data.

Providing reconciliation via a remote or virtual InfoProvider is another common method. This process involves creating a virtual view of source data on the SAP ECC or SAP R/3 system. This view can be used as a DataSource to look into the SAP ECC or SAP R/3 system. For example, the sales data can be sourced as a DataSource and this DataSource queried in SAP NetWeaver BW as a virtual InfoCube. Comparison queries can then be created to verify this data and compare it with its source data. Figure 8.5 shows a generalized data flow diagram for data reconciliation.

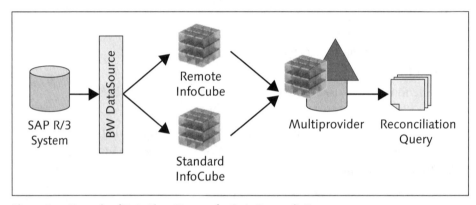

Figure 8.5 Example of Data Flow Diagram for Data Reconciliation

This method involves some development on the source system to create the view needed to look at the data. However, once this view is established, this method provides a user-friendly reconciliation of data because SAP NetWeaver BW queries can be run by the COE to compare the data in the various systems to ensure that they match.

The biggest issue that occurs with most reconciliation is that SAP NetWeaver BW is a batch system. It gets its loads periodically, typically nightly. When reconciling, however, it is looking at live data. To properly reconcile, the latency of the SAP NetWeaver BW solution must be considered in the reconciliation process. Most of the time, this means that data from the current day is excluded from the reconciliation process. This is typically done because that data has not been loaded to SAP NetWeaver BW.

This subsection summarizes some of the typical issues with reconciling data to SAP systems. In most projects, there are also non-SAP systems that need to be checked. There are other methods that are used to reconcile these systems.

8.4.3 Reconciling Data to External Systems

Reconciling SAP NetWeaver BW data to external systems is much more difficult. Most projects opt to run either standard or custom reporting programs on the external source system and compare that to the data in the PSA or via queries on the SAP NetWeaver BW system.

However, this process is completely reliant on the toolset provided in the external system to create a reconciliation process. Because many external systems use flat files to load data into SAP NetWeaver BW, this provides a place to do some reconciliation. Periodic checking of the flat files against the SAP NetWeaver BW data helps to ensure a level of accuracy.

External systems should have some process to reconcile their data against the SAP NetWeaver BW system and a periodic audit of the data to ensure that the users are seeing the data properly.

Along with data reconciliation, there are other ongoing tasks that the COE needs to either perform or oversee other groups' performance to support the system. In the next section, we highlight some of the most popular periodic processes that need to be performed.

8.5 Periodic Jobs to Run in an SAP NetWeaver BW Environment

To keep an SAP NetWeaver BW system running properly, there are several ongoing and periodic jobs that need to be planned and scheduled. Here are the most important periodic jobs:

▶ **System Backup (Daily)**
All SAP NetWeaver BW environments need to be backed up and a backup-and-recovery strategy should be implemented and tested periodically.

▶ **Basis Monitoring (Daily)**
All system logs (Transaction SM21), ABAP runtime short dumps (Transaction ST22), operation monitor (Transaction ST06), and database monitor (Transaction DB02) should be checked daily to assess the overall health of the SAP NetWeaver BW system.

▶ **Application Load Monitoring (Daily)**
All process chains used for the loading of SAP NetWeaver BW data should be monitored for errors. Any errors in data loads should be logged and fixed. This often means reloading or re-running a delta load process again to fix an error.

- **Run Database Statistics (Daily)**
  The database statistics are vital to ensuring that the underlying database optimizer can determine the proper run path for queries. This should be run on all InfoCubes, DSO/ODS tables, and any other large or dynamic tables in the SAP NetWeaver BW system. In some cases, this is run from the SAP NetWeaver BW application; in others, it is run from the database system.

- **Load-Performance Statistics InfoCubes (Daily)**
  The performance statistics InfoCubes are used to report and measure performance. All InfoCubes and ODS structures should be turned on for reporting and all performance InfoCubes should be loaded in batch nightly. In order to use these statistics InfoCubes, they need to be activated from the Business Content.

- **Compression**
  This is done periodically, typically daily. Compression should be performed on the data packages in SAP NetWeaver BW to speed the query performance and reduce the data volume in the InfoCubes.

- **Aggregate Rollup (Daily)**
  When data is loaded into an InfoCube that contains aggregates, the data must be rolled up into the aggregates before the new data is available to be reported. This rolling up of the data must occur after each data load.

- **Query-Performance Monitoring (Periodically)**
  The statistics InfoCubes should be monitored to determine the level of query performance. Those queries that are performing poorly should be tuned.

- **View SAP EarlyWatch Alerts (Weekly)**
  SAP provides a service called EarlyWatch that can provide some system monitoring and warnings. The report should be checked and any recommended actions be performed. This is typically run and monitored by the technical Basis team and not by the applications team, because most of the recommendations are more technical in nature.

- **RSRV Checks (Periodically)**
  There are many checks in the Transaction RSRV. This transaction can be used to check the overall health of the SAP NetWeaver BW system. In many cases, the system has a function to fix any issues that are shown during the checks. These processes can either be run manually or scheduled periodically.

- **Check InfoCube Fact-to-Dimension Ratio (Periodically)**
  The optimal fact-to-dimension table ratio in any InfoCube is 10%. If a dimension table goes beyond this limit, query and load performance can suffer. To monitor the fact to dimension table ratio, the program SAP_INFOCUBE_

DESIGNS can be run. This is run using Transaction SE38. For this program to work, all database statistics must be run first. This program gives the current ratio of all SAP NetWeaver BW InfoCubes. To fix any skewed dimension, the InfoCube can be dumped and characteristics can be shuffled. In the NW 2004s release, the remodeling workbench can be used to shift the dimensions without dumping and reloading data.

▶ **Purge the Persistent Staging Area (Periodically)**
The PSA tables can become large. After data loads have been verified, the persistent staging area is typically not necessary. This frees up some disk space in the system, and keeps the file system from filling up.

▶ **Check and Verify Aggregates (Periodically)**
Aggregates can help query performance; however, any aggregate that is being used infrequently or not at all causes unneeded overhead in the system. Thus, all aggregates should be checked periodically to determine their usefulness. The aggregates can either be checked via the statistic queries or via the aggregate-maintenance screen.

▶ **Delete DTP Temporary Storage (Periodically)**
In the NW 2004s version, the Data Transfer Process (DTP) has temporary storage tables that can be used for troubleshooting. The deletion of temporary storage can be set from DTP maintenance by following this menu path: SETTINGS FOR DTP TEMPORARY STORAGE • DELETE TEMPORARY STORAGE.

▶ **Delete Unused Queries and Workbooks (Periodically)**
Transaction RSZDELETE allows unused queries to be removed periodically.

▶ **Near-line Storage (Periodically)**
SAP NetWeaver BW allows for near-line storage of data. This means that a subset of some little-used data is offloaded to another storage device. This allows this data to be available for reporting; however, using an alternate storage device, the data is taken off of the primary database server. Typically, queries of this near-line data are slower than the data in the primary database server, but offloading that data does allow for the primary database server to perform faster.

▶ **Archive Data (Periodically)**
Archiving of data reduces the data volume and thus allows for better performing system. An overall archive strategy should be developed and implemented.

Another responsibility and ongoing task is to apply the various support packages when they become available. Determining when to apply and how to perform the needed regression testing on the solution often involves the development, Basis, and COE teams. Developing a sound strategy to continually keep up-to-date with support packages is crucial.

8.6   Develop an Ongoing SAP NetWeaver BW Support Package Strategy

Developing an ongoing support-package strategy is important to the overall health of the SAP NetWeaver BW system. There are several components of a typical SAP NetWeaver BW system, and each requires support packages for the following:

► Java support packages (NW 2004s and above)
► ABAP support packages
► Basis support packages
► BW content support packages
► BW frontend support packages

> **Tip**
>
> To find out the timing of and get information about each SAP support package, visit SAP's Service Marketplace website at *www.service.sap.com/bi*. This site gives information in detail on all support packages.

SAP delivers fixes to the software via individual SAP Notes. Periodically, SAP gathers up all relevant SAP Notes and provides an ABAP support package as one large grouping of many fixes to the software. The ABAP support packages are designed to fix or enhance the software application and have the biggest direct impact on the support team of all the support packages.

The frequency of the ABAP support packages depends on the stability of the software and the complexity of the related area. This support package schedule is arbitrary and is set based on SAP's support timetable.

Often, there are a few prerequisites and dependencies in the SAP NetWeaver BW support packages. Proper care should be taken to assure that all the dependencies are satisfied prior to installing a support package. SAP has developed a support-stack strategy for recommending the various Basis, ABAP, and Java support packages that are needed and should be upgraded together. This takes some of the guesswork out of determining which components should be upgraded together.

Each support stack is tested manually and via automated tools by SAP NetWeaver BW support. Because of the complexity of the product and the many different ways that customers use and configure the SAP NetWeaver BW product, however, there are often new issues that occur with each new support stack.

For this reason, each new support stack requires regression testing prior to implementation in the production environment. Because this effort can be so time consuming, customers often find themselves many support stacks behind, despite SAP's recommendation that they stay no more than two support stacks behind. Regression testing of SAP NetWeaver BW is split into two specific types, as seen here:

▶ **Data Loading**
Typically, the data loading testing is done using process chains. Most customers simply run their normal batch processes in the development and/or QA testing environment for several weeks under the new support stack to ensure that it does not adversely affect the batch loading.

▶ **Query Processing**
Query processing testing is much more difficult and time consuming. Most automated testing tools do not work well for regression testing. This is because SAP NetWeaver BW query regression testing requires a lot of user interaction regarding different queries and comparison of these results with other queries and with the source system itself. Automated testing tools typically do not allow for a great deal of user interaction, so most SAP NetWeaver BW query testing is done manually.

To test the query results, the query statistics can be used to determine the most-used reports and the focus of the testing can be on the most mission critical and most-used queries. These queries should be run with a series of different users with different authorizations. This will allow the security authorizations to be checked along with the query data.

Typically, support stacks are added first to the development system and tested in some detail. After a few weeks of stabilization, the support stack is applied to the QA system. The testing occurs again with QA data. This support stack is then stabilized until it can later be added to production.

The latency of the support stack allows for a challenging production support environment. If the development, production, and QA systems are not using the same support stack, testing issues can be hard to resolve because the systems often do not act the same way under different support stacks.

For this reason, many customers opt to wait until any new major functionality is being developed for SAP NetWeaver BW prior to upgrading the support stack. This allows them to create a new completely separate SAP NetWeaver BW development environment. This new environment can be upgraded to the newest support stack while leaving the production support development, QA, and production at the old support stack.

When the new development is ready for cutover, the production environment is then upgraded to the newest support stack. This strategy has several advantages. It allows the support stack to be implemented in an environment outside of the production support environment, ensuring the integrity of that system. It also allows for new development to occur on the newest support stack. If issues occur, SAP Notes can be applied to the new development landscape independently of the production support systems.

Because all new development needs to be regression tested prior to bringing the functionality to the production system, this regression testing serves two purposes. It tests the new functionality that is being delivered and also tests the new support stack to determine its stability and validity.

This strategy only works for those environments that perform new development in a new separate SAP NetWeaver BW environment. If this is not feasible, the only other strategy is to stagger the support stacks as stated above and regression test in each environment. This also assumes that any risk of the development, QA, and productive systems being at a different support stack is understood.

There are also other non-SAP patches needed in any implementation. These include kernel patches, operating system patches, database patches, etc. These should not be overlooked when developing a support-stack strategy.

8.6.1   Frontend Support Packages

Frontend support packages are challenging in an SAP NetWeaver BW environment. This is because these frontend packages are required to be loaded on the various desktops that are using and accessing SAP NetWeaver BW. Although the SAP NetWeaver BW frontend support packages are typically small, the process of pushing out the support packages to a large audience can be challenging.

The frontend support packages are only needed if users are developing or accessing SAP NetWeaver BW reports via the BEx Analyzer. If the users are not developing queries and all queries are accessed via the Java or ABAP Web interface, the frontend patches are not needed for these users.

The frontend patch is only used during query development and running using the BEx Analyzer. Because the Web queries are being processed in the Web browser and nothing else is running on the desktop, the frontend patch is not needed for these users.

To support those users who need the frontend patches, most SAP NetWeaver BW customers use a push technology to send these patches to the various desktops in their organization. There are several software packages that allow the pushing out of these patches to the end user. This allows the packages to be organized, scheduled, and queued for periodic rollout out to the end users.

For those project organizations that do not want to deal with the overhead of the frontend patches for all users often use a Citrix or other shared environment. This environment allows multiple users to run the same frontend patches to keep some consistency for these users. If there is an upgrade necessary, only one instance needs to be upgraded. This reduces the overhead of rolling out multiple frontend patches to users.

No matter which access method is used, a clear frontend strategy should be decided on and planned as part of the SAP NetWeaver BW implementation to ensure that new frontend patches can be pushed out to the end users.

One of the other tasks that should be performed after go-live is a lessons-learned session. The goal of this session is to go over the implementation and determine where the process could have been more efficient and highlight some of the things that were done well. This helps to make sure the team can build on some of the lessons of the past.

8.6.2 Conduct a Lessons-Learned Session

A lessons-learned session is important to gather, analyze, and document feedback on events that happened during the SAP NetWeaver BW project so they may be beneficial to others in the future. During these sessions, it is important not only to speak about some of the things that the project could have done better but also to focus on the things that went well.

Conduct this session as soon as possible after go-live to get the clearest and most pertinent feedback. Include the project management and the stakeholders in the discussion. If possible, it helps to have a facilitator who has not been directly involved in the project.

Set some guidelines and rules for the lessons-learned session to ensure that the discussion stays focused. Keep the focus on the process not on the people involved in the process. Where possible, in addition to the discussion with the group, allow people an opportunity to provide anonymous feedback.

These sessions can either be run with the entire project team or with each process group. There have been many projects where these sessions are used to find issues with the entire project as one group. It's also not uncommon to find yourself working in teams where the SAP NetWeaver BW team held these sessions to look at only the SAP NetWeaver BW implementation issues. The lessons-learned discussion should include the following:

- What went well, and what steps should continue in future implementations?
- Are we doing things the right way?
- What recommendations would you have for others that would do a like project?
- Are we focusing on the right things?
- What did not go well? How would you have changed it?
- Are we getting the benefits that we expected?

After the lessons-learned session, document the feedback and provide a clear action plan on how the lessons will be included in future implementations. Communicate this to the project team.

This is often where the lessons-learned process breaks down. To have a clear and effective strategy for learning from past implementations, a formal plan and communication medium need to be developed. This shows the team members that any feedback that is given is used constructively to build a stronger team.

Take the example of a long-term implementation that continually scheduled these sessions after large go-lives. The change-management group met with many of the key project members to get their input in several group settings. These were then assimilated into one large document of all the feedback from all the groups.

The problem was that this feedback was then never acted on by the project management staff. This was extremely frustrating because many of the issues and problems were then repeated in the next implementation. For example, one of the big issues was a lack of a consolidated project plan and many issues with lack of business involvement in decision making. After the session, the next phase of the implementation started. It started without a consolidated project plan and with little business involvement. This was extremely frustrating for the team because these challenges had been addressed clearly in the lessons-learned sessions.

However, the change management team was not able to convince the project management staff to find a systematic way of implementing the suggestions. The team would have been less frustrated had the project management organization explained why suggestions were not being implemented. Simply ignoring the lessons-learned sessions caused a lot of frustration within the team.

The most important step in the lessons-learned process is to clearly spell out all the things that were mentioned and give clear steps on how these will be implemented or what steps are being taken in the future to make the process more efficient.

This helps to keep the staff motivated and helps retain good team members. There are other things that can be done to retain good team members. Let's explore some in the next section.

8.7   Retaining and Motivating Staff for Future Rollouts

After the go-live has occurred and the initial software issues have been addressed, the pressure starts to mount again. Often, there is functionality that was not addressed in the first go-live and that has been delayed for a subsequent release. Typically, there are also some elements that require a redesign or change based on user feedback.

To provide these changes and also roll out future functionality, a new project-scoping exercise and new staffing plan are needed. Often, the people that worked on the first project may be slated to return back to their original jobs, or they may be burned-out from the hours spent getting to the latest go-live.

To retain the staff, it is imperative that the people that made the go-live successful are rewarded for their work. There are several actions that help to motivate and recognize those that were vital to the project:

▶ Provide some money in the form of travel vouchers to use on vacation travel. This helps to recognize the employees and their families' sacrifice for the project.

▶ Create a wall of fame for outstanding project team members.

▶ Have various members of the team present some lessons learned to upper management. This gives some credibility and recognition to the team in front of their top managers.

▶ Provide project-related items such as shirts, mugs, etc. Although this seems like a small gesture, an unexpected gift like this can sometimes go a long way.

▶ Set a meeting time and use this time to thank individuals for their contributions. Do not discuss any other issue at this meeting.

The main thing to understand is that often those employees who were the most productive now have valuable skill sets. The management team needs to recognize and understand that keeping these people motivated and challenged will go a long way toward retaining them.

Once the staff has been chosen, the next step is to prepare for rolling out new functionality. There are several things to keep in mind about rolling out new functionality. Let's discuss this process next.

8.8   Prepare for Future Rollouts

SAP NetWeaver BW projects are seldom considered completely finished. Often, after a go-live, there is a hand-off process to production support and then an evaluation of the existing environment and a prioritization of the unfilled analysis needs. In many cases, the existing reporting environment may need to either be enhanced or redesigned.

Although frustrating, this is typical. Once the business users begin to see the information provided by SAP NetWeaver BW and start to use this to aid in business decision making, the emphasis and focus often shifts to other areas of improvement in the same functional area. Depending on the scope of the initial implementation, this may require redesigning the existing environment to provide this analysis need. This should be considered normal and should be expected.

Of course, the more the SAP NetWeaver BW team is able to foresee any new analysis needs, and incorporate this into the existing design, the better the team will be able to meet new demands.

8.9   Conclusion

Understanding and providing a clear go-live strategy requires careful planning before the go-live to make sure that the COE can provide definite value to the end user. This is often the only view that the user gets of the implementation team. It is important that, through the proactive steps mentioned, the COE provides value to the organization and helps to keep the users focused on their responsibilities and not on issues with the software.

Now, let's proceed to Chapter 9, where you'll learn about the different Six Sigma techniques to achieve excellence in SAP NetWeaver BW maintenance projects.

This chapter introduces a few basic Six Sigma methodologies that can be used in an SAP NetWeaver project to enhance the quality of data.

9   Enhance Quality: The Six Sigma Way

In this chapter, you'll learn about the simple statistical tools that are used in Six Sigma implementations and can be used in your SAP SAP NetWeaver BW project to improve the overall quality of the SAP NetWeaver BW objects.

9.1   Introduction to Six Sigma

In this section, we'll discuss some of the important terminologies and statistical tools of Six Sigma.

9.1.1   History

In 1980, Six Sigma started in Motorola as the company fought for its survival against the fierce competition of other Japanese companies. Motorola quality engineer Bill Smith presented a solution that reduced the defects dramatically in eight years. Motorola implemented Six Sigma as the philosophy of the company. Honeywell and General Electronics are among the early adopters of this methodology. Today, Six Sigma enjoys widespread acceptance across all sectors. Earlier adopters of Six Sigma were primarily found in the manufacturing sectors; however, today, the IT industry has also adopted Six Sigma as their primary tool to optimize and improve processes.

9.1.2   Definition

Six Sigma is a set of quality management methods and statistical tools used to improve the quality of the process output by identifying and removing causes and defects of the process.

Six Sigma methods cannot be implemented for problems that are not measurable. Using the statistical tools, we can derive the improvements that are quantifiable metrics (see Figure 9.1).

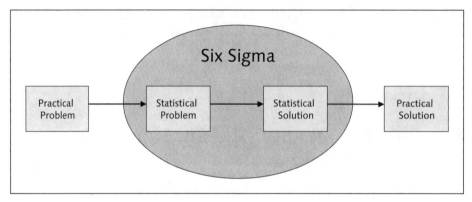

Figure 9.1 Overview of Six Sigma Approach

9.1.3 Six Sigma Methodology – DMAIC

DMAIC is as **D**efine, **M**easure, **A**nalyze, **I**mprove, and **C**ontrol (see Figure 9.2).

Figure 9.2 Six Sigma Steps

▶ Define the goal of your project.
▶ Measure the metrices of the project and collect required data.
▶ Analyze the collected data and decide on various solutions.
▶ Improve the current process/project.
▶ Control the improved process/project.

9.1.4 Six Sigma Terminologies

Defect

Anything that dissatisfies your customer, for example, functional requirements, performance, service failure, wait time, cycle time, etc., is known as a defect. In SAP NetWeaver BW projects, such defects are included in Table 9.1:

Unit

The numbers of objects that are checked for defect is called a *unit*. For example: There are 5 reports out of 25 reports giving the wrong result. Here, the unit is 25. So, defects per unit (DPU) will be 5/25 = 0.2. DPU can also be called *defect density per unit*.

SAP NetWeaver BW Defect Types	Customer Reaction	Measurement
Data Mismatch	I am not getting a correct picture of sales figure in my department.	How many records are mismatching?
	I am losing confidence in SAP NetWeaver BW reports.	How many data mismatch tickets are opened? (mismatch discovered by customer)
Delay	I always have to wait a long time to retrieve data from BI report.	What is the time taken to run the report? (SAP NetWeaver BW Statistics can be used to retrieve this kind of information.)
Design	It is difficult to navigate through the SAP NetWeaver BW report.	What time is taken by the new users to learn the navigation in an SAP NetWeaver BW report.

Table 9.1 Different Types of Defects in an SAP SAP NetWeaver BW Implementation

Opportunity

Anything that you measure is called an *opportunity*. For example: There are 25 reports that are based on two InfoCubes. The two InfoCubes have approximately 10,000 records. These 25 reports are giving nearly 2,000 erroneous records. Here, the opportunity is 10,000 and the defect per opportunity (DPO) = 2,000/10,000. DPO can also be called *probability of defects* (p(d)). The value of p(d) will be between 0 and 1. If p(d) = 0, then there are no defects, and if p(d) = 1, then all records are defective.

Take a closer look into the examples mentioned in Table 9.2. Calculation of defects and opportunities are different in both examples. In the first example, opportunity is calculated by multiplying the number of finished goods and number of checking criteria. So, the total number of defects will never exceed the total number of opportunities. In the second example, the reports will fetch maximum the total number of records in the cube. That's why the total number of records is considered an opportunity.

DPO and DPU Formula

`Total Opportunity (TOP)` = (No of Unit checked) × (No of opportunities of failure per unit).

`Probability of Defect, p(d)` – (# Defects) / (# Opportunities). P(d)=[0,1]. p(d) is also termed as *DPO*.

`Defects per million opportunity (DPMO)` = p(d) × 1,000,000. It is easier to work with DPMO when DPO is small.

Example 1	
In a production plant, each finished packaged is checked for four types of criteria. Total production of finished package in each day is 1000. Out of these packages, there are five defective packages in two types of criteria.	Unit = 1000
	Opportunities = 1000 × 4 = 4000
	Total Defects = 5 × 2 = 10
	DPU = 10/1000 = 0.01
	DPO or p(d) = 10/4000 = 0.0025
	DPMO = 0.0025 × 1,000,000 = 2500
Example 2	
There are 10 reports based on a specific InfoCube. The InfoCube consists approximately of 500,000 records. Among the 10 , 2 reports are not giving results correctly. In the first report, 100 records are wrong, and in the second report, 400 records are wrong.	Unit = 10
	Opportunities = 50,000
	Total defects = 100 + 400=500
	DPU = 500/10 = 50
	DPO or p(d) = 500/500,000=0.001
	DPMO = 0.001 × 1,000,000=1000

Table 9.2 Different Examples to Determine Key Terminologies

Upper Specification Limit (USL) and Lower Specification Limit (LSL)

Specification limits may be called *borders* and any values beyond this border will be known as *defects*. Let's try to understand this with the following examples:

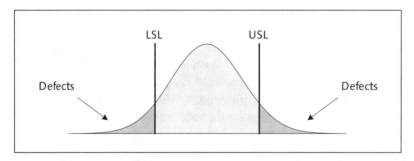

Figure 9.3 Determination of Defects with Respect to LSL and USL

▶ Metrices with only Upper Specification Limits: These types of metrices only have upper specification limits. For example: Cycle Time, Wait time, Response time, Cost, Price. SLA Time to resolve a ticket always have upper limits, but there should not be any lower limits.

▶ Metrices with only Lower Specification Limits: SLA compliance always should have lower specification limits. Another example is system downtime.

▶ Metrices with Upper Specification Limits and Lower Specification Limits: Delta schedule timings, effort always have upper and lower specification limits.

9.1.5   Basic Statistics

Extensive usage of statistical tools and methodologies is the main essence of a Six Sigma project. In this chapter, we'll look at some of the basic statistical terminologies. In statistics, calculated data can be distinguished in two types: *continuous* and *discrete*. Table 9.3 outlines the differences of these types of data.

Continuous Data	Discrete Data
They are real numbers.	They are whole numbers.
Normally, they are measured values with reference to other parameters.	Normally, they are counted values.
The efforts of a specific resource can be distinguished as continuous values because efforts are referenced with hours. Hours of efforts can be any real number, for example, 5.5, 3.4, 1.2, etc.	The number of deliverable objects has to be a whole number, for example, 1, 2, 3, etc. Here, the data type is discrete.

Table 9.3   Difference Between Continuous and Discrete Data

Mean

Summation of all values divided by the numbers of values signifies as mean or average.

Median

This is the value that has an equal number of values above it and below it, when arranged in ascending order. In other way, median is whatever value that splits a distribution in half, with equal number of observations lying above and below.

Example to Calculate Median
Example: If the number of defects occurred in a report for a week beginning from Sunday to Saturday are 1, 16, 18, 20, 33, 48, 68, then the median defect will be 20 and mean is (sum of defects)/7=29.
If you have excluded the Sunday data, then the list will be 16, 18, 20, 33, 48, 68 (Monday to Saturday). In this case, median will be (20+33)/2=26.5.

Mode

This is the value that occurs with the highest number of frequencies.

Standard Deviation (SD)

Standard deviation is commonly used in Six Sigma and takes all observed values in account. SD is a kind of average amount by which all values deviate from the mean. In Figure 9.4, we'll try to understand how SD is calculated.

Consider the population of defects
16, 18, 20, 33, 48, 68

$$\text{Mean} = \frac{16+18+20+33+48+68}{6}$$

To calculate the population standard deviation, we compute the difference of each data point from the mean, and square the result

Values	Difference from Mean		Square of the Difference
16	16-29	-13	169
18	18-29	-11	121
20	20-29	-9	81
33	33-29	4	16
48	48-29	19	361
68	68-29	39	1521
Sum of squared values			2269
Calculated Standard Deviation $\sqrt{(2269/6)}$			19.45

Below is the generalized formula of SD

$$\sqrt{\frac{1}{N}\sum_{i=1}^{N}(x_i - \bar{x})^2}$$

Where, N = total number of population,
$\bar{x}$ Is arithmetic mean of population

$$\bar{x} = \frac{x_1 + x_2 + \cdots + x_N}{N} = \frac{1}{N}\sum_{i=1}^{N}x_i$$

Figure 9.4   Calculation of Standard Deviation

Calculate Sigma Rating

If you know the *sigma rating (Z)* of a process, you can easily establish the rejections that can be expected from a process. See Table 9.4 to calculate the sigma ratings.

Identifiers	Values	Excel Functions and Formula
Normal Continuous Data with Upper Specification Limits		
Mean, m	100	AVERAGE(number1,number2,...)
Std Dev, s	10	STDEV(number1,number2,...)
USL	120	Customer defined constant
Z	2	Z = (USL − m)/s
p(d)	2.28%	p(d) = 1-NORMSDIST(Z)
Normal Continuous Data with Lower Specification Limits		
Mean, m	100	AVERAGE(number1,number2,...)
Std Dev, s	10	STDEV(number1,number2,...)
LSL	90	Customer defined constant
Z	1	Z = (m − LSL)/s
p(d)	15.86%	p(d) = 1-NORMSDIST(Z)
Normal Continuous Data with Both Specification Limits		
Mean, m	100	AVERAGE(number1,number2,...)
Std Dev, s	10	STDEV(number1,number2,...)
LSL	90	Customer defined constant
USL	120	Customer defined constant
ZL	1	Z = (m − LSL)/s
p(d),L	15.86%	p(d) = 1-NORMSDIST(Z)
ZU	2	Z = (USL − m)/s
p(d),U	2.28%	p(d) = 1-NORMSDIST(Z)
p(d),T	18.14%	p(d),T = p(d),L + p(d),U
ZB	0.91	ZB = NORMSINV(1 − p(d)T)

Table 9.4 Calculation of Sigma Rating

From the example in Table 9.4, you can say that your process has nearly 1 sigma rating.

9.2 Reasons to Implement Six Sigma in an SAP NetWeaver BW Project

In this section, we'll discuss a few of the most important reasons to implement Six Sigma in an SAP NetWeaver BW project.

9.2.1 Six Sigma is a Pro-Active Approach

In any SAP NetWeaver BW maintenance project, at first sight, daily activities like loading of data, successful completion of all process chain means that the project is running smoothly. True, there might be no big issues around SAP NetWeaver BW report. But today's competitive market demands you to offer more to your customer so that they feel special for you. If you ask for feedback from the end users and work on those feedbacks using Six Sigma, it will add much value your service to your customer.

9.2.2 Talking in Customer's Language

Six Sigma methodologies were first introduced in the manufacturing industry to cut down the costs occurring because of defects in products. Today, most of the production companies as well as service sector companies are well aware of Six Sigma and few of them adopted Six Sigma as their corporate strategy toward quality. So, when you are using Six Sigma to address various issues in a SAP NetWeaver BW project, customers will also be happy to see the results and documents because they are masters in this.

9.2.3 High level of Correctness

Six Sigma does not work with any qualitative problems; instead, the whole process is fully statistical result oriented. It has robust and well-proven methodologies that will drive your processes to perform with the best results.

9.2.4 Happy Strategic Users — A Foundation for New Business Opportunities

Most end users of the SAP NetWeaver BW report are the top management of the company. Based on the SAP NetWeaver BW reports, they only take important strategic decisions. If you can provide visually intriguing, user-friendly, and correct results, it will have a direct, positive impact on your service and eventually will lead new to avenues of businesses.

9.3   Phase 1: Define

Define is the first phase of DMAIC architecture in Six Sigma. Although it is not possible to discuss everything of Six Sigma in a single chapter, here we'll familiarize with some basic important steps (see Figure 9.5).

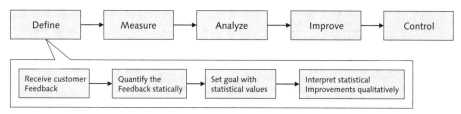

Figure 9.5   Steps for DEFINE Phase of Six Sigma

9.3.1   Voice of Customer and Voice of Business

Any comprehensive feedback received from a customer(s) is called *Voice of Customer (VOC)*. VOC contains feedback and suggestions about the application or process, for example:

▶ Sales department is not able to get a correct picture of sales figures in SAP NetWeaver BW reports.

▶ SAP NetWeaver BW reports are taking too much time to load.

▶ SAP NetWeaver BW reports are not user friendly.

Requirement or feedback of the customer's business as whole is known as *Voice of Business (VOB)*, for example:

▶ The company needs to cut down costs on SAP NetWeaver BW.

▶ SAP NetWeaver BW end user training costs need to be minimized.

9.3.2   Critical to Quality (CTQ)

CTQ is derived from the VOC and VOB after applying different statistical tools (see Figure 9.6). So, a quantified value that covers most critical aspects of VOC and VOB is known as *CTQ*.

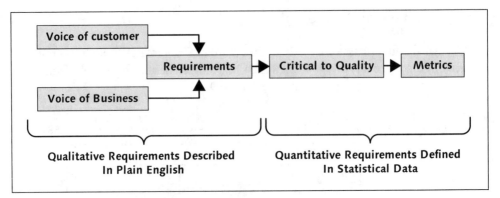

Figure 9.6   Translation of VOC into CTQs

9.3.3   CTQ Tree

The CTQ tree translates broad customer/business requirements into specific CTQ requirements (see Figure 9.7). It helps the team to move from high-level requirement to small specific requirements. The main objective of CTQ is to ensure that all aspects of the needs are addressed.

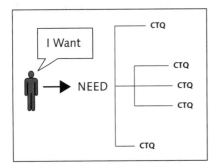

Figure 9.7   Derivation of CTQ Tree

9.3.4   Project Charter

Preparation of project charter is the main output of the define phase. The project charter contains information related to team structure, problems, and goals (see Figure 9.8).

▶ In the *Champion* field, enter the name of the mentor who will be helping you throughout the project. In general, champions are master black belt in your organization.

▶ Stake holders are the end users who are directly affected by the change.

▶ In general, a Six Sigma project should have a sponsor. However, because this tool will be used proactively, there might not be a sponsor (see Figure 9.9).

▶ Figure 9.8 depicts a listing of a CTQ definition. However, there could be more than one CTQ derived from the CTQ Tree.

▶ Use Microsoft Excel formulas to calculate the different parameters of the CTQ definition.

▶ Figure 9.8 shows a standard Microsoft Excel sheet. It's not mandatory to fill in all of the fields. You can use your own version in accordance with your requirement.

▶ Take confirmation sign-off from your customer about the goal statements.

▶ Target performance values should not be overambitious. There could be numourous unforeseen factors that can generate defects in your system.

▶ Take help from a champion (master black belt) before finalizing the *Define phase*.

Six Sigma Project Charter
Title: Increase % SLA Compliance

Business Case	(Compelling reasons for doing the project)		
Voice of Customer	Reduce Cost	**Voice of Business**	Increase profitability
	Increase overall SLA compliance		
Project Team			
Champion		Team Leader	
Team Members			
Customers			
Stake Holders	(The name of end users of BI application)		
Sponsors	(Customer or the company which may fund this activity)		

Figure 9.8 Project Charter with Team Information

389

Six Sigma Project Charter
Title: Increase % SLA Compliance

	(Plain English)		(Plain English)
Problem Statement	SLA Compliance not met with	**Goal Statement**	Penalties due SLA breach will be reduced
	priority one ticket		
AS IS (CTQ Terms)	92% of P1 ticket take > 4 hrs	**TO BE (CTQ Terms)**	96% of P1 ticket take > 4 hrs
	with average of 3 hrs		with average of 2 hrs
IN Scope		**OUT Scope**	

CTQ Definitions	
Definition of Opportunity	Every P1 ticket supported by team
Definition of unit	Every P1 ticket supported by team
Definition of defect	Response and resolution breach per ticket

Present performance		Target performance	
DPO		**DPO**	
DPMO		**DPMO**	
Z-Bench		**Z-Bench**	
If data is continuous		If data is continuous	
Mean		**Mean**	
Median		**Median**	
P05		**P05**	
P95		**P95**	
Q1 or P25		**Q1 or P25**	
Q3 or P75		**Q3 or P75**	

Figure 9.9   Project Charter with Problem and Goals

9.4   Phase 2: Measure

In the measure phase, we'll look into the methodologies to get the detailed view of a process and will try to find out the root cause of defects.

9.4.1   SIPOC – Supplier Input Process Output Customer

SIPOC (Supplier Input Process Output Customer) diagram is a high-level view of process flow from supplier to customer (see Figure 9.10).

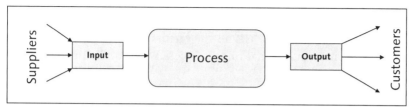

Figure 9.10 High-level SIPOC Diagram

Ask a few questions before preparing the SIPOC diagram:

- ▶ Why this process exists?
- ▶ What is the main purpose of this process?
- ▶ At what point does the process starts?
- ▶ What are the inputs of the process?
- ▶ Where do the inputs affect the process flow?
- ▶ What happens to each inputs?
- ▶ What conversion activities take place?
- ▶ What are the outputs of the process?
- ▶ At what point does the process ends?

If you know the answers of the above questions, you can easily create the block diagram of the process. The idea behind is to identify the steps in the whole process that are causing or influencing the defects. Figure 9.11 depicts the Microsoft Excel template of SIPOC for the example in the Define phase in the previous section.

SIPOC

Who are the		What do the suppliers provide to my		What are the start and end points of the	What product or service does the		Who are the customers for our	
Suppliers		**Input**		**Process** (High Level)	**Output**		**Customers**	
1 Client problem Ticket	1	Support Center	Start Point:	1	Detail activity Report	1	BW report user
	2	Applications (BW)	End user sends mail about the issue to raise ticket			2	
	3			2	Cycle time	1	Project Manager
2 System Events	1	Support Center				2	
	2	Applications (BW)	Operation or Activity	3	Service metric	1	Project Manager
	3		1 Receive Ticket			2	
3	1		2 Categorize Ticket type	4	Documents	1	Project team members
	2		3 Determine SLA			2	
	3		4 Document the incident	5		1	
4	1		5 Assign resource			2	
	2		6 Determine root cause	6		1	
	3		7 Fix the problem			2	
			8 Mail to end user				
			9				
			10				
			11				
			End Point:				
			Confirmation mail about the solution from end user and close the ticket				

Figure 9.11 Microsoft Excel Template for SIPOC

9.4.2 Analyze Process — Fishbone Diagram

The *Fishbone* diagram identifies and lists all the factors that impact the problem and identifies the potential causes that impacts overall output. Figure 9.12 is the example of the SLA problem.

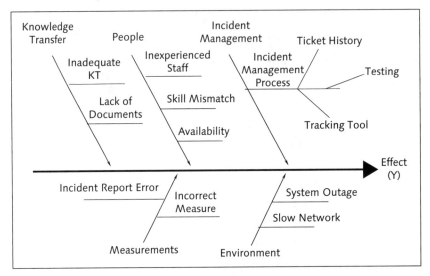

Figure 9.12 Fishbone Diagram

9.4.3 Cause and Impact Analysis

While drawing the fishbone diagram, include all the factors regardless of their feasibility. You get detail and a complete view of the causes that results defect (see Figure 9.13). The next step after the fishbone analysis is to analyze the feasibility of the causes derived during fishbone analysis. The idea behind this analysis is:

▸ Identify and fix the causes that are less cost effective and have high impact on the CTQ.

▸ Do not implement the causes that are costly and have less impact on the CTQ.

Prioritizing the implementation of the potential causes is entirely dependent on the requirement and severity of the defects. There could be some defects that completely shut down the system. In that case, go for the implementation of the causes regardless of the cost involved.

At the end of the measure phase, collect the data from the process to derive the sigma level.

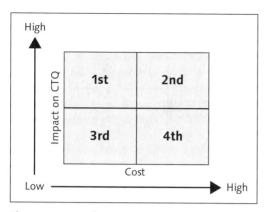

Figure 9.13 Graph to Prioritize the Causes Derived from Fishbone Diagram

9.5   Phase 3: Analyze

In this phase, we'll analyze the data collected during the define and measure phases with the help of some basic charts, including basic charts and a few complex charts.

9.5.1   Pie Chart

A pie chart is one of the most common types of all the charts used in Microsoft Excel. This type of chart can compare relative magnitude or percentage among various sectors. You need to sort the data either in ascending or in descending order to analyze a vital few out of trivial many.

9.5.2   Bar Charts

Bar charts compare the values of different items in specific categories or at discrete points in time.

Do and Don'ts:

▶ Use various color options to highlight importance.

▶ Don't use this type of charts if there are too many segments.

▶ In a pie chart, use the Explode option to draw attention to a particular segment, as shown in Figure 9.14.

393

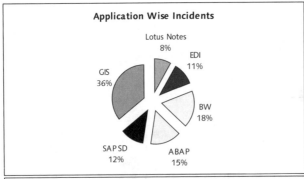

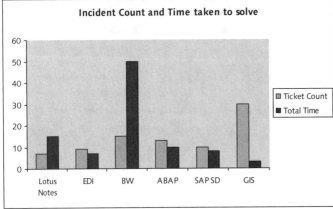

Figure 9.14 Example of Pie and Bar Chart

9.5.3 Pareto Chart

Pareto charts visualize defect symptom type or cause type in decreasing order of number of occurrences to separate the vital few from the trivial many. The Pareto principle says that 80% of problem happens from 20% of the causes. Let's try to understand the Pareto chart with the SLA problem example in Figure 9.15.

Inadequate Skill and Understanding are the main two causes for which 80% of SLA breaches are happening.

The Pareto chart is the most important tool in Six Sigma. With this chart, you can easily figure out what are the few reasons for most of the problems.

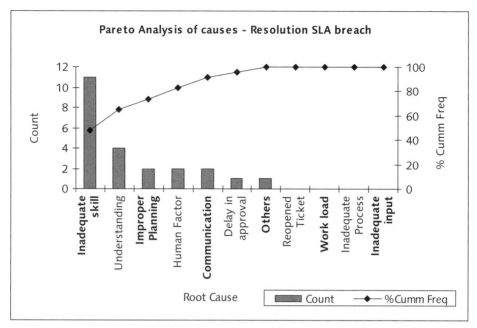

Figure 9.15 Pareto Chart Example

9.5.4 Histogram and Box Plots

Histogram represents the frequency of the occurrences as bars in the chart. The main advantage of histogram is that you can visualize the densities of different occurrences.

In Figure 9.16, three histograms were created for the tickets with Simple, Medium, and Complex category. The X axis represents the average effort per ticket and Y axis is the frequency of such tickets.

Box plots are another way of representation for a histogram. It shows spread of data with outliers. It can be used to do segmentation and narrow down problem areas, as seen in Figure 9.17.

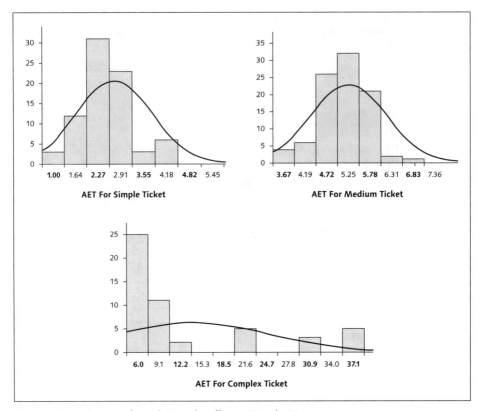

Figure 9.16 Histograms for Tickets with Different Complexities

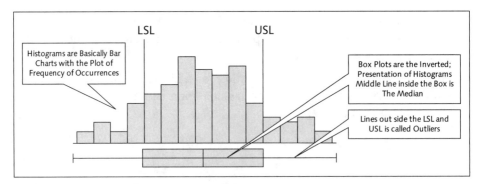

Figure 9.17 Conversion of Histograms to Box Plot

Now using this example, we'll create the box plots, as seen in Figure 9.18.

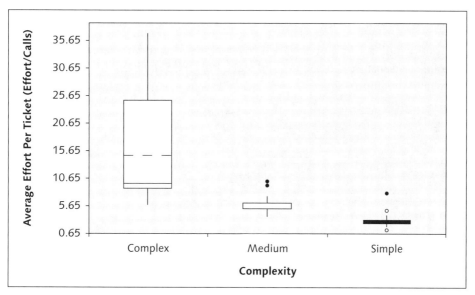

Figure 9.18   Box Plot Example

According to Figure 9.18:

▶ Simple, Medium, and Complex tickets are non-overlapping.

▶ Average Effort per Ticket (AET) spread of complex tickets are the most.

> **Tip**
>
> The Pareto chart, histogram, and box plots are the most important and frequently used tools in Six Sigma. However, creating this chart in Microsoft Excel is tedious. You can download and install tools like SigmaXL to create this kind of chart. Also, you can find numerous free guides and tools on the Internet.

9.5.5   Conclusion of Analyze Phase

Until now, we have used several charts to analyze the SLA problem. Using these tools, we have reached the following conclusions:

▶ The most time is spent on SAP NetWeaver BW tickets (Figure 9.14).

▶ Inadequate skill and understanding of the tickets are the main casuses of SLA breach (Figure 9.15).

▶ Most of the SLA breaches are happening with complex tickets (Figure 9.18)

If you upgrade the skill of SAP NetWeaver BW consultants to solve complex tickets, you will definitely reduce the number of SLA breaches.

9.6   Phase 4: Improve

The idea behind the improve phase is to generate ideas and implement those ideas with full consensus of customers and stake holders. See Figure 9.19 for the steps to execute the improve phase.

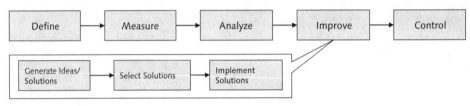

Figure 9.19   Steps to Execute Improve Phase

9.6.1   Brain Writing

Brain writing is a unique method of generating ideas where a group of people write their ideas in a piece of paper for a particular problem. This method helps those people who are particularly shy or concerned to speak in an open forum to express their views without competing to each other. Below are the steps for brain writing:

▶ Give a card to the team members.

▶ Team members write their ideas on the card.

▶ Now, each team member passes those cards to each other.

▶ The next team member will add more ideas on those cards.

▶ Repeat the prior two steps until all team members have seen and added to all cards.

▶ Consolidate all ideas in a single paper and remove duplicate ideas.

9.6.2   Brain Storming

Unlike brain writing, brain storming is the process to generate ideas where team members will voice their ideas and a facilitator of this session writes them on board (see Table 9.5). Below are the steps for brain storming:

▶ Prepare the group by talking about the problems or writing the problems on the board.

▶ List down the ideas on the flip chart.

▶ There should not be any debate or criticism within the team members.

▶ Separate and regroup the ideas.

Brain Storming	Brain Writing
Fragile process and intends to be free-flowing, non-judgmental exchange	Writing your ideas is better than speaking them
Impact of what other person says funnels down ideas rather than opening it up	Brain writing generates 40% more creative ideas than brain storming.
Normally shy people often shut down completely in an open forum	Uniform participation within the group

Table 9.5 Difference Between Brain Writing and Brain Storming

9.6.3 Select and Implement Ideas

It's not always possible to implement all ideas generated from brain storming or brain writing sessions. You have to start the cost and benefit analysis on all ideas. First, prioritize the proposed solutions based on the benefits from the solution and difficulty to implement the solutions. Then, analyze the key stake holders affected by the Six Sigma project. There could be a situation where some of them will be extremely supportive to the proposed solutions and some may not. Analyze the type of resistance shown by the key stake holders and build the strategy to gain acceptance for the proposed solution.

9.7 Conclusion

This chapter introduced a few basic Six Sigma methodologies that can be used in an SAP NetWeaver project to enhance the quality of data through fewer defects, shorter cycle times, increased capacity and throughput, lower costs, higher revenues and reduced capital expenditures.

In this chapter, we'll look into the latest reporting tools offered by SAP, including integration aspects of SAP NetWeaver BW with SAP Business-Objects and BEx tools.

10   Reporting and Analytics in an SAP NetWeaver BW Environment

SAP BusinessObjects is widely recognized as a pioneer in the business intelligence space with solutions spanning information discovery to delivery. SAP acquired Business Objects to tap the high potential business intelligence market by integrating the Business Objects tools with their existing SAP NetWeaver BW reporting portfolio. In the following sections, you'll learn how the SAP NetWeaver BW reporting tools can be integrated with the SAP BusinessObjects tools to enable reporting from SAP and non-SAP data sources.

10.1   SAP + BusinessObjects

Synergy between the best SAP ERP solution provider and the best business intelligence solution provider results in the most effective and robust information analysis platform available (see Figure 10.1). Today, any enterprise needs better clarity into its operations to survive the competitive market and SAP's comprehensive tool set is the best-suited solution to provide transparency across the enterprise with heterogeneous system architecture.

Figure 10.1 Synergy of SAP and Business Objects

10.2 SAP SAP NetWeaver BW Presentation Layer

Figure 10.2 shows a complete reporting scenario of SAP NetWeaver SAP NetWeaver BW, including the SAP BusinessObjects tools. Leveraging the SAP BusinessObjects Data Service tool will enable you to integrate data from third-party data into SAP NetWeaver BW. The SAP BusinessObjects Data Service tool can also cleanse and enrich master data from various source systems.

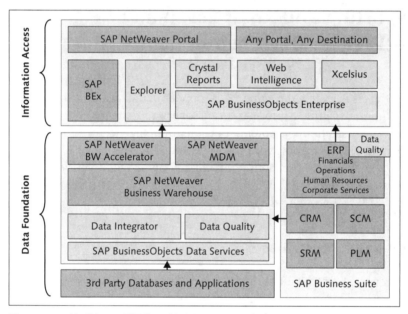

Figure 10.2   NetWeaver BW Reporting Layer Data Flow Diagram

In SAP BusinessObjects reporting architecture, data can be retrieved from SAP NetWeaver BW through a semantic layer called a *Universe*. Universes can be defined on various SAP SAP NetWeaver BW objects such as InfoCubes, DSOs, and SAP NetWeaver BW Queries. It's also possible to integrate various SAP ERP systems and databases into a Universe. Web Intelligence reports can be built on these universes, resulting in a combined delivery of data from SAP ERP systems and SAP NetWeaver BW systems. Crystal Report, the industry standard for formatted reporting, can also be built on Universes as well or on SAP ERP directly. Xcelsius, a Microsoft Excel–based dashboard creation tool, can create great data visualization and intuitive navigational elements. In next two subsections, we'll discuss the architecture of SAP BusinessObjects and SAP BEx tools.

10.2.1   SAP NetWeaver BW Standard BEx Reporting

Business Explorer (BEx) is SAP's homegrown business intelligence tools and provides flexible reporting and analysis tools. These tools include query, reporting, and OLAP functions. With proper authorization, you can evaluate old and current data to varying degrees of detail and from different perspectives using BEx Web and BEx analyzer.

As shown in Figure 10.3, you can see that the BEx reporting tools are tightly integrated with the SAP NetWeaver BW environment. So, if you have only SAP systems to support your business activity throughout the organization, adopting the BEx tools for reporting will be the best and most cost-effective approach. While SAP has indicated that the SAP BusinessObjects tools are the future of their business intelligence portfolio, the BEx tools will be supported through 2016, although no further development will occur.

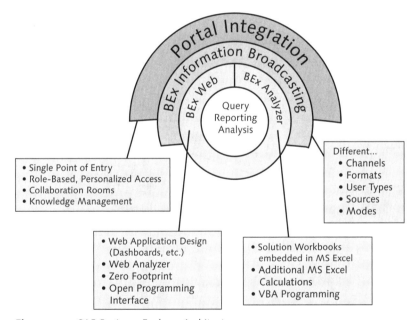

Figure 10.3   SAP Business Explorer Architecture

10.2.2   Reporting with SAP BusinessObjects

Figure 10.4 outlines the different connectivity options available in SAP BusinessObjects to integrate SAP NetWeaver BW, SAP ECC, and third-party database systems. The *SAP Business Intelligence Integration Kit* acts like a connection agent between source systems (SAP NetWeaver BW, SAP ECC, and third-party database) and different BO client/server components.

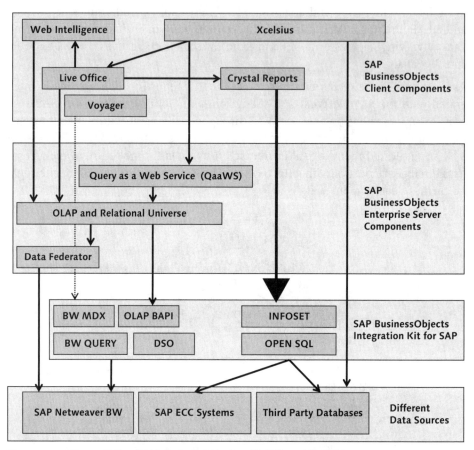

Figure 10.4 Connectivity of SAP BusinessObjects with Different Data Sources

Let's briefly discuss the SAP BusinessObjects components:

▶ **Universe (Semantic Layer)**
Using Universe Designer, you can build a data abstraction layer on top of your database. This layer provides a unified view of your data regardless of the source.

▶ **Web Intelligence**
This tool allows information users to build queries easily on data and choose how to graphically display that data. Users can dynamically build tables, charts and other views without requiring in-depth knowledge of the underlying table

structures. The simplicity of Web Intelligence is due to Universe, which reduces the complexity of the metadata into a format that business users can understand.

▶ **Crystal Reports**
This powerful, yet easy-to-use, reporting tool allows end users to construct and view highly formatted reports. This tool can access data from any source using the SAP integration kit.

▶ **Live Office**
This is a connectivity tool that allows a live link from the content of a Universe to Crystal Reports or Web Intelligence.

▶ **Xcelsius**
This CEO-friendly, data-visualization tool consumes data from Microsoft Excel, Crystal Reports, or Web services, to build a visual dashboard delivered as Flash content, that can be embedded in a Web page or even a Microsoft PowerPoint file, while still retaining flash interactivity.

▶ **Voyager**
This OLAP analysis tool offers more advanced analytical capabilities beyond ad-hoc reporting. Voyager is a tool to answer questions and help discover trends and anomalies within the data. Features of Voyager include data mining, navigation of multidimensional data sets, and analysis of data leveraging statistical functions.

▶ **Polestar**
A visualization tool that leverages the Universe semantic layer and interprets the data to determine common dimensions to display. End users can easily navigate data, compare different dimensions, drill down, and chart. You do not need to be a BI tools expert to use Polestar.

▶ **Data Federator**
This tool can access different SAP NetWeaver BW InfoProviders directly.

10.3   SAP BusinessObjects Installation Guides

In this section, we'll provide an overview of an SAP BusinessObjects installation, which can be broken down into server side SAP BusinessObjects Enterprise (BOE) installations, SAP BO client installations, and SAP BO Integration Kit for SAP Solutions.

Note

A full installation guide is available in *http://service.sap.com/bosap-instguides*. You can also get more detail information in the SAP PRESS book Integrating *SAP BusinessObjects XI 3.1 Tools with SAP NetWeaver* by Ingo Hilgefort.

10.3.1 SAP BusinessObjects Enterprise Server Installation

Figure 10.5 gives an outline of the SAP BOE server installation steps. We strongly recommend referring to the installation guides available at *http://service.sap.com/bosap-instguides* for more details.

1	• Validate system requirements from http://service.sap.com/bosap-support
2	• You should have administrative privilege in the system
3	• Access to all machines via TCP/IP
4	• Access to supported web application server
5	• Access to supported database systems
6	• Run installation file in your server
7	• Install SAP GUI on BOE server
8	• Install SAP Java Connector (sapjco.jar) in web application server shared library folder
9	• Install SAP BusinessObjects Integration Kit for SAP on BOE server
10	• Configure SAP BW and BOE server for Crystal Reports Publisher settings

Figure 10.5 SAP BusinessObjects Server Side Installation Steps

10.3.2 SAP BusinessObjects Client Installation

The SAP BusinessObjects client side tools include Crystal Reports, Xcelsius, SAP BusinessObjects Live Office, and Universe Designer. Installation of these tools is easy and straight forward, like any typical software installation. Figure 10.6 shows the overview of the steps required to install SAP BusinessObjects client tools.

1	• Install client side components of SAP BusinessObjects Integration Kit for SAP solution
2	• Install Crystal Reports, Xcelsius, SAP BusinessObjects Live Office, and Universe Designer
3	• Install ABAP connectivity transports in your SAP NetWeaver BW system
4	• Verify your installation by connecting with your SAP BW and BOE server

Figure 10.6 SAP BusinessObjects Client Side Installation Steps

10.4 OLAP Universe Design Based on SAP NetWeaver BW

SAP BusinessObjects Universe Designer is used to build OLAP Universes on top of SAP NetWeaver BW InfoProviders such as SAP NetWeaver BW Queries, Info-Cubes, and MultiProviders. You can also create a Universe based on other data sources such as SAP ECC Systems, third-party databases, and flat files (XML, Excel, CSV, etc). Before using SAP NetWeaver BW Queries as OLAP Universe, you have to configure it to allow external access via property window on SAP NetWeaver BW Query Designer (see Figure 10.7). OLAP Universe leverages all SAP NetWeaver BW query features, except those listed below:

▶ Time characteristics and key figures type is not supported by OLAP Universe.

▶ Personalization values cannot be accessed in OLAP Universe.

▶ Variables defined on hierarchy versions are not supported by OLAP Universe.

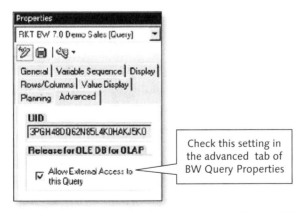

Figure 10.7 Allowing External Access of SAP NetWeaver BW Queries

In next sub-sections, we will create a Universe on SAP NetWeaver BW Query and will change few settings of an OLAP Universe.

10.4.1 Creating OLAP Universe Based on SAP NetWeaver BW Queries

In this subsection, we'll see how an OLAP Universe can be created on a SAP NetWeaver BW Query. Below is a simple, step-by-step, approach to building a Universe.

1. **Launch Universe Designer**
   On your windows desktop, follow the path START • PROGRAMS • BUSINESS-OBJECTS XI 3.1 • BUSINESSOBJECTS ENTERPRISE • DESIGNER. Enter user name and password and select system (see Figure 10.8). If you select Authentication as Standalone, then you need not to enter the user id and password.

Figure 10.8 Universe Designer Logon Screen

2. **Launch New Connection Wizard**
   Select menu FILE • NEW. A new dialog box will be opened. Enter the name of the new Universe and click the New button to launch the new connection wizard (see Figure 10.9).

3. **Create a New Connection with an SAP NetWeaver BW Query**
   After clicking the Next button in the New Connection Wizard introduction screen, you will get a list of available connection types. Under SAP connection type, select SAP Client inside the SAP Business Warehouse. Then choose the Next button to enter SAP server information, user id, and password. This information is the same as you enter in the SAP logon pad (see Figure 10.10).

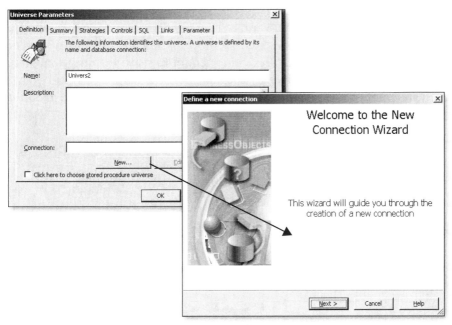

Figure 10.9 Launching the New Connection Wizard

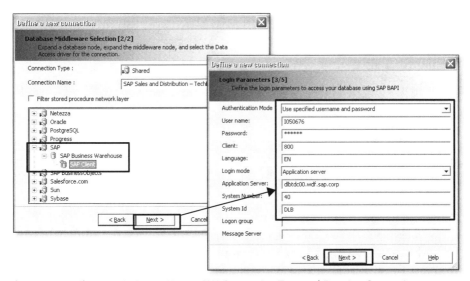

Figure 10.10 Choosing SAP NetWeaver BW Connection Type and Entering Connection Parameters

4. **Finalizing Universe Connection**

   After entering the user id, password, and SAP system information, you'll get a dialog window showing all the InfoCubes in your SAP NetWeaver BW system. Go to the your required InfoCube and expand it to select the query on which you want to build your universe. Clicking the Next button will lead you to enter different parameters for timeout and record size. Click the Finish button to complete your Connection definition wizard (see Figure 10.11).

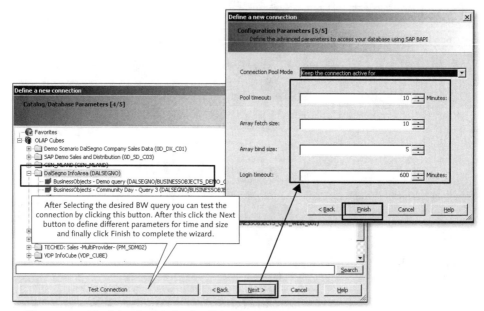

Figure 10.11 Finalizing Connection for Universe

5. **Completion of Universe**

   After defining the connection, you can see the Universe Parameters dialog screen where you can see that the connection field contains a newly created one. Now, go to the Controls tab and uncheck different limit parameters (see Figure 10.12).

6. **Save and Export Newly Created Universe**

   After pressing the OK button, you can save the newly created Universe in your local desktop as well as you can export it to BOE server by accessing the menu path FILE • EXPORT. The exported Universe can be accessed by InfoView on the BOE server. In the next subsection, we'll discuss different options related to the generation of a Universe. Figure 10.13 shows the generated Universe based on a SAP NetWeaver BW Query.

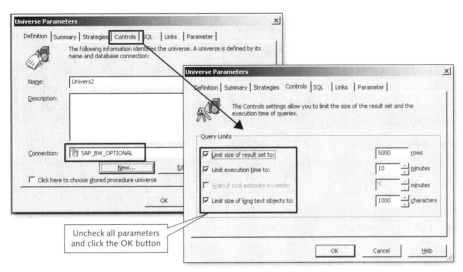

Figure 10.12 Changing Parameters for New Universe

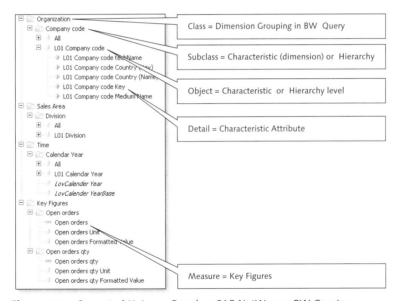

Figure 10.13 Generated Universe Based on SAP NetWeaver BW Queries

10.4.2 Setting OLAP Universe Generation Options

Universe generation options can be changed via accessing the menu path Tools •
Options • OLAP tab. If you need to change any default settings, then change these

values before generating the Universe (see Figure 10.14). Let's discuss the meaning of each option individually:

- **Generate technical name as detail**
  This option enables a user to decide to create a detail object in the universe for each level. The definition of that detail object is based on technical name like the key. The detail object does not replace the key; it is created in addition to the key. This option is common to all OLAP data sources.

- **Set measures aggregation to delegated**
  This option is most useful when you are using nonaggregated key figures. It is used to set aggregation function of measures in the universe to be delegated to the database. This function directly impacts the way Measures are calculated in the Web Intelligence report. If you do not select this option, Sum will be the default aggregation function. Aggregations will be computed by the Web Intelligence calculator and not the database. Setting the aggregation to "Database delegated" is useful in the case of measures like ratios, weight, percentage, etc.

- **Replace Prefix L00, L01**
  With this option, you can set your own prefix for levels instead of "L." If you put "Level" in the "New Prefix" field, the generated universe will contain levels renamed as "Level 00," "Level 01," etc.

Figure 10.14 Defining Universe Generations Options

► **Generate Level 00**

SAP always provides Level 00 and Level 01 for characteristics, whereas level 00 is equivalent to "All characteristic members." In general, SAP users are not aware of this level and don't use it.

► **Rename Level 00 to ALL**

If the option "Generate level 00" is set Level 00, it will be renamed to "All."

10.4.3 Customizing OLAP Universe

Several new fields can be added in the Universe level. You can add a new Measure (Key Figures) and create a mandatory filter on Universe level.

Adding Calculated Measures

1. Right-click on the Key figures class and select the menu option Object... In the *Definition* tab of the editor pane, enter the name and type of the new Measure.

2. In the Properties tab, select Measure as Qualification of the object and function as Database Delegated.

3. Return to the Definition tab and click ">>" for the Select field. A new dialog will open to enter your calculation function. Here, you can formulate your MDX formula to calculate a new key figure. (See Figure 10.15.)

> **Note**
>
> To know more about MDX, refer to online documentation of universe designing on *http://help. sap.com/businessobjects*.

Creating a Filter

1. To create a filter, select the radio button filter at the bottom of the Universe business layer.

2. Right-click on a class and select menu the option Condition....

3. Enter the name of the filter name.

4. Check the option Use filter as mandatory in the query and select the option Apply on Universe (see Figure 10.16).

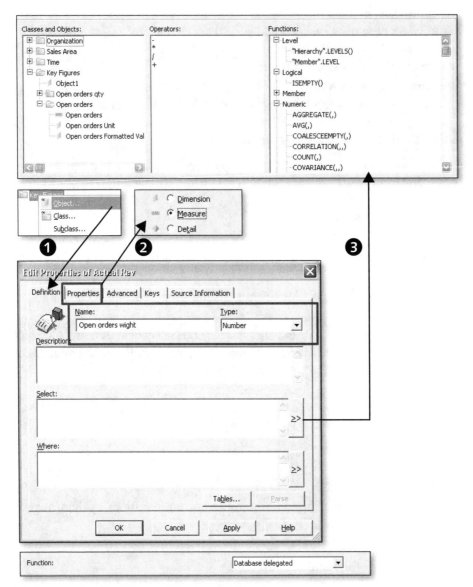

Figure 10.15 Creating Calculated Measures in Universe

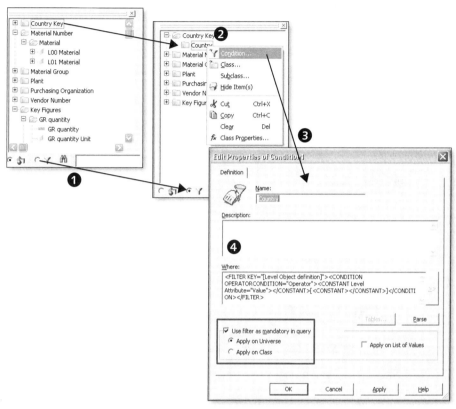

Figure 10.16 Creating Filter Based on a Universe

Checking Integrity of the Universe

You can parse the whole Universe for correctness from the Universe designer as shown in Figure 10.17. Checking integrity is most important if you have several complicated calculated measures and filters on your Universe. You can access the integrity check option from the toolbar as well as from the menu shown in Figure 10.17.

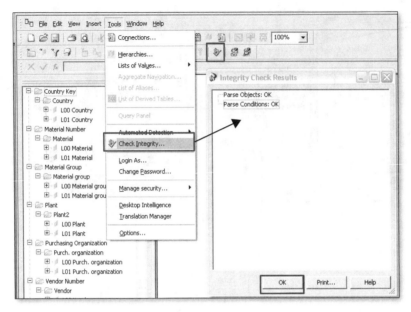

Figure 10.17　Checking Integrity of a Universe

10.4.4　Leveraging SAP NetWeaver BW Query Variables in Universe

Most SAP NetWeaver BW query variables are supported in Universe and can be used in any Web Intelligence report based on the Universe. A few points should be remembered while using SAP NetWeaver BW queries in SAP BusinessObjects:

▶ Use Optional variables because mandatory variables will always load a list of values.

▶ Use inclusive filters instead of exclusive.

▶ Ensure that the user can only select values from the actual LOV (List of values).

▶ Check the delegated search option in the properties of Universe. This option forces the Universe to delegate the search in the SAP NetWeaver BW system.

▶ Define the primary keys in the Key tab of properties of Universe objects. This feature ensures access to indexes.

Table 10.1 shows different types of SAP NetWeaver BW query variables that are supported in SAP BusinessObjects.

Variable Type	Processing Type				
	User Entry/ Default Value	Replacement Path	Authorization	Customer Exit	SAP Exit
Characteristics	Supported	Supported	Supported	Supported	Supported
Text	Not Supported	Supported	N/A	N/A	N/A
Formula	Supported	Supported	N/A	Supported	Supported
Hierarchy	Supported	N/A	N/A	Supported	Supported
Hierarchy Node	Supported	N/A	N/A	Supported	Supported

Table 10.1 Supported SAP NetWeaver BW Query Variable Types in SAP BusinessObjects

10.4.5 OLAP Universe: Best Practice and Guidelines

▶ We strongly recommend using SAP NetWeaver BW queries as a data source for Universes. Adding Calculated, Restricted Key Figures and SAP variables is a flexible option in SAP NetWeaver BW Query designer, which can be leveraged in Universes.

▶ While creating a Universe connection, always use Secured connection. Universe built on secured connection can be exported in SAP BusinessObjects Enterprise server.

▶ Adopt proper naming conversion to define the Universe connection names so that the underlying database can easily be traced.

▶ Because a Universe is used as a semantic layer for ad-hoc reporting by information users, proper documentation and naming conversions should be adopted for each of the class and objects. You can use the description field for documentation of each object so that information users will know the purpose and meaning of the object's runtime.

▶ Never use duplicate object names in different classes.

▶ Always apply an aggregation function for each measure (Key Figure) object.

▶ Always do the integrity check of Universe before exporting it to the BOE server.

▶ Do not turn on every SAP NetWeaver BW queries for external access. So, don't create too many Universes to confuse information users.

▶ Create calculated key figures at the SAP NetWeaver BW Query level. With this approach, information users don't need to create calculated key figures every time they do ad-hoc reporting.

▶ Do not create only one query above one SAP NetWeaver BW InfoProvider because document level data in Query can add significant processing time even if you are not using all fields in Web Intelligence report.

▶ The implementation strategy should focus on limiting the number of SAP NetWeaver BW queries and Universes that shares common elements.

▶ Set the property Use Selection of Structure Members in Transaction RSRT for the query to ensure that structure elements are sent to the database for processing.

10.5   Web Intelligence Report Design on Universe

Web Intelligence is an SAP BusinessObjects reporting tool that can leverage Universe created on different type of data sources.

10.5.1   In Which Scenario Can Web Intelligence be Used?

▶ The SAP BusinessObjects Web Intelligence tool can create ad-hoc reporting from Universes. These Universes act as a semantic layer and hide underlying complexity of data in databases.

▶ You can combine data from SAP and non-SAP such as XLS, CSV, and Text Files.

▶ Web Intelligence can be accessed from Web (InfoView) as well as from your desktop.

10.5.2   Creating a Web Intelligence Report

1. To run Web Intelligence Rich Client, follow the path in your start menu PROGRAMS • BUSINESSOBJECTS XI 3.1 • BUSINESSOBJECTS ENTERPRISE • WEB INTELLIGENCE RICH CLIENT. Enter your user id and password if you are connecting to SAP BusinessObjects Enterprise Server. If you are connecting in standalone mode, then you don't have to enter the user id or password (see Figure 10.18).

2. After clicking the Logon button, you'll have to choose the Universe already saved in your local desktop. You can also select Universe from enterprise server if are already logged in Enterprise with your credentials.

3. After choosing your desired Universe, you will be taken to a new screen as shown in Figure 10.19. Drag and drop the fields that you want to see in the reports to the right of the results object panel.

4. After adding your desired fields, click the Run Query button at the upper right corner of the screen (Figure 10.19).

5. A new dialog will open to show the progress (Figure 10.19).

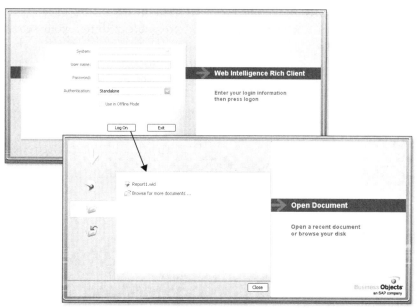

Figure 10.18 Logging in Web Intelligence Tool

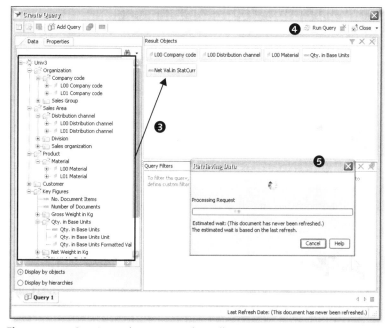

Figure 10.19 Creating and Running Web Intelligence Query

In the next screen, you'll see the report retrieved from the data source. See Figure 10.20. This is a rich report development tool where you can design your report according to your industry requirements. You can also apply a template in your existing reports. In next few subsections, we look into how a Web Intelligence report can be retrieved from Enterprise server, how Alerts can be designed in Web Intelligence reports, etc.

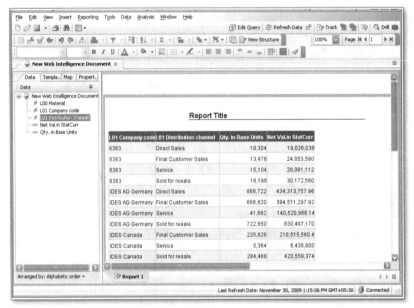

Figure 10.20 Web Intelligence Report Designer

10.5.3 Exporting Web Intelligence Report in Enterprise CMS

You can export Web Intelligence Reports in InfoView so that information consumers can access this report. To export the Web Intelligence report, follow the steps:

1. Go to menu File • Export to CMS.

2. A new screen will be opened to select the location of the report to be saved.

10.5.4 Define Alert in Web Intelligence Report

An alert in the Web Intelligence report is much similar to Exceptions in BEx Queries. The following steps refer to Figure 10.21.

1. In the toolbar, click the Alert icon as shown in Figure 10.21.

2. In the next screen, click the New button.

3. In the Alerter Editor screen, select fields for which you want to define an alert.

4. Select Operator in the operator drop down.

5. In the operands field, enter the value to be compared.

6. Click the Format button to define the color and format.

7. Finally, click OK.

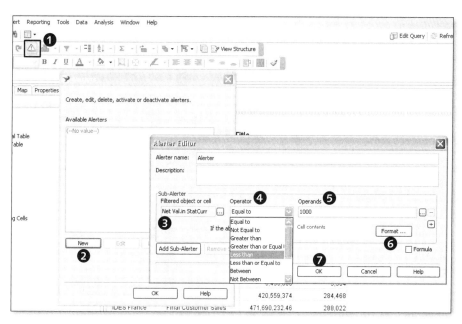

Figure 10.21 Defining Alert in Web Intelligence Reports

10.5.5 Accessing Web Intelligence Reports from InfoView

You can access SAP BusinessObjects InfoView by entering *http://<BOE Server>/Info-ViewApp/logon.jsp* in Microsoft Internet Explorer. In the Login page of InfoView, enter your BOE credentials. The following steps refer to Figure 10.22.

1. In the home page of InfoView, click the Document List link.

2. In the next screen, browse to the folder where you saved the Web Intelligence reports and click that folder.

3. In the right pane, you can see all your reports inside the designated folder. Double click on the report to run it.

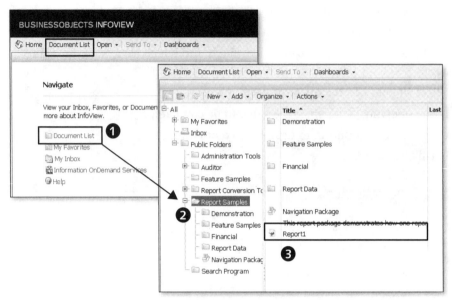

Figure 10.22 Accessing Web Intelligence Reports from InfoView

10.5.6 Opening and Saving Web Intelligence Report in Different Modes within InfoView

Web Intelligence document can be viewed or saved in different formats based on your requirement. Figure 10.23 relates to the following steps.

1. In Web Intelligence Interactive, select the report tab of the report that you want to view.

2. Click the arrow next to the View button on the main toolbar above the report.

3. Select the viewing mode.

4. Web Intelligence Interactive displays the report in the selected viewing mode.

5. In the Java Report Panel, use Switch Page/Quick Display on the Reporting toolbar to alternate between Page mode and Quick Display mode.

6. You can save the report in the same way. (See Figure 10.23.)

Saving reports in different modes

Viewing reports in different modes

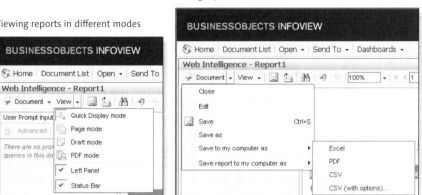

Figure 10.23   View and Save Web Intelligence Reports in Different Modes

10.5.7   Displaying Track Changes in Web Intelligence Report

Using this functionality in Web Intelligence reports, you can track the changes in data within the report. Using this option, it is possible to highlight the changed, created, and deleted records in the report. Figure 10.24 corresponds to the following steps:

1. Click Track on the main toolbar to display the Activate Data Tracking dialog box.

2. Select options in the dialog box, as in Table 10.2.

Option	Description
Auto-update the reference data with each data refresh	With each data refresh, current data becomes the reference. With this option, you can see the difference between the most recent data and the last refresh data.
Use the current data as reference data	Current data becomes the fixed reference data and remains as the reference for further data refreshes.

Table 10.2   Options While Refresh for Track Changes

3. Click Refresh Now to refresh the data when the dialog box closes.

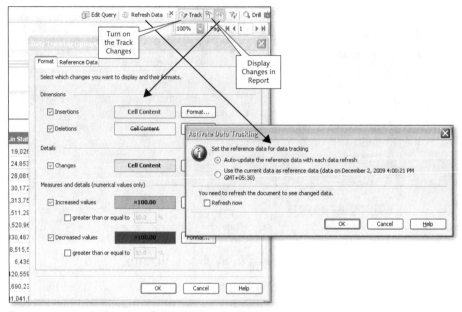

Figure 10.24 Track Changing of Web Intelligence Reports

10.6   Query as a Web Service (QaaWS)

Query as a Web Service (QaaWS) is an SAP BusinessObjects application that allows business users to quickly create queries and publish them as Web services.

The QaaWS is available to any application that uses Web services, and allows users to access data returned by the query from within the application. It allows information to be securely delivered to any application that can consume Web services.

10.6.1   Starting QaaWS Tool

To create a QaaWS, you have to start the client tool and meet the following prerequisite to create a QaaWS.

▶ Your SAP BOE user id should be included in QaaWS Group Designer or Administrator user group.

▶ You have to define a server host to store the query Web service. You do this when you start Query as a Web Service for the first time or at any other time by adding a host in the Edit a Host dialog box. See Figure 10.25.

Note

If you are creating QaaWS for testing purposes in your machine, then you can give the host address of your tomcat server where SAP BusinessObjects Enterprise CMS resides.

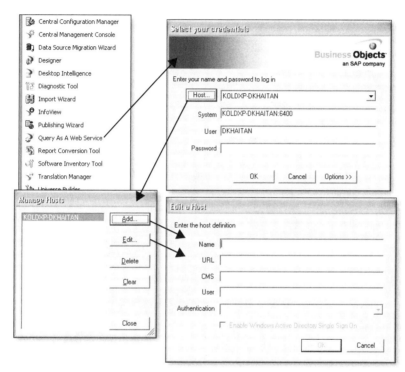

Figure 10.25 Logging into QaaWS Tool

10.6.2 Steps for Creating a New QaaWS

Follow the steps below. Figure 10.26 corresponds to the following steps.

1. Select QUERY • NEW QUERY. The Publish as a Web Service Wizard opens to the Description page. You can enter the name, description, and advanced parameter information on this page. Press the Next button.

2. Click a Universe in the list. A description of the selected universe appears in the description box. Press the Next button.

3. The Query page of the wizard appears. Drag and drop the required fields in the Result and Filter pane. You can define different parameters (Duplicate rows, Max. fetched time, Max. rows fetched, Sample result set) for performance of

the Web service. You can also set the sort order of the fields by clicking the Sort button in the upper left corner of the screen. Press the Next button.

4. You will get a preview of your newly created QaaWS. Press the Publish button to complete the wizard.

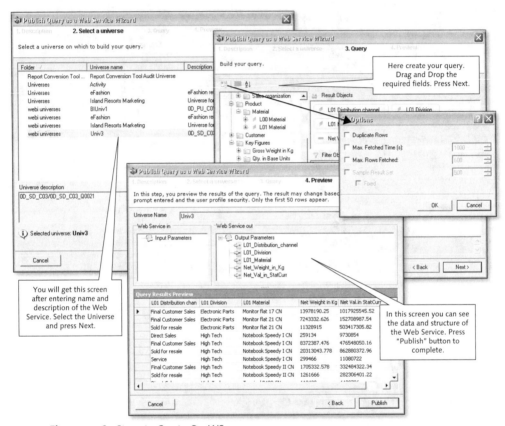

Figure 10.26 Steps to Create QaaWS

10.6.3 Business Scenarios Where QaaWS is Required

▶ QaaWS is a gateway to the external applications to interact with SAP Business-Objects. Any external tool or websites that supports Eeb service can utilize QaaWS to get data from SAP BusinessObjects.

▶ Crystal reports and Xcelsius can leverage QaaWS via the SOAP protocol to display up-to-date data from SAP or other data sources.

10.6.4 Implementation Best Practice for QaaWS

▸ Fetch the data that you need for your use. The time consumed will be higher with the more data you fetch.

▸ Aggregate the data as much as possible to keep the number of records small.

▸ Create more queries with less information rather less queries with more information.

▸ Restrict your number records within 500.

10.7 Xcelsius

Using Xcelsius, you can create visually stunning and interactive dashboards and applications. Xcelsius leverages technology from Microsoft Office Excel and Adobe Flash Player. This breakthrough technology builds the bridge between data analysis and data visualization. You don't need to learn a programming language to build beautiful, user-friendly dashboards for your strategic users. In this section, we'll dive into the Xcelsius tool to create some basic dashboards and integration aspects for various data sources including SAP SAP NetWeaver BW.

10.7.1 Different Types of Flavors to Suite Your Need

SAP BusinessObjects provides different types of Xcelsius based on the user expertise and project requirements.

▸ **Xcelsius Present**
It is a basic level version and intended for the users who will create dashboards on Microsoft Excel data only. This version does not offer any connectivity options with external data sources.

▸ **Xcelsius Engage**
This version has everything of Xcelsius Present and has options to connect to external data sources.

▸ **Xcelsius Engage Server**
This version has everything of Xcelsius Engage and you'll have tools to deploy your dashboards in your portal.

▸ **BusinessObjects Xcelsius Enterprise**
This version provides everything from Xcelsius Engage Server. In addition, SAP BusinessObjects Xcelsius Enterprise integrates with the SAP BusinessObjects platform, including QaaWS, LiveOffice, and Crystal Reports.

10.7.2 Creating a Simple Xcelsius Application Based on QaaWS

Before creating Xcelsius dashboards, you first need to create a Universe and QaaWS (see Figure 10.27). For our example, we created a Universe based on query 0D_SD_C03/0D_SD_C03_Q0021 and created a QaaWS, which shows sales amounts against company code and sales group.

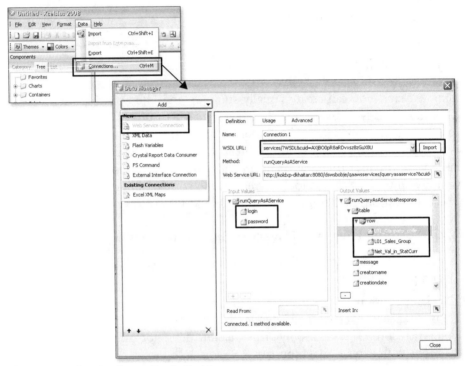

Figure 10.27 Creating Connection in Xcelsius

1. Run the Xcelsius tool from your start menu with the path ALL PROGRAMS • XCELSIUS • XCELSIUS 2008. Also, open the QaaWS tool to copy the path of the Web Service.

2. After opening the QaaWS tool and providing the user id and password, you can see the QaaWS created previously. At the right lower part of the screen, press the To Clipboard button to copy the QaaWS path.

3. In the Xcelsius tool, follow the menu path DATA • CONNECTIONS. A new screen will open to define your connection with the data source (see Figure 10.28).

4. Select Web Service Connection by pressing the Add button at the upper left corner of the screen. You'll see a dialog with three tabs and connection fields at the right panel (see Figure 10.28).

5. Enter the name of the connection and paste the QaaWS address, which was copied in Step 1.

6. Press the Import button. The Input Values and Output Values areas are filled (see Figure 10.28).

7. Map the input and output fields with an embedded Microsoft Excel sheet within the Xcelsius tool. Select fields in output values area and click the small icon beside the Insert in field. Select cells in the A column up to the maximum number of rows that QaaWS will fetch. See the Figure 10.28.

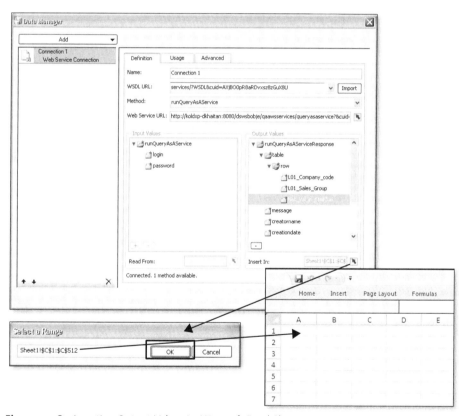

Figure 10.28 Inserting Output Values in Microsoft Excel Sheet

8. In the Usage tab of the *Data Manager* screen, check Refresh on load so that whenever the application loads the data will be refreshed.

9. Close the Data Manager screen.

10. In the main workspace area, in the Components panel, select the Tree tab and expand the Selectors folder.

11. Drag the List View component to the center of the workspace area. See Figure 10.29.

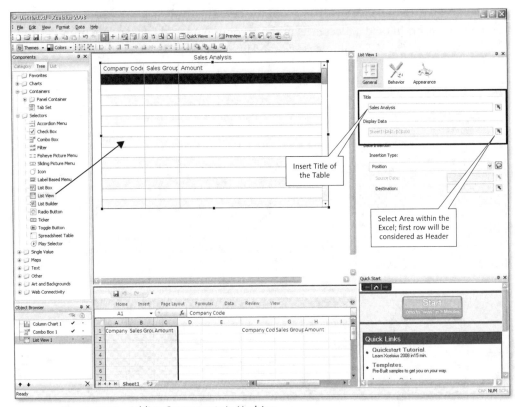

Figure 10.29 Adding Components in Xcelsius

12. In the general properties of the List View component, enter the title and select cells in Microsoft Excel by clicking the button near the Display Data field.

13. Save your Xcelsius file.

14. Export the Xcelsius file in SWF format to see it in Microsoft Internet Explorer. Export the SWF file in an http folder of the server you are having the QaaWS.

In our example, it'll be the same Tomcat server root folder. This is required to prevent the error message related to cross domain. See the flash tutorial to know more about this and how to solve this issue.

15. Open Microsoft Internet Explorer and type in *http://<server-name>:8080/<folder>/<file>.swf*. See Figure 10.30.

Sales Analysis

Company Code	Sales Group	Amount
IDES AG Germany	Donald Wachs	299688576.28
IDES AG Germany	Natascha Abercomb	227478343.34
IDES AG Germany	Scott Right	284709418.76
IDES AG Germany	Mario Bridget	701729193.38
IDES AG Germany	Chris Smith	286227662.26
IDES UK	Edward Anderson	41240063.78
IDES UK	Donald Wachs	320394960.18
IDES UK	Natascha Abercomb	196298547.78
IDES UK	Phil Coopers	72832760.16
IDES UK	Chris Smith	125915890.58
IDES UK	Michael Rey	174679974.42
IDES France	Edward Anderson	113403143.14
IDES France	Donald Wachs	399687734.5
IDES France	Natascha Abercomb	397404419.76
IDES France	Chris Smith	62236864.16
IDES US Inc.	Edward Anderson	125933611.36
IDES US Inc.	Donald Wachs	467610890.78
IDES US Inc.	Natascha Abercomb	524050875.02

Figure 10.30 Output of Xcelsius Application

10.7.3 Xcelsius Best Practices

In this subsection, you're going to learn some best practices that should be followed while creating a dashboard with the Xcelsius tool.

Because Xcelsius is tightly integrated with Microsoft Excel, follow a few basic rules to design your data in a spreadsheet to ease your dashboard development.

- Xcelsius does not support all Microsoft Excel functions while generating a SWF file for your dashboard. Generally, avoid functions like SUMIF, COUNTIF, HLOOKUP, and VLOOKUP. For more detailed information see the help file (press F1).
- Different Microsoft Excel formatting options should be followed to identify data in the sheet. For example, the cells with input values are formatted with bright yellow and output value cells should be formatted with green. See Figure 10.31.

	A	B	C	D	E	F	G	H	I	J	K	L	M
1													
2													
3	Selector 2	Option 1	Option 2	Option 3	Option 4								
4	Dynamic Visibility	1											
5	Department 1	$ 926	$ 773	$ 162	$ 929	$ 102	$ 311	$ 97	$ 906	$ 327	$ 768	$ 737	$ 911
6	Year To Date Values	$ 926	$ 1,699	$ 1,861	$ 2,790	$ 2,892	$ 3,203	$ 3,300	$ 4,206	$ 4,533	$ 5,301	$ 6,038	$ 6,949
7							ACTUAL						
8	Department	Jan	Feb	Mar	Apr	May	Jun	Jul	Aug	Sep	Oct	Nov	Dec
9	Department 1	$ 926	$ 773	$ 162	$ 929	$ 102	$ 311	$ 97	$ 906	$ 327	$ 768	$ 737	$ 911
10	Department 2	$ 322	$ 576	$ 36	$ 664	$ 393	$ 502	$ 57	$ 992	$ 241	$ 441	$ 992	$ 826
11	Department 3	$ 725	$ 618	$ 578	$ 850	$ 30	$ 483	$ 43	$ 817	$ 50	$ 138	$ 979	$ 85
12	Department 4	$ 825	$ 331	$ 66	$ 587	$ 98	$ 399	$ 604	$ 659	$ 480	$ 531	$ 596	$ 471
13	Department 5	$ 111	$ 11	$ 286	$ 4	$ 666	$ 358	$ 837	$ 709	$ 148	$ 104	$ 20	$ 470

Figure 10.31 Sample Microsoft Excel Sheet for Xcelsius

▶ Organize your data in a Microsoft Excel sheet in a logical manner so that the design time will be reduced significantly while creating a complex dashboard application.

▶ Use multiple tabs to store your data. A huge single sheet containing all information is not helpful to debug the dashboard at design time.

▶ Most frequently used data should be kept at the top of the sheet for overall performance of the dashboard.

▶ If you are creating an Xcelsius dashboard from Web Services or another database that fetches data at runtime, you can mock up some data in Microsoft Excel to test your visualization. However, don't forget to delete all mockup data before exporting your dashboard.

▶ The easiest way to embed your dashboard in your Web page is to export the Xcelsius file as HTML and use the code in a generated HTML file.

▶ Do not over-fetch data in Xcelsius because it supports only 500 lines.

▶ If you are hosting the SWF file on a Web server, make sure that the server from which you are getting the live data has a crossdomain.xml file in its root folder. To know more about crossdomain.xml, you can get help from the Adobe website.

10.8   Microsoft Office Integration with Live Office

SAP BusinessObjects Live Office is another tool built in the Microsoft Office environment to integrate the data in various Microsoft Office applications like Excel, Word, PowerPoint, and Outlook. Live Office is most similar to SAP BEx Analyzer, and using this tool, you can integrate data from various sources like Universe, Web Intelligence Report, and Crystal Reports as shown in Figure 10.32.

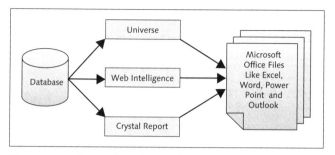

Figure 10.32 Connectivity Options for SAP BusinessObjects Live Office

10.8.1 Live Office Ribbon within Microsoft Office Applications

SAP BusinessObjects offers a Ribbon for Microsoft Office 2007 applications from where you can integrate and manage documents with BOE server. The functionality of each button is mentioned in Figure 10.33.

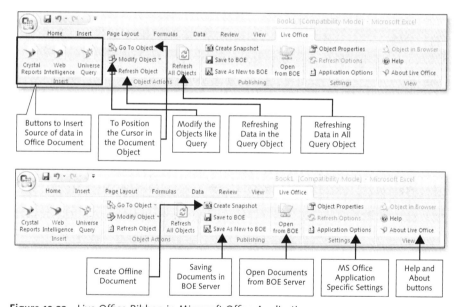

Figure 10.33 Live Office Ribbon in Microsoft Office Applications

With current Live Office tools, you can integrate the data from SAP systems also. If you want to put SAP SAP NetWeaver BW data in Microsoft Excel by using Live Office, then first you have to create a Universe on the SAP NetWeaver BW Query and the Universe then can be utilized in a Live Office application. In a first look, you may be wondering about the difference between Live Office and BEx Analyzer. Let's discuss the comparison between them:

▶ Using Live Office, you can integrate data from various source systems including SAP NetWeaver BW, but BEx Analyzer is only able to present SAP NetWeaver BW data through SAP NetWeaver BW Queries.

▶ Live Office provides a unified view of data regardless of the source.

▶ Apart from Microsoft Excel, Live Office can also be used in Microsoft Word, PowerPoint, and Outlook. However, BEx Analyzer only runs on Microsoft Excel.

10.8.2 Logging in SAP BusinessObjects Enterprise from Live Office

In this subsection, you're going to log in to SAP BOE server from Live Office.

1. Launch Microsoft Excel, Word, or PowerPoint from your Windows start menu.

2. Click Application Options within Settings area of Live Office Ribbon. The Option dialog box will open.

3. In the Enterprise tab of the Options dialog box, check Use specified logon criteria and enter the BOE user id and password.

4. In the Web Service URL field, enter the Web Service URL. If your CMS and Web Service server is the same, then enter *http://<Your CMS URL>:8080/dswsbobje/services/session*.

5. Enter your BOE CMS name in the System field and finally select Enterprise from the Authentication drop downbox. Press OK.

10.8.3 Inserting Crystal Reports Content in Live Office Document

To insert Crystal Reports data in your Microsoft Office application, click the Live Office ribbon and then Crystal Reports within the Insert area. A wizard dialog will be opened, which contains the following steps in Table 10.3:

Wizard Page	Activity
Choose Document	1. Browse the BOE server folder structure and locate your Crystal Reports.
	2. Enter logon credentials for the selected Crystal Report.
	3. Press the Next button.

Table 10.3 Inserting Crystal Reports: List of Activities

Wizard Page	Activity
Specify Parameter Values	4. This page will appear if your selected Crystal Reports have parameters defined.
	5. Choose parameter values from a pre-selected list of values.
	6. Specify whether you are prompted each time data is refreshed.
Choose Data	7. In the Choose Data page of the Live Office Insert Wizard, select the Switch to Fields option.
	8. In the Available Fields list, click a field that you want to include in the Report object, and then click the right arrow (>). The selected fields appear in the Selected Fields list.
	9. Use the up and down arrows to change the order of the included fields, as required.
	10. Click the Next button.
Set Filters	11. In the Set Filters page of the Live Office Insert Wizard, click the field that you want to filter.
	12. Select a suitable operator from the Operators dropdown list on the right.
	13. Select a value from the dropdown list of values for the operator you chose, and click Add Filter.
	14. Click the Next button.
Summary	15. From the Summary page, name your Live Office object and verify its path in the SAP BusinessObjects repository.
	16. Click Finish to insert your Live Office object into your Microsoft Office document.

Table 10.3 Inserting Crystal Reports: List of Activities (Cont.)

10.8.4 Inserting Web Intelligence Content in Live Office Document

Web Intelligence reports that are stored in the BOE server can be inserted in your Microsoft Office application by selecting the button in the Insert area of the Live Office ribbon. Table 10.4 shows the steps:

Wizard Page	Activity
Choose Document	1. Browse the BOE folder structure to locate your Web Intelligence report. 2. Press the Next button.
Specify Query Context	3. This dialog will appear if your query has more than one context. 4. Choose the available context. 5. Press the Next button.
Specify Prompt Values	6. Enter values for the selection criteria of the Web Intelligence report. 7. Press the Next button.
Choose Data	8. In this wizard page, select the table that contains data. 9. Press the Next button.
Summary	10. Enter the name of the Object. 11. Verify the Web Intelligence report path in the BOE server. 12. Press the Finish button.

Table 10.4 Inserting Web Intelligence Report: List of Activities

10.8.5 Inserting Universe Query in Live Office Document

Table 10.5 shows the steps to be performed to insert data from Universe.

Wizard Page	Activity
Choose Universe	1. Locate the Universe in the BOE server folder structure. 2. Press the Next button.
Specify Query	3. Drag and Drop the Universe objects in the Result area. 4. Drag and Drop the Universe objects in the Filter area if you need to restrict the result based on some selection criteria. 5. Select filter values as Constant, Prompt or List of values. 6. Press the Next button.
Specify Prompt Values	7. Choose a prompt value from a pre-selected list of values. 8. Press the Next button.
Summary	9. Specify the name of the object in a Live Office document. 10. Press the Finish button.

Table 10.5 Inserting Universe Query: List of Activities

10.9   Crystal Reports

In this section, we'll discuss about integration aspects of Crystal Reports with SAP system. Crystal Reports is a widely accepted tool to create highly formatted reports.

10.9.1   Crystal Reports Connectivity Options with SAP

Crystal Reports offers six connectivity drivers to integrate SAP systems. Using these drivers, you can connect SAP NetWeaver BW as well as SAP ECC systems to generate highly formatted reports.

▶ **MDX Driver**
This driver can connect SAP NetWeaver BW systems through SAP NetWeaver BW queries. Its most enhanced version supports all features of SAP NetWeaver BW Queries. It is highly recommended to use this driver to connect SAP NetWeaver BW system.

▶ **SAP NetWeaver BW Query**
This is another driver to connect SAP NetWeaver BW system through SAP NetWeaver BW Queries; however, it's not as efficient as MDX driver and lacks some performance issues. Many features aren't supported in this driver, for example, multiple structure and display attribute.

▶ **Infoset**
Whenever reporting is required off an SAP R/3 system, you can use this driver. This driver allows access to pre-built views in SAP R/3 system.

▶ **ODS**
As the name suggests, the ODS driver connects ODS in SAP NetWeaver BW system where detail reporting is required. The main disadvantage of this tool is the performance is degraded if you are fetching a large amount of data.

▶ **ABAP Functions**
Use this driver when complex logic should be implemented before reporting. Using this driver, you'll have flexibility to use ABAP features within the function modules.

▶ **Table and Cluster**
Use this driver to access SAP R/3 tables directly in your Crystal Reports. Main disadvantage of this driver is that you will don't have any options to format the data. However, the advantage lies in its simplicity of use.

Pay special attention while choosing the driver for your Crystal Reports. A selected driver can be the main performance factor for your Crystal Reports.

10.9.2 SAP Toolbar in Crystal Reports

Crystal Reports offers a typical SAP toolbar similar to BEx analyzer. You can open/ save Crystal Reports documents in the same way as Work Books. See Figure 10.34.

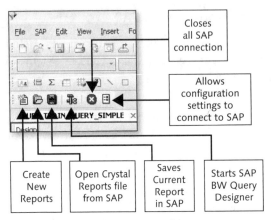

Figure 10.34   SAP Toolbar in Crystal Reports

10.9.3 General Steps to Create A Simple Report Based on SAP NetWeaver BW Query

The complexity of Crystal Reports development depends on your reporting requirement. The development of complex Crystal Reports requires a dedicated resource who has sufficient knowledge on this tool. In the following steps, we'll discuss how to create a simple Crystal Reports based on SAP NetWeaver BW.

1. Start Crystal Reports Designer by accessing the menu path START • PROGRAMS • CRYSTAL REPORTS 2008.

2. In Crystal Reports Designer application, select the menu path File • NEW • STANDARD REPORT.

3. Click on CREATE NEW CONNECTION.

4. In the Available DataSource area, select SAP NetWeaver BW MDX Query.

5. In the next screen, select your SAP NetWeaver BW system.

6. Enter your logon credential, which is similar to a normal SAP logon pad.

7. Click the Finish button.

8. In the Available DataSource Area, select your SAP NetWeaver BW system under SAP NetWeaver BW MDX Query.

9. Select your SAP NetWeaver BW Query. Press the Next button.

10. Select required fields from the selected SAP NetWeaver BW Query. Press the Next button.

11. If grouping is required, then select the fields. Press the Next button.

12. Choose a template for your Crystal Reports. Press the Finish button.

10.9.4 Crystal Reports Best Practices

Below, we're going to discuss some of the best practices that must be followed while developing Crystal Reports on an SAP system:

▶ Leverage ABAP function module driver if you have to implement complex business logic. Within ABAP code, you can join several tables and perform complex transformation easily.

▶ Before preparing Crystal Reports, clearly determine the reporting requirement. Use the paper-pencil approach to determine the output format of the report.

▶ Clearly define the output format of the report. Crystal Reports has the ability to export the report in different formats, for example, Adobe PDF, Microsoft Word, Microsoft Excel, Rich Text, etc.

▶ The reporting strategy for BEx and Crystal Reports should not be the same.

▶ Avoid using a large dataset within Crystal Reports. This may downgrade the performance. Use filters and restrictions as much as possible to reduce the volume of data.

▶ If you need to report on transactional data, use an ODS driver instead of SAP NetWeaver BW Query driver.

▶ Ensure that a clear security plan is defined before rolling out the reports in production.

10.10   Information Discovery with Polestar

Polestar is the most innovative offering of SAP BusinessObjects where you can retrieve answers to your business questions quickly through searching. In this section we will look into how to create Spaces within Polestar to enable data searching facility.

Using Polestar, information becomes more accessible and can be directly analyzed.

10.10.1 What is Information Space?

Polestar leverages Information Space objects that contain data for searching and analysis. Information Spaces can be created out of pre-built Universes and indexed on the BOE server for faster retrieval of data.

10.10.2 Accessing Polestar

1. Go to *http://<BOE SERVER>:8080/polestar.*
2. Type the name of your BOE server in the System field.
3. Enter the SAP Business Objects Enterprise user id and password.
4. Select Enterprise in the Authentication dropdown box.
5. Press the Logon button.

10.10.3 Creating Space

In this subsection, we'll see the steps to create a Space.

1. Select the Manage Spaces button at the upper right corner of the home page.
2. A new tab will open. In this tab, you'll see a panel on theleft side called Sources. You'll see the Universe Tree from the BOE server.
3. In the right panel area, you can see all the Spaces created on the Universe. Press the Create New button.
4. In the Properties tab of the new Space creation dialog box, enter the name of the space and description. Verify other information like Regional settings, Universe Name, and Universe description. Figure 10.35 corresponds to Steps 1 to 4.
5. Go to the Objects tab.
6. Move the Universe Objects to the right panel by Clicking > button. At least one Measure object and one Dimension object are mandatory. If there are any SAP key date objects that require your input, you're prompted to choose a value. If you selected any Universe objects that require your input, you're prompted to choose values.
7. Click the Validate button to check your selection.
8. Now go to the Scheduling tab. In the scheduling page, you can enter the timings when the Space Index will be refreshed. Figure 10.36 corresponds to Steps 5 to 8.

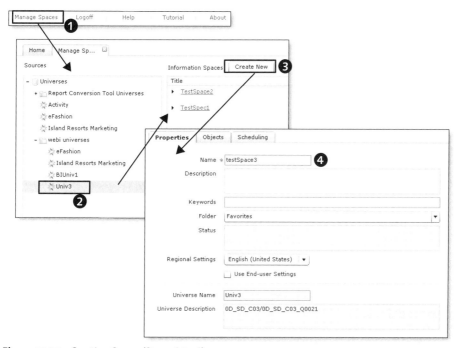

Figure 10.35 Creating Space (Steps 1 to 4)

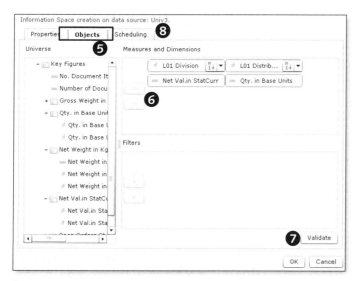

Figure 10.36 Creating Space (Steps 5 to 8)

9. Click OK to save the Information Space.

10. The dialog box disappears and you are returned to the Manage Spaces tab. The new Information Space appears within the right pane of the Manage Spaces tab.

11. If the Space was created from a Universe and you wish to index the Space immediately, click Index Now next to the Space.

10.10.4 Information Search Features in Polestar

Polestar provides the following search features to quickly recognize the most relevant information. Figure 10.37 shows an example of search results in Polestar.

▶ **Search Content**
You can search the data within the Information Spaces. For example, if you want to see information related to company code, just give the name of the company code and Polestar will provide related data in Information Spaces.

▶ **Highlighting Matched Words**
Text key entered as search criteria will be highlighted in the search result.

▶ **Ranking the Search Result**
On the Search results tab, each object is assigned a score rating ranging from 1 to 5. Each score rating is represented with a set of graphical bars, for example, a score of five bars signifies that the object is a strong match. A score of one signifies a weak match.

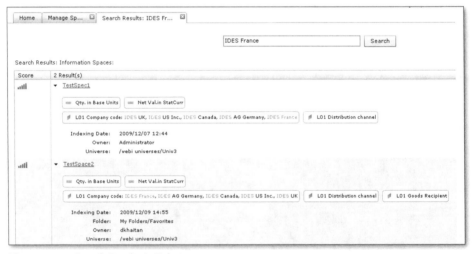

Figure 10.37 Search Results in Polestar

10.10.5 Guidelines and Best Practices for Polestar

The following guidelines must be adhered to while creating Information Spaces in Polestar.

▶ Polestar leverage Indexes to search the data. Only the Spaces that are indexed can be used for searching. Be aware of Memory and Disk Space requirements before implementing Polestar.

▶ Business requirements should be well understood before creating the Information Space. Every Information Space costs indexing time, memory, and space on the server.

▶ Implement several small Information Spaces rather than one big Information Space.

▶ Use a filter to restrict the data for indexing.

▶ Schedule the indexing of Information Spaces at the time when the least number of users is using Polestar. It is preferable to schedule indexing at off business hours.

▶ All Information Spaces should be secured.

10.11 Pioneer: The Best of the Both Worlds

Many reporting tools comprising BEx and SAP BusinessObjects may raise confusion among customers about adoption of best in class software for their reporting needs. As shown in Figure 10.38, functionalities of many BEx reporting tools are almost similar to SAP BusinessObjects tools. For this reason, SAP has come up with a project to integrate all these tools in a single platform called *Pioneer*. This tool is under development in SAP and is planned to be released in Q4 2010. Using Pioneer, it will be possible to integrate SAP BusinessObjects and BEx in a single platform. Pioneer can be used for Microsot Excel as well as for Web pages.

Below are the key features and benefits of Pioneer:

▶ Tailored Support for multiple user roles

▶ Focus on the Business Analysts (Microsoft Excel/Web) but also extend the footprint of advanced analysis through ease of use and tool interoperability

▶ Easy migration for existing SAP NetWeaver and Voyager customers

▶ Openness: Can run either with BOE or SAP NetWeaver

▶ Ability to fully leverage SAP in-memory analytic engine capabilities

▶ Basis for next-generation SAP embedded analytics offerings

▶ Lower TCO – Single architecture

▶ Full Pioneer Suite runs on BOE, can run side-by-side with SAP NetWeaver

▶ Pioneer leverages BOE platform services (LCM, persistency, authentication, etc.)

▶ The Pioneer Web Server component can be optionally installed on SAP NetWeaver J2EE 7.1 or higher or on any J2EE supported by BOE

▶ Pioneer query views, workbooks, and workspaces stored in BOE repository

▶ Pioneer Office Lean allows direct connectivity to SAP NetWeaver BW and storage of SAP NetWeaver BW–based views in SAP NetWeaver BW

▶ Web applications built with BEx WAD are compatible with Pioneer Web

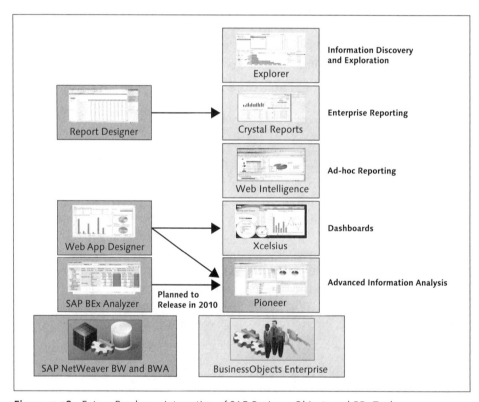

Figure 10.38 Future Roadmap: Integration of SAP Business Objects and BEx Tools

10.12   Other Tools Provided by SAP BusinessObjects

In earlier sections, we discussed many important tools provided by SAP Business-Objects. However, the list does not end here. Following is a list of other tools that are equally important for your information processing.

10.12.1   SAP BusinessObjects Data Services

SAP BusinessObjects Data Services provides a broad set of tools in the area of ETL (Extract, Transform, and Load) and data quality. This desktop tool provides an intuitive environment where you can create data transformation logic easily. Moreover, Data Services is able to extract data from virtually any source and it is also tightly integrated with SAP SAP NetWeaver BW system. The Data Services tool can receive data from SAP SAP NetWeaver BW through an Open Hub object and data can be pushed into SAP NetWeaver BW through External Source System. Data Services offers many data transformation and enriching features that are not possible in SAP NetWeaver BW. Table 10.6 shows the ETL capability difference between SAP NetWeaver BW and Data Services.

Scenario	SAP NetWeaver BW Possibility	Data Services Possibility
Referential Integrity	Y	Partial
Plausibility Check	-	Y
Pattern Matching	-	Y
Lookups	Y	Y
Master data attribute derivation	Y	-
Profiling	-	Y
Address Cleansing	-	Y
Data Cleansing	-	Y
Data Matching	-	Y

Table 10.6   ETL Capability Comparison Between SAP NetWeaver BW and Data Services

10.12.2   SAP Business Objects BI Widget

BI Widget is another innovative offering from SAP BusinessObjects. BI Widgets provides access to your Business Intelligence content as desktop widgets. It leverages Web Intelligence Reports and Xcelsius dashboards. BI Widgets automatically updates the widget on your desktop, providing you with up-to-the-minute data at your fingertips.

BI Widget includes the following features:

▶ BI Widget leverages information access through Web Intelligence reports and Xcelsius dashboards.

▶ It has Microsoft WindowsVista's look and feel.

▶ Microsoft Windows Vista sidebar gadgets are supported by BI Widget.

▶ Leverages user rights and permissions from SAP BusinessObjects Enterprise Configuration Management Console.

10.12.3 Voyager

Multi-Dimensional data can be analyzed easily through the Voyager tool. You can access this tool from SAP BusinessObjects Enterprise InfoView. Information Analysts can create Voyager workspaces and can be saved in SAP BusinessObjects Enterprise server. Voyager is purely Web enabled; you don't need to install any software to run the Voyager Client tool. All user rights are maintained in the SAP BusinessObjects Enterprise server.

10.12.4 SAP BusinessObjects Data Federator

Data Federator is an Enterprise Information Integration tool that provides uniform and integrated view of data located in heterogenous systems. Unlike various ETL tools, Data Federator does'nt store data anywhere in the system; instead, it maintains a virtual database and reduces the space and meintenance costs significantly. Data Federator works in between your source of data and your buisiness intelligence applications. Data Federator uses virtual tables and mappings to present the data from your sources of data in a single virtual form that is accessible to and optimized for your applications.

10.12.5 SAP BusinessObjects LifeCycle Manager

LifeCycle Manager acts as a migrator of your Business Intelligence objects. Different objects created with the SAP BusinessObjects tool can be moved from one system to another system using LifeCycle Manager. LifeCycle Manager comes as a plugin for SAP BusinessObjects Enterprise.

There are many more innovative tools available from SAP BusinessObjects. Giving information about all those tools is out of the scope of this chapter. See the SDN for more updated information on SAP BusinessObjects. From SDN, you can get more information of installation guides and security-related guidelines.

10.13   Summary

In this chapter, we gave you the snap shot of the SAP BusinessObjects offerings. SAP BusinessObjects strengthens SAP's vision to make its customer enterprise clear, where decision making and day-to-day work can be performed without any ambiguity and assumptions. Business Intelligence offerings from SAP is not limited to SAP only; it reached beyond bounderies of complex heterogenous enterprise architecture to bring data in single platform–enabling efficient and reliable decision making.

Even after go-live, your work isn't complete. It's now time to work with your BW system and help it achieve your business goals.

11   Epilogue

BW implementations are often complex and can easily become quite political because of the analytical needs that are involved. Understanding these needs and planning to meet the challenges help to make sure that the project manager handles them gracefully.

This involves understanding the typical issues and mistakes that are commonly made as well as the most common systems issues that are encountered. Familiarity with these allows the project manager to make good decisions and steer the team quickly toward resolution.

This book walked through many of the challenges that are typically faced in the implementation process. Of course, every project has its own particular challenges and unforeseen issues. However, a clear methodology, as spelled out in the preceding chapters allow the project to clearly assess the scope, deal with new scoping questions, prioritize, and implement a solution. It also aids with the transition from development to production support.

11.1   Using this Book

The various methods outlined in this book to help with requirements gathering, transport management, cutover, etc., should be used to develop the end-to-end project management strategy. This book can help you to highlight the most important challenges and recommendations, this information can be used along with knowledge of the various project requirements to create and evolve a clear implementation methodology. A large part of this methodology involves gaining understanding of the typical challenges and planning properly how to respond when faced with these issues.

Another important goal is to make sure that the requirements-gathering process is clearly understood and well planned. There are several documentation templates in the appendices of this book that will also help with building and defining this strategy. You can return to this book at any time, using it as a reference guide.

We would now like to give you some additional insight into the common issues and challenges you are likely to face in your BW project.

11.2   Common Issues and Challenges

In general the most common issues that BW projects face is typically not in the actual configuration tasks of the BW system. Many of the biggest challenges are typically project management, scope, and requirements-gathering issues. That is the main reason this book focused more on project management and not as much on the functionality and system configuration features.

SAP provides many classes and documentation on the features of the software; however, there is very little emphasis on the tools and methods needed to successfully implement the product. Ironically, these are the most common reasons that projects fail. They rarely fail because the system cannot satisfy clearly understood requirements. They fail because these requirements are either not understood or there is not a clear direction to scope, prioritize, staff, and implement these requirements.

These tasks are where a project defines its success. This means providing sound tools in order to capture the current requirements in detail and modelling the solution so as to meet not only these needs but also the unnamed needs that will emerge in the future.

The best way to understand these needs is to clearly understand today's needs and work with the business users to help predict the future requirements. We hope this book provided some guidance on typical issues encountered and methods for requirements-gathering and scope management. These should give your project a head start on their methodology decisions.

Let's now recap the important things to remember for your BW project.

11.3   Important Things to Remember

There are several important things to understand and remember during any BW project. We have covered these in the subsections that follow.

11.3.1   More Challenging than an ECC or R/3 Project

The reasons for these challenges lie in the extreme flexibility of the BW product and many different systems involved. Most ECC or R/3 projects do one conversion of data from external systems during the go-live phase. In a BW project, these conversions happen nightly. Added to this is the political nature of BW projects and the diverse audience that it addresses, which can make project management difficult. The most important thing to remember is to have a clear communication with the business partners to ensure you have their full understanding and guidance.

11.3.2 Management Commitment Needed from the Beginning

Projects need the right sponsorship to get over the inevitable issues that will occur. Management needs to be updated frequently. This commitment is built through establishing clear missions and strategies for data acquisition and data delivery and also through a thoughtful prioritization of scope. This prioritization should take place under the guidance of management to ensure its buy-in and also to ensure that the steering committee understands how BW would address some of the business pain of the organization.

11.3.3 Project Management: User-Focused, Not Technology Focused

Sometimes teams focus too much on the system issues and the technology and not enough on the business drivers behind the solution. This can cause the team to deliver a product that does not match the end user requirements. Understanding and keeping the team focused on the end solution can keep the team working toward this solution. In many ways, the technology issues are more micro in nature compared with the macro issues of meeting the end user needs. Project management needs this macro-focused approach.

11.3.4 Clear Methodology Needed to Determine Requirements

Many projects attempt to begin configuration too early. This forces them to make decisions on the user requirements before they understand them. Having a clear methodology with clear ways to document and agree on scope can help this process. Often, the more time spent up front developing these methodology documents, the better the end result.

11.3.5 Understanding Data Load Volume and Granularity

Once the data volume is known, it is much easier to develop a sound data model. One factor that directly impacts the volume is the granularity of the data. This is important because it impacts the overall loading time and query performance. It also sets the scope for user reporting in the future. This is because the decisions made early in a project regarding the level of granularity affect the availability of data in the entire solution. Knowing as much as possible about the volume and granularity requirements help to ensure that data is loaded and analyzed properly.

11.3.6 Manage Expectations for BW

BW should not be considered the only reporting solution. Proper management of expectations can make sure that the transactional data process teams do not assume that BW will provide their end users with all the reporting they need. Although BW does excel at many analysis tasks, there is some reporting that is better left on the transactional system. Recognizing this early in the project will help to keep the scope of BW better matched to its strengths.

11.3.7 Fix Bad Data at Its Source

From the beginning of a BW project, there is pressure to fix data that is incorrect on the source systems. Mainly, this pressure comes from the source system teams because they do not want to spend the effort fixing data that is already complete. Instead they look for the BW solution to fix this data. What starts as a few lines of code to make a few fields consistent often turns into complex logic and custom coding. Setting the precedent early that data should be fixed at its source helps to reduce or even eliminate the data-fixing process.

11.3.8 Build a BW System, Not a Series Of Data Marts

There is a temptation to maintain the BW system as silos of data in the same way as do the transactional systems from which BW sources. This is a mistake. The more the BW solution works to consolidate data from multiple sources and report this data together, the better the solution will be at providing a clear picture of the business as a whole.

11.3.9 When the BW System Is Live, the Solution Isn't Finished

The work is not done after go-live. A sound BW system is constantly evolving with enhancements to the existing solution and new scope added. This should be expected and embraced.

11.4 Conclusion

We hope this book fulfilled your BW project-management needs. Remember that your work is not complete, even after go-live. It is now time to work with your BW system and to help it achieve your business goals.

We welcome any feedback or questions you have on the book and hope that you gained valuable insight that can be applied to your project.

Appendices

A   Sample Project Plan

This is a sample project plan that can be used as a base for developing your project plan or for understanding the typical tasks involved in project planning. The core of this project plan came from an initial project plan developed by SAP. We've changed several tasks, reordered others, and added typical tasks needed in a SAP NetWeaver BW project. This can be used to help in planning or for reconciling with your project plan.

A.1   Phase 1: Project Preparation and Planning

A.1.1   Create and Issue Project Charter

Project Mission Statement	▶ The mission statement should be brief — between one and four sentences. It should be a bird's view of project goals.
Business Warehouse Project Objectives	▶ How different landscapes will be integrated? ▶ How data will be harmonized? ▶ How will reporting users be benefited?
Business Drivers	▶ Why SAP NetWeaver BW is implemented? ▶ How the SAP NetWeaver BW implementation will help organization to take strategic decisions? ▶ What will be the cost benefit to the organization?
Business Measurements	▶ What are the Key Performance Indicators? ▶ Define key figure matrix.
Project Measurements	▶ What are the criteria for the project success?
Project Charter	▶ Who are stakeholders? ▶ What is the project scope? ▶ What are the assumptions and dependencies? ▶ What are the constraints? ▶ Define milestone. ▶ Define resource plan.
Approvals	▶ Get approval from stake holders.

A.1.2   Define and Review Implementation Strategy

Basic Requirements	▶ This should be a brief statement, which will describe basic requirements and expectations of the customer.
End User Requirements	▶ What are the expectations of end users from this implementation?
Data Requirements	▶ How will different systems be integrated and data will be harmonized to meet the end user's expectation?
Technical Landscape	▶ What will be the whole technical landscape? ▶ Define DEV, QA, PROD, Training, Sandbox, and Production Support systems.
Implementation Approaches	▶ How will the SAP NetWeaver BW project be executed with respect to SAP R/3 implementation?
Transport Strategy	▶ Define transport path. ▶ How will the transport be moved to next environment? ▶ Define process for troubleshooting and documentation of the transports.
Authorization Strategy	▶ Define authorization requirements for end users. ▶ Define authorization for different roles within project team.
Reporting Strategy	▶ How will data be presented? ▶ Which tools will be used? ▶ Define query development and Web template strategy.
Team Structure	▶ Define team structure. If offshore development is involved, then define the scope for them.

After completing the strategy document, review it and get approval from the customer.

A.1.3   Establish Project Team Working Environment

Plan Environment	▶ What should be the operating system of the server? ▶ Which tools will be used for managing the project?
Set Up Environment	▶ How will the environment be set up? ▶ Who will set up the environment?

A.1.4 Determine Project Organization

Organization and Roles	▶ Create Organizational Structure.
	▶ Define the roles in detail for each node of the Organizational Hierarchy.
Assign People to Roles	▶ Assignment of people to different roles.
Project Team	▶ Define project team in detail.
	▶ What is the experience of SAP NetWeaver BW consultants?
	▶ Communication details of every project team members.

A.1.5 Prepare Project Plan

Work Plan	▶ This should describe all deliverables with planned completion date. This document should be updated during whole the lifecycle of the projects to track deliverables.
Budget Plan	▶ How will the budget be utilized?
Resource Plan	▶ Assign resources to the roles.
	▶ How will roles be rotated?
	▶ How will trainings be tracked?
	▶ Define Skill Matrix.

A.1.6 Create Project Team Training Plan

Training Requirements	▶ Define Skill Gap for the development team.
	▶ Identify SAP NetWeaver Business Warehouse Training Requirements.
Workshop	▶ Evaluate Need for SAP NetWeaver Business Warehouse Workshop.
Training Plan	▶ Define extensive training plan for project resources.
	▶ This plan should be revised over time periodically as the project moves on.
Schedule Training	▶ Define detailed training schedule for project resources.
	▶ Main objective of the training plan is to manage deliverables effectively when resources will be in training.

A.1.7 Approve Project Planning Documents and Project Procedures

Define Project Management Standards and Procedures

Communication Plan	▶ Define communication plan with stakeholders and other team members in detail. ▶ Define frequency of meetings.
Issue Management Plan	▶ Define plan to address different issues. ▶ Define Escalation Matrix.
Scope Management Plan	▶ How will scope changes be addressed?
Team Building Plan	▶ How will different teams be built, for example, Basis Team, EDW Team, Reporting Team, etc.? ▶ Define detail hierarchy for the entire team.
Monitoring Standards	▶ Define Inspection Checklist for deliverables. ▶ Define process to monitor technical systems.
SAP Service	▶ Define Strategy for Using SAP Services.
Quality Management	▶ Define standards to maintain quality in all deliverables. ▶ How will data quality be defined? ▶ What proactive measures will be taken to enhance quality?
Procedures Document	▶ Define process to handle daily project management tasks. ▶ Define tools to implement project management procedures.

A.1.8 Define Implementation Standards and Procedures

Configuration Standards	▶ Develop SAP NetWeaver Business Warehouse System Configuration Standards.
Functional Model	▶ Determine functional model of Data Warehouse.
Documentation	▶ Define End User Training and Documentation Strategy.
Quality Standards	▶ Define Quality Assessment Process and Parameters. ▶ Conduct Quality Assessment. ▶ Create Project Preparation Quality Assessment Document. ▶ Define testing strategies.
Post Implementation Service and Support Strategy	▶ How will incidents be tracked and closed? ▶ Define SLA. ▶ How will change requests be handled?

Authorization Standards for Project Team	▶ Which systems will be accessed by whom? ▶ How will systems be used by different team members?
Error Handling	▶ How will errors be tracked and closed? ▶ Define escalation matrix.
Change Request Approval Process	▶ Define the Transport approval process. ▶ Define process to get approval from stakeholders for a change. ▶ Define Transport Steward Process (if applicable).
Naming Standards	▶ Define naming standards for various SAP NetWeaver BW objects.
Data Lifecycle	▶ Define Data Archival process.

A.1.9 Approve Project Procedures Documents

Project Kickoff

Figure A.1 Project Kickoff

A.1.10 Technical Requirements Planning

Identify Technical Requirements

Technical Questionnaires	▶ How many reporting users? ▶ What is the scope for operational data reporting? ▶ What will be the look and feel of the reports? ▶ Granularity of the report? ▶ Identify record counts approximately for each data load. ▶ Which systems will be harmonized? ▶ How many non-SAP data sources will be used?
Technical Infrastructure Needs	▶ Prepare a document to describe the infrastructure requirement based on technical questionnaires.

Hardware Procurement Process

Figure A.2 Hardware Procurement Process

Project Preparation Phase Quality Assessment Process

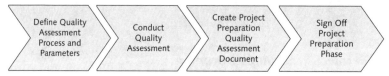

Figure A.3 Quality Assessment Process

A.2 Phase 2: Business Blueprint and Analysis

A.2.1 Project Management Business Blueprint Phase

Conduct Project Team Status Meetings

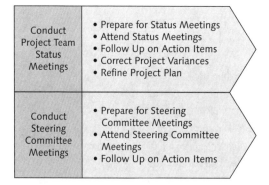

Figure A.4 Conducting Project Team Status Meetings

Steering Committee Meeting Focus Points	▸ Overall project status
	▸ Schedules/Milestones
	▸ Deliverables
	▸ Completion Status (% complete)
	▸ Financial Status
	▸ Staffing
	▸ Customer responsibilities
	▸ Scope controls
	▸ Management action items

General Project Management

▸ Change Management.

▸ Conduct Team-Building Activities.

▸ Define End User Roles and Responsibilities.

Project Team Training Business Blueprint Phase

Training Schedule	▸ Refine the training schedule defined during project preparation phase.
Prepare for Training	▸ Preparation of the training system.
	▸ Assign trainer.
Attend Training and Assess Post-Training Skills	▸ Complete feedback should be taken and recorded on the training given.
	▸ Measure effectiveness of the training.

Business Process Analysis Phase

Prepare for End User Requirements Workshops	▸ Schedule Requirements Workshops Based on Categorization of Key End Users.
	▸ Develop Agenda and Approach for Each Workshop.

Conduct Key End User Requirements Workshops	▶ Review/Refine Business Drivers and Critical Success Factors. ▶ Determine Executive Information Needs and Key Measurements. ▶ Determine and Document Decision Support and OLAP Requirements. ▶ Determine and Document Operational Reporting Requirements. ▶ Determine and Document Application Functional Areas Involved. ▶ Determine Cross Application Functional Areas Involved. ▶ Determine and Document Global Decision Support Requirements. ▶ Complete Functional Model Document.

A.2.2 Assess Current Data Warehouse and Information Access Environment

Identify and Assess Current SAP and Non-SAP Reporting Environment

Identify SAP Sources	▶ Identify Information in SAP R/3 or SAP ECC Sources Necessary to Satisfy Requirements. ▶ Complete SAP R/3/SAP ECC DataSource Section in Functional Model Document.
Identify Non-SAP Sources	▶ Identify Data from Non-SAP Sources Necessary to Satisfy Requirements. ▶ Develop Plan for Capturing Non-SAP Source Data into Flat Files. ▶ Assign Resources to Obtain the Data. ▶ Complete external DataSource Section in Functional Model Document.
Identify Master Data Requirements	▶ Create Master Data Requirements Document.
Define Data Conversion Rules	▶ Define Transformation Rules. ▶ Define Aggregation Rules. ▶ Define Staging Requirements. ▶ Define Granularity Rules. ▶ Estimate Volume. ▶ Define Filtering Rules. ▶ Complete Data Section of Functional Model Document.

A.2.3 Business Process Analysis Documents and Business Warehouse Design

Data Design for Each Functional Area

Key Figures	▶ Identify Key Figures Required for Each Functional Area.
Characteristics	▶ Identify Characteristics Required for Each Functional Area.
Dimensions	▶ Identify Dimensions Required for Each Functional Area.
Compound Characteristics	▶ Identify Compound Characteristics Required for Each Functional Area.
Calculated Key Figures	▶ Identify Calculated Key Figures Required for Each Functional Area.
Hierarchies	▶ Identify Hierarchies Required for Each Functional Area.
Business Rules	▶ Identify Business Rules by Field for Each Functional Area.
Data	▶ Create Data Design Document.
Data Access Design	▶ Identify Presentation/Layout Preferences.
	▶ Identify Summarization Level Requirements.
	▶ Identify Data and Retention Requirements.
	▶ Complete Analysis Section of Functional Model Document
Model Business Warehouse Environment	▶ Determine Uses of Business Content DSO, InfoCubes, and Reports.
	▶ Identify New InfoProviders to be Created.
	▶ Define and Document SAP NetWeaver Business Warehouse Data Model.
	▶ Identify Data Integration Requirements.
	▶ Create Business Warehouse Environment Document.
Create Technical Design	▶ Identify Major Technical Components Required (Hardware/Software/Network).
	▶ Identify Technical Components Not Required in SAP-Only Solution.
	▶ Develop Plan for Assessment of Non-SAP Technical Components.
	▶ Assess and Select Non-SAP Technical Components.
	▶ Define Printing Infrastructure.
	▶ Define Network Topology.
	▶ Define SAP NetWeaver Business Warehouse Interfaces.
	▶ Define Change Request Management.

- ▶ Define Release Management Strategy.
- ▶ Determine Desktop Deployment Strategy.
- ▶ Define Desktop Management Strategy.
- ▶ Design Archiving Management Strategy.
- ▶ Define SAP NetWeaveer Business Warehouse Detailed Physical Technical Design.
- ▶ Create Technical Design Document.

Technical Components Procurement Process

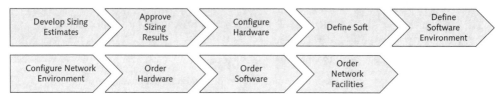

Figure A.5 Technical Components Procurement Process

Establish Business Warehouse Development Environment

- ▶ Install Initial Hardware.
- ▶ Install Operating System on Business Warehouse Server.
- ▶ Install Business Warehouse Software.
- ▶ Install Business Information Warehouse Plug-in on SAP ECC or SAP R/3 System.
- ▶ Establish ALE System Connectivity.
- ▶ Install Desktop Components for Project Team.
- ▶ Install Additional Components for Project Team.

System Administration

- ▶ Define System Administration for Business Warehouse.
- ▶ Define Business Warehouse System Monitoring Strategy.
- ▶ Define Backup Strategy.
- ▶ Define Table Space and Reorganization Strategy.
- ▶ Verify System Administration Functions.
- ▶ Define Periodic System Maintenance Procedures.

Approve Business Warehouse Documents

▶ Business Blueprint Phase Quality Assessment.

▶ Define Quality Assessment Process and Parameters.

▶ Conduct Quality Assessment.

▶ Create Business Blueprint Quality Assessment Document.

▶ Sign Off Business Blueprint Phase.

A.3 Phase 3: Realization/Build

A.3.1 Project Management Realization Phase

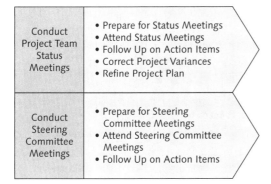

Figure A.6 Project and Steering Committee Meetings

Initial Planning for Production Support and Cutover

▶ Determine Production Support Plan

▶ Determine Cutover Plan

Conduct Project Team Training

▶ Refine Training Schedule

▶ Prepare for Training

▶ Attend Project Team Training

▶ Review and Assess Post-Training Skills

A.3.2 System Management

Develop System Test Plans	► Develop Unit Test Plan.
	► Develop Volume Test Plan.
	► Develop Integration Test Plan.
	► Develop Stress Test Plan.
Define Service-Level Commitment	► Determine Possible Failure Scenarios.
	► Define Disaster Recovery Procedures.
	► Establish Service Level Commitment.
	► Create Service Level Commitment Document.
Define Service-Level Commitment	► Determine Possible Failure Scenarios.
	► Define Disaster Recovery Procedures.
	► Establish Service Level Commitment.
	► Create Service Level Commitment Document.
Establish Business Warehouse Administration Functions	► Develop Testing Procedures for Business Warehouse Objects.
	► Develop System Monitoring Procedures.
	► Develop Database Reorganization Procedures.
	► Verify Transport Procedures.
	► Verify Backup and Recovery Procedures.
	► Create SAP NetWeaver Business Warehouse Administration Functions Document.
Create Functional Model	► Develop ETL (Extraction/Transformation/Loading) Document.
	► Develop DSO Functional Model Document.
	► Develop InfoCube Functional Model Document.
	► Develop InfoSet Functional Model Document.
	► Develop Master Data Spreadsheet.
Build Development Environment	► Activate DataSources in the SAP ECC/SAP R/3 System.
	► Replicate DataSources.
	► Activate Business Content.
	► Create InfoObjects.
	► Configure DSO Objects.
	► Configure DSO Transformation.
	► Configure InfoCube Objects.
	► Configure InfoCube Transformation.
	► Configure InfoSet Objects.
	► Configure Analysis Query Objects.
	► Configure Master Data Loads.
	► Configure Process Chains.
	► Load Development System.

Establish Business Warehouse Administration Functions	▶ Develop Testing Procedures for Business Warehouse Objects. ▶ Develop System Monitoring Procedures. ▶ Develop Database Reorganization Procedures. ▶ Verify Transport Procedures. ▶ Verify Backup and Recovery Procedures. ▶ Create Business Warehouse Administration Functions Document.
Set Up Quality Assurance Environment	▶ Verify Business Warehouse Systems Technical Environment. ▶ Install Quality Assurance System. ▶ Set Up User Master Records. ▶ Secure Quality Assurance System. ▶ Set Up Client Management and Transport System.
Define Productive System Management	▶ Define Productive System Security. ▶ Define Productive Operating Procedures. ▶ Define Productive System Administration. ▶ Define Productive System Printing Environment. ▶ Define Productive Database Administration Procedures. ▶ Create SAP NetWeaver Business Warehouse Systems Operations Manual. ▶ Create Productive System Management Document.
Set Up Production Environment	▶ Install Production Hardware. ▶ Verify Production Systems Technical Environment. ▶ Install Production System. ▶ Install and Configure Network Environment. ▶ Install Desktop Hardware and Components. ▶ Secure Operating System and Database. ▶ Install Printers and Configure Printing Services.
Conduct Business Warehouse Unit Testing in Development	▶ Resolve Discrepancies from Unit Testing. ▶ Prepare Transport List and Reconcile with Basis Group.
Approve System Management Documents	▶ Migrate Objects to QA Environment: Troubleshoot Transports. ▶ Build and Load the QA Environment.
Conduct Integration Testing	▶ Resolve Discrepancies from Unit Testing. ▶ Sign off on Integration Testing.
Migrate Objects to Production	▶ Troubleshoot Transports.

Prepare Final Confirmation	▶ Prepare Final Confirmation Scenarios.
	▶ Develop Final Confirmation Agenda.
	▶ Prepare for Final Confirmation Session.
Perform Final Confirmation	▶ Perform Final Confirmation Scenarios.
	▶ Review and Sign Off Final Confirmation.

Develop Production System Environment

Process Chains	Schedule Process Chains.
Data	▶ Test Data Extraction.
Authorization Detailed Design	▶ Review Company Security Philosophy.
	▶ Define Access Required by Job Functions.
	▶ Conduct Authorization Interview with Data Owners.
	▶ Identify General Information Access and Service Usage.
	▶ Create Authorization Management Procedures.
	▶ Create Authorization Detailed Design Document.
Implement Authorization Concept	▶ Create Activity Groups.
	▶ Generate Authorization Profiles.
	▶ Create User Master Models for Job Roles.
	▶ Test User Masters.
	▶ Create Authorization Profiles and Job Roles Document.
Validate Authorization Concept	▶ Identify Activity Groups for Individual Users.
	▶ Create All User Masters.
	▶ Validate User Masters for Job Functions.
	▶ Refine Authorization Design.

End User Documentation and Training Material

Prepare End User Documentation Development Plan	▶ Define End User Documentation Requirements.
	▶ Create End User Documentation Development Plan.
	▶ Approve End User Documentation Development Plan.
Create End User Documentation	▶ Conduct End User Documentation and Training Workshop.
	▶ Create End User Documentation.
Develop End User Training Materials	▶ Create End User Training Materials.
	▶ Create End User Training Instructors Guide.

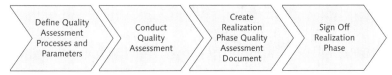

Realization Phase Quality Assessment

| Define Quality Assessment Processes and Parameters | Conduct Quality Assessment | Create Realization Phase Quality Assessment Document | Sign Off Realization Phase |

Figure A.7 Realization Phase Quality Assessment Process

A.4   Phase 4: Final Preparation

The main activity for this phase is to train end users with a new solution and prepare for cutover.

A.4.1   Project Management Final Preparation Phase

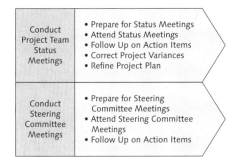

Figure A.8 Meetings for Final Preparation

End User Training

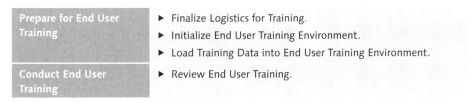

469

System Management

Establish Productive System Administration	▶ Configure SAP NetWeaver Business Warehouse System Monitoring for Production Environment. ▶ Configure Productive System Printing and Spool Administration. ▶ Train System Administration Staff.
Conduct System Tests	▶ Conduct Volume/Stress Test. ▶ Conduct System Performance Tuning (if needed). ▶ Implement BI Accelerator. ▶ Conduct System Administration Tests. ▶ Conduct Disaster Recovery Test. ▶ Conduct Going Live Check.
Create/Refine Cutover Plan	▶ Create Conversion Checklist. ▶ Determine Production Readiness. ▶ Approval for Cutover.

Create/Refine Production Support

▶ Define Help Desk Procedures.
▶ Create Help Desk Facility.
▶ Reorganize Team for Post Live.
▶ Staff Help Desk.
▶ Define Long-term Production Support Strategy.
▶ Create Production Support Plan Document.

Cutover

Perform Cutover to Production System	▶ Transport to Production Environment. ▶ Perform Load Conversions. ▶ Perform Manual Entries.
Final Approval for Going Live	▶ Approve the Production System. ▶ Secure Productive Environment. ▶ Verify Users are Ready.
Final Preparation Phase Quality Assessment	▶ Define Quality Assessment Process and Parameters. ▶ Conduct Quality Assessment. ▶ Create Final Preparation Phase Quality Assessment Document. ▶ Sign Off Final Preparation Phase.

A.5   Phase 5: Go-Live and Support

In this phase, new SAP NetWeaver BW systems are working in production efficiently. The following details are management activities to be performed after go-live.

A.5.1   Production Support

Provide Production Support	▶ Direct Problem and Issues. ▶ Manage and Resolve Problems.
Validate Live Business Process Results	▶ Monitor Daily and Weekly Transactions. ▶ Resolve Issues. ▶ Confirm Live Environment.
Optimize System Use	▶ Conduct Early Watch Sessions. ▶ Optimize Technical Environment. ▶ Optimize SAP NetWeaver Business Warehouse Data Model Star Schema.

Post Go-Live Activities

Follow Up Training	▶ Attend Advanced Training. ▶ Train New Employees.
Define Long-Term Plans	▶ Refine Technical Upgrade Plan. ▶ Create Enhancements or Additional Implementations Document. ▶ Execute Long-Term Service and Support Strategy.
Upgrade Live System Landscape	▶ Conduct System Upgrade. ▶ Conduct Database Upgrade. ▶ Execute New Release Migration Plan. ▶ Perform User Acceptance Testing.
Perform On-Going System Operations	▶ Perform Computer Center Daily Operations. ▶ Perform Database Administration Daily Operations. ▶ Refine System Administration Procedures.
Project Review	▶ Review and Close Open Issues. ▶ Review Business Benefits. ▶ Sign Off and Close Issue List. ▶ Conduct Lessons-Learned Session.

B   Important Checklists

This appendix contains important checklists that you can use during the course of your SAP NetWeaver BW project implementation.

B.1   New SAP NetWeaver BW System Validation Checklist

This is a preliminary checklist that can be used to make sure that the initial system settings are enabled and correct before the system is used. This assumes that the system has been installed properly and should not be considered an exclusive list.

B.2   Preliminary Checks (Prior to Any Transports)

- All users created are in the system with proper security.
- Connections to each source system are established.
- SAP Notes have been applied in development and QA systems applied to production.
- All kernel/DB patches are applied in development and QA systems applied to production.
- Check of each source system performed as green (RSA1 • Tools • Manage Source Systems).
- Replication green for relevant source systems (RSA1 • Tools • Manage Source Systems).
- Source system name assignment (RSA1 • Tools • Source System Assignment).
- Transfer global settings are complete on each system (Source System).
- The number of parallel processes limit checked (coordinate with Basis for this).
- Conversion of local systems names are set, only on a development system (RSA1 • Tools • Conversion of Local System Names).
- Printers are set up (Transaction SPAD).
- Permitted character settings (Transaction SPRO).
- Default packet size checked (Transaction SPRO—Links to Other Systems – Maintain control parameters).
- Flat file parameters checked (Transaction SPRO).

- Switch off all system traces. Trace status should be set to Trace switched off (Transaction ST01).
- Check trace tool — verify there are no users activated for logging (Transaction RSRTRACE).
- SAP ECC or SAP R/3 Source System load parameters (Transaction SBIW in SAP ECC or SAP R/3).

B.3   SAP NetWeaver BW Object Check Before Transports

Check all SAP NetWeaver BW objects before releasing them from development environment. It is particularly important to reduce effort spent on analysis of failed transports.

- Check objects are active.
- Newly created dependent objects are also included in the same transport request.
- Check objects in Transport Connection (Transaction RSA1 — Transport Connection).
- Reporting Objects are checked thoroughly in Transport connection. Make sure variables used in the reports are collected by transports.
- Documents related to new/changed objects are created/updated in designated document repository.
- All objects are developed according to naming standard document.

B.4   Query/Portal Checks

- Check mail server to see if active (Transaction SPRO).
- Check Internet Graphics Server (IGS) to see if active (Transaction SPRO).
- Check Web template to see if active (Program SE38 RS_TEMPLATE_MAINTAIN_70).
- Activate personalization in BEx (Transaction SPRO).
- Check OLAP Cache global settings (Transaction RSRT).

B.5   Loading Checks

- Check traffic light color settings (Transaction SPRO).
- Set traffic light waiting time (Transaction SPRO).

▸ Check permitted character settings (Transaction SPRO).

▸ AL11 flat file locations setup.

▸ ALEREMOTE and connection user IDs set up with proper security.

B.6   Transport Settings

▸ Development package established.

▸ Function groups created.

B.7   SAP NetWeaver BW Query Development Checklist

This checklist serves as a design standard and validation procedure for good query development standards. Make sure that queries are following good SAP NetWeaver BW query standards.

▸ Query design should be consistent with the requirements document and the functional model document and should be reviewed often with the business SME(s). This allows the query development to stay in sync with the business requirements.

▸ Naming standards of the query matches naming standards document for all key figures, characteristics, query technical name, and description.

▸ Abbreviations of key figures and characteristics are consistent within the same queries and existing queries and follow standard project abbreviations. For example, amount = Amt, Count = Ct, etc.

▸ Capitalization of key figures and characteristics are consistent to give the user the same look and feel for each query.

▸ Queries should utilize variables. This ensures that all queries include a variable screen. This encourages filtering of the data for performance purposes.

▸ Mandatory variables exist to limit the first view of data for performance, if applicable. This is typical for higher-volume MultiProviders.

▸ Mandatory variables should appear at the beginning of the variable list that is presented to the end user. This prevents the mandatory variables from being found in the middle or at the bottom of the variable screen.

▸ Variables are in order of most commonly used and should appear at the top of the variable screen. Because almost all queries are filtered by date, this typically means that the date variables appear first in all query variable screens.

▶ InfoObjects related to the variables should be checked to ensure that their F4 settings are consistent with the user values. If there is no preference, the setting to *show only values in the InfoProvider* should be used. This setting is found in the InfoObject screen (Transaction RSD1). This option tells the system if all master data values or just the InfoProvider relevant values should be shown when the user hits the F4 button in the variables.

▶ The initial view of data should be limited; the user should be encouraged to filter and/or drill the report by the free characteristics for better performance. Typically, this means that the fewer data values that are pre-drilled down in the rows, the better the performance of the query.

▶ The developer should be mindful of the totals shown and verify that the user needs to see result totals. Result subtotals at a detailed level can be distracting.

▶ UOM and currency queries should present the data in a consistent UOM or currency value, if possible. This ensures the consistency of the data in the report.

▶ Initial sorting of the query should be logical based on business needs.

▶ OLAP cache should be turned on for the query in Transaction RSRT.

B.8 SAP NetWeaver BW Data Model Conceptual Review Checklist

This checklist includes all tasks that need to be completed for the SAP NetWeaver BW Data Model conceptual review.

B.8.1 Items Needed Prior to Conceptual Data Model Review

▶ Completed key figure matrix: detailed documentation of the key figures that will be used and their calculations

▶ Completed SAP NetWeaver BW functional model document

▶ Understanding of current reporting requirements

▶ Understanding of the DataSources

▶ Mockups of the reporting requirements (either physical or conceptual)

▶ Preliminary data model diagram complete (this will be the foundation for the review)

B.8.2 Conceptual Data Model Review

▶ Analyze preliminary data model diagram and discuss touchpoints with other functional models.

▸ Ensure that the overall model is reviewed for any possible reuse of existing data. This can be reconciled against the global data model data diagram.

▸ View all DataSources to determine which sources are new and which are leveraged from existing feeds or from other models.

▸ Analyze the data model diagram to determine if data is integrated or siloed. Where should the various information from differing sources be joined and how?

▸ Discuss how the levels of granularity differ in the sources and how this can present a challenge in the consolidation of the data.

▸ Discuss need for a conceptual DSO layer and where this might aid the future requirements. This is a layer of the DSO that consolidates data from multiple areas for a more holistic view of data. There are multiple ways of doing this, but each requires some thought on the consolidation of that data. The integration of this data should be understood, and the linking of the data should be verified.

▸ Ensure that the cross-model requirements provide an end-to-end view of the data (if applicable) and establish the owner of the end-to-end view of data.

▸ Ensure that every key figure in the key figure matrix has a clear owner.

▸ Ensure that the data model goals are clearly understood by developing a mission statement for the data model review. What questions are the model supposed to be answering? How will this provide business value now and in the future?

▸ Discuss the possible future requirements. What are the reports that will likely be required or needed for future analysis?

B.9   SAP NetWeaver BW Data Model Review Checklist

The SAP NetWeaver BW Data Model Review is designed to check the planned data model after the configuration build is complete and before any transports are sent. This allows the data model to be verified against typical best practices to ensure that the model is sound and sustainable.

B.9.1   Items Needed Prior to SAP NetWeaver BW Data Model Review

▸ Completed documentation, including functional model document and any other related functional specifications

▸ Detailed knowledge of the source data volumes

▶ Knowledge of the source data relationships including data dependencies, compounding characteristics, parent-child relationship, and hierarchies

▶ Diagram of InfoCubes and DSO that are being planned (Microsoft Visio diagram)

▶ Knowledge of the business requirements and DataSources for the purpose of answering questions about how the information will be used and the data will flow.

B.9.2 Items Checked During SAP NetWeaver BW Data Model Review: Overall

▶ All required documents are completed.

▶ Master data feeds are documented on the master data lists for use creating process chains; all master data fields are configured and tested.

▶ All data is loaded to the first-level DSO without transformation (or extremely minimal transformation) on first pass of data into SAP NetWeaver BW.

▶ All objects follow SAP NetWeaver BW naming standards per the naming standards document.

▶ Security strategy is clearly understood and included in the design.

▶ Reflexive or recursive loads on transactional data are avoided for performance reasons.

▶ Data volume of rows coming into SAP NetWeaver BW for transactional and master data is understood. This is used to ensure that the performance of the model will be sound.

▶ Model is checked for possible dump and reloads later via restatement. This requires the developer to understand the possibility for restatement.

▶ Navigational attributes are included when necessary and/or required.

▶ SAP NetWeaver BW database storage parameters are updated on all objects.

▶ Logical partitioning is used, if necessary, to allow for parallelization of queries across multiple InfoProviders.

▶ Loading requirements are documented and implemented into process chains.

▶ SAP ECC job requirements are captured and implemented into SAP ECC loading schedules.

▶ ABAP Code review is complete; all ABO follows good ABAP standards for performance, syntax, and documentation.

B.9.3 DataSources/Feeds

▶ Generic DataSources are delta-enabled, where applicable.

▶ Flat files use ASCII (text) files, not CSV (if possible, for performance).

▶ FTP procedure determined and planned for flat files; if archiving is needed, this is planned and implemented.

B.9.4 DSO

▶ DSO settings are checked for reporting, data quality flag, etc., to see if these settings are correct.

▶ DSO key is verified to ensure that no entries are lost.

▶ DSO key figures are checked to determine overwrite vs. addition.

▶ DSO delta capabilities are properly designed.

B.9.5 InfoCube/InfoSets/MultiProviders

▶ InfoCube dimensions were reviewed for multiplying effect between characteristic values; this includes checking for the 10% rule on dimensions.

▶ InfoCubes designed for multiple use (i.e., not one InfoCube for one query, etc.).

▶ InfoCube key figures were reviewed to verify/understand the needs (summarization versus non-cumulative).

▶ Check that MultiProviders meet the requirements.

▶ Physical partitioning is implemented on each InfoCube (if applicable).

▶ InfoCube compression is planned.

▶ Aggregates are implemented (if applicable, data volume).

B.9.6 Query Processing Checklist

▶ Check for NOT clause in filters; remove if possible.

▶ Initial query result should be limited in number of rows.

▶ Summation should be suppressed if not needed.

▶ Read mode should be set to H (Transaction RSRT).

▶ Cache mode should be set to cache the query, if query is reusable and large results are expected.

▶ No virtual key figures or virtual characteristics should be used, if possible.

▶ Initial view of query should hit aggregate, if applicable (Transaction RSRT).

B.10 Cutover Plan Checklist

This checklist highlights the most common tasks needed in an SAP NetWeaver BW project before cutover. Often projects have other specific tasks that are unique to their implementations, so this list should not be considered complete for all projects. However, it can serve as a template for a project cutover plan.

B.10.1 Administrative Tasks

- Schedule downtime of SAP ECC or SAP R/3 systems for initial loads.
- Determine test queries to be used for data validation.
- Schedule application resources for cutover.
- Schedule Basis resources for cutover.

B.10.2 Security Requirements

- Set up cutover role for SAP NetWeaver BW.
- Set up cutover role for source systems.
- Assign user authorizations for portal (if applicable).
- Set up ALEREMOTE and connection user Ids with proper security.
- Test cutover roles.

B.10.3 System Requirements

- Verify that technical steps for connections to source systems have been completed.
- Set up SAP NetWeaver BW systems and make all connections to source systems.
- Validate source system connections.
- Check FTP directory for flat files (Transaction AL11).
- Manually configure in SAP NetWeaver BW via Transaction RS_PERS_ACTIVATE per SAP Note 754206.
- Apply all SAP Notes to production that have been applied to test and development systems.
- Apply all database/kernel patches to production that have been applied to test and development systems.
- Check the number of parallel processes limit.
- Set up printers (Transaction SPAD).

▶ Permitted character settings (Transaction SPRO).

▶ Check default packet size (Transaction SPRO—Links to Other Systems—Maintain control parameters).

▶ Check flatfile parameters (Transaction SPRO).

▶ Switch off all system traces. Trace status should be set to Trace switched off (Transaction ST01).

▶ Check trace tool. Verify there are no users activated for logging (Transaction RSRTRACE).

B.10.4 Transport Requirements

▶ Change source system name after transport (Transaction RSA1).

▶ Maintain source system IDs (Transaction RSA1).

▶ Transport SAP R/3 or SAP ECC DataSources.

▶ Transport DataSources in SAP ECC.

▶ Replicate DataSources in SAP NetWeaver BW to keep systems consistent.

▶ Transport InfoObjects.

▶ Validate InfoObjects.

▶ Transport InfoProviders.

▶ Validate InfoProviders.

▶ Transport transformations.

▶ Validate transformations.

▶ Transport data transfer processes (DTP).

▶ Validate data transfer processes (DTP).

▶ Transport or manually create InfoPackages.

▶ Validate InfoPackages.

▶ Transport process chains.

▶ Validate process chains.

▶ Transport queries and query elements.

▶ Transport reporting roles.

▶ Transport Web templates.

▶ Validate reporting.

B.10.5 Portal Requirements

▶ Set up portal system.

▶ Technical setup of portal.

- ▸ Save Iviews to portal.
- ▸ Set up personalization and history.

B.10.6 Prior to Load Checks

- ▸ Check traffic light settings (Transaction SPRO).
- ▸ Set traffic light waiting time (SPRO).
- ▸ Check permitted character settings (Transaction SPRO).
- ▸ Lock users out of SAP ECC system (except ALEREMOTE and Admin users) for initial loads.
- ▸ Transfer global settings complete on each system (Source System tab).

B.10.7 Prior to Query Testing

- ▸ Check OLAP cache settings for each query (Transaction RSRT).

B.10.8 Validation

- ▸ Validate reporting roles.
- ▸ Validate Web template (if applicable).
- ▸ Validate process chains.
- ▸ Validate data loads.
- ▸ Validate queries and analysis.

B.10.9 Data Loads

- ▸ Run setup programs in SAP ECC for initial loads (if applicable).
- ▸ Schedule jobs for V3 updates on SAP ECC system (if applicable).
- ▸ Run delta initializations for master data deltas.
- ▸ Run delta initializations for transactional data.
- ▸ Schedule periodic loads.
- ▸ Schedule process chains.
- ▸ Monitor loads.
- ▸ All queries should come from a multi-provider, even if only reporting from one underlying InfoCube.

B.11   SAP NetWeaver BW Performance Checklist

This checklist can be used to check the various performance settings in SAP NetWeaver BW. It is broken down into loading and query performance. Often, there are several reasons for performance issues, so all should be checked. The most common cause of poor performance is the data model. In general, it is better to have many smaller objects than a few larger objects. This checklist gives the most common things to check when experiencing slow or substandard performance in SAP NetWeaver BW.

B.11.1   Overall Tasks

▸ Turn on statistics for all queries (RSA1 • TOOLS • SETTINGS FOR BI STATISTICS).

▸ Install all performance InfoCubes and DSO structures (NW 2004S STATISTICS FOUND IN THE BUSINESS INFORMATION WAREHOUSE • BI STATISTICS INFOAREA).

▸ All ABAP coding should be tuned per ABAP best practices and standards.

B.11.2   Query Performance

▸ Check data model to ensure that volume is not too great. When in doubt, use logical partitioning to separate data into multiple InfoProviders.

▸ Check the InfoProvider, and if running from an ODS/DSO, make sure indexes are added to query access fields. If possible, build queries from InfoCubes and not DSO/ODS objects. The star schema model is typically faster for performance than the relational model. Thus, InfoCubes are typically faster than DSO/ODS structures.

▸ Eliminate the volume in the query by reducing the data in the rows and columns. Make the query less granular for the initial view, and add fields as free characteristics. This forces the user to choose the characteristics they want. This typically reduces the volume.

▸ Check the query read mode (TRANSACTION RSRT • PROPERTIES).

▸ Reduce the number of navigational attributes that are used in the query.

▸ Suppress totals lines, if not needed.

▸ Check database statistics; make sure they are up-to-date for the query Info-Provider.

▸ Check support package, and get to newest support package. There are many performance enhancements with each support package.

▸ Check database settings to ensure that tuning is optimal for star joins, etc.

- If running a query from an InfoCube, implement compression to reduce the data volume and utilize partitioning.
- Eliminate Not Equal To logic in queries. This can increase performance degradation substantially.
- Eliminate virtual characteristics and virtual key figures.
- Eliminate before aggregation key figures.
- Turn on OLAP cache for each query (TRANSACTION RSRT • PROPERTIES).
- Check the partitioning setting of the InfoCube; if data query performance is substandard, this can be activated via a transport for most databases.
- Implement aggregates to reduce the volume of data being accessed. To determine if aggregates are needed, use TRANSACTION RSRT: EXECUTE AND DEBUG • DISPLAY AGGREGATE FOUND.
- Check the authorizations. A complex authorization strategy can cause query performance degradation.
- Implement line-item dimensions in the InfoCube or shuffle the InfoObjects in the dimensions, if dimension to fact table ratio exceeds 10%.
- Keep non-cumulative data in InfoCubes to a lower level of granularity.
- Implement pre-cache of query, to prime the OLAP cache.
- Implement pre-calculated Web templates.
- Reduce the number of cell calculations in the query.
- Examine hardware and memory.
- Examine network latency.

B.11.3 Load Performance

- Check the data model to make sure data is segregated so that more parallel loading is possible.
- Use delta loading whenever possible.
- Drop indexes before high-volume loads.
- Check process chains to ensure parallel processing.
- Reduce granularity in the data model.
- Implement load balancing.
- Check customer enhancements and custom code to determine where bottlenecks exist.
- Eliminate LIS as a source for data, wherever possible.

- Load master data before transactional data.
- If loading high-volume master data, buffer the number range table.
- If loading very high-volume transactional data, buffer the number ranges for the dimension tables.
- If load is slow on the change run (apply job), implement parallel activation.
- If load is slow on the change run, reduce the number of navigational attributes in the aggregates.
- If load is slow on the DSO/ODS, turn off reporting flag in the DSO/ODS if possible.
- Reduce the time-dependent fields in the data model, if possible.
- Implement line-item dimensions.
- Implement PSA partitioning.

B.12   Checklist for ABAP Codes used in SAP NetWeaver BW

The following checklist corresponds to ABAP codes used in SAP NetWeaver BW projects.

- TYPE (data element) command is used while declaring the fields whenever feasible instead of LIKE.
- Internal Table is defined with TYPE STANDARD TABLE OF and Work-Areas is used instead of header lines.
- In SELECT statement, only the required fields are selected in the same order as they reside in underlying database table.
- Use SELECT INTO TABLE rather than SELECT INTO CORRESPONDING FIELDS OF TABLE.
- No SELECT * is used
- Delete adjacent duplicate entries from internal table before selection from database table using FOR ALL ENTRIES statement.
- SORT inside a LOOP is not used.
- After the APPEND statement inside a loop, the work area that has been appended is cleared.
- Do not delete the records of internal table inside the Loop.
- For copying internal tables, use '=' operator instead of Looping and Appending.

B.13 Checklist for SAP BusinessObjects

If you're implementing SAP BusinessObjects as a reporting tool for SAP NetWeaver BW, clear guidelines and checklists should be prepared beforehand. A complete checklist for SAP Business Objects will help you to move the settings smoothly in production and there will less post-production issues.

B.13.1 Checklist for Universe Connection

- Make sure Universe Connection is defined as a Secured connection.
- The Universe Connection name should be descriptive enough to recognize the source of data.

B.13.2 Checklist for Universe

- Universe classes are named as per business naming convention so that business users can understand meaning of each Universe fields.
- Proper business meaning is provided in each Class/Subclass definition.
- Integrity Check is performed before exporting the Universe in CMS.

B.13.3 Web Intelligence Report Checklist

A comprehensive checklist is required for Web Intelligence reports so that it can run in production without any issues. The main objective of this checklist is to ensure that the report is running with optimal performance. Below is the checklist for Web Intelligence reports:

- Report is not fetching unnecessary data that is not required in the report.
- Description is well written and understandable to business users.
- Proper header and font is used in the report.
- Stress test is performed based on maximum record output.
- All report items are named correctly.
- Syntax errors are checked for calculated values and input variables.
- Business Standards are maintained for report colors, fonts, logo, etc.

C   Document Templates

This appendix gives you information about the various documents that you will need to create for your SAP NetWeaver BW project. You can use the information contained in each section in this appendix as a template for these documents. There are four types of documents needed, which are:

- Functional Model Template
- Data Store Object (DSO) Template
- InfoCube Template
- Extraction, Transformation, and Loading (ETL)

Each of these is discussed in this appendix.

C.1   Functional Model Template

The goal of this document is to allow the functional business process teams to communicate their needs. Basically, this functions as a requirements document. Once complete, it serves as a functional specification for SAP NetWeaver BW. Once SAP NetWeaver BW is determined to be in scope for a process, this should be the first document completed.

This document allows the SAP NetWeaver BW team to clearly understand the requirements of the process teams. The most difficult part is to make sure that all sections are filled out with the proper level of detail so that you can later model the solution in SAP NetWeaver BW.

There should be one functional model document for each subject area used for analysis in SAP NetWeaver BW. This subject area is not always easy to define. The goal is that the functional model document gives the requirements for one logical grouping of functionality. Examples include: *Sales Analysis Reporting Functional Model* or the *Demand Planning Functional Model*.

The functional model document is not designed to provide information about InfoCubes or DSOs, etc. The goal, instead, is to get agreement on the scope for the subject area. It can then be used as the main input to determine the physical model structures that need to be created in the SAP NetWeaver BW system.

This document should be listed and tracked as a process team deliverable. The reason for this is considered a process team deliverable and not a SAP NetWeaver BW team deliverable to shift the analysis gathering and ownership to the process teams. This gives these teams the incentive to gather and own the functional model document, because without a completed functional model document, no development can take place in the SAP NetWeaver BW system.

Refer to Chapter 5 for some details about this document such as its timing, and some information about major sections of this document. Now, let's examine some of the important sections of this document.

Document Information

Each functional model document should cover one subject area. This section should detail the SAP NetWeaver BW and the business owner of the model. It should also give a name and brief description of the model and its complexity. This section should have information on the process team that owns it, such as *finance* or *sales*. This helps to group the functional model documents.

Functional Model Description and Audience

In this section, a few paragraphs should be written that clearly state the overall goal of the functional model and why it is being implemented. This helps to gain some understanding of why the functional model is needed, who is the intended audience, and the roles of the analysis users.

Related Documents

This section can list and attach any preliminary requirement documents and/or other supporting documents that help to explain the scope and needs of this subject area. In some cases, these are samples of legacy reports and other similar information to help the SAP NetWeaver BW team understand the analysis needs.

Document History and Signoff

This section tracks any versions of the document. Each edit document should be assigned versions so that changes can be tracked. This is designed to determine who made edits to the document at any stage. This section is also reserved for the signoff. Projects differ on who signs off on this document. However, at the very least, the signoff should be the SAP NetWeaver BW data architect, the process team representative, the process team manager, and the SAP NetWeaver BW project manager. The signoff conveys that these team members have read and understand the structure and data contained in this structure.

Business Functionality Description: Business Questions Asked and Answered

This section gives an overall understanding of the business and the questions that this functional model should answer once implemented. Although this appears to be a easy section to complete, it's often the one that process teams have trouble completing fully.

These business questions will also be used as a foundation for the test cases in the future. This ensures that the physical model, once implemented, does answer the questions posed in this section.

Transformations

Often, there is some type of transformation of data that is required to meet a business need. This transformation often requires significant time from the SAP NetWeaver BW development team. It's difficult to determine all transformations of data until the data is loaded. However, the transformation that is known early should be clearly spelled out in this section. Some common transformations include unit of measure (UOM) conversion and currency conversion. There is typically more significant transformation with legacy data than with SAP data because it typically requires harmonization with the SAP data.

Filters

If data is to be filtered from the source, this should be documented in this section. This helps to determine if the full or a subset of the source data is needed.

Reconciliation, Validation Needs, and Error Handling

This section should include any potential errors or validation issues. If the data needs to be validated or checked against existing data, this should be clearly stated.

Test Criteria

Any special test criteria can be listed here. The test criteria will also be developed based on the business questions mentioned in the functional model document.

Dependencies and Constraints

Typically, in any model, there are some dependencies. The more important dependencies include external jobs that need to run before the data can be loaded. For example, an external invoice creation program needs to run before the legacy invoice data is loaded. There will be similar constraints on the SAP ECC or SAP R/3 transactional systems to complete certain jobs before SAP NetWeaver BW loads the data. This ensures that SAP NetWeaver BW is getting the most current data. This helps to determine when the data loads should be scheduled and also points out potential issues that can occur if these dependencies do not run or fail.

Compliance Requirements

Apart from other compliance requirements, this section is also where any Sarbanes-Oxley (SOX) or validation requirements should be documented.

Assumptions

Any assumptions about the data model, data validity, or any processes outside of the team's control that need to be assumed should be mentioned here. This helps to show any outside risk.

DataSource Profiles

This is the most important section of the document because the DataSources make up one of the biggest inputs into scope and timeline. It is very important, therefore, that all DataSources used to load this data are clearly recognized and documented. There are several things that should be documented about each source, which are:

- DataSource Name
- Source System (SAP ECC or Flat File, etc.)
- DataSource Description
- Data anomalies or specific information about DataSource that should be known
- Dependencies for this DataSource
- Frequency of loading
- Key Contact for access
- Update Type (Delta/Full Load)
- Data Granularity
- Volume Expected
- History Needed
- Notes about this DataSource

Because this section is so vital, all these subsections should be clearly filled out for each DataSource. This information is only required for each transactional Data-Source, not for each maser data source. If the data is being loaded from the SAP ECC or SAP R/3 system and if there are similar DataSources, these can be combined into one list. The goal is to understand the main DataSources that will be used as an input to the flow.

Data Flow Diagram

A data flow diagram is helpful to see the flow of data and sources feeding this data. This helps to understand that the feed of the data might come from SAP. However, the data may have originated in a legacy system first, then fed to SAP SAP ECC, and then onto SAP NetWeaver BW. Understanding the flow of the data through the organization allows for a clearer understanding of the dependencies involved.

Frequency and Timing

Understanding the frequency and timing of the data loading process and the query analysis timing helps to plan how the model will be loaded. For example, SAP NetWeaver BW is typically loaded once per day, nightly. If the data needs to be loaded multiple times per day, or real-time data is needed for the model, this section can help the SAP NetWeaver BW team understand the requirement. It also helps to determine how the users will use the queries. Do they use them only at month-end or daily? It also helps determine how often they are used.

History Requirements

The history requirements help to define the information and source of data for the solution. If history is required, it's important to understand what history and how much history is required to complete the model. This is most important when there are legacy systems involved.

Security

Because SAP NetWeaver BW security should be considered early in the data modeling process, this section is important to understand any security requirements. These might be role, by query, or by individual characteristics or key figure values. For example, if users should only be able to see selected company codes, this security requirement should be listed. It is understood that security could differ by report. However, this section gives an overall view of the security for the Functional Model so it can be included in the SAP NetWeaver BW data model.

Sample Reports and Output

This section shows some of the sample analysis reports required in this subject area. Although there can be many queries associated with the model, this section is designed to list a few of the most important analysis queries. In many cases, these sample reports are created with the use of Microsoft Excel to show the SAP NetWeaver BW team what to expect.

Issues

Any open issues should be documented here. Any issues should also be entered into the central issues database maintained by the project.

Appendix

Any attachments or other design documents can be linked. Any supporting documents can also be linked or attached here.

C.2 DSO Document Template

The purpose of the DataStore Object (DSO) Document Template is to provide some guidelines for documentation of the DSO or Operational Data Store (ODS) structures used in a data model. It helps to record the business purpose of the structure, its design, and use. It should be completed and signed off prior to any configuration in the SAP NetWeaver BW system.

One document should be completed for each DSO used in the data model. This is an ideal document for transitioning a data model from the development team to the production support team. Figure C.1 shows the table of contents for a DSO/ODS document template.

Document Information

This section should list the name of the DSO—both technical and functional—and describe the SAP NetWeaver BW team owner and the business SME owner. It should also describe at a high level the subject matter and intent of the DSO.

Related Documents

All related documents should be listed in this section. These include documentation on any other InfoProvider(s) (InfoCube, DSO) that is fed or feeds this DSO. This would also include the ETL document(s) that show this DSO as part of its flow. This section is useful to determine where this DSO fits in the entire data model.

Contents

1 DOCUMENT INFORMATION
- *1.1 Document Information*
- *1.2 Document History*
- *1.3 Approval*

2 OVERVIEW
- 2.1 Diagram & Data Flow
- 2.2 Business Content
- 2.3 Sources of Data
- 2.4 Data Profile
- 2.5 Historical Data Profile
- 2.6 Reporting
- 2.7 Queries Created above ODS/DSO
- 2.8 Issues

3 TECHNICAL SPECIFICATION
- *3.1 DSO Definition*
- *3.2 Settings*
- *3.3 Key Fields*
- *3.4 Data Fields*
- *3.5 Navigation Attributes*
- *3.6 Indexes*

4 DATA TRANSFORMATION
- *4.1 Update Rules*
  - *4.1.1 Update Rule – Data Fields Calculation*
    - 4.1.1.1 Formula
    - 4.1.1.2 Routine
  - *4.1.2 Update Rule – Key Fields Calculation*
- *4.2 Report To Report Interface*
  - *4.2.1 Sender Assignment*
  - *4.2.2 Receiver Assignment*
  - *4.2.3 Assignment Details*
- *4.3 Security*

5 OTHERS
- 5.1 Metadata Repository and Other Links

APPENDICES

Figure C.1 Table of Contents for DSO/ODS Design Document

Document History and Signoff

This section tracks any versions of the document. Each edit to the document should be assigned versions so that changes can be tracked using these versions. This will show who made edits to the document. This section is also reserved for the signoff. Projects differ on who signs off on this document. However, the signoff should at least include the SAP NetWeaver BW data architect and the SAP NetWeaver BW project manager. We recommend that a representative from the business also signs off. The signoff communicates that these people have read and understand the structure and the data contained in this structure.

Business Functionality Description

This section shows the business reason for the DSO in paragraph format. It describes why the DSO was created and gives some details about the data being stored in the structure.

Diagram and Data Flow

This diagram shows the flow of data in graphical format from the DataSource through this DSO as well as any other structures that are fed from this DSO. This section helps to illustrate where the DSO falls into the data model and what downstream and upstream objects in the data flow are affected by its use.

Business Content

If the DSO is activated or copied from Business Content, this section can show that original Business Content object. This helps you to understand the origin of the structure. If the DSO is completely custom created, this should be noted here.

Sources of Data

Understanding the sources of data used to fill the DSO is important to understanding the purpose and use of the DSO. This section describes the DataSources used to fill the DSO. If the data is being filled by an SAP ECC or SAP R/3 DataSource, the DataSource name, description, and a brief summary of the extracted data should be documented. If the DataSource is related to an external source, this section should also describe the external source system and the data being fed from this system.

DataSource Profile

This is the most important section of the document. It describes each DataSource that feeds this DSO, in detail. It shows each source, the type of data, frequency, and method of loading (flat file, DBConnect, SAP API, etc.). The goal is to know the type(s) of data being loaded into the DSO.

Historical Data Profile

If historical data is being loaded into this DSO, this should be noted here. This section is useful if a new DSO is being created and legacy data needs to fill the DSO. For example, a new sales order DSO is created, once SAP ECC is live. It will be filled with SAP ECC orders. Before the SAP ECC system is live, the historical order data needs to be loaded from the legacy system.

This historical data should be documented in detail. Some of the more common issues involving DSOs are with the harmonization of data with other sources and with the SAP ECC system data. This section helps to document historical data challenges and its content.

DSO Data Profile

This section describes the data that will be loaded into the DSO. It should be used to describe the key fields of the DSO and its overall data design.

Reporting

Most DSO structures are not used for reporting. Although the DSO is not intended to be the main reporting tool in SAP NetWeaver BW, it can be used to report some detailed data to the users, if needed. The goal for this section is to delineate some of the reporting needs of the DSO. This can affect how the DSO is set up and the various indices that might be needed.

Queries Created Above the ODS/DSO

List all the queries created above the ODS/DSO. This tracks the complete dataflow if users report errors in SAP NetWeaver BW reports.

Issues

Any open issues should be documented here. Any issues should also be entered into the central issues database maintained by the project.

Appendix

Any attachments or other design documents can be linked. Any supporting documents can also be linked or attached here.

Metadata Repository Link

The Metadata Repository is a documentation tool in SAP NetWeaver BW that is automatically updated with the latest SAP NetWeaver BW configuration. Because the SAP NetWeaver BW system is self-documenting and the Metadata Repository can be exported to HTML, this can be linked in the document to provide details on the specific InfoObjects and flow of data used in the SAP NetWeaver BW system. This prevents all objects from being listed manually in this document.

C.3 InfoCube Document Template

The purpose of the InfoCube Document Template is to provide some guidelines for the documentation of the InfoCubes or InfoSets used in a data model. It helps record the business purpose of the structure, its design, and use. It should be completed and signed off prior to any configuration in the SAP NetWeaver BW system. One document should be completed for each InfoCube or InfoSet used in the data model. This is an ideal document for transitioning a data model from the development team to the production support team.

Document Information

This section should list the name of the InfoCube, both technical and functional, and describe the SAP NetWeaver BW team owner and the business SME owner. It should also describe, at a high level, the subject matter and intent of the InfoCube (see Figure C.2).

Related Documents

All related documents should be listed in this section. These include documentation on any other InfoProvider(s) (InfoCube, DSO) that is fed or feeds this InfoCube. It should also include the ETL document(s) that show this InfoCube as part of its flow. This section is useful to determine where this InfoCube fits in the entire data model.

Document History and Signoff

This section tracks any versions of the document. Each edit to the document should be assigned versions and changes tracked using these versions. This shows who made edits to the document. This section is also reserved for the signoff. Projects differ on who signs off on this document. However, the signoff should at least include the SAP NetWeaver BW data architect and the SAP NetWeaver BW project manager. A representative from the business should also sign off on this document. The signoff conveys that they have read and understand the structure and the data contained in this structure.

Business Functionality Description

This section shows the business reason for the InfoCube in paragraph format. This describes why the InfoCube was created and some details about the data that is being stored.

Contents

1 DOCUMENT INFORMATION
- 1.1 DOCUMENT PROPERTIES
- 1.2 DOCUMENT HISTORY
- 1.3 APPROVAL

2 OVERVIEW
- 2.1 DIAGRAM AND DATA FLOW
  - 2.1.1 Data Flow
  - 2.1.2 Star Schema
- 2.2 BUSINESS CONTENT
- 2.3 SOURCES OF DATA
- 2.4 DATASOURCE PROFILE
- 2.5 HISTORICAL DATA PROFILE
- 2.6 INFOCUBE DATA PROFILE
- 2.7 PARTITIONING
- 2.8 REPORTING
- 2.9 ISSUES

3 TECHNICAL SPECIFICATION
- 3.1 INFO CUBE DEFINITION
- 3.2 STORAGE PARAMETERS
- 3.3 CHARACTERISTICS
- 3.4 DIMENSION
  - 3.4.1 Characteristics - Dimension Assignment
- 3.5 NAVIGATION ATTRIBUTES
- 3.6 TIME CHARACTERISTICS
- 3.7 KEY FIGURES
- 3.8 PARTITION
- 3.9 UPDATE RULES
  - 3.9.1 Update Rule – Key Figures
  - 3.9.2 Update Rule – Characteristics
  - 3.9.3 Update Rule – Time Reference
- 3.10 AGGREGATES
- 3.11 REPORT TO REPORT INTERFACE
  - 3.11.1 Sender Assignment
  - 3.11.2 Receiver Assignment
  - 3.11.3 Assignment Details
- 3.12 SECURITY

4 OTHERS
- 4.1 META DATA REPOSITORY LINKS
- 4.2 APPENDIX

Figure C.2 Table of Contents for InfoCube Design Document

Diagram and Data Flow

The diagram illustrates the flow of data, in a graphical format, from the DataSource through any other structures to this InfoCube. It should also show any other structures that feed or are fed to/from this InfoCube. This section helps to determine where the InfoCube falls into the data model as well as the downstream and upstream objects in the data flow affected by its use.

Business Content

If the InfoCube is activated or copied from Business Content, this section can show the original Business Content object that has been copied. This helps to clarify the origin of the structure. If the InfoCube is completely custom created, this should be noted here as well.

Sources of Data

Understanding the sources of data used to fill the InfoCube is important. It helps with understanding the purpose and use of the InfoCube. This section describes the DataSources used to fill the InfoCube. If the data is being filled by an SAP ECC or SAP R/3 DataSource, the DataSource name, description, and a brief summary of the extracted data should be documented. If the DataSource is related to an external source, this section should also describe the external source system and the data that is being fed from this system.

DataSource Profile

This is the most important section of the document. It describes each DataSource that feeds this InfoCube in detail. It shows each source, the type of data, frequency, and method of loading (flat file, DBConnect, SAP API). The goal of this section is to lay out the type(s) of data being loaded into the InfoCube.

Historical Data Profile

If historical data is being loaded into this InfoCube, this should be noted here. This section is useful if a new InfoCube is being created and legacy data needs to fill the InfoCube. This historical data should be documented in detail.

InfoCube Data Profile

This section describes the data that will be loaded into the InfoCube. This describes the various key performance indicators (KPIs) that will be loaded and/or used when reporting from this InfoCube. It also lists the most important characteristics and the granularity level of the InfoCube.

Partitioning

This section describes any partitioning needed in the InfoCube for faster query performance. Partitioning is only recommended if the volume of data is large. This section describes the InfoObject to be used for partitioning and the number of partitions made.

Reporting

The reporting needs of the InfoCube are important to ensure that the design is sound. This section describes some of the analysis that is needed from the Info-Cube and some mock-up reports, if possible. The more detailed understanding of the reporting requirements, the more useful this document becomes.

Issues

Any open issues should be documented here. Any issues should also be entered into the central issues database maintained by the project.

Appendix

Any attachments or other design documents can be linked. Any supporting documents can also be linked or attached here.

Metadata Repository Link

As discussed in Section C.2, the Metadata Repository is a documentation tool in SAP NetWeaver BW that is automatically updated with the latest SAP NetWeaver BW configuration. Because the SAP NetWeaver BW system is self-documenting and the Metadata Repository can be exported to HTML, this can be linked in the document to provide details on the specific InfoObjects and flow of data used in the SAP NetWeaver BW system. This prevents all objects from being listed manually in this document.

C.4 ETL (Extraction, Transformation, and Loading) Document Template

The purpose of the ETL document template is to provide some guidelines for the documentation of the SAP NetWeaver BW data model as a whole. Documenting the model includes having one overall diagram of the entire landscape. However, it is also helpful to understand each process and the loads required for each separate function and how this data is loaded and transformed in the model. Without this document, it is difficult to piece together the many DSO, InfoCube documents that make up the model and to understand how the data flows.

This document helps to record the technical flow of the design and use. It should be completed and signed off prior to any configuration in the SAP NetWeaver BW system. One ETL document should be completed for each subject area used in the data model. This is an ideal document for transitioning a data model from the development team to the production support team.

Document Information

This section should list the name of the subject area defined by the ETL flow. Examples include the *Purchasing/Vendor Performance ETL Model* or *Sales Analysis ETL Model*. This section can also list the process team and the SAP NetWeaver BW developer or steward responsible for the ETL flow from end to end.

Related Documents

All related documents should be listed here. These include documentation on all InfoProvider(s) (InfoCube, DSO) that are mentioned in this ETL document. It could also include any other related ETL document(s).

Document History and Signoff

This section tracks any versions of the document. Each edit should be assigned a version. Changes can be tracked using these versions. This shows who made edits to the document. This section is also reserved for the signoff. Projects differ on who signs off on this document. However, the signoff should at least include the SAP NetWeaver BW data architect and the SAP NetWeaver BW project manager. A representative from the business should also sign off. The signoff conveys that these individuals have read and understand the structure and data contained in this structure.

Business Functionality Description

This section shows the business reason for the DSO in paragraph format. This describes why the DSO was created and gives some details about the data that is being stored in the structure.

ETL Diagram and Data Flow

The ETL diagram is the most important part of the ETL document. It shows the flow of data graphically, from the DataSource all the way to the InfoProvider. Typically, the queries are not listed or mentioned in this document. However, any MultiProviders that are related to the model should be shown along with all associated InfoProviders.

This section illustrates the data from beginning to end. It should clearly show all related data model structures for the associated subject area and what downstream and upstream objects in the data flow are affected by its use. Typically, these diagrams are done using Microsoft Visio to allow as much detail as possible to be shown in one clear document.

Sources of Data

This section should clearly state each DataSource used to load the data and the source system that has the data. It should also detail the approximate volume that is loaded and if the load is a full or delta load.

Destinations of Data

This section lists the various destinations of data. Typically, these are DSOs or InfoCubes.

Data Transformation

All custom transformations should be detailed in this section. The goal is to make sure that any custom transformation logic is clearly understood. Any custom start routines, end routines, expert routines, or transformation routines should be documented in detail. Each should show the source of data, the transformation logic used, the purpose, and who requested the transformation. The goal is not to show the actual ABAP code. The primary goal is to understand why, where, and how the transformation was done. This allows anyone troubleshooting the design to see where anything outside of standard mapping occurs.

This section can get long and involved depending on how complex the transformation is in the model. However, it allows one place to look for any custom logic and makes the handoff of the design much easier than looking through multiple documents.

Dependencies and Constraints

Typically, in any model there are some dependencies. These are tasks and loads that have to take place before others can begin. Some of these are rather obvious, as shown in the ETL diagram. For example, an InfoCube may not be loaded before its source, the DSO.

These need not be listed here. The more important dependencies are external jobs that need to run before the data can be loaded. For example, an external invoice creation program needs to run before the legacy invoice data is loaded. There will also be similar constraints on the SAP ECC or SAP R/3 transactional systems to complete certain jobs before SAP NetWeaver BW should load the data. This ensures that SAP NetWeaver BW is getting the most current data. This helps to determine when the data loads should be scheduled and also points out potential issues that can occur if these dependencies do not run or fail.

Issues

Any open issues should be documented here. These issues should also be entered into the central issues database maintained by the project.

Appendix

Any attachments or other design documents can be linked. Any supporting documents can also be linked or attached here.

Metadata Repository Links

As seen earlier, the Metadata Repository is a documentation tool in SAP NetWeaver BW that is automatically updated with the latest SAP NetWeaver BW configuration. Because the SAP NetWeaver BW system is self-documenting and the Metadata Repository can be exported to HTML, this can be linked in the document to provide details on the specific InfoObjects and flow of data used in the SAP NetWeaver BW system. This prevents all objects from being listed manually in this document. Typically, there are multiple links associated with each ETL document.

C.5 SAP BusinessObjects Template

In this section, we'll see templates on Universe Connection, Universe, and Web Intelligence reports. The main purpose of these documents is to let the business users know about SAP BusinessObjects settings so that they can execute Business Objects reports without any help from technical consultants.

Universe Connection Pool

Before creating Universe in SAP BusinessObjects, you have to create a Universe Connection. This document will contain different connectivity settings information to fetch data from SAP or non-SAP data sources into SAP BusinessObjects. Any changes in source systems connectivity settings should also be reflected in this document.

Your Universe Connection pool document should contain the following sections:

- Diagram and Data Flow
- Sources of Data
- Data Profile
- Business Requirements
- Connection Pools—In this section, list all Universe connections defined in your implementation. Table C.1 is a simple example of a template for listing your Universe Connections.
- Issues
- Appendix

<Name of the Universe Connection>	
Description	
Connection Type	
Connection Properties	If SAP connection, provide SAP logon pad information
Pool Timeout	
Array Fetch Size	
Array Bind Size	
Login Timeout	

Table C.1 Table to Record Universe Connection Information

Universe

Universe is a logical view of data from different sources. The main purpose of Universe is to provide a uniform business view of the data collected from heterogenous system landscapes.

Documents on SAP BusinessObjects Universe should contain the following sections:

▶ Document properties and change history
▶ Business Requirements
▶ Data Flow Overview
▶ Universe Connection Name
▶ Different Universe Connection parameters like type, timeout, etc.
▶ List of Web Intelligence reports and Web services built on the Universe
▶ List of Classes and Objects
▶ List of Measures
▶ List of Calculated Measures
▶ List of Filters
▶ Issues
▶ Appendix

Web Intelligence Reports

Web Intelligence reports represent data from Universe. Because the complexity of the underlying data is hidden through Universe, many information users can use this tool to create ad hoc reports. However, you may need to create a few stored reports for the users who are not much familiar to the Web Intelligence reporting tool. The following sections should be furnished in your Web Intelligence report document:

- Document overview
- Business requirements and purpose
- Report properties
  Report Name
    - Name of the Universe on which the report is built
    - Report title, subtitles
    - Input variables
    - Rows, columns
    - Alert requirements
    - Sort requirements
    - Chart requirements
- Issues
- Appendix

D   Common Issues When Upgrading from SAP NetWeaver BW Version 3.x to NW 2004s

Upgrading SAP NetWeaver BW can be a challenging task. When setting up a project plan for an upgrade project, it helps to know some of the common issues faced by others when developing your plan. This helps not only to estimate time for each activity but also allows the team to be proactive in its overall planning to avoid or mitigate some of the common issues with the upgrade.

In most cases, the actual system time needed for the upgrade is approximately one week. This includes just the loading of the software, Java, etc. This time varies depending on the expertise of the team and the size of the database that needs to be upgraded. During the time the upgrade is loading, no activity can take place on the SAP NetWeaver BW system. This can cause some issues with the end users. Therefore, some project organizations have opted to upgrade a shadow system and cutover from the shadow system to the production system when complete. This lessens the downtime for the upgrade. Other projects accept the downtime and communicate the need for it well in advance.

The NW 2004s system allows configuration running in the 3.x method of modeling (with InfoSources, transfer rules, and update rules). This means that any existing configuration in the 3.x system will continue to work in the NW 2004s system. For this reason, many project organizations opt for a technical upgrade, in which the configuration is moved to the new release, but the data model does not take advantage of the new loading methodology, Java functions, etc. This allows for a quicker and less risky upgrade because there are fewer changes to the application.

Listed in this appendix are some of the typical challenges in the 3.x-to-NW 2004s projects. The issues are broken down by project subject area. These include some of the issues that have occurred during upgrade projects, including some of the areas that are particularly challenging.

D.1   System, Basis-Related Issues

The following challenges are related to the system:

▶ **NW 2004s Involves Database Upgrade**
The database administrator should be involved as early as possible during the

upgrade process to plan and implement any database upgrade that is needed to support NW 2004s. The list of the compatible and recommended database versions can be found in the SAP Service MarketPlace at *www.service.sap.com/pam*.

▶ **Recommended Database Settings**
SAP has provided notes to communicate the best database options and settings. These differ by database platform and have changed often. These settings need to be verified and checked. This is a task that often gets overlooked because the database administrator does not always get the list of recommended settings. A coordinated effort needs to be established to ensure that the database team knows about these settings.

▶ **Differing Database Settings**
In some cases, data settings differ from SAP ECC and SAP R/3 to the SAP NetWeaver BW system. These settings are a result of SAP suggestions. Expect that there could be some different database settings between the SAP ECC and SAP R/3 system and the SAP NetWeaver BW system. Previously, many customers used identical or similar settings between the two environments.

▶ **Tools Checked for Compatibility**
There are several new tools in the NW 2004s environment. Each needs to be checked to ensure that all components on the server and desktop are compatible. Some common issues involve integration with Adobe, BEx Analyzer, and Visual Composer.

▶ **Additional Requirements for Upgrade**
There are specific system requirements to complete the upgrade. There are also other applications that run in conjunction or communicate directly on the SAP NetWeaver BW base. Some popular components are XI, APO, CRM, etc. These should be checked to determine the necessary patch level before the upgrade is planned on their underlying SAP NetWeaver BW system.

▶ **Larger Databases Take Longer**
In some cases, larger databases can take a long time to complete the upgrade process. To reduce the time that is required, a database reorganization should be planned prior to the upgrade. This allows the database to be optimally organized to begin the upgrade process.

▶ **Upgrade Process Slows Periodically**
The upgrade process changes the database tables rather dramatically. Periodically running the database statistics during the upgrade process on the tables and dictionary helps the database optimizer plan and execute tasks much more quickly.

▶ **Java Expertise Required**

There are many Java tuning parameters associated with the NW 2004s system. If there are plans to render the analysis using Java, this area needs to be tuned properly. Sub-optimal tuning slows performance and can even make the system unstable for the end user.

SAP should be involved in this tuning and stress testing be performed on the system. In one case, a customer found multiple new issues with the environment after running a stress test. The system appeared to work fine with few users, once many users joined the system, performance issues surfaced.

D.2 SAP NetWeaver BW Application-Related Issues

Let's look at SAP NetWeaver BW application-related issues related to the NW 2004s upgrade:

▶ **Large Number of SAP Notes**

This release is an extensive and complex release, which leaves a potential for substantial software issues. SAP is releasing a large number of SAP Notes for each support stack. The team needs to keep the system updated as often as possible. Regression testing needs to be planned after each support-stack upgrade.

▶ **Java Analysis Queries Need Proper Planning**

Java analysis queries can sometimes gather huge volumes of data, depending on their design. In some cases, this can monopolize the Java server, causing performance issues for everyone. This can be compensated for by good user training and intelligent query design. The query design element forces the user to utilize jump queries to get detailed data. This can keep the users from running large queries and taking up a large share of the Java server.

▶ **Common Access Tools Issues**

Project organizations that use the 3.x BEx Browser and/or the Web menu item will find these are not included in the current version of NW 2004s. This may mean that the upgrade requires a new way for the users to launch queries to be developed. This can pose a difficult change management issue.

▶ **Data Loading Issues**

Any ABAP transformation using update rules, transfer rules, start routines, etc., must be re-coded if the project wishes to implement the loading using the NW 2004s methodology of loading.

There are two main ways of loading data in the NW 2004s system. Data can be loaded using the 3.x methodology, using InfoSources, update rules, and transfer rules. It can also be loaded using the NW 2004s methodology, using a mandatory persistent staging area (PSA) and transformation logic.

If the 3.x configuration is switched to the NW 2004s methodology of loading, any ABAP code must be revisited. This is because the NW 2004s system using ABAP OO (object-oriented) coding to transform data. It is not mandatory to switch the configuration to the NW 2004s methodology, and SAP plans to continue to support the 3.x methodology of loading in the NW 2004s system.

If the model is to be upgraded to the new loading methodology, however, this code needs to be revisited and converted to the ABAP OO. No mass-conversion program from ABAP to ABAP OO currently exists.

▶ **Conversion of Queries**
Each query that is converted from the 3.x to the NW 2004s query processing method needs to be re-saved in the NW 2004s version. There is currently no mass-level program to provide this conversion. Depending on the number of queries, this effort can be substantial.

▶ **BI Accelerator Pricing Model**
The BI Accelerator is a tool designed to provide faster query performance. It's a hardware appliance used to supplement SAP NetWeaver BW by providing faster indexes on the data. The current pricing model for the BI Accelerator makes it quite expensive for many projects. This should be investigated before using the tool in any implementation.

D.3 Security-Related Issues

Now let's look at security-related challenges in the NW 2004s upgrade:

▶ **3.x Method of Authorizations Not Supported**
After the upgrade, project teams should quickly migrate the authorization security to the NW 2004s Analysis Authorization security functionality. This can involve a large effort depending on the complexity the 3.x security model. In most cases, this should be managed as a separate project because of the effort involved.

▶ **Security Migration Tool**
This tool does not always convert everything. SAP has provided a tool to convert existing 3.x security to the NW 2004s model. This program is RSEC_MIGRATION. It does not always convert all security; most customers report that it is converting about 80% to 85% of security. This means some of the migration needs to be done manually. All security requires a regression test to ensure that the migration was successful.

▶ **Regression Testing for Analysis Authorizations**
This is really time consuming. The only way to really understand any issues that may result from the transition from the 3.x authorizations is to regression test fully. This is a labor-intensive process involving creating many user ids and manually testing the SAP NetWeaver BW functionality to verify that the authorizations are set up correctly.

D.4   Portal-Related Issues

Now let's examine issues related to the portal:

▶ **Integration with Portal**
This is much more vital in the NW 2004s release. There are many more touchpoints between the SAP NetWeaver BW application team and the Portals team. The SAP NetWeaver BW team needs to determine what strategy is to be used for publishing queries to the portal.

The portal team needs to develop a clear strategy in conjunction with the SAP NetWeaver BW and SAP ECC or SAP R/3 transactional teams to provide clear content to the end user. In the 3.x version, the SAP Enterprise Portal (EP) was not as tightly integrated with SAP NetWeaver BW. In the NW 2004s version, the integration is more dramatic.

▶ **Federated or SAP NetWeaver BW Portal Strategy**
This federated or SAP NetWeaver BW portal strategy needs to be developed. If the project team plans to use the SAP EP functionality to provide the end user access point for SAP NetWeaver BW, several important decisions need to be made by the portal team. The portal can be run either from the SAP NetWeaver BW system or from a centralized federated portal. There are advantages to each approach. There are several whitepapers that detail this decision on the SAP developer network website (SDN) at *www.sdn.sap.com*.

E Sample SAP NetWeaver BW Naming Standards Document

The purpose of the naming standards document is to ensure that the project team is consistent in their approach to naming custom objects in SAP NetWeaver BW. This document can serve as a template to create an SAP NetWeaver BW naming standards document. This naming document should be established early in the project to keep naming consistent, allow for easy tracking of objects in SAP NetWeaver BW and to allow a basis for authorizations, if needed. Let's take a look at some naming standards now:

Objects	Standards	Meaning
InfoObject Catalogs	▶ ZXXXXX_CHAR ▶ ZXXXXX_KF ▶ Description: Free	▶ All custom InfoObject Catalogs should begin with Z. ▶ XXXXX should describe the business area associated with the change. Because there is no need to separate out the InfoObjects into many separate catalogs, most projects simply have two custom InfoObject Catalogs, one for characteristics and one for key figures.
Characteristics InfoObject	▶ Technical: ZXXXXXXXX. ▶ Description: Free	▶ All custom InfoObjects should begin with the letter Z. ▶ The rest of the technical name is freely determined to suite business understandings. ▶ The description should reflect the business meaning of the Characteristics InfoObject.
Key Figure InfoObject	▶ Technical: ZXXXXX_<TT> ▶ Description: Free	▶ All custom InfoObjects should begin with the letter Z and should have a descriptive name. ▶ XXXXX is to be freely determined to identify the business area of the Key Figure. ▶ <TT> values should end with a consistent value to denote the following: QT—Quantity, AT—Amount, CT—Count, PT—Percentage.

Objects	Standards	Meaning
ODS/DSO	▸ Technical: Zff_Dnna ▸ Description: Free	▸ Custom ODS/DSO should start with Z. ▸ *ff*—Functional Name—FI for Finance, AM for Asset Management, etc. ▸ D – To identify the object as DSO/ODS ▸ nna— Unique Number. A, B, C, etc. This is needed if there are several identical DSO/ODS structures, used for logically partitioning the DSO/ODS structures.
Standard InfoCube	▸ Technical: Z_ff_Cnna ▸ Description: Free	▸ Custom InfoCube should start with Z. ▸ ff—Functional Name—FI for Finance, AM for Asset Management, etc. ▸ nna—Unique Number. A, B, C, etc. This is needed if there are several identical Info-Cubes, used for logically partitioning the InfoCube data.
MultiProvider	▸ Technical: Z_ff_Mnn ▸ Description: Free	▸ Custom Multiprovider technical name should begin with Z. ▸ ff—Functional Name—FI for Finance, AM for Asset Management, etc. ▸ nn—Unique Number.
Query/ Query View	▸ Query Technical: Z_ff_XXXXXXXXQnn Y_ff_XXXXXXXXQnn X_ff_XXXXXXXXQnn ▸ Query View Technical: X_ff_XXXXXXXX-Vnn ▸ Description: Free	▸ Begin queries with Z if they have been transported from development. ▸ Begin queries with Y if they have been developed in production (if allowed). ▸ Begin X with queries that have been developed in production and are considered ad hoc. In case of Query views, most of the time they are created in the production system. ▸ ff—Functional Name—FI for Finance, AM for Asset Management, etc. ▸ XXXXXXX represents a description/type/business area of the query. You can give the technical name of the InfoProvider in this area. ▸ Q – to identify the object as Query and V – as Query View. ▸ nn – unique number.

Objects	Standards	Meaning
Web Template	▶ Technical Name: Z_tXXXXXXXXX ▶ Description: Free	▶ Web templates should begin with Z and end with a descriptor of the web template.
Roles	▶ Technical Name: ZccT_ff_ XXXXXXXXXXXXXX ▶ Description : Free	▶ All custom roles should begin with Z. ▶ cc—country code. ▶ t—Role Type (C—Composite, S—Single). ▶ ff – functionality of the role. ▶ XXXXXXXXXXXXX—Description of role.
Restricted Key Figures	▶ Technical Name: RXXXX ▶ Description : Free	▶ Restricted key figures should begin with R and end with a descriptive value.
Calculated Key Figures	▶ Technical Name: CXXXX ▶ Description : Free	▶ Calculated key figures should begin with C and end with a descriptive value.
Variables	▶ Technical Name ZoXXXXX ▶ Description : Free	▶ Variables should begin with Z and end with a description of the variable. ▶ o—Optional or Mandatory.
InfoPackages	▶ Technical Name: System Generated ▶ Description: <Data-Source>_<DataSource Type>_<Update Mode>_XXXX	▶ <DataSource> – Technical name of the data source ▶ <DataSource Type> – TRAN – Transaction Data, ATTR – Masterdata Attribute, TXT – Masterdata Text, HIER – Masterdata Hierarchy ▶ <UpdateMode> – FULL – Full Update, DELTA – Delta Update, INIT – Initial data upload ▶ XXXX – Free text.
Application Components	▶ Technical Name: ZXXXXXX	▶ The application component should begin with Z and end with a clear description of the component.

F   SAP NetWeaver BW Integration Test Script

This document can be used as an integration test script for the SAP NetWeaver BW data against the source data being loaded. All steps to load the data and run any analysis should be clearly spelled out in the integration test script. It is typically a best practice that the author does not run his own test scripts. This ensures that the test script is written to a detailed level and that there are multiple sets of eyes on the data reconciliation.

The data must be reconciled against the source data. This typically means that the tester loads the SAP NetWeaver BW data model, PSA, DSO, InfoCube, etc. An associated query would then be run on this data model, which should be reconciled against a report or list within the SAP ECC or SAP R/3 system to verify that the data is consistent. It is vital that the test script not only reconcile data within the SAP NetWeaver BW system. More importantly, this data must be reconciled back to the source data to ensure data integrity.

Adopt a clearly specified and agreed strategy for SAP NetWeaver BW integration testing. A successful integration testing requires massive collaboration with various teams of the project. Figure F.1 shows the generic process to be followed while performing SAP NetWeaver BW integration tests.

Data	• Receive data which fed into R3/ECC system • Test Data should be recorded in Excel for ease to prove pass/fail of the test case
Load	• Load ECC/R3 data by scheduling the Jobs in R3/ECC systems and Process Chains in BW
Test	• Depending on your strategy (Manual or Automatic), check integrity of data received from R3/ECC system • Verify all transformation logics are working properly
Record	• Put BW data and ECC/R3 data in same excel file as test evidence • You can also record the screen shots if required.

Figure F.1   General SAP SAP NetWeaver BW Integration Testing Procedure

SAP NetWeaver BW Integration Test Script

The SAP NetWeaver BW integration test script includes the following sections, which must be filled in with as much detail as possible:

- Test Case Title
- Author
- Date Created
- Team
- Executed By
- Execute Date
- Approved By
- Approval Date
- Test Case Description
- Prerequisites

Table F.1 describes the various steps you need to go through and also gives you the expected and actual results.

Step Description	Expected Results	Actual Results	Condition Tested
▸ Include step number, step description, and necessary input data. ▸ Create specific lists of steps required in order to load data and reconcile the data against the source. ▸ This should include specific loading, activation, rollup, etc., to get the data fully loaded. ▸ It may also include steps to start a process chain to load data. ▸ It should be very specific (including transaction codes, etc.) to show how data is reconciled to the source from the loaded data or from a specific query.	▸ Describe verification steps	▸ Document actual results, document numbers, report that was executed, etc. ▸ ERecord issues in issue tracking database	▸ OK or Issue

Table F.1 Description of Steps and Results

After the test script is run, you can then proceed with the other requirements of the test script as described in the following subsections

Comments

Any comments after running the test script should be placed here. Did the test script perform as designed? Were there any issues? If any issues occurred, these should be tracked separately in the issues database. All steps should have a screen print. These screen prints should be placed in this section with a clear link back to the test script and a clear explanation of the data being reconciled or collected. This will allow someone at a later time to see the full testing procedure and get proof that the data was reconciled properly.

Issues

All issues should be tracked in this section. These clearly show any issues that caused the test to fail. These should also be entered into the issue tracking database so they can be resolved separately.

Pass/Fail

Indicate if the test script passed or failed and if the test script should be re-run. You can create a template for integration test script similar to shown in Figure F.2.

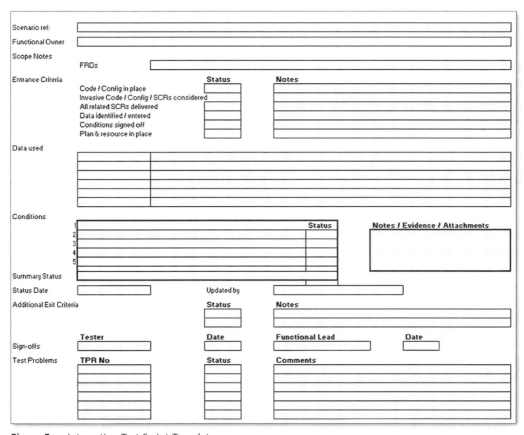

Figure F.2 Integration Test Script Template

G   Bibliography

McDonald, K., Dixon, D. C., Wilmsmeier, A, and Inmon, W. H. (2006): *Mastering the SAP Business Information Warehouse: Leveraging the Business Intelligence Capabilities of SAP NetWeaver (2nd edition)*. Wiley.

Egger, N., Fiechter, J., Rohlf J., Rose, J., and Schrüffer, O. (2006): *SAP BW Reporting and Analysis*. SAP PRESS.

TDWI's Data Quality Report—Data Quality and the Bottom Line: Achieving Business Success through a Commitment to High Quality Data (2002). The Data Warehousing Institute.

Eckerson, E. (2004): *In Search of a Single Version of Truth: Drivers of Consolidating Analytic Consolidation*. The Data Warehousing Institute.

Ingo Hilgefort (2009): *Integrating SAP BusinessObjects XI 3.1 Tools with SAP NetWeaver*. Galileo Press.

H   The Authors

Highly regarded as an expert in his field, **Gary Nolan** is an SAP NetWeaver BW certified independent consultant specializing in implementation. He excels at evaluating customer requirements, configuring SAP NetWeaver BW, and providing SAP NetWeaver BW project management consulting in all areas of Business Intelligence. He also provides project expertise and consulting in SAP NetWeaver BW performance management, data architecture, and data modeling.

A former Platinum Consultant with SAP America, Inc., he has over 10 years of SAP experience. He has worked with SAP NetWeaver BW since version 1.2B. He has served as the lead consultant in many Fortune 500 company projects for the planning, system configuration, and testing phases, through go-live and post-implementation support. Gary has written over 20 articles for the *SAP NetWeaver BW Expert* and *SCMExpert* newsletters and is also a technical advisor for these publications. He was a moderator on SAP's internal message board, and has spoken at Sapphire, ASUG, Managing SAP Projects conferences, SAP InfoDays, and SAP SAP NetWeaver BW and Portals conferences.

He can be reached at: *gary.nolan@melvanconsulting.com*.

An SAP Certified Professional, **Debasish Khaitan** has over five years of experience in Data Warehousing and SAP NetWeaver BW. He has worked on many SAP NetWeaver BW implementation projects where his main responsibilities were to gather client requirements, analyze the customer's legacy data warehousing system for migration in SAP NetWeaver BW, prepare SAP NetWeaver BW technical specifications, end-to-end integration testing, SAP NetWeaver BW performance optimization, etc.

Apart from regular project works, he is an active contributor in SDN and writes how-to guides on different innovative integration technologies with SAP NetWeaver BW.

He can be reached at: *admin@dkhaitan.com*

Index

Exporting, 420
Opening and Saving, 422
Track Changes, 423
Web reporting, 34
Web-reporting tools, 165
Web Services, 30
Web templates, 258, 334
Web Template Strategy, 108
Web tools, 165
Workbooks, 258
Workflow, 138
Write Optimized DSO, 300

Best Practices, 431
Xcelsius Engage, 427
Xcelsius Engage Server, 427
Xcelsius Present, 427
XML interfaces, 280

Z

Zero Elimination, 313

X

Xcelsius, 402, 405, 427

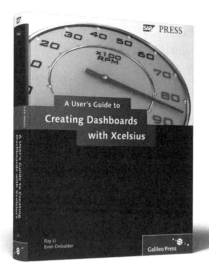

Explains how to use all of the features in Xcelsius

Teaches you how to build and customize interactive dashboards to effectively visualize your key business data

Provides guidance on using Xcelsius in an SAP environment

Evan Delodder, Ray Li

A User's Guide to Creating Dashboards with Xcelsius

Learn how to build your own Xcelsius dashboards, with this practical book. It explains how to use Xcelsius in an end-to-end, linear "common usage" manner, while highlighting typical scenarios where each feature can be used to solve business problems. It also gives you detailed, step-by-step guidance and best-practices for each feature, along with hands-on exercises that will help you begin creating dashboards and visualizations quickly. And if you're more advanced, you'll learn how to customize the Xcelsius components, themes, and data connections so you can use Xcelsius to the fullest extent.

approx. 620 pp., 49,95 Euro / US$ 49.95
ISBN 978-1-59229-335-3, Sept 2010

>> www.sap-press.com

Discover how to develop and implement successful BW data models

Find complete explanations of key topics including: Architecture, Information Objects, Info Providers and SAP Business Content

Learn about Business Intelligence (BI) planning and related Business Object innovations

Frank K. Wolf, Stefan Yamada

Data Modeling in SAP NetWeaver BW 7.1

This book provides consultants, project/implementation teams and IT staffs with clear guidance on how to develop, implement, maintain, and upgrade SAP data models. The book starts by explaining the entire data modeling process, from the logical design of a model through enterprise requirements, technical framework, and implementation requirements. It then moves into a more in-depth review of the technical/component requirements and maps the technologies to the specific business requirements outlined in the first chapter. The next several chapters focus on the primary foundations of a data model (i.e. Info Objects, Key Figures, Data Store Objects, etc.) and the principles of data modeling, including data architecture, data loading and transformation. The book also provides coverage of SAP's predefined data models (known as SAP Business Content), advanced topics, data modeling for planning applications, and a roadmap for continued maintenance and development of your data models.

approx. 450 pp., 79,95 Euro / US$ 79.95
ISBN 978-1-59229-346-9, Aug 2010

>> www.sap-press.com

 **PRESS**

Explains what Explorer is and how it can be used in daily business activities

Details how to integrate and get Explorer up and running quickly

Uses real-world scenarios to show how it works in financials, HR, CRM, and retail

Ingo Hilgefort

Inside SAP BusinessObjects Explorer

With this book you'll learn what SAP BusinessObjects Explorer is, and find out how to install, deploy, and use it. Written for people who are interested in bringing Business Intelligence to business users, this book will teach you how to use it in your SAP environment and address specific questions about how it works with your existing SAP tools and data. After reading this book, you'll understand why and how to leverage Explorer to bring quick and easy access to data analysis to users throughout your company.

307 pp., 2010, 69,95 Euro / US$ 69.95
ISBN 978-1-59229-340-7

>> www.sap-press.com